Enter this rich labyrinth of wisdom prepared to review every aspect of your own calling as a priestess, from lore to scholarship, scent alchemy to song, personal shadow work to utter jubilation. This is the new required reading for anyone who feels the call to serve in the often misunderstood, always sacred, role of priestess.

—**Holli Emore**, executive director of Cherry Hill Seminary

Stepping Into Ourselves captures, in a collage of personal essays, poems and academic works, contemporary women's connection with the divine. The collective voices presented here are a vibrant, harmonious chorus singing the ancient song of the priestess. Use this book on your own journey toward empowerment, for the archetype of the priestess is a powerful template available to us all.

—**Lisa Levart**, *Goddess on Earth: Portraits of the Divine Feminine*

This is a rich and inspiring offering, a wonderful compendium of creative talent, scholarship, spirit and wisdom. The papers in this anthology combine to illustrate that this world is a sacred place that women may help to heal if we but serve it as priestesses.

—**Miriam Robbins Dexter**, *Whence the Goddesses: A Source Book and Sacred Display: Divine and Magical Female Figures of Eurasia*

This eclectic collection of personal narratives, poetry, history, guidelines and suggestions provides a wealth of fascinating international perspectives on what it means to be a priestess. As the role is being reconstructed and recreated to fit today's world, this book belongs on the bookshelf of every woman who believes herself to be on the Priestess Path.

—**Wendy Griffin**, Professor Emerita, California State University Long Beach

A book for women who have dared to be religious leaders and priestesses of the ancient pre-Christian faiths, who, led by some deep mysterious impulse, have travelled forth on their own without role models.

In essays interlaced with feminist rhetoric, each contributor reminds us that these powerful, self-directed women still live in a male society that often seeks to suppress female talents. Despite the obstacles, like stubborn weeds emerging from cracks in cement, the power and grace of these women bleed through; grieving, healing, celebrating, speaking to the Divine and dancing change into the world.

There are wise words here for those of us who have been burned, and soaring words for those who aspire to step into the title of "Priestess." This book is a balm for those of us who have held positions of power and then still had to carry out the garbage, and find a way to navigate through the deep projections of others. Neophytes and Elders alike will find wise guidance within.

—**Ellen Evert Hopman**, herbalist, Druid Priestess, and author of the *Priestess of the Forest* trilogy of Celtic novels and other volumes

Praise for *Stepping Into Ourselves: An Anthology of Writing on Priestesses*

To read this book is like attending a luscious and well-appointed buffet dinner, where one can sample a variety of tasty foods. This feast of knowledge includes scholarly essays, juicy stories, and thoughtful reflections, as well as personal poems, songs and prayers expressing what it means to be a Priestess. It is quite a satisfying meal!

—**Vicki Noble,** co-creator of *Motherpeace*,
and author of *Shakti Woman* and *The Double Goddess*

Welcome the new generation of Goddess culture makers! All that was taken away from women—our Heras, their names and deeds, the inventors of poems and prose, rituals and dances—we could still not fill the the gaping, empty space if we published a million more books like this. But it is something. This work will be seeding the generations after us to continue the research, the relentless reclaiming, the constant agitation, to re-create sisterhood.

—**Z Budapest,** Spiritual Elder of the Dianic Tradition
The Holy Book of Women's Mysteries

Every woman, it is said, is a priestess at her own altar. Some of us are priestesses at more public altars. In this excellent book, priestesses tell their tales, and in scholarly articles discuss priestesses through history (and pre-history) around the world. There is also a useful how-to section and a toolkit. This book is a must-read for beginning and mature priestesses. And be sure to read Abbi Spinner McBride's "Dream"—-in half a page, she says it all.

—**Barbara Ardinger**
Pagan Every Day

Stepping Into Ourselves celebrates the extraordinary diversity and depth of priestess traditions and practices from around the world. The reader is treated to historical records and contemporary stories, ancient rituals and current priestess practices that lift up the lives of women everywhere. This book is an opportunity to encounter deeply spiritual women from different religious and cultural traditions who are empowering women to celebrate the priestess in all of us.

—**Rabbi Lynn Gottlieb**, *She Who Dwells Within: A Feminist Vision of Renewed Judaism* and *Trail Guide to the Torah of Nonviolence*

This volume is a veritable witches' cauldron of brewing bits of nourishment and mystery.

—**M. Macha NightMare (Aline O'Brien)**, witch-at-large, author, ritualist and interfaith activist

As you turn these pages, you enter into a Sis-Star-hood guided by a sense of Fierce Compassion, traveling deep into the personal and collective experience of our modern-day practice. Each in her own presence, these priestesses are influencing a deeper resonance with the divine. I highly encourage you to saturate yourself in this Living Anthology of Priestess Sis-Stars who are gathering, actualizing and sharing what it means to embody the presence, power and position of the Priestess.

In essence, this anthology reflects what we found on the path of our practices: as we embody the ancient wisdom of the Divine Feminine, we become that wisdom and we must share what we have learned. I invite you to drink deeply and allow your/our voices to serve as validation of what you already know in your heart to be true. Whether for a moment, or for many lifetimes, if you feel the call of the priestess, make the time to walk with us as we share our journeys and invite HER to continue to animate our lives.

—**Mz. Imani, ceremonial musician, sacred activist and shamanic healer,** and author of *They Dreamt of Us*

Stepping Into Ourselves
An Anthology of Writings on Priestesses

Edited by
Anne Key and Candace Kant

Copyright © 2014 by Anne Key and Candace Kant

All rights reserved. No part of this book may be reproduced in any form or by an electronic or mechanical means, or the facilitation thereof, including information storage and retrieval systems, without permission in writing form the publisher, except by a reviewer, who may quote brief passages in a review.

Printed in the United States of America
ISBN: 978-0-9833466-5-4

Published by
Goddess Ink, Ltd.
Las Vegas, NV
www.goddess-ink.com

Designed by Soujanya Rao.

Front cover artwork by Betty LaDuke, www.bettyladuke.com.
All rights reserved, used with permission.

Photo by Robert Jaffe. All rights reserved, used with permission.

Title page artwork by Katlyn Breene, www.mermadearts.com.
All rights reserved, used with permission.

"Animal, Vegetable, Mineral Offerings" by Anne Key. From *Desert Priestess: A Memoir.* Las Vegas, NV: Goddess Ink, © 2011. All rights reserved, used with permission.

"Answering the Call of Service: Dianic Tradition and Women's Mysteries," "The Dianic Priestess," "Hearing the Call of Service," "Priestessing Yourself," "Priestessing Ritual" and "Models of Leadership" by Ruth Barrett. *From Women's Rites, Women's Mysteries: Intuitive Ritual Creation* © 2007. Llewellyn Worldwide, Ltd. 2143 Wooddale Drive, Woodbury, MN 55125. All rights reserved, used by permission.

"Ammachi: In the Lap of the Mother" by Linda Johnsen. *From Daughters of the Goddess: The Women Saints of India.* St. Paul, MN: Yes International Publishers, © 1994. All rights reserved, used with permission.

"The Art of Disappearance" by Lorraine Schein. From *Women Artists Datebook 2004.* New York: Syracuse Cultural Workers, © 2004. All rights reserved, used with permission by the author.

"Calypso's Island," "She Who Watches and Holds Still," "Wisdom of Elders," "Forest Rules" and "She Who Hexes Newscasters" by Patricia Monaghan. *From Seasons of the Witch: Poetry and Songs to the Goddess.* Cottage Grove, WI: Creatrix books, © 2004. All rights reserved, used with permission by the author.

"Discovering The Priestess Within: The Origins of a Thriving Women's Ministry" by IONE. From *Spell Breaking: Remembered Ways of Being. An Anthology of Women's Mysteries.* Kingston, NY: Ministry of Maat/Deep Listening Publications, © 2013, used with permission by the author.

"Garden-ing" by Andrea Goodman. *From Spell Breaking: Remembered Ways of Being. An Anthology of Women's Mysteries.* Kingston, NY: Ministry of Maat/Deep Listening Publications, © 2013, used with permission.

"Generating Stillness: Creating Sacred Space" by Kathy Jones. *From Priestess of Avalon, Priestess of the Goddess: A Renewed Spiritual Path for the Twenty-first Century.* Glastonbury, England: Ariadne Publications, © 2006. All rights reserved, used with permission.

"Holy Bite" and "Minoan Snake Priestess" by Le'ema Kathleen Graham. *From Dancing the Inner Serpent: Memoirs of a Snake Priestess.* Goddesswork, © 2009, 2013. All rights reserved, used with permission by the author.

"It's Easier to be a Priest than a Priestess" by Nano Boye Nagle/Ziji Salaam. Based on "Queer Spirituality" in *MatriFocus: Cross-Quarterly for the Goddess Woman* (Lammas 2003), www.matrifocus.com/LAM03/queer.htm. All rights reserved, used with permission by the author.

"Mourning-Woman-Priestess" by Jill Hammer and Holly Taya Shere. From *The Hebrew Priestess*. Teaneck, NJ: Ben Yehuda Press, © 2013. All rights reserved, used with permission by the author.

"Priestess: Born Unto Herself" by Pamela Eakins. A longer version of this article appears in *Priestess: 3000 BCE to The Future*. CreateSpace, © 2013. (Originally published as *Priestess: Woman as Sacred Celebrant*. Newburyport, MA: Weiser Books, © 1996.) All rights reserved, used with permission by the author.

"Questions for the Oracle" by Lorraine Schein. From *Vallum,* 8, no. 1, © 2010. All rights reserved, used with permission by the author.

"Raising the Sacred Fire: How to Build and Move Energy in Ritual" by Shauna Aura Knight. *From Circle Magazine: Celebrating Nature, Spirit, and Magic,* 105 (Winter 2009). All rights reserved, used with permission by the author.

"Ritual Design and Facilitation: Chanting that Works" by Shauna Aura Knight. From *Circle Magazine: Celebrating Nature, Spirit, and Magic.* All rights reserved, used with permission.

"Sacred Prostitutes" by Johanna Stuckey. From *MatriFocus: Cross-Quarterly for the Goddess Woman* (Samhain 2005), www.matrifocus.com/SAM05/spotlight.htm. All rights reserved, used with permission (Line drawings accompanying "Sacred Prostitutes" © Stéphane Beaulieu [2005]. All rights reserved, used with permission.)

"Temple Weaving: Jewish Weaver-Priestesses and the Creation of the Cosmos" by Jill Hammer. From *The Hebrew Priestess* by Jill Hammer and Holly Taya Shere. Teaneck, NJ: Ben Yehuda Press, © 2013. All rights reserved, used with permission by the author.

"The Role of the Priestess" by Delphyne Platner. Excerpted from "Conjuring the Priestess to Heal and Empower Young Women," in *She is Everywhere: An Anthology of Writings in Womanist/Feminist Spirituality,* edited by Lucia Chiavola Birnbaum. Berkeley: Belladonna, © 2005. All rights reserved, used with permission.

"The Stuff of Life: Clay Figurines and Priestesses in Mesoamerica" by Anne Key. From *She is Everywhere: An Anthology of Writing in Womanist/Feminist Spirituality* Volume III, edited by Mary Saracino and Mary Beth Moser. Bloomington, IL: iUniverse, Inc., © 2012. All rights reserved, used with permission.

"The Technology of Rhythm" by Layne Redmond. From *When Drummers were Women: A Spiritual History of Rhythm.* New York: Three Rivers Press, © 1997. All rights reserved, used with permission by the author.

"Wings of Augury" by Lorraine Schein. From *The Beltane Papers,* no. 8, ©1995. All rights reserved, used with permission by the author.

We have followed the footprints of those who walked this path before us. To all of those on the path now and all who will come after us, we dedicate this anthology to you.

CONTENTS

PREFACE xix

LINEAGE OF THE PRIESTESS

    CALYPSO'S ISLAND   Patricia Monaghan 5

    I, ENHEDUANNA   Jezibel Anat 6

    INANNA'S CHANT   Janine Canan 11

    SACRED PROSTITUTES   Johanna Stuckey 13

    SHE WHO WATCHES AND HOLDS STILL   Patricia Monaghan 25

    JOB DESCRIPTIONS FOR THE PRIESTESS   Asia Shepsut 26

    THE VOYAGE OF HATHOR TO SEE HER SEVEN SISTERS
        Normandi Ellis 42

SECRETS OF THE GREAT MOTHER   Normandi Ellis 49

THE KOHANOT: KEEPERS OF THE FLAME   D'vorah J. Grenn . . . 50

MOURNING—WOMAN—PRIESTESSES   Jill Hammer. 60

SHECHINAH   Geela Rayzel Raphael 76

TEMPLE WEAVING: JEWISH WEAVER-PRIESTESSES AND THE
    CREATION OF THE COSMOS   Jill Hammer 78

HOUSE OF THE VESTALS   Janine Canan 95

THE DREAM OF THE SNAKE PRIESTESS
    Le'ema Kathleen Graham 96

YOGINIS OF ANCIENT INDIA   Jalaja Bonheim 98

INVOCATION   Andrea Goodman. 105

THE STUFF OF LIFE: CLAY, FIGURINES AND PRIESTESSES
    IN MESOAMERICA   Anne Key 107

MY FAMILY'S LINEAGE OF PRIESTESSES   Carmen Roman . . . 120

ALOHA PRIESTESS PATH   Leilani Birely 125

CENTURIES   Janine Canan 129

THREE TIMES A PRIESTESS   Jade River 131

ANSWERING THE CALL OF SERVICE: DIANIC TRADITION AND
    WOMEN'S MYSTERIES   Ruth Barrett. 139

LUCK   Susan Levitt 144

DISCOVERING THE PRIESTESS WITHIN: THE ORIGINS OF
A THRIVING WOMEN'S MINISTRY Ione 145

THE ART OF DISAPPEARANCE Lorraine Schein 148

FOR APHRODITE AT THE WATER WHEEL Rachel Koenig 149

ROLES OF THE PRIESTESS

QUESTIONS FOR THE ORACLE Lorraine Schein........... 159

WALKING THE PRIESTESS PATH ALisa Starkweather 161

THE ROLE OF THE PRIESTESS Delphyne Platner 172

THE PATH OF PRIESTESS AND PRIEST: INITIATION INTO AN
ANCIENT TRADITION Jalaja Bonheim 175

PRIESTESS OF KALI Chandra Alexandre 185

AMMACHI: IN THE LAP OF THE MOTHER Linda Johnsen 191

THE DREAM Abbi Spinner McBride 209

PRIESTESS: BORN UNTO HERSELF Pamela Eakins 211

GARDEN-ING Andrea Goodman 216

I AM THE EARTH: THE PRIESTESS IN SERVICE TO COMMUNITY
Deirdre Pulgram Arthen 219

WISDOM OF ELDERS Patricia Monaghan............... 226

ON BECOMING A TREE PRIESTESS Kathryn Ravenwood 228

WINGS OF AUGURY Lorraine Schein.................. 234

THE STORY OF MY FIRST AND SECOND URBAN STREET TREES
    Jennifer Jones............................ 236

THE FOREST RULES Patricia Monaghan................ 242

THE DIANIC PRIESTESS Ruth Barrett................. 243

IT'S EASIER TO BE A PRIEST THAN A PRIESTESS
    Nano Boye Nagle........................... 247

I AM A PRIESTESS OF SHECHINAH Geela Rayzel Raphael ... 256

RECLAIMING ADAM AND EVE: THE WORK OF A PRIESTESS IN
    ISRAEL Hava Montauriano....................... 258

FLAMEKEEPER: PRIESTESS OF BRIGHID Erin Lund Johnson . 270

HOLY BITE Le'ema Kathleen Graham................. 273

THE UNFOLDING ONE Jill Hammer.................... 276

THE PRIESTESS AS WEDDING CEREMONIALIST
    Josephine MacMillan......................... 277

SHE HEXES NEWSCASTERS Patricia Monaghan.......... 283

TOOLKIT

THE STAR CHALICE Katie Anderson................... 291

THIN PLACES Breyn Marr 292

HEARING THE CALL OF SERVICE   Ruth Barrett 294

PRIESTESSING WITH INTEGRITY   Sylvia Brallier 309

PRIESTESSES I HAVE KNOWN   Calypso 313

THE HIEROSGAMOS OF HATHOR AND HORUS   Normandi Ellis . 324

THE CIRCLE OF THEATER AND RITUAL   Nan Brooks 327

MINOAN SNAKE PRIESTESS   Le'ema Kathleen Graham 336

RAISING THE SACRED FIRE: HOW TO BUILD AND MOVE ENERGY
   IN RITUAL   Shauna Aura Knight 339

PRIESTESSING RITUAL   Ruth Barrett 346

THE TECHNOLOGY OF RHYTHM   Layne Redmond 350

RITUAL DESIGN AND FACILITATION: CHANTING THAT WORKS
   Shauna Aura Knight 361

THE PERFECT PRAYER: INCENSE AND SCENT CRAFTING
   Katlyn Breene 368

PRIESTESS OF THE DOORS   Kathryn Ravenwood 380

PRIESTESS ME   H.D. Artemis 383

ANIMAL, VEGETABLE, MINERAL OFFERINGS   Anne Key 385

PRIESTESSING YOURSELF   Ruth Barrett 391

GENERATING STILLNESS: CREATING SACRED SPACE
   Kathy Jones 393

CRONE'S CAULDRON OF CHANGES Abbi Spinner McBride ... 396

GROUPS, POWER AND PRIESTESSING
    Shekinah Mountainwater........................ 398

AS WITHIN SO WITHOUT: SOME PSYCHOLOGICAL ASPECTS OF
    PRIESTESSING Kim Duckett...................... 408

WHO AM I Martina Steger 428

BUILDING A WORKING RELATIONSHIP WITH DEITY
    Mary Moonbow 430

SACRED VOWS Katie Anderson 438

WHAT SHE SPEAKS WHEN I TEND HER FLAME
    Erin Lund Johnson 439

RE-DISCOVERING YOUR WILD PRIESTESS POWER
    Gloria Taylor Brown 441

ROOFTOP POEM AT DENDERA Normanda Ellis 447

THE BODY IS MY BIBLE Vajra Ma.................... 448

DANCE WITH ME Martina Steger..................... 457

MODELS OF LEADERSHIP Ruth Barrett................ 458

THE WICCAN PRIESTESS AS INITIATOR: THE PSYCHOLOGY OF
    THE INITIATORY PROCESS Vivianne Crowley 464

ON ORDINATION Andrea Goodman 478

STEPPING INTO OURSELVES

THE BOOK OF EARTH   Jill Hammer 484

THE MOTHER OF US ALL   Tamis Hoover Rentería 489

CREDITS AND ACKNOWLEDGEMENTS

ACKNOWLEDGEMENTS 511

ABOUT THE EDITORS 513

ABOUT THE CONTRIBUTORS 515

APPENDICES

SUGGESTED READINGS 539

A GUIDE TO INCENSE BOTANICALS 549

READER'S GUIDE

QUESTIONS FOR DISCUSSION 564

Preface

This work was conceived at the bar in the lobby of the Doubletree Hotel in San Jose, California. Imbibing several glasses of red wine after leading a powerful ritual for Sekhmet at Pantheacon in February of 2012, we asked each other, "What shall we do next?" In unison, we said, "How about an anthology on priestesses?" Little did we know what that would entail over the next two years. We immediately began writing lists of possible contributors on the bar napkins. Our husbands just continued drinking and chatting with each other, as they often have to do in these situations. We were on a roll.

The first question we tackled: "What is a priestess?" Is she a ritualist? A leader? A shaman? A role model? A coach? A soothsayer? A sybil? Or is she all of these, or some of these, or none of these?" As good academics, our next step was to look in the dictionary. Oh my, what a surprise! The best example of what we found comes from the *Cambridge Dictionary*[1], which defines priestess as: "A woman in particular non-Christian religions who performs religious duties."[1] But we also found that a priestess was a variety of a fancy pigeon having a bald pate with a crest or peak at the back of the head, a small club used to kill fish, a rock band, an Armenian film and a Tarot card.

More to the point, we asked ourselves, what exactly did we want to accomplish with an anthology on priestesses? We wanted women to step into their power, and we wanted to make it easier for them to find the tools they need, both external and internal, to help them in their roles as priestesses or in becoming priestesses. We wanted to enhance women's authority and voices in spiritual contexts.

The title of priestess is an ancient one. We want this book to be a part of the movement that is bringing this enduring vocation into a living existence in the 21st century. The colorful tapestry of voices in this anthology displays the diversity of the roles and perspectives of priestesses and different ways of priestessing, and how they weave together to create the beautiful fabric of women's spiritual authority. Differing opinions exist without crushing each other.

Because traditional and mainstream religions do not recognize the spiritual authority of women in the role of priestess, we must move away from those structures and fashion our own. The definition of priestess may be unique to each individual, comprising different facets, but the common thread is service.

This anthology engages many topics. How does one become a priestess? What does she do? What qualities does she need? What skills are useful? Many questions remain. By what authority can she call herself priestess? Can a man be a priestess? We look to others to offer answers to these questions in future works.

Many women currently serve as priestesses. We honor their work and that of each of our contributors in this book. We intend this book to be helpful in recognizing and sustaining them.

This book is edited by two women of similar backgrounds: both white, educated, married, middle class women, both living in the Southwest of the United States, both priestesses of Sekhmet, both academics, feminists and trailblazers. We put the call for contributions for this anthology on our own networks, which often include women of similar backgrounds. This anthology is not representative of all the aspects of priestessing, nor all the lineages; it is Euro/Amero-centric, with a heavy emphasis on the modern Pagan, Wiccan and Goddess movements.

The threads that bind this work with other women in the world are the voices of these priestesses, these women who have accepted roles of spiritual leadership—practicing priestesses who are walking the barely discernible dusty path, detecting the faint trails of lost lineages, following them and creating new ones. This anthology is only the beginning. Many future works on priestesses will expand our work here to include other voices, and other traditions.

Endnotes

1 *Cambridge Advanced Learner's Dictionary*. 3rd ed. Cambridge: Cambridge University Press, 2008.

Lineage of the Priestess

Lineage of the Priestess

The story of priestesses begins at the dawn of humanity, and perhaps before. There is evidence of women in sacral roles in the Paleolithic including the bas relief on the cave of Laussel, the female figurines from Malta, graves in the Czech Republic and in Israel, and more. There were women in religious authority in the Neolithic in places such as Catal Huyuk, and later in Mesoamerica, among other places. An ancient lineage of priestesshood can be traced through many spiritual traditions such as Hinduism, Judaism and Hawaiian Huna.

The priestesses' written history begins with Enheduanna, priestess and poet of ancient Mesopotamia. The desert civilization of Egypt was familiar with priestesses, who played a prominent and significant role in Egyptian spiritual life. The Middle Eastern regions of Syria, Canaan and Israel also provide records of female religious leaders. Women played pivotal roles in early Hebrew temples, and the Roman Empire boasted of its Vestal Virgins, who kept the flame alive. Certainly, the island of Crete is replete with examples of women with spiritual presence, and even Classical Greece can provide models of priestesses.

With the emergence of patriarchal monotheisms and the diminishment of women's authority, the role of the priestess was eclipsed by that of male spiritual leadership; for a time, the priestess seemed to disappear. Yet, in the middle 20th century, women once again stepped into the role of priestess, reclaiming their spiritual authority.

The essays and poems in this first section are only a slight slice of the history—no, the herstory—of priestesses. The section opens with the poignant yearning of women remembering:

> This is the dream of the women
> sleeping in the rock, hair
> disheveled, breasts bare.
> This is the dream of the women
> in towns, in cities, everywhere.
> —*Patricia Monaghan, "Calypso's Song"*

The historical record of priestesses in Mesopotamia forms the bedrock. Reclamation of ancient roles in Judaism, speculations on the evidence of priestesses in Mesoamerica and the lineage of family priestesses in Mexico further expand the view. The resurgence of Wicca and the Dianic tradition in the United States has rebirthed the role of priestess, and it has flourished through the waves of the women's movement. This section ends with the longing of contemporary priestesses, the women carving a place where one once existed, weaving faded threads into vibrant cloth:

> Great Goddess
> Ignite
> the emptiness!
> Pour the Great
> Bliss through Your faithful.
> —*Rachel Koenig, "For Aphrodite at the Water Wheel"*

Calypso's Island*
By Patricia Monaghan

Animals always lead the way
into the earth. Down, down,
wolves lead the women,
down to the cave-heart,
back to their origin.

It has always been so
on this island of caves:
Animals lead the way,
women follow, becoming
animals and holy.

Into the black water go
the seal-women. Into
the cliff winds go the birds.
The horsewomen rear.
They have fled beyond words.

This is the dream of the women
sleeping in the rock, hair
disheveled, breasts bare.
This is the dream of the women
in towns, in cities, everywhere.

---

* From *Seasons of the Witch: Poetry and Songs to the Goddess* (Cottage Grove, WI: Creatrix Books, 2004).

I, Enheduanna
By Jezibell Anat

Enheduanna (ca. 2285–2250 BCE) was a priestess, princess and poet of ancient Mesopotamia, the area between the Tigris and Euphrates Rivers now known as Iraq. Here, centuries before her birth, the Sumerians developed a sophisticated urban civilization. They invented one of the first known systems of writing, the cuneiform script, so named because the characters consisted of wedge-like strokes formed by reed pens on clay tablets.

Early Sumerian goddesses were credited with the invention of arts such as writing and healing, but in later myths these roles were subsumed by gods. The one goddess who gained power and continued to flourish in the Sumerian era was Inanna. Personified as the morning and evening star (the planet Venus), she did not conform to the traditional feminine role of wife and mother. She was the Goddess of Love and War and eventually became Queen of Heaven and Earth.

Enheduanna's father was Sargon, King of the Akkadians, a Semitic people who lived north of Sumer. According to legend, Sargon's mother was a priestess of Inanna and was not supposed to bear children. In order to save her son's life, she placed the infant into a basket lined with pitch and set it adrift in the Euphrates, where the infant was rescued by a royal gardener. (This is one source of the Hebrew story of Moses, since the pitch that caulked both Sargon's and Moses' baskets was common in Mesopotamia but not found in Egypt.)

After becoming King of the Akkadians, Sargon conquered Sumer and established the first empire in Mesopotamia. The Akkadians adapted Sumerian mythology and culture, and maintained the Sumerian language as a sacred script. Sargon appointed Enheduanna as High Priestess in the city of Ur, in the heartland of Sumer, where many of the natives still resented their Akkadian conquerors. Combining political and spiritual authority, Enheduanna's task was to provide theological unification as well as to uphold her father's sovereignty.

Besides her administrative duties, Enheduanna composed poems and hymns for the deities, and she is the first recorded writer in history. Much of her poetry centered upon Inanna, whom she connected with the Semitic Goddess Ishtar. Enheduanna depicts Inanna with a wide range of attributes, from loving to ferocious. This priestess described her personal relationship with her beloved Goddess, introducing an emotional depth of expression that had not appeared in previous literature.

In a time when many of the functions and powers of the Mesopotamian goddesses were waning, Enheduanna's work maintained the presence of the divine feminine and established Inanna-Ishtar as one of the most widely worshiped deities. Her popularity endured throughout the subsequent Babylonian and Assyrian Empires. Enheduanna's position as High Priestess of Ur became a hereditary role of royal daughters, which gave them a great deal of power and influence.

Enheduanna's stories, poems and songs were used in ritual and for scribal study for centuries after her death, and became a model for other hierological compositions. She has been described as the Shakespeare of Mesopotamian literature.

I am Enheduanna, Ornament of Heaven, High Priestess of the Moon God Nanna in the city of Ur in Mesopotamia. I pour the lustrations from the holy water, bear the smoking incense, present the libations, lead the prayers, keep the feasts. To be a priestess is to live in the giparu, the sacred enclosure, among the pure ladies. Here the people bring the fruits of the harvests for us to tabulate and allocate.

I am the eldest daughter of Sargon of Akkad, First of the Kings, whose life became the stuff of legend. His mother was a priestess consecrated to Inanna, a naditu priestess, who was not supposed to bear children, but still she conceived. Luckily it was winter when her belly swelled, so she could conceal her secret in her cloak. When she gave birth in the spring, she hid her baby in a basket of reeds, lined the basket with pitch to make it waterproof, and offered her precious burden to the river. The king's gardener found the baby boy and raised him in the royal household.

Surely my father was specially favored by Inanna, for when he grew up, he joined the king's army and then he became its commander. With the support of his troops, he claimed the throne of Akkad, and then he conquered all of the territory between the Tigris and Euphrates Rivers. Here the Sumerians had developed a splendid civilization, but their feuding cities had nearly destroyed each other in war. Father wanted a unified land and an integrated culture, where the people could live in harmony, crops and flocks could grow in peace and trade could thrive.

We admired the Sumerians for their accomplishments, in agriculture, architecture, textiles and ceramics, but most particularly in literature, for their language is sacred to the divinities. From the mud of the river, they baked tablets of clay. From the reeds of the marsh, they cut pens to make marks in the clay, first to account for the grain and goods in the temple storehouses, and then to write the deeds of deities and rulers: stories and songs of praise and lamentation.

When I became chief priestess, it was my task to ensure that the rituals were rightly done, so that the hearts of the gods rejoiced. Not only did I choose the liturgy; I created it. I began to write new poems and songs for the rituals, and I was the first to take my pen and inscribe my name upon the wet clay to identify myself as the author. My father had no qualms about telling the world about his exploits, and so I proclaimed mine, declaring that I, Enheduanna, Moon Priestess of Ur, composed these texts.

As royal priestess, I served all the gods, for I understand the numinous powers that shape the universe. I wrote a hymn *for every god and goddess in every city of Mesopotamia, and then I went to each temple and sang each hymn with my drum, playing the rhythms that resounded in the heart. I raised my voice in praise and I moved my body in exultation; when the god or goddess was satisfied, I taught my song to the priests and priestesses. Thus my hymns became part of the temple literature, uniting the Akkadians and Sumerians in worship. My name was known, and my father's rule was stabilized.*

I was officially the priestess of Nanna, the Lord of the Moon, but though I watched his path every night, Nanna was not my personal deity. My heart followed the path of Inanna, Sumer's Queen of Heaven and Earth, and I saw her appear in the morning star that heralds the dawn and the evening star that acclaims the darkness. In my time, the popularity of the ancient goddesses was waning, fading into the background as gods began to subsume their roles and powers. But Inanna had been the protector of the Sumerian Kings, and she had blessed my own father as well.

I restored Inanna to the forefront of our theology, linking her to our Akkadian Ishtar. To the nobles, this Goddess demonstrated queenship, and to the peasants she embodied fertility. I wrote of her power as the Great Thundering One of ardent love and violent rage. I made sure that she was known in every shrine, as lover, warrior, prophetess. She became my inspiration, not merely in traditional myth, but as a vital, visceral force. She manifested as the shy maiden, the bold prostitute, the cunning trader, the fierce warrior, the prosperous farmer, the skillful musician, the mourning widow.

Inanna was not an easy Goddess to follow. She could be honey-sweet, but just as often she was demanding and cruel. I loved her wildness, her rebellion, her pride, for she did not conform to the ordinary. She was innin-sagura, the Lady of Largest Heart, and that heart beat fiercely, encompassing the full range of expression. In describing her, I did not repeat ritual formulas but shared my own feelings and my personal experience of her divinity, for I was her chosen priestess and she filled my heart.

Thus I reached between the worlds around me and I became a bridge: between Sumer and Akkad, between the priests and priestess of the different cities, between the clergy and the royals, between the gods and the people, and between Inanna and the other gods. My father's empire lasted decades. My songs and poems remained in the liturgy and in the temple schools for centuries. My writing set the standard, and my name was invoked for inspiration.

Inanna-Ishtar endured as the greatest Goddess of the Fertile Crescent and beyond, not just among the Akkadians, but among the Babylonians and the Assyrians, until the followers of Zarathustra and Jesus and Allah brought in their armies of intolerance and demanded absolute obedience. Like me, they wanted their religion to unite the people, but their vision was far narrower and their religions did not allow priestesses.

Now the Goddess is denied, the Fertile Crescent is a desert and the women of Mesopotamia are veiled. But my works have resurfaced, my ideas are in circulation and the Goddess is returning. I am Enheduanna, and what I have done, no one has done before.

Inanna's Chant
By Janine Canan

Heaven is hers, Earth is hers.
She is a warrior, She is a falcon,
She is a great white cow.

She fought the dragon and slew it.
She seduced the scorpion and tamed it.
The golden lion sleeps at her side.

She is the singer. She is desire.
She is the mountain of silver and gold and lapis.
On her hips tall trees grow, and grasses.

From Her, waters spout and savory grains.
Her lap is holy, her lips are honey,
her hand is law.

Her breast pours heavenly rain.
She is the healer. She is life-giver.
She is the terror, the anger, the hunger.

Fierce winds blow from her heart.
Hers is the thunder, the lightning, the glory.
She is the morning, She is the evening, She is the star.

STEPPING INTO OURSELVES

She wears the gown of mystery.
Heaven is hers! Earth is hers!
Who can argue?

Sacred Prostitutes*
By Johanna Stuckey

Figure 1. *"Woman at the Window," often interpreted as a prostitute, sacred or not, soliciting clients, but actually, in all likelihood, the Mesopotamian goddess Kilili, an associate or aspect of Inanna/Ishtar. One of many such ivory inlays of the same motif found in Mesopotamia, but probably made in Phoenicia/Canaan. Dated about 900 BCE. © S. Beaulieu, after Shepsut, 1993:115, Fig. 3.*

An "improbable percentage of the population [of Mesopotamia and Syria-Canaan] must have been either secular or religious prostitutes of some sort," wrote Beatrice Brooks in 1941.[1] She was drawing conclusions from the writings of predominantly male scholars who accepted without question the concept of "sacred, cult, or temple prostitutes." Female temple functionaries, they maintained, regularly engaged in sexual intercourse in return for a payment to their temples. Female devotees of Inanna/Ishtar, the Mesopotamian goddess of sexuality and love, were "immediately" suspect of such behavior.[2] Until recently, most scholars took this view for granted, and some still do.

---

* Originally published in a slightly different form in *MatriFocus: Cross-Quarterly for the Goddess Woman* (Samhain 2005), www.matrifocus.com/SAM05/spotlight.htm. Reprinted with permission.

In the nineteenth century, scholars thought Mesopotamia to be a hotbed of "naive and primitive sexual freedom."[3] Members of the then-new discipline of anthropology, such as Sir James Frazer of *The Golden Bough* fame, made matters worse by presenting for readers' delectation the orgiastic rites of fertility cults.[4] The result was a fertility-cult myth which took hold among scholars.[5] A number of ancient sources were ultimately responsible for the concept of "sacred prostitute": the Hebrew Bible; later Greek writers like Herodotus (ca. 480–425 BCE), Strabo (ca. 64 BCE–19 CE) and Lucian (ca. 115–ca. 200 CE); and early Christian churchmen. They greatly influenced later writers.[6]

Herodotus reported a "wholly shameful" custom by which every woman "once in her life" had intercourse near the temple of Aphrodite (Ishtar) with the first stranger who threw "a silver coin" into her lap.[7] Similarly, Lucian described the punishment of women who declined to shave their heads in mourning for Adonis: "For a single day they [had to] stand offering their beauty for sale . . . [in a] market . . . open to foreigners only, and the payment [became] an offering to Aphrodite [Astarte]."[8] The Christian writers accused pagans of indulging in orgies in honor of Aphrodite, ritual pre-marital sex, and "cult prostitution."[9]

It is true that much ritual activity in the ancient Eastern Mediterranean focused on promoting the fecundity of the land. In early Mesopotamia, for instance, the Sacred Marriage, with its fertility focus, could possibly have involved a "sacred prostitute."

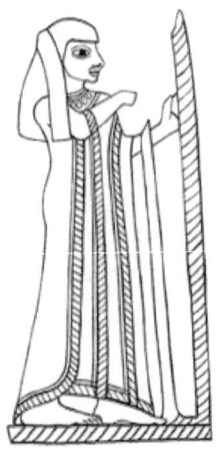

Figure 2. Canaanite dignitary with staff, possibly a priestess or queen. Ivory plaque carved on both sides. Probably a furniture inset. Pupils of eyes inlaid with glass. Megiddo, Israel. Dated about 1350–1150 BCE. © S. Beaulieu, after Pritchard 1969:38, Fig. 125.

Webster's English Dictionary defines a prostitute as, first, ". . . a woman who engages in sexual intercourse for money; whore; harlot"; second, ". . . a man who engages in sexual acts for money."[10] According to one scholar, "Cultic prostitution is a practice involving the female and at times the male devotees of fertility deities, who presumably dedicated their earnings to their deity." The Sacred Marriage rite was one of "the motives of the practice, particularly in Mesopotamia," where the king had intercourse with "a temple prostitute."[11] Obviously, most scholars did not distinguish between ritual sex and sexuality for pay.[12] However, ritual sex would not have been prostitution even if the act produced an offering for a temple.[13] Rather, it would have been an act of worship.

In the Hebrew Bible, the word normally translated as "sacred or cult prostitute" is *qedeshah/qedeshot* (feminine singular/plural) and *qadesh/qedeshim* (masculine singular/plural). These four titles do not occur very often in the Hebrew Bible.[14] The root, *qdsh*, means "set apart, consecrated."[15] For the most part, the terms occur in books from Deuteronomy through to II Kings, the so-called Deuteronomistic History, which is especially nationalistic, polemical and denunciatory of Canaanite religion.[16] The assumption that "sacred prostitution" had not only occurred, but had happened in the context of fertility cults, resulted from the Hebrew Bible's deliberate association of *qedeshah* (sacred/consecrated woman) with *zona* (prostitute).[17]

Figure 3. Seated North Syrian lady holding a goblet. Perhaps a priestess or a queen, who would also have been a priestess as a result of her queenship. Fragment of ivory carving found in Assyria, but probably made in Syria-Canaan. © *S. Beaulieu, after Shepsut 1993:168, Fig. 62.*

Thus, an important category of cult functionary called *qedeshah* existed in Canaan.[18] Otherwise, why would the Bible need to discredit such women? Their function in Canaanite religion is not known, but they were "consecrated women," probably priestesses.

When the archives of Ugarit, an ancient Semitic-speaking city in Syria, began to be interpreted, it quickly became evident that the religion of Ugarit was similar to the Canaanite religion vilified in the Hebrew Bible. Thousands of clay tablets dated to the Late Bronze Age (specifically to ca. 1300–1200 BCE, the last hundred years of the Late Bronze Age) were found to contain, among other things, lists of gods, offerings and religious functionaries.[19] None of the priestly titles in the texts is grammatically in the feminine gender, but they could have included women if the masculine form included the feminine, as it used to do in English.[20]

Figure 4. *Lady from Mari in northern Mesopotamia, now in Syria. Probably a priestess. Detail of main figure in a procession depicted in white shell inlay on slate. Found at Mari. Dated ca. 2600–2400 BCE. © S. Beaulieu, after Shepsut 1993:33, Fig. 7.*

The word *qdshm* (consecrated ones), designated important functionaries: ". . . we find [them] listed second after the *khnm* 'priests.'"[21] *Qdshm* had high status, could marry and establish families, and could hold other offices.[22] There is no suggestion that the ritual role of the *qdshm* was sexual; nor, indeed, is there any evidence to date of "sacred prostitution" at Ugarit.[23]

In Mesopotamian lists, the Semitic word *kharimtu*, usually translated as "prostitute," was often written with, or close to, the titles of female cultic personnel. As a result, the latter became "tainted" by proximity.[24] Thus, not only *qadishtu* but other female cultic titles were translated as "sacred or temple prostitute."[25]

The Mesopotamian Semitic titles, which have usually been translated as "sacred prostitute," include *naditu, qadishtu and entu*.[26] In general, *naditu* priestesses were high-status women who were expected to be chaste.[27] At Sippar in Old Babylonian times (ca.1880–1550 BCE), they included royal and noble women.[28] There is no evidence that a *naditu's* duties included ritual sex.[29] The title *qadishtu* (holy, consecrated or set-apart woman) has the same root as the Hebrew *qedeshah*.[30] After scholars have carefully scrutinized "extensive evidence of [the *qadishtu's*] cultic and other functions,"[31] it is clear that the *qadishtu* was no "cult prostitute."[32] Indeed, it is likely that most Mesopotamian priestesses, with one possible exception, were expected to be pure and chaste.

Figure 5. *Enthroned lady, probably a high priestess, found in the Ishtar temple at Mari in northern Mesopotamia. Alabaster statue. Dated ca. 2600–2400 BCE. © S. Beaulieu, after Shepsut 1993:33, Fig. 6.*

The one exception might have been the *entu*, whom the Sumerians called Nin.Dingir, which means "lady deity" or "lady who is goddess."[33] If the Sacred Marriage rite ever involved human participants, this priestess might, as Inanna, have had ritual intercourse with the king. However, the *entu* had very high status[34] and, according to Mesopotamian law codes, had to adhere to "strict ethical standards."[35] Whatever else she was, she was not a prostitute.

For a certain period, the Sacred Marriage was an important fertility ritual in Mesopotamia.[36] As a result of the king's participation, whatever form it took, he became Inanna's consort, sharing "her invaluable fertility power and potency," as well as, to some extent, her divinity and that of her bridegroom, Dumuzi.[37] Unfortunately, no text tells us what happened in the temple's ritual bedroom, not even whether the participants were human beings or statues.[38] However, in a persuasive article, Douglas Frayne argues that, at least in early times, the participants were human: the king and the Nin.Dingir or *entu*.[39]

In the Sacred Marriage material, the female participant is always called Inanna, so her human identity is obscured.[40] That is not surprising, for I suspect that, during the ritual, the only female present was Inanna. What I am suggesting is that the Nin.Dingir or *entu* was a medium. Through talent and training, she went into a trance and allowed Inanna to take over her body. Then the Goddess could actually be present during the ritual. To a greater or lesser degree, the king could similarly have embodied the God Dumuzi.

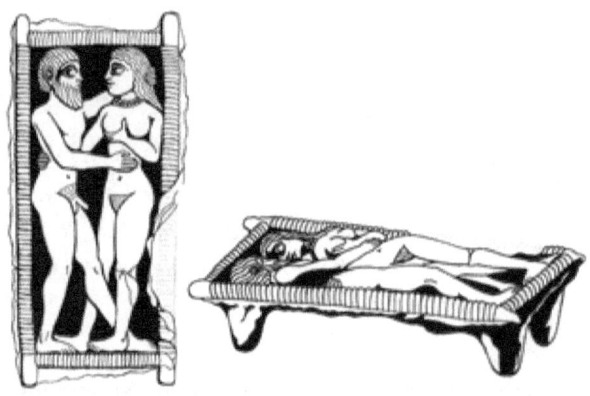

Figure 6. One of a large number of terracotta images of lovers on beds found in Mesopotamia. Often understood as connected to the Sacred Marriage rite, with the woman seen as a "sacred prostitute." Dated to the third millennium BCE. © S. Beaulieu, after Teubel 1984:117, Plate 19.

A medium is ". . . a social functionary whose body only, the person's awareness suppressed while in an ecstatic state, serves as a means for spirits to assist and/or communicate with members of the medium's group in a positive manner."[41] The "witch of Endor" in the Hebrew Bible

(I Samuel 28:725) was likely a medium; other ancient examples include the oracular priestesses through whom Apollo spoke at Delphi, and the Maenad devotees of Dionysus.[42] Today, mediums function in many religions rooted in many regions, including China, Korea and Africa, as well as in African-Christian religions of the Americas.[43] Interestingly, most contemporary mediums are female.[44]

Ancient Mesopotamia, like most other cultures, had its prophets and seers.[45] A number of them probably worked through trance. Indeed, ". . . ecstatic religious functionaries, that is, those whose religious functioning involves trance, are virtually ubiquitous in human cultures".[46] So it would not surprise me to discover that the Inanna of the Sacred Marriage rite was properly named, because the Goddess was using the body of a willing and devout ecstatic and priestess, who was certainly not a "cult prostitute." On the contrary, she would have had extremely high status and have been deeply revered, for she was chosen of the Goddess. Finally, then, the identity of the human female participant in the ritual is irrelevant. She was Inanna!

"Tragically," says one contemporary scholar, "scholarship suffered from scholars being unable to imagine any cultic role for women in antiquity that did not involve sexual intercourse."[47] However, recent scholars are fast setting the record straight. Even if ancient priestesses were involved in ritual sex, even if they received offerings for their temples, they were not prostitutes but devotees worshipping their deity.

Endnotes

1 Beatrice A. Brooks, "Fertility Cult Functionaries in the Old Testament," *Journal of Biblical Literature* 60 (1941): 231.
2 Julia Assante, "The kar.kid/[kh]arimtu, Prostitute or Single Woman? A Reconsideration of the Evidence," *Ugarit-Forschungen* 30 (1998): 6.
3 Ibid., 5–6.
4 Julia Assante, "From Whores to Hierodules: The Historiographic Invention of Mesopotamian Female Sex Professionals," *Ancient Art and Its Historiography*, ed. A.A. Donahue and Mark D. Fullerton (Cambridge/New York: Cambridge University, 2003), 22–24; Robert A. Oden Jr., *The Bible Without*

Theology (Urbana, IL: University of Illinois, 2000), 136–138.

5 Johanna H. Stuckey, "Ancient Mother Goddesses and Fertility Cults," *Journal of the Association for Research on Mothering* 7 no.1 (2005): 32–44. Julia Assante, "From Whores to Hierodules: The Historiographic Invention of Mesopotamian Female Sex Professionals," *Ancient Art and Its Historiography*, ed. A.A. Donahue and Mark D. Fullerton (Cambridge/New York: Cambridge University, 2003), 24–25; Wilfried G. Lambert, "Prostitution," *Aussenseiter und Randgruppen: Beiträge zu einer Sozialgeschichte des Alten Orients, ed.* V. Haas (Konstanz: Universitatsverlag, 1992), 136.

6 Robert A. Oden, Jr., *The Bible Without Theology* (Urbana, IL: University of Illinois, 2000), 140–147; Julia Assante, "The kar.kid/[kh]arimtu, Prostitute or Single Woman? A Reconsideration of the Evidence," *Ugarit-Forschungen* 30 (1998): 8; Richard A. Henshaw, *Female & Male, the Cultic Personnel: The Bible and the Rest of the Ancient Near East* (Allison Park, PA: Pickwick, 1994), 225–228; Edwin M. Yamauchi, "Cultic Prostitution: A Case Study in Cultural Diffusion," *Orient and Occident: Essays Presented to Cyrus H. Gordon*, ed. H. Hoffner (Neukirchen-Vluyn, Germany: Kevelaer, 1973), 216.

7 On Herodotus's "wholly shameful" Babylonian custom, Tikva Frymer-Kensky comments: "No cuneiform text supports the idea that the women of Assyria or Babylon did this." She adds that Herodotus wanted to demonstrate "the superiority of Greeks," and possibly "to show the horrible results that could follow if proper women were not kept as guarded and secluded as they were in Greece." Significantly, according to Yamauchi, late commentaries such as that of Herodotus are the "most explicit texts describing sacred prostitution in Mesopotamia." Herodotus, *The Histories*, trans. A. de Selincourt, rev. A.R. Burn (New York: Penguin, 1983), 121–122, vol. I: 199; Tikva Frymer-Kensky, *In the Wake of the Goddesses: Women, Culture, and the Biblical Transformation of Pagan Myth* (New York: Free, 1992), 200; Edwin M. Yamauchi, "Cultic Prostitution: A Case Study in Cultural Diffusion," *Orient and Occident: Essays Presented to Cyrus H. Gordon,* ed. H. Hoffner (Neukirchen-Vluyn, Germany: Kevelaer, 1973), 216.

8 Lucian, *The Syrian Goddess* (De Dea Syria), ed. and trans. H.W. Attridge and R.A. Oden (Missoula, MT: Scholars, 1976), 13–15.

9 Oden, Robert A., Jr, *The Bible Without Theology* (Urbana, IL: University of Illinois, 2000), 142–144.

10 *Webster's Encyclopedic Unabridged Dictionary of the English Language* (Avenel, NJ: Gramercy Random House, 1996), 1553.
11 Edwin M. Yamauchi, "Cultic Prostitution: A Case Study in Cultural Diffusion," *Orient and Occident: Essays Presented to Cyrus H. Gordon,* ed. H. Hoffner (Neukirchen-Vluyn, Germany: Kevelaer, 1973), 213.
12 Cooper, J. S., "Prostitution," *Reallexicon der Assyriologie.* 1932 – Founding eds. Erich Ebeling and Bruno Meissner. (Berlin/Leipzig: de Gruyter, 2006-2008), XI, 12-21.
13 Wilfried G. Lambert, "Prostitution," *Aussenseiter und Randgruppen: Beiträge zu einer Sozialgeschichte des Alten Orients*, ed. V. Haas (Konstanz: Universitatsverlag, 1992), 136.
14 For examples of *qedeshah*, see Gen. 38:21–22, Dt. 23:18; of *qedeshot*, see Hos. 4:14; of *qedesh*, see Dt. 23:18, 1K. 22:46; of *qedeshim*, see 1K. 14:24, 1K. 15:12, 2K. 23:7. The Jewish Publication Society translation of the Hebrew scriptures renders the female term "cult prostitute" into "prostitute," and the male term "cult prostitute" into "male prostitute." Richard A. Henshaw, *Female & Male, the Cultic Personnel: The Bible and the Rest of the Ancient Near East* (Allison Park, PA: Pickwick, 1994), 218–221.
15 The King James Bible translates *qedeshim* as "sodomites." F. Brown, S.R. Driver, and C.A. Briggs, ed. *A Hebrew and English Lexicon of the Old Testament* (Oxford: Clarendon, 1978), 871–874.
16 Robert A. Oden Jr., *The Bible Without Theology* (Urbana, IL: University of Illinois, 2000), 131, 132; Saul M. Olyan, *Asherah and the Cult of Yahweh in Israel* (Atlanta, GA: Scholars, 1988), 3.
17 Some scholars are even questioning the translation of term *zonah* as meaning "common prostitute, whore, harlot." See Julia Assante, "From Whores to Hierodules: The Historiographic Invention of Mesopotamian Female Sex Professionals," *Ancient Art and Its Historiography*, ed. A.A. Donahue and Mark D. Fullerton (Cambridge/New York: Cambridge University, 2003), 39, note 31. Phyllis Bird, "'To Play the Harlot': An Inquiry into an Old Testament Metaphor," *Gender and Difference in Ancient Israel*, ed. Peggy L. Day (Minneapolis, MN: Fortress, 1989), 76.
18 Richard A. Henshaw, *Female & Male, the Cultic Personnel: The Bible and the Rest of the Ancient Near East* (Allison Park, PA: Pickwick, 1994), 235–236.

19 Michael C. Astour, "Ugarit and the Great Powers,"*Ugarit in Retrospect: Fifty Years of Ugarit and Ugaritic,* ed. Gordon D. Young (Winona Lake, IN: Eisenbrauns, 1981), 4; Lete Gregorio del Olmo, *Canaanite Religion According to the Liturgical Texts of Ugarit* (Bethesda, MD: CDL, 1999); Jean-Michel de Tarragon, *Le Culte à Ugarit d'apres les textes de la pratique en cuneiformes alphabetiques* (Paris: Gabalda, 1980).

20 Jean-Michel de Tarragon, *Le Culte à Ugarit d'apres les textes de la pratique en cuneiformes alphabetiques* (Paris: Gabalda, 1980), 7, 8, 139ff.

21 Richard A. Henshaw, *Female & Male, the Cultic Personnel: The Bible and the Rest of the Ancient Near East* (Allison Park, PA: Pickwick, 1994), 222–225; Jean-Michel de Tarragon, *Le Culte à Ugarit d'apres les textes de la pratique en cuneiformes alphabetiques* (Paris: Gabalda, 1980), 134, 141; Edwin M. Yamauchi, "Cultic Prostitution: A Case Study in Cultural Diffusion," *Orient and Occident: Essays Presented to Cyrus H. Gordon*, ed. H. Hoffner (Neukirchen-Vluyn, Germany: Kevelaer, 1973), 219.

22 Jean-Michel de Tarragon, *Le Culte à Ugarit d'apres les textes de la pratique en cuneiformes alphabetiques* (Paris: Gabalda, 1980), 141.

23 Ibid., 139, 140; Edwin M. Yamauchi, "Cultic Prostitution: A Case Study in Cultural Diffusion," *Orient and Occident: Essays Presented to Cyrus H. Gordon*, ed. H. Hoffner (Neukirchen-Vluyn, Germany: Kevelaer, 1973), 219.

24 Julia Assante, "The kar.kid/[kh]arimtu, Prostitute or Single Woman? A Reconsideration of the Evidence," *Ugarit-Forschungen* 30 (1998): 11.

25 Julia Assante, "From Whores to Hierodules: The Historiographic Invention of Mesopotamian Female Sex Professionals," *Ancient Art and Its Historiography*, ed. A.A. Donahue and Mark D. Fullerton (Cambridge/New York: Cambridge University, 2003), 32.

26 Robert A. Oden, Jr., *The Bible Without Theology* (Urbana, IL: University of Illinois, 2000), 148–150; Julia Assante, "The kar.kid/[kh]arimtu, Prostitute or Single Woman? A Reconsideration of the Evidence," *Ugarit-Forschungen* 30 (1998): 9; Wilfried G. Lambert, "Prostitution," *Aussenseiter und Randgruppen: Beiträge zu einer Sozialgeschichte des Alten Orients*, ed. V. Haas (Konstanz: Universitatsverlag, 1992), 137–141.

27 Julia Assante, "The kar.kid/[kh]arimtu, Prostitute or Single Woman? A Reconsideration of the Evidence," *Ugarit-Forschungen* 30 (1998): 38–39;

Richard A. Henshaw, *Female & Male, the Cultic Personnel: The Bible and the Rest of the Ancient Near East* (Allison Park, PA: Pickwick, 1994), 192–195.

28 Rivkah Harris, "The Naditu Woman," *Studies Presented to A. Leo Oppenheim*, edited E. Reiner (Chicago: University of Chicago, 1960), 109, 123ff.

29 Robert A. Oden, Jr., *The Bible Without Theology* (Urbana, IL: University of Illinois, 2000), 148.

30 Julia Assante, "The kar.kid/[kh]arimtu, Prostitute or Single Woman? A Reconsideration of the Evidence," *Ugarit-Forschungen* 30 (1998): 44–45; Richard A. Henshaw, *Female & Male, the Cultic Personnel: The Bible and the Rest of the Ancient Near East* (Allison Park, PA: Pickwick, 1994), 207–213.

31 Mayer I. Gruber, "Hebrew Qedeshah and her Canaanite and Akkadian Cognates". *Ugarit-Forschungen* 18 (1986): 139.

32 Robert A. Oden, Jr., *The Bible Without Theology* (Urbana, IL: University of Illinois, 2000), 149.

33 Richard A. Henshaw, *Female & Male, the Cultic Personnel: The Bible and the Rest of the Ancient Near East* (Allison Park, PA: Pickwick, 1994), 47; Douglas Frayne, "Notes on the Sacred Marriage Rite," *Bibliotheca Orientalis,* no. 42 (1985): 14.

34 Richard A. Henshaw, *Female & Male, the Cultic Personnel: The Bible and the Rest of the Ancient Near East* (Allison Park, PA: Pickwick, 1994), 46.

35 Stephen M. Hooks, *Sacred Prostitution in Israel and the Ancient Near East*, PhD dissertation (Hebrew Union College Cincinnati, OH: 1985), 13.

36 Douglas Frayne, "Notes on the Sacred Marriage Rite," *Bibliotheca Orientalis,* no. 42 (1985): 6.

37 Samuel N. Kramer, *The Sacred Marriage: Aspects of Faith, Myth and Ritual in Ancient Sumer* (Bloomington, IN: Indiana University, 1969), 57.

38 Stephen M. Hooks, *Sacred Prostitution in Israel and the Ancient Near East*, PhD dissertation (Hebrew Union College Cincinnati, OH: 1985), 29.

39 Douglas Frayne, "Notes on the Sacred Marriage Rite," *Bibliotheca Orientalis,* no. 42 (1985): 14.

40 Yitschak Sefati, *Love Songs in Sumerian Literature: Critical Edition of the*

Dumuzi-Inanna Songs (Ramat Gan, Israel: Bar-Ilan University, 1998), 305.
41 Jordan Paper, "The Role of Possession Trance in Chinese Culture and Religion: An Overview from the Neolithic to the Present," *The People and the Dao: New Studies in Chinese Religion in Honor of Daniel L. Overmeyer*, ed. Philip Clart and Paul Crow (Sankt Augustin, Germany: Monumenta Serica Monograph, 2009), 87.
42 Ross S. Kraemer, "Ecstasy and Possession: Women of Ancient Greece and the Cult of Dionysus," *Unspoken Worlds: Women's Religious Lives*, ed. Nancy A. Falk and Rita Gross (Belmont, CA: Wadsworth, 1989), 49.
43 Jordan Paper, *Through the Earth Darkly: Female Spirituality in Comparative Perspective* (New York: Continuum, 1997), 95. Susan S. Sered, Priestess, Mother, Sacred Sister: *Religions Dominated by Women* (New York/Oxford: Oxford University, 1994), 181–193.
44 Jordan Paper, *Through the Earth Darkly: Female Spirituality in Comparative Perspective* (New York: Continuum, 1997), 95.
45 Joan G. Westenholz, "[Religious Personnel:] Mesopotamia" *Religions of the Ancient World: A Guide*, ed. Sarah I. Johnston (Cambridge, MA: Harvard University Belknap, 2004), 295.
46 Jordan Paper, "The Role of Possession Trance in Chinese Culture and Religion: An Overview from the Neolithic to the Present," *The People and the Dao: New Studies in Chinese Religion in Honor of Daniel L. Overmeyer*, ed. Philip Clart and Paul Crow (Sankt Augustin, Germany: Monumenta Serica Monograph, 2009), 95, 104–107, 222–226,303; Susan S. Sered, *Priestess, Mother, Sacred Sister: Religions Dominated by Women* (New York/Oxford: Oxford University, 1994), 181–193.
47 Mayer I. Gruber, "Hebrew Qedeshah and her Canaanite and Akkadian Cognates," *Ugarit-Forschungen* 18 (1986): 139.

She Who Watches and Holds Still*
By Patricia Monaghan

From the top of the round tower
a naked woman looked down
upon the darkening road north.

Little whirlwinds blew across the road,
little vortices of wind and sand.
She held her arms up to the sky.

The white sky tilted towards blue.
Horsemen appeared, riding steadily.
She watched with no fear, no fury.

She stood there fearless as the star fell
high above the tower. She stood there
as the wind rushed up the tower wall.

Now she is sleeping on the parapet,
the winds still and calm, the riders encamped,
the stars holding their places in the sky.

---

† From *Seasons of the Witch: Poetry and Songs to the Goddess* (Cottage Grove, WI: Creatrix Books, 2004).

Job Descriptions for the Priestess
By Asia Shepsut

The British Press announced in November 1992 that the General Synod of the Church of England had finally agreed to ordain women to the priesthood—by a margin of two votes. Those women who had decided to take that route were ecstatic, but the anomaly of the word "priesthood" struck me at the time with a sense of disappointment, since it meant women would be allowed only on sufferance into an establishment that was founded as a male-run organization, initiating further conflict in a tradition already riven by controversies. (The same is true for rare female rabbis, such as London's Julia Neuberger, while there is absolutely no possibility of a Muslim woman acting as an Imam; likewise within Sikhism, Zoroastrianism and all branches of Middle Eastern and Orthodox Christianity.)

In Journey of the Priestess, written before that year from a study of records of temple life in the ancient world, I had noticed that, as far back as 3000 BCE, Uruk, in southern Iraq, had one temple dedicated to Anu, the Sky God, run by males,[1] which ran in parallel with a second one dedicated to Inanna/Venus and run by females. I noted then that there was something to be said for keeping distinct the fundamental polarity between priesthood and priestesshood.[2] Commonly, in the largest *temenoi*[3] of Egypt, Sumer and the Levant, both priests and priestesses played their parts together in the complex hierarchy of one temple, but in this scenario priestesses never had overall administrative control. (Even today, a convent headed up by an abbess can only celebrate Holy Communion administered by a visiting priest or bishop.)

I would like to arrive at some criteria for the job of priestess for those who feel the calling, since there is no one simple formula and it depends on each person's gifts and level of development. I believe sometimes unconscious, or even conscious, memories from a past life can account for a natural inclination toward a role often quite outside one's own immediate life situation today.

2000 CE: Current Perspectives "Priestess"
Perusing current news items about women still trying to keep alive ancient traditions from eras before the rise of the monotheistic religions, I found an article published in 1995 about Maddula Venkataratnam of southern India, aged 75, who is described as a *devadāsī* seeking to pass on her dying tradition of sacred sex and temple dancing, now long desecrated by corrupt priests who began selling these young girls, dedicated to the God for life, into prostitution; genuine priests at temples such as the Jaggannath at Pūri say they now cannot properly perform their rituals without their participation. My next story, from 1996, described how the wife of a well-known British TV script-writer was ordained as a Buddhist Lama. From 1993, I have a magazine story about Susan Noble, an American who decided her karma was to become a Buddhist nun in the Shingon Japanese sect: after extreme austerities, she qualified as the head of the Daifukuji temple at Koryo. A magazine feature from 1997 related the story of Heather Campbell, a suburban English woman who trained with the Deer Tribe in California to become a medicine woman, and is now advising business executives back in Britain.

When it comes to the survival of priestess graves, a feature in a 1998 newspaper described the discovery in the Takla Makan desert, Central Asia, of the mummy of a shamaness from the first millennium, still wearing a blouse, long skirt and leather boots; astonishingly, she has European features and two plaits of pale hair, and tattoos on her hands, forehead and cheeks. In fact, the skulls of a priest and priestess of the previous millennium from Minoan Arkhanes in Crete served as the basis for the reconstruction of the faces of a pair of actual celebrants at an altar of sacrifice. These led me to consider, through artefact and text, the more usual links to individuals whose bodies have long since turned to dust.

For those interested in resurrecting pre-monotheistic ways and taking the freelance option, or even pioneering independent female temples, I propose to seek guidance from what priestesses used to do within the Western Tradition of the ancient Near East, of which Europe is part, with particular reference to Sumer, Syria and Greece. Mainly I consider known individuals who might serve as prototypes. Factual knowledge about these women has been revealed over the past two centuries through archaeology, giving a sense of the modes and levels of priestesshood and how (depending on the type of person you are) they could be adopted and adapted to our own times. This information is often buried in scholarly journals, a high percentage of which still need to be dug out of obscurity for general consumption by a new generation of researchers.

4000 BCE: Uruk and the Moon Priestesses of Ur

Uruk's history started in the fourth millennium BCE, when two separate temples were established with *ziggurats* for astronomical observations to keep the calendar accurate. Alongside the *ziggurat* of Anu were the living quarters of its priests, whose head was known as an *en*, or leader. We know the *en* would represent the God at the new year in the sacred marriage when he would symbolically ensure the fertility of the land with an act of ritual sex, probably with the Priestess of Inanna; inherited from the Neolithic Period, we might call this "cosmic sex." The inherent risks for abuse are obvious, and as time went on the physical rite was replaced by other ways of celebrating the male-female polarity on higher planes. The recent rejuvenating effect of a royal marriage on Britain, with ripples reaching to most English-speaking parts of the world, provides an idea of how potent the ancient act was intended to be.

From later in the fourth millennium BCE and into the third, and slightly farther afield, we have the archaeological remains of priestess quarters from temple sites in Iraq, at Khafaje Tell Aqrab and, most notably, Ur, which came under the direct jurisdiction of Uruk for its moon observations. In "The Giparu at Ur," Penelope Weadock gathered all the textual and archaeological information known about life in these quarters (*giparu* literally means "storehouse"), where this time it was a high priestess (*entu*) who would represent not only the consort of the Moon God Nannar (Ningal), but also his daughter Inanna (her brother being Shamash, the sun); note how at Ur the moon was regarded as male and seen as superior even to the sun and Venus.[4] An *entu's* duties included adorning Ningal's statue and making offerings to it of valuable objects (much like the practice involving Hindu temple statues today), as well as taking part in the sacred marriage rite at the new year, probably conducted with the King (who on that day took on the role of *en*, standing in for Nannar himself).

From the confusing plethora of archaeological information in Weadock's paper, we can assess the work of an *entu* and her entourage as a template for our work as priestesses. Since the Sumerians imagined their gods as being like human, the *giparu* was laid out as Ningal's house. Its square ground plan adjacent to the *ziggurat* survives. It was subdivided into many chambers, the most important being Ningal's official shrine. Smaller rooms were assigned to minor gods and to the graves of former *entus*, who were honoured with memorial rites (much like saints today) and offerings of cheese, butter and dates. So closely enmeshed with their lives was an *entu's* role as "upholder of the temple" that it is thought, in one or two cases, all those in her immediate entourage were compulsorily entombed with her when she died, along the lines of the occupants of the Royal Tombs of Ur themselves. Several rooms were assigned to her and her staff, and the entire establishment was run like an ordinary domestic house with a kitchen, storage rooms, a dining room and individual bedrooms.

Texts reveal that the words *en* and *entu* were bound up with the priest or priestess's far-reaching authority in managing local land and the produce it yielded, a day-to-day activity that took up most of her time. This provides the idea that we could run our own homes like a *giparu*: on the foundations of routines of housework, we could open up our homes to the conscious cultivation of divine presence, with the focal point being a special room or altar—the prototype of a convent, where a high priestess lived her entire working life as a Bride of Nannar, just as nuns today live as Brides of Christ. It also shows that, in high-day rituals, the role of a high priestess was closely connected to the state government itself. How we can make that link in the Age of Aquarius is open to development, but the initial step could simply be to let the running of our households on both practical and spiritual lines have a knock-on [secondary] effect on our neighbours.

3000 BCE: Enheduanna, High-Priestess at Ur in Turbulent Times
Enheduanna (*hedu-anna* means "ornament of heaven") was the most outstanding *entu* of Ur. She probably first served at Uruk, briefly; her father, King Sargon, placed his daughter in this position around mid-millennium, at a time when he was quashing rebellions and fighting enemies on all sides. Over about five hundred years, there were several other distinguished *entus* whose names we know. One of their main functions was to pray daily to Nannar for the success of the King, while another was to pass back his divine utterances in oracular fashion. Most high priestesses of Ur were royal women so, through them, temple life was bound to state control. Three cylinder seals, belonging to her vizier, scribe and hairdresser, survive with Enheduanna's name on them. In the University of Pennsylvania Museum of Archaeology, there is a circular limestone plaque (representing the full moon, one writer thinks) showing a side view of Enheduanna in a fleece robe and turban; it shows her taking part, with her retinue, in a ceremony that involved a naked male priest watering a young date palm. The palm represented (among other things) the Goddess Inanna (Venus) in fertility mode, often depicted with six braids of long hair, wheat ears sprouting from her shoulders and a date cluster in her hand (Figure 7).

Figure 7. *Drawing by Katlyn Breene*

Enheduanna wrote hymns and poetry addressed to Inanna. Her father wanted her to blend the cults of Sumerian Inanna (Venus) and Akkadian Ishtar; these two different peoples worshipped Venus, whose synodic cycle dovetailed with the cycle of the sun and moon, keeping the calendar synchronized and typifying Venus' central identity as the Goddess of Life and Harmony. Articulate, artistic and an effective administrator of the lands around Ur, Enheduanna was the most intellectually gifted to hold the position. While ensuring the upkeep of the fabric of her own temple, she also collected and edited, on one tablet, the hymns sung in the temples of the city states of Sumer and Akkad surrounding Ur.

Given that Enheduanna so identified herself with Inanna, the dimension of her life I dwell on here concerns the myth called "Inanna's Descent to the Underworld" because it is useful to us as a template to determine what levels of work are open to a priestess. As she reveals in her poem, "Nin-Me-Sharra" which means "Inanna, illustrious lady of measures," after the sack of Ur by Lugalanna (a rival king), Enheduanna was stripped of her position and lost everything. This parallels the Inanna story where, as she descends through seven levels of darkness seeking her beloved Dumuzi, she is gradually stripped of all items of apparel by the minions of her sister, Ereshkigal, the Queen of Hell. Then, as Inanna makes the return journey, one by one each piece of her apparel is restored. In terms of Hindu practice, we can look at the myth as a journey through the seven chakras of the body, as summarized in Table 1.

For us, these can represent seven key modes of priestesshood, or indeed stages in our own spiritual journeys, like the notes of the octave in music. We can ponder these levels in ourselves to consider whether we are happiest working at spiritual, psychological, intellectual or more material levels; at the same time, we can take into account that any one level is the gateway to those above and below it, due to the nature of the correspondences between, for instance, astrology, music, colour, plants and inert substances, our minds and bodies (the Mesopotamians consciously cultivated these correspondences to a complex degree).[5]

Level of Inanna's Descent	Type of Adornment Stripped from Inanna on the Downward Journey, and Restored on Her Upward Return	Main Corresponding Chakra
One	Turban, the pure headdress	Crown chakra
Two	Wig for her forehead	Brow chakra
Three	Small lapis lazuli beads for her neck	Throat chakra
Four	Twin egg-shaped beads on her breast and breastplate	Heart and lungs chakra
Five	Gold ring on her hand	Navel chakra
Six	Lapis lazuli measuring rod and circle in her [other] hand	Sex, bodily movement and rhythm chakra
Seven	The robe of ladyship	Root chakra

Table 1.

Priestesses today may not need to clock in to the powers of the planetary pantheon to keep the calendar on track, but the gods are still there and the great cycles of time and feasts of the year based upon them need to be upheld and celebrated: they represent the archetypal concordances between realms of spirit and psyche, which manifest in the world of matter that a priestess needs to understand if she is to help guide souls to their true home, by all modes possible. Here I see a split between priestesses who are more like civil servants, keeping the routines going without always understanding them (hence the value of working within a tradition, such as a church), and those who actually experience higher worlds and can speak from personal example in giving spiritual guidance and healing for journeys of the soul.

The top chakra would be open to those women with a truly spiritual nature, connected first-hand to divine worlds, and often needing to sacrifice the lower chakras (by not having children, remaining unmarried or giving housework a low priority, for instance) in order not to lose focus. Clearly, it is the high priestess who consciously maintains the doors opening to pure spirit, fostering a full spiritual tradition within the community and operating on several levels, as Enheduanna did, even if needing to delegate lesser tasks to other members of her group.

STEPPING INTO OURSELVES

In the ancient Near East, the term "priestess" covered an entire hierarchy from the top down to assistants of all kinds. Not all were equal to each other in spiritual capacity—some were perhaps only centred on one chakra—but all were essential for the greater glory of the god or goddess. For instance, I would put the *devadāsī* role at chakra six, since its underlying principle is to maintain the connection with rhythm and pattern, whilst chakra three covers singing and, when linked to the brow chakra, teaching and intellectual life. Someone who works predominantly from the heart chakra would influence others to offer devotion and enthusiastic praise in their spiritual life rather than relying on logic and metaphysics. Certainly, in the case of Enheduanna, we have a huge amount of evidence to show she was someone who operated on several levels, not only as a civil servant of the state, but also as a mystic and prophetess passing on the messages of the gods, a role she particularly regretted losing as it truly lived up to her rank.

Each priestess must consider whether she would prefer to be an assistant or junior priestess rather than the top lady—whether she'd prefer to be a foot soldier than to have the responsibility of queen bee. Everyone benefits from shared rituals, whether working in the kitchen, keeping everything clean or ordering supplies; all contribute, and there is also the option of taking turns in different roles. Though dress is probably no longer an animal skin, a priestess might decide to choose an item of dress or adornment that expresses her main work; I have a fond idea that any priestess can indicate her calling by wearing a necklace. A priestess may want to reflect, through ornament and fabric, the splendour, beauty and dignity of the Divine; but there must also be substance behind the dressing up, and simply being clean and tidy (pure) is important. For a guerrilla warrioress working invisibly within society in Amazon mode (Enheduanna often appealed to Inanna in her aspect as Warrior Goddess), the ordinary dress of the time may be most effectively innocuous.

At whatever rank, if a woman works to mirror the correspondences transmitted between heaven and earth, and vice versa, whether she is major or minor, she is a servant of heaven, for only as ends in themselves do "lower tasks" become profane. Perhaps the most interesting item Inanna loses and then regains during her journey to the underworld are the rod/ruler and circle of the *Me*, the measures of cosmic order that come under chakra six. She is depicted on seals conferring kingship with this regalia, which represent any rule or measure that keeps things together, from the regular motions of the stars and planets to the tools of geometry or the reproductive cycles that uphold order in human life. Women, through their biology, naturally have a sense of these rhythms, including the routines of meals and bringing up children, as well as defense and protection. We know from another Inanna myth that she did not wait for Ea, God of Wisdom, to give the Me to her; she simply took them. The very words "mother" and "mater" refer to someone who measures and regulates life for others. Finally, to be a priestess of the root chakra is extremely powerful; it is to maintain solitary contact with the Great Mother of the Universe as a hermit in order to transmit her Shaktic Being onwards: the hyperactive and materialistic West is completely unaware of the contribution the closed orders make through their deep silence.

2000 BCE: The Installation of the High Priestess of Baal at Emar
Syria in the second millennium perpetuated Mesopotamian traditions. We know, for instance, that *entus* like Enheduanna, with their fitness for the position having been decided by divination and astrology, were ordained on the authority of the Moon God, Nannar. From accounts about them, we have some ideas about the many rituals in Enheduanna's life, such as ablution rituals using water (the element of the moon), for frequent hand washing; and eating and drinking ceremonies, similar to events we celebrate today by eating and drinking (Holy Communion, for example). We also know she would have worn special priestess garb, and the enclosed nature of her life would have been crucial for its subtle infusion into the machinery of state.

In the past two decades, we have learned more about the life of a high priestess in Emar (Syria) from a text giving the order of events to be followed for the installation of a new lady to the office, chosen from already existing temple personnel or the local community.[6] For Emar, the God in question was Baal, the equivalent of Zeus/Jupiter in the classical world of the next millennium. Since it takes twelve years for Jupiter to travel through the entire circuit of the zodiac, one sign per year, by this time, this God, blended with the Sky God Anu, had superseded the moon in importance for regulating the calendar. In his everyday Weather God form, Zeus/Jupiter was depicted as a warrior with an axe, a sword or a mace representing thunder, lightning and rain. At Emar, the new priestess was described as fully representing Baal's consort, Ishtar/Venus, leaving behind the lunar character of the gods of Ur. The gist of the Emar text follows, with emphasis on the new points, based on Daniel E. Fleming's translation of the slightly damaged text in *The Installation of Baal's High Priestess at Emar*.[7] Each phase of her installation, which lasted many days, was interspersed with washing or anointing ceremonies, lavish animal sacrifices, offerings of drink and food to the gods and an astonishing amount of human feasting and drinking.

On the first day, "the sons of Emar" would perform a divination ceremony before Baal in order to identify "the daughter of any son of Emar" for the position, and an aromatic unguent would be poured over the chosen woman's head to sanctify her. The following day, her hair would be shaved off and, with a procession of singers, she would proceed to Baal's temple, where his weapon was kept. Her father would look after this sceptre of office and hold it while wine was passed round and a feast in honour of Baal took place: one table was presided over by the new priestess's predecessor, another by priestesses from neighbouring towns, and others for the officiating priest, the king of Emar and princes from the neighbouring areas. At the end of the day, at the gate of the temple, they would again anoint the new priestess and accompany her back to her father's house.

On the following day, all the gods of Emar would be offered bread and beer and then, in her father's house, they would dress the Nin-Dingir, or "God's lady," in a red wool robe specially brought in from the temple. In the temple, they would set up four tables: one each for Baal and his consort, and two on the ground for the underworld gods. Further feasting and propitiation ceremonies would go on for seven days. On the seventh day, the Nin-Dingir/priestess, followed by a procession of singers, would libate oil at city shrines of other gods, ending at Baal's temple, his weapon now solemnly carried behind Ishtar; after more offerings to him, his weapon would be handed to her. After much coming and going between shrines, with the Nin-Dingir still holding Baal's sceptre, she would go into his temple. While incense burned, yet more offerings would be made and more feasting would take place to sorrowfully commemorate Baal's disappearance in his journey to the underworld and then to celebrate his return and union with his beloved consort, who had made the journey to find him, thus re-enacting the Inanna-Tammuz story cycle of the passing of the seasons and the death and resurrection of plant and animal life. As the evening came to an end, the Nin-Dingir would be enthroned (the second-millennium Syrian cylinder seal in Figure 8, nicely matches this phase of the ritual), and then her own table/altar would be set up in the temple.

Figure 8. *From the Kunsthistorisches Museum. Used with permission.*

Now the officiating clergy would insert a pair of gold earrings in her ears, place the gold ring of Baal on her right hand and wrap her head in a red woollen headdress. Protective amulets of silver and gold would be affixed, with the city notables making offerings of silver and gold to her. "Two of her brothers [would] carry her on their shoulders," taking her back again to her father's house, still in procession with the singers and Baal's weapon carried immediately behind her. A further seven days of feasting would follow, ending with the enthroned Nin-Dingir offering to statues of Baal and his wife "two gold figurines of one shekel weight." Finally, the red vestment she had worn would be returned to its temple, and "when the Nin-Dingir [left] her father's house [for the last time], they [would] cover her head as a bride" and "her two maids will embrace her as a bride." She would once again do the rounds of the shrines ending at Baal's temple where, after yet further feasting, the notables attending would "give her one bed, one chair and one footstool. On that bed they [would] lay out one . . . blanket for her pure bedroom." Accompanied by singing, "her sisters [would] wash her feet and they [would] place one silver ring . . . in the water that washed her feet." Finally, "the Nin-Dingir [would] ascend her bed and lie down." Remember the bed of Nannar mentioned in the Ur texts, set up in the *giparu* for the entirely secret rite enacted upon it to celebrate the start of the new year. Then she would be allotted dowry rations: bales of wool, jars of oil, aromatics, wine, beer, milk and fruit, along with "two pairs of sandals, two pairs of boots, two gazelles, two fish and four pigeons." The text ends on this final note: "When the Nin-Dingir goes to her fate . . . the house of her father [would] take her ritual equipment—and the city gets nothing."

Here is a model whereby, even as a priestess, a woman had no position other than in relation to male relatives (a culture at least half the women in the world live by), and where, even if they do not like it, they have no choice but to go along with it and thereby still serve a purpose.

1000 BCE: Athens and Delphi: Administrative v. Oracular Priestesses
This is not the place to unravel the European, Egyptian and Asian roots of the Greek tradition of priestesshood: however, one or two details should be enough to convey continuity within the temple traditions of those lands. In passing, I cannot resist mentioning the bronze mirror in one of the smaller museums at Athens bearing the name and title in both Greek and Egyptian of a priestess of Hathor/Venus who owned it.[8]

Our exercise here is to roughly contrast what we might call the tamed respectability of the priestesses of Athena at the Parthenon (a word referring to its young virgin community) in fifth century BCE Athens, and their limited position in male-dominated Attic society, with the wilder modes of divine possession cultivated by the Delphic priestesses, which was in turn inherited from the prophetess Cassandra of Troy, who was brought back to Mycenae as a war trophy by Agamemnon. Cassandra appears in Aeschylus' tragedy, *Agamemnon*, describing the pain of giving birth to her prophecies as if giving birth to Apollo's child, whilst the last play in the *Oresteia* trilogy shows the Goddess, Athena, addressing the wild women of ancient tradition, the Furies, now renamed the *Eumenides*, to play their role in a more rational society based on public trial and the rule of law. This was the way to break the endless chain of revenge following

Agamemnon's sacrifice of his daughter, Iphigenia at the start of the Trojan War: his murder by her avenging mother Clytemnestra; her murder in turn by their avenging son, Orestes; Athena herself absolving Orestes' guilt by arguing that a woman's death was less important than a man's. (According to the story, Athena herself was born, not of a woman's womb, but from the head of Zeus.)

Where the priestesses of the Parthenon and Athena Nike on the Acropolis at Athens worked within the orbit of Athens and Eleusis (the latter still performing the secret rituals of the Mysteries with a virtual experience of the underworld that left its adherents unafraid of death), the Delphic Oracle under the aegis of Apollo perpetuated divination in terms of instinctual utterance. Even if the prophecies were in later times manipulated by its priests, its scope was international, consulted by kings throughout the immediate Near East, as far afield as Egypt and Sicily, and all around the Mediterranean. Even great philosophers like Pythagoras and Socrates were known to take advice from the Delphic or Athenian priestess of their time.

Herodotus described the encounter between Kleomenes, the Spartan general, and a current priestess of Athena: For when he went up to the Acropolis intending to seize it . . . the Priestess rose up from her throne before he could pass through the door and said, "Stranger from Sparta, go back and do not enter the holy place . . ."[9]

She certainly had authority within her own territory. The head priestess was usually a married woman belonging to the aristocracy, and in the British Museum the marble head of an elderly lady, labelled "Priestess of Athena," indicates she was venerable enough to have been sculpted. Indeed, like the *entus* of Ur, priestesses like Myrrhine, First Priestess of Athena Nike, were commemorated in death, in her case by a huge marble urn showing her led by the hand by Mercury, Leader of Souls, on her entry to the underworld, with a separate chiselled epitaph recounting her deeds.

The priestesses of Delphi operated in an entirely different way, pointing us towards the more instinctual path for those with clairvoyant gifts. The priestess was reportedly positioned in the cave below the Temple of Apollo, perched on a tripod over a fissure in the earth from which issued the sulphurous fumes of the underworld domain of Gaia/Mother Earth. She had a huge snake, originally associated with Delphi, an idea inherited from Babylon (where Marduk fought the female monster, Tiamat, splitting her in two to create Heaven and Earth); Apollo, who had usurped the site, grappled with the snake annually. The priestess' ability to channel the wishes of Apollo may have been enhanced not only by inhaling the natural gases but by chewing the leaves of the laurel plant (Apollo's plant). This leads to thoughts about shamanic use of mind-enhancing substances: while it is profane to use them merely for egotistical pleasures, within a full tradition, shamanesses used such substances to gain access to higher worlds.

2000 CE: Changing Perspectives

Before the rise of the monotheistic religions, hundreds, if not thousands, of women operated in society as priestesses. From Neolithic times, they took their cue from the animal world: goats are led by the nanny; bee hives centre on the queen bee, ants on the queen ant; the female wolf is head of the wolf pack. Most prominent of all are the lioness and her sisters, who run the pride and do the hunting; the lion is only needed for fathering cubs. Of course, there are examples from the animal world, too, where the male leads the pack and is involved in many different possibilities of partnership with the female. I believe our lesson here is that it is unwise to go against nature, and that there is room for all these differing power structures to co-exist.

If we wish to relink ourselves to ancient Near Eastern traditions, we can see how many options there are for priestesshood. It is safer to be attached to a living tradition because its infrastructure has weeded out an acceptable body of knowledge and practice, giving protection from self-serving deviation. It also provides the authority by which a person is placed in office, guaranteeing fitness for the job. But the monotheistic traditions of Judaism, Islam and Christianity—in comparison with the high status of priestesses in the ancient world—have all deliberately suppressed official female power. Perhaps this was accomplished initially as a reaction to the decadence that priestesshood had reached by the last centuries of the first millennium, visible in Athena's instructions to the

Eumenides. I do think it important not to disable men's natural operation and to leave them alone if they want to be. We must not wage war on them; we love them. There are more than enough men who want to cooperate with women without losing their manliness. Again, it depends on the human type they are, and on their gifts.

Taking a bird's eye view of ancient history, we must conclude that, at some point, pre-monotheistic traditions emerged gradually out of the life circumstances of the Neolithic agricultural revolution, and then out of the urban revolution from the fourth millennium BCE. We are again in the position today of needing to take into account our unprecedented situation as members of the hugest, most urbanised population the world has ever known. Coupled with seepage of the more damaging aspects of the media into every corner of one's psyche, this has caused great distortions of soul: never has there been such wholesale need for spiritual healing, on both ancient and modern lines.

Maybe it is time, not to put new wine into old wineskins, but to make new wineskins too. Women are now in a position to search out a middle way, either alone or in a group, and with men or without them. Although many readers may not think they have the capacity to be high priestesses, they certainly will have a talent that could be used somewhere in a network, and if so they should consciously step forward to their work without needing to be aggressive about it. Above all, it is important not to try to be men, but to persist in gaining acceptance for the ways we naturally approach things. Wherever the universe places us, we must work from that platform. Looking at the fourth millennium BCE Sumerian cylinder seal impression in Figure 9, with a wise old woman on her platform outside a reed shrine accepting offerings, we bear in mind that, from such beginnings, the great temples of the ancient world arose.

Figure 9. Photo by the author. Used with permission.

Endnotes

1 *Journey of the Priestess* is now out of print but available used from Amazon. Asia Shepsut, *Journey of the Priestess*. London: Aquarian/Thorsons, 1993.

2 Maybe a solution for the Protestant Church would be to have male-run churches and female-run ones.

3 "Temenoi," the plural form of "temenos," refers to sacred land set off as an official domain for political and religious leaders.

4 Penelope N. Weadock, "The Giparu at Ur," *Iraq*, vol. 37, no. 2 (Autumn, 1975): 101–28.

5 Full details are documented in Booklet 7A on www.cosmokrator.com.

6 We know much of this information due to emergency archaeology at new sites in Syria unearthed by dam-building along the Euphrates.

7 Daniel Fleming, *The Installation of Baal's High Priestess at Emar: A Window on Ancient Syrian Religion* (Atlanta: Harvard Semitic Studies, 1992).

8 The Egyptian word for a mirror is "Ankh," the familiar Egyptian hieroglyph for life, perhaps because the reflection in it is so lifelike.

9 Herodotus 72:3.

The Voyage of Hathor to See Her Seven Sisters*
By Normandi Ellis

A third voyage of Hathor follows on the heels of the other two voyages, lasting for the week (ten days) between Mechir 21 and 30. This time, Hathor sails north from her temple in Dendera to the Temple of the goddess at Beni Hassan to see the Seven Hathors.[1] The Seven Hathors were said to be the goddesses of fate and destiny who appeared after the birth of the holy child. They functioned rather like fairy godmothers, blowing their breath of life gently into the child's face and bestowing upon the babe its true human destiny, foretelling the future and even the moment of death. Sometimes they appeared as seven cow goddesses who suckled the holy child; sometimes they appeared as dancing maidens whose music and belly dances assisted the mother in childbirth.

Each goddess had her own secret name, by which she might be summoned: Lady of the Universe, Sky Storm, She from the Land of Silence, She from the Land of Khem (Egypt), She with Red Hair, She with Bright Hair, She Whose Name Flourishes through Skillfulness.[2] Like their older sister Hathor, these gentle, beautiful maidens could be appealed to by women in love in order to perform a love spell. Protective and powerful of magic, it was said that the red hair ribbons of the Seven Hathors could bind dangerous spirits and keep one from harm.[3] On many occasions, Hathor's priestesses wore red sashes imitating the girdles of these seven goddesses.

---

† Originally published in a slightly different form in *Feasts of Light: Celebrations for the Seasons of Life Based on the Egyptian Goddess Mysteries* (Wheaton, IL: Quest/Theosophical Publishing House, 1999). Reprinted with permission.

On the walls of goddess temples or within the tombs, the Seven Hathors often appeared as singers, dancers and priestesses assuming human form. In the Old Kingdom, *mastaba* (a flat-roofed Egyptian tomb) images of Hathor and her sisters were not uncommon. Carved on the walls of the tomb of Qar and Idut, a nobleman and his wife, one finds the seven goddesses making merry for the couple. Four goddesses dance the dance of life, while the other three measure time by clapping. The inscription reads: "Hail to you in life, Hathor, the places of your ka [soul] are propitiated that you should grow in what the goddesses desire."[4] Even in Ptolemaic times, the Seven Hathors retained their popularity as an image of the good life. On the sarcophagus of a nobleman named Unnefer appears a description of the Seven Hathors, who richly blessed Unnefer's life:

> Singers and maidens gathered together, making acclaim like that of Meret [goddess of music]. Braided, beauteous, tressed, highbosomed, priestesses richly adorned, anointed with myrrh, sickles. In Greece at temples dedicated to Artemis and perfumed with lotus, their heads garlanded with wreaths, all together drunk with wine and fragrant with the plants of Punt (myrrh), they danced in beauty, doing my heart's wish, their rewards were on their limbs.[5]

Not much is known about the long-standing festival of the people mentioned in the Dendera Calendar. In this season, equated with Egypt's spring, the priestesses of Hathor went abroad, dressed in colorful gowns, beautiful jewels and garlands of flowers. The rites they performed during this public festival would be the equivalent of what we might call "committing acts of random, senseless beauty." Wandering through town, singing and dancing, the priestesses occasionally stopped in the street or at the communal well, or knocked upon a door to single out a particular person to receive blessings from the goddesses. This transmission of divine grace was bestowed by a simple touch of the hand or lips, with some emblem of the goddess, perhaps the *sistrum* or *menat* (a musical instrument and necklace, respectively, connected with Hathor), perhaps a papyrus flower or lotus.[6]

Like the three wise men who journeyed from afar to bequeath the destiny of the infant Jesus with their gifts of gold, frankincense and myrrh, these goddesses likewise traveled from Dendera throughout Egypt to bless all mothers and their children. It may be the memory of this "voyage of Hathor to see her seven sisters," and the associated idea of bestowing gifts and blessings, that is connected to the Christian celebration of Little Christmas on January 7.

As beautiful and loving as the Seven Hathors could be, as goddesses of fate, they also possessed fierce aspects. The heinous fate that befell Osiris at the hands of his brother might well happen to a mortal being. In the underworld, the dead had to know the sacred names of the Seven Hathors and pass their tests before entering into eternal life. Upon meeting the goddesses in the underworld, the soul of the deceased cried out:

> Hail, ye seven beings who make decrees, who support Ma'at
> on the night of judgment of the *uatchat* [wadjet], who cut off
> heads, who hack necks to pieces, who take possession of hearts
> by violence and rend the places where hearts are fixed, who
> make slaughterings in the Lake of Fire, I know you. I know your
> names.[7]

Seven was a powerful number in woman magic throughout the ancient and classical world. In Arabia, the Seven Imams or Seven Sages were also thought to be seven mothers who make decrees. The seven *krittikas* of pre-Vedic India were called the "razors of the world," who possessed the power to judge men and cut them down with moon-shaped sickles. In Greece, at temples dedicated to Artemis and Athena, seven *caryatid* stood as the columns of the temples, much like the columns of Hathor that support Egyptian temples. These Caryatids were moon priestesses, the seven high priestesses who were the pillars of wisdom, called the "seven mothers." In Greek mythology, the "seven sisters of the Pleiades" were a flock of doves born to Aphrodite, a Greek goddess equivalent to Hathor. In Old Babylon, the new year originally began with the rising sign of Pleiades, rather than the later, more traditional sign of the Ram.[8]

In Egyptian mysticism, seven was the number of creative process and progression. There are also seven sacred vowels in the ancient language, seven chakras or wheels of light in the etheric body, seven notes in the musical scale and seven veils that robed the Goddess in light. In the language of architecture, the Egyptian pyramid had three angles and four faces, which equaled seven; that is, the number seven related to the energy of creative motion (three, or heaven) combined with stability (four, or earth).[9] The festival also occurred during a time of year when the Pleiades, the constellation that represented the Seven Hathors, was prominent in the eastern evening sky.

As an image of the union of spirit and matter, the Goddess, Seshat, the recording angel or scribe, appeared as an aspect of Hathor. A companion of Thoth, God of wisdom, Seshat inscribed one's life deeds in the *akashic* records (mystical knowledge encoded on the astral plane); she was often depicted making notches in a palm frond with her stylus to record the years of one's life, or writing in letters of gold on the leaves from the Tree of Life. Upon her head she wore a seven-petaled flower, protected by the inverted cow horns of Hathor.

The Egyptians assigned to Hathor and her seven sisters the art of divination and the transmission of wisdom, the magical mirror of Hathor being but one way to contact the spirit dimension. The Incans bear similar kinds of legends, as do the Greeks. The wise Egyptian always sought the truth and relied upon the knowledge that truth is often more than one thing.

Using Hathor's Magic Mirror

The British Museum of London houses a fine example of Hathor's magical mirror. Typically, Hathor's mirrors were made of bronze, and the handle of the mirror was shaped with Hathor's full form or with just her face at the top. The mirror itself was the image of Hathor's diadem, a lunar disk surrounded by crescents. Thus, the magic mirror and Hathor's energies were linked with the moon. The highly polished and reflective side was used for the age-old art of self-contemplation known as *scrying* (see below), while the other scoured or dented side collected negative energies and rebounded or dispersed them. The polished side aided one in viewing distant events, as well as gazing into the past and future. The scoured side became the means of dispelling inharmonious energy.

Invocation to Hathor

> *Sweet Hathor, queen of beauty, protector of the weak, shield us against the enemies of light. Adorn us in the raiment of truth and nourish and support us when our strength fails. Guide us in the interpretation of the heavenly signs and assist us in the daily routine of our earthly lives.*[10]

Hathor's Mirror for Self-Contemplation

Scrying is an ancient form of meditation that involves learning to still conscious thought and to focus one's subconscious mind on the mirror. One learns to sit quietly, focusing on the breath, the eyes slightly out of focus. To *scry* into a mirror, try gazing beyond or peering in through the object, as opposed to looking at the reflection. If you cannot get beyond the surface image, focus your vision at a point between the two eyes. Begin by invoking Hathor, then simply breathe awhile into the mirror, imagining your life's breath carrying the record of your spirit outward into visible manifestation. Repeat your own name while holding your focus. It may take a while to get the hang of scrying, of learning to see true, but keep practicing. Keep a pencil and paper handy, for when the meditation is finished and you find yourself back in focus gazing into your own face, you'll want to jot down whatever fleeting thoughts or images have occurred to you. These will form a record to which you can refer later to determine the accuracy of your visioning.

Hathor's Mirror for Self-Protection

The great talent of Hathor's mirror is its ability to deflect negative vibrations. In any dream or altered state, it is important not to look into the eyes of one whom you suspect is sending you bad energy. Once you know the problem—the negative energy may manifest as recurrent computer malfunctions, or cars constantly pulling out in front of you—then visualize the situation and write the problem on a piece of clean white paper. Gazing into the polished side of the mirror, hold the paper with the written problem to the other side. Invoke Hathor as your protection. Raise the mirror as you gaze into it, holding it almost as a shield. State firmly that you send the unkind thoughts and energy back to their origin, then respectfully ask Hathor to be the messenger. End with a ritual blessing, perhaps burning the image of the negative energy in a brazier and making an offering of thanks. Since the mirror's job is to force one to look truly at oneself and one's reflection, placing the mirror in your windows will keep intruders from your home, as well as other forms of psychic invasion, such as spirit manifestations.

Seeing Afar

Again, invoking Hathor and entering a tranquil meditative state, gaze into the mirror, focusing beyond it and allowing your mind to go blank. Do not attempt to force any image to appear. Simply let the magic work. The image may cloud over as energy gathers in the mirror. Some people see the vision directly inside the mirror; others close their eyes and see with the third eye. When the mirror clouds over a second time, the energy is dispersing. Cover the mirror with a dark cloth and thank Hathor for your vision.

Endnotes

1 Rosalie David, *The Ancient Egyptians: Religions, Beliefs, and Practices* (London: Routledge & Kegan Paul, 1982), 125.
2 Margaret A. Murray, *Egyptian Religious Poetry* (London: John Murray Publishers, 1949), 96.
3 Irmgaard Woldering, *The Art of Egypt* (New York: Crown, 1963), 127.
4 Author's translation of Pyramid Text Utterance 269. See R.O. Faulkner, *The Ancient Egyptian Pyramid Texts* (Oxford: Clarendon Press, 1969).
5 James Breasted, *Ancient Records of Egypt* (Chicago: University of Chicago Press, 1906), 2: 318.
6 Ibid., 332.

7 Lawrence Durdin-Robertson, *The Year of the Goddess: A Perpetual Calendar of Festivals* (Wellingsborough, Northhampshire: Aquarian Press, 1990), 131. "Wadjet" refers to a snake-headed Egyptian goddess, the protector of Egypt and closely associated with Hathor.

8 James Breasted, *Ancient Records of Egypt* (Chicago: University of Chicago Press, 1906), 2: 359.

9 Ibid., 4: 134–141.

10 Ibid., 141.

Secrets of the Great Mother
By Normandi Ellis

Last night when Egypt danced
The Goddess smiled.
Her face grew bright as silver.
She lifted Her skirt to reveal
a fecund body filled with stars.
In the market, She was anise;
She was cardamom and lemon.
All night She listened to my secrets.
"O Mother, I am wounded," I said.
"Yes," She said. "That's the nature of Love."
I sensed my Beloved everywhere—
glistening on the bodies of lovers,
intoning in the throats of frogs,
rustling in dark sycamore leaves
like thoughts turning over at night.
I saw Her face awakened and golden,
opening like night becoming day,
like lanterns alive inside the houses.
She blew her sweet breath
and stroked the hair of my neck.
She offered me sunlight and advice.
"Awaken now and repeat after me:
'For this day I was born.
I am a godded one, too.'"

The Kohanot: Keepers of the Flame
By D'vorah J. Grenn

We are keepers of the flame, eshet lapidot . . .
—Rabbi Lynn Gottlieb,
"Prayer for Lighting the Fires of the New Moon"

Inside our hearts is a flame that must be kept burning. That fire is our passion for Life, our yearning for God, our curiosity about the mysteries, our sparkle of humor, our enthusiasm for the Work. We keep that fire burning by engaging in spiritual practice.
—Rabbi Shefa Gold[1]

For those who may be floundering in search of a connection to the divine, and who feel alienated from Judaism because of its frequently patriarchal voice, there are ways to excavate and celebrate a deep closeness to the Ein Sof (that which cannot be named), to our ancestry and our soul's most insistent longings. Imagining and configuring the role of a contemporary Jewish priestess, a *kohenet*, can be a way to strengthen the umbilical cord connecting us to our heritage.

The re-emergence of the *kohenet* is one of the most exciting developments in Jewish and feminist conversation and practice in the past fifteen years, in a religious tradition that in contemporary times has no priests and has rarely acknowledged the possibility of independent priestesses. Women as oracles, healers, magicians and sorceresses have been known from the time of the Hebrew Bible; however, their roles have never been viewed as indicative of priestly qualities or functions but rather as threatening and "other."

The role of priestess in the ancient Temple of Solomon is usually described, when it is mentioned at all, as one fulfilled only by the wife or daughter of a priest. The word *kohenet* is a feminized form of the word *kohen*, a member of the priestly class headed by Moses' brother Aaron (from whom a lineage can be traced) in which the sons (and potentially the daughters) of a *kohen* inherited the role of priest. (*Kohanot* is the plural form of the word.) It is likely women also trained and performed as priestesses independent of any officially sanctioned structure. I believe this because I have witnessed rituals and liturgy that some of us have created, rituals that were doubtless inspired—often in undefinable, ineffable ways—by our ancestors and the rites they performed thousands of years ago.

What was the role of the ancient Israelite priestess, the *kohenet*? Could anyone step forward or be appointed to serve the needs of their community? What of the women who functioned daily as priestesses long before the 10th century BCE, when Solomon's Temple was built—what were they doing? Technically, these women would not have been called *kohanot* if they lived before Aaron, but I want to include the question here to stimulate our thinking.

I suspect the construction of Solomon's Temple as the official center of Judaism did not drastically change women's practices; sacrifices would have been made and divinations performed, for instance, long before the Temple existed. Indeed, it seems the priests were co-opting these functions while quoting scripture forbidding others to perform these rites as a way to ensure their new power structure stayed in place. Also forbidden were ancestor worship and other activities commonly practiced by oracles, healers and those often demonized in the literature as witches, magicians and sorceresses, all of whom were regularly consulted by both the monarchy and the people. It is interesting to note that many of these practices are the same healing and magical functions co-opted by the Church starting in the 12th century CE, and throughout the Inquisition we know all too well as "the burning times."[2]

The Holy of Holies in Solomon's Temple could only be entered by the high priest once a year, for deep prayer and communication with the Divine on behalf of all, on the high holy day of Yom Kippur. Yet today we know women would have congregated around their own Holy of Holies, whether that was in their domestic sphere, in a grove of trees, at oceans and rivers or on hills, where prophetesses consulted Huldah, and sacred Asherah poles have been found.[3] One can easily imagine that these prophetesses were also priestesses, and that people brought offerings and libations for Asherah, Shekhinah or other deities to these sacred sites. There is a vivid description of the destruction of symbols of Asherah in the second book of Kings, which describes it with such vitriol that there is little doubt Asherah and these sites, considered sacred by the people—in addition to or perhaps in lieu of the Temple—posed a threat, as did the priestesses who tended them.[4]

With few easily discernible precedents or writings to guide us, today's priestesses often feel as if we are making it up as we go along. We cannot readily capture an oral transmission on what it meant to be a priestess in ancient times, except through deep meditation to call on our primal, cellular memories, intuition, dreams and other non-verbal means of communication. We must pay close attention to signs and symbols, literary and other kinds of clues, and to the work of such women as Savina Teubal and Bernadette Brooten.[5]

Because the dearth of unbiased—or any—information about our foremothers' spiritual roles leaves us ignorant of much of our heritage, it often feels as if parts of ourselves are missing, buried or hidden along with customs and rituals that had to go underground because they endangered the status quo. As we unearth material culture and re-interpret the incomplete reports and "findings" of those male historians, theologians and archaeologists who did not include women's perspectives in their work, we encounter ourselves. As we piece the puzzle together, we are re-producing age-old rites of passage and creating new ceremonies relevant to our lives, taking inspiration from the words and acts of our ancestors, by using the *mikvah* ritual bath outside the customary context of menstrual separation within heterosexual marriage, for instance, to heal from rape or abortion.

Fictional but well-researched reconstructions of the past, such as *The Red Tent* by Anita Diamant, allow us to imagine what might have been. Rabbi and Kohenet Jill Hammer has written, "I am proud and grateful to have received the title rabbi, and I am dedicated to the task of creative interpretation that the title implies. Yet I have often felt there is something missing. How does this title connect me to my female ancestors, who were spiritual practitioners and ritual experts?"[6]

It is interesting to also note Starhawk's comment that, as she grows older, both her Jewish and Pagan identities grow stronger.[7] She is comfortable celebrating both Chanukah and Winter Solstice and has modeled the ability to hold both, while declaring herself a priestess in an earth-based tradition with many similarities to early Judaic traditions.

Kohenet D'vorah K'lilah, liturgist and teacher, has written, adapted and translated hundreds of prayers embracing both ancient and contemporary traditions, hopes and concerns. She co-led services/rituals with me at Mishkan Shekhinah in San Francisco in 2007, and holds Rosh Chodesh ceremonies in her home/temple. One of the first *kohanot* to be initiated, in 2009, through Rabbi Jill Hammer and Holly Taya Shere's Kohenet Priestess Training Institute, D'vorah teaches ancient Judaic practices and is preparing a book of ritual practices for publication.[8]

DeAnna L'am, an international pioneer in Menstrual Empowerment, as well as an educator, ceremonialist and peacemaker, is a Romanian-born Israeli Jew living in California; although she does not practice contemporary Judaism, she feels deeply connected to pre-Judaic Middle Eastern goddesses dating to times long before recorded Jewish traditions. Raised as a secular Jew in Israel, she does not see Judaism as an essential part of her identity. Growing up, she celebrated Jewish holidays both in school and at home, not as spiritual activities but rather as "a cultural thing." Today, DeAnna raises a daughter with her husband in a home steeped in multicultural spiritual roots; she recently noted, "My spiritual practice is rooted in Paganism, and earth-based traditions."[9]

DeAnna's priestessing includes her work on rituals and "healing work for women of all ages around their first menses, holding Red Tent retreats, coming of age ceremonies, and mother-daughter work, as well as training other women to do this work in their communities."[10]

It stands to reason that many of the roles we perform today were also performed by the ancient priestesses outside the Temple space, where they were not allowed to perform cultic functions. In the books of Kings and Chronicles, these functions are often attributed to sorcerers, magicians, diviners and prophetesses, so sometimes we have to read between the lines, recognizing that the activities of a prophetess or diviner often overlapped with those of priestesses, and that we are working with the challenges of semantics and androcentric bias. There are ample references in the literature to functions performed by priestesses. They included, but were by no means limited to:

- Preparing sacrifices; making animal, meal and incense offerings; baking cakes for the Queen of Heaven.[11]
- Chanting repetitive, trance-inducing litanies.[12]
- Serving as oracles, diviners and guides.[13]
- Writing and delivering prophylactic incantations, and invocations at births and other times.[14]
- Speaking to the ancestors and angels on behalf of the community.[15]
- Drumming; playing tambourine.[16]
- Offering wine, water and honey libations.[17]
- Serving as scribes; writing as well as performing the reading of sacred texts, writing and vivifying amulets, incantation bowls and other prophylactic devices.[18]

Many of the above-mentioned roles continue in the work of contemporary *kohanot*. "Cultic or priestly functions could have included singing psalms, providing musical accompaniment, performing priestly blessings, examining the priestly offerings and animals and performing sacrifices."[19]

In my own practice, I build altars, light the lamps, create amulets and invocations, give food offerings, offer libations and drum ritually; I have coordinated goddess-centered Shabbat dinners, and conducted prayer ceremonies and a variety of rituals, including weddings and baby blessings. Little of my work revolved around death rites until my father's passing. Now I do mostly private rituals honoring my ancestors and, when I was gathering prayers for my own Mishkan Shekhinah *siddur* (prayer book), I brought in the sacred feminine by adapting the Jewish Mourner's Kaddish, later published in *Festival of Bones 2: What is Remembered Lives*[20] and *Talking to Goddess*.[21] Like my colleagues, I have worked privately with young women to imagine and shape rites of passage, including rites which are either alternative to or can accompany a Bat Mitzvah.[22]

At one time, it felt sacreligious to invoke my ancestors; it has been affirming to discover that my ancestors did so. Certainly, honoring our ancestors through yearly remembrances, and marking an ancestor's *yahrzeit* (death anniversary), are embedded in the tradition, and this has become a place where my Jewish and African practices can come together strongly. There are differences in the two traditions, to be sure; for example, within Ashkenazic Judaism, we do not prepare food for our ancestors and most do not intentionally set up an "ancestor altar" *per se*, but this priestess does.[23] If we look at the practices of Lemba South African Jews, the indigenous Igbo Jews in Nigeria or the Abayudaya of Uganda, we certainly see ancestral communication in the form of food offerings and libations. Among the Lemba, we see direct communications from women doing call-and-response to the ancestors in a beer-and-snuff ritual, for instance, and in the offering of special foods.[24]

Our roles today may include many or all of the above-named functions, as well as creating blessings for one another in groups, rewriting male-dominated liturgy and re-creating rituals for lifecycle events, including menarche rites and the use of the *mikvah* ritual bath, mentioned earlier, not just within marriage or as a wedding or pre-birth rite, but also to celebrate a new job or new home, to acknowledge menopause or other transitions, or as a healing ritual in response to such events as miscarriage, divorce or death.

Was there an ancient role for a priestess if she was single, or married to someone not a priest? How would different Jewish women define the role of *kohenet*? Of course, the answer depends on whom you ask, but most would agree on a number of roles. For some contemporary priestesses, empowered action comes from re-envisioning rituals, in writing new blessings and in a feminist re-reading of sacred texts. For others, finding and including the female aspect of deity in worship is crucial. Space constraints do not allow me to elaborate here, but I invite readers to explore these questions further, to expand what are always juicy conversations.

How do we move forward from here? Being a priestess can be exhausting. Without proper shielding and protection, women can find their precious energies only going out, and too rarely being replenished. We must continually find new and effective ways to guard against becoming depleted. Every day, we witness the positive, transformative effects of "restoring women to ceremony," to use Lynn Gottlieb's phrase, another reason it is vital that we continue our work. But to do so, we must protect our spirits, psyches, hearts and time[25]; those who have been spiritual leaders for some time are well aware of the pitfalls of not doing so. Since others rely on our strength and clarity, this is not a task to be postponed or ignored. We must carry and pass on the knowledge of how to take better care of ourselves, along with our spiritual teachings.

When we recite the litany of Inanna's powers—the *me*, the Thunder, Perfect Mind, an *oriki* (a type of Yoruba praise song or prayer) to Yemaya or our own blessings—we hear the female voice of deity speaking to us with strength and power. She is beyond time, definition or the confines of any religious construct. It is through her voice, combined with our deepest senses, that we can access our own sacrality, a prerequisite to leading others.

Without knowing exactly what spiritual leadership roles women played within the Hebrew/Israelite community 3,000 years ago, we can be left with the mistaken impression that only men led worship, both inside and outside the official Temple, the impression that only men connected with deity and that men were the predominant shapers of culture. Correcting these still-common misconceptions is a vital part of our work as priestesses, scholars, writers and theologians.

There is reason to be hopeful that our numbers will grow, that *kohanot* and priestesses in other traditions will begin to lead more often, within and outside of traditional religious spaces. If we can work less in isolation and more in collaboration, and as we hold cross-cultural, cross-millennial conversations with other priestesses and healers, we will support each other while expanding recognition of what female spiritual leadership looks like. When the work goes slowly, or is not understood, when we come under attack or feel alone, it is critical that we seek such connection, to preserve our ability to serve the larger community as catalysts for spiritual growth, justice and positive social change.

Endnotes

1 Lynn Gottlieb, *She Who Dwells Within: A Feminist Vision of a Renewed Judaism* (San Francisco: HarperSanFrancisco, 1995), accessed November 2012 at www.rabbishefagold.com/FireOnTheAltar.html and excerpted with permission; and Shefa Gold, personal communication.

2 See Donna Read and Erna Buffie, *The Burning Times* (Toronto: National Film Board of Canada, 1990).

3 Johanna Stuckey, *MatriFocus* web magazine 3–4 (Lammas 2004) accessed January 2013, http://www.matrifocus.com/LAM04/spotlight.htm

4 2 Kings 23:4–7, 23:15.

5 Savina Teubal, *Sarah the Priestess: The First Matriarch of Genesis* (Athens, Ohio: Swallow Press, 1984); Bernadette Brooten, *Women Leaders in the Ancient Synagogue* (Atlanta: Scholars Press, 1982).

6 Rabbi Jill Hammer. "Faces of the Shekhinah: Thirteen Archetypes of the Priestess from Jewish Tradition," *Kohenet: The Hebrew Priestess Institute,* accessed December 2012, www.kohenet.org/articles/.

7 Melissa Raphael, *Introducing Thealogy: Discourse on the Goddess* (Sheffield: Sheffield Academic Press, 2000), 41.

8 Personal communications, 2012.

9 Personal communications, 2008, 2012.

10 Personal communication, 2012.

11 John Bodel and Saul M Olyan, eds. *Household and Family Religion in Antiquity (*Hoboken, NJ: Wiley-Blackwell, 2008), 147–148; Ziony Zevit, *The Religions of Ancient Israel: A Synthesis of Parallactic Approaches* (New York and London: Continuum, 2002), 508, 569; William G Dever, *Did God Have a Wife?: Archaeology and Folk Religion in Ancient Israel* (Grand Rapids and Cambridge: William B. Eerdmans Publishing Company, 2008); Rabbi Jill

Hammer. "Faces of the Shekhinah: Thirteen Archetypes of the Priestess from Jewish Tradition," *Kohenet: The Hebrew Priestess Institute*, accessed December 2012, www.kohenet.org/articles/.

12 Max Dashu, personal communications, 2002, 2008.

13 Bernadette Brooten, *Women Leaders in the Ancient Synagogue* (Atlanta: Scholars Press, 1982); Rabbi Jill Hammer. "Faces of the Shekhinah: Thirteen Archetypes of the Priestess from Jewish Tradition," *Kohenet: The Hebrew Priestess Institute*, accessed December 2012, www.kohenet.org/articles/; Hennie J. Marsman, *Women in Ugarit and Israel: Their Social and Religious Position in the Context of the Ancient Near East* (Boston: Brill, 2003).

14 Gideon Bohak, *Ancient Jewish Magic: A History* (Cambridge: Cambridge University Press, 2008); Hennie J. Marsman, *Women in Ugarit and Israel: Their Social and Religious Position in the Context of the Ancient Near East* (Boston: Brill, 2003); Karel Van der Toorn, *From Her Cradle to Her Grave: The Role of Religion in the Life of the Israelite and Babylonian Woman* (Sheffield: Sheffield Academic Press/JSOT Press, 1994).

15 Savina Teubal, *Sarah the Priestess: The First Matriarch of Genesis* (Athens, Ohio: Swallow Press, 1984).

16 Carol Meyers, "Women with Hand-Drums, Dancing: Bible," *Jewish Women's Archive*, accessed February 2013 www.jwa.org/encyclopedia/article/women-with-hand-drums-dancing-bible; Exodus 15:20–21.

17 Philip J. King and Lawrence E Stager, *Life in Biblical Israel* (Louisville: Westminster John Knox Press, 2002); John H. Walton, Victor H. Matthews, and Mark W. Chavalas, *The IVP Bible Background Commentary: Old Testament* (Downers Grove, IL: IVP Academic, 2000).

18 Hennie J. Marsman, *Women in Ugarit and Israel: Their Social and Religious Position in the Context of the Ancient Near East* (Boston: Brill, 2003); Erica C.D. Hunter, "Who Are the Demons? The Iconography of Incantation Bowls," Instituto de Estudios Islámicos y del Oriente Próximo, accessed January 2013 at www.ieiop.csic.es/pub/08hunter.pdf

19 Bernadette Brooten, *Women Leaders in the Ancient Synagogue* (Atlanta: Scholars Press, 1982).

20 Maes Valdez Xochipala, *Festival of Bones 2: What is Remembered Lives* (Oakland: Ile Orunmila Oshun, 2011).

21 D'vorah Grenn, *Talking to Goddess* (Napa and San Mateo: The Lilith Institute, 2009).

22 Max Dashu, independent scholar and founder of the Suppressed Histories Archives, has spent more than forty years researching women's religious roles around the world. She believes the priestess would have been responsible for the singing of chants—often used as conduits for incantations—prophecy, divination, communion with the spirits of the dead, divine litanies, attendance at birth and death and going into trance states for oracular purposes. When I first spoke with Max of priestly roles and ancient ancestor reverence practices, she noted that dislocation of ancestor reverence occurs early on in the Bible with references to the Witch of Endor. Personal communications, 2002, 2008.

23 The Ashkenazim are Jews who come from Germany, France and Eastern Europe. Other major groups are the Sephardim, who come from Spain and Portugal, and the Mizrahim, of North Africa and the Middle East.

24 Deborah Grenn-Scott, For she is a tree of life: Shared roots connecting women to deity. An organic theological inquiry into identities, beliefs and practices among South African Lemba and European-American Jewish women (doctoral dissertation), accessed from ProQuest Dissertations and Theses database (AAT #3078795), 2003.

25 Lynn Gottlieb, *She Who Dwells Within: A Feminist Vision of a Renewed Judaism* (San Francisco: HarperSanFrancisco, 1995), 119.

Mourning-Woman-Priestess*
By Jill Hammer

On Tisha b'Av, the summer night when Jews mourn the destruction of both the first and second Temples in Jerusalem,[1] the Kohenet Institute—a group of Jewish women learning priestessing in a Jewish context—led a service for the entire community at the Isabella Freedman Jewish Retreat Center. We appointed some of our students as spiritual guardians. They stood at the door of the synagogue, served bread we had just baked with ashes (a traditional Ashkenazi dish for Tisha b'Av) and anointed everyone who entered with the ashes from the bread-baking. The reading of the book of Lamentations began.

At the center of the room was a design made out of river stones—a kind of mandala. We invited everyone present to come and take a stone at some point during the reading. This represented the destruction of Jerusalem: the removal of its walls, foundations and inhabitants. The stones were also a reminder of present reality: people starving, enslaved, at war or expelled from their homes.

Surrounding the mandala were four women, covered in *tallitot* (prayer shawls), who acted as our *mekonenot* (mourning women). As the reading began, the women keened and vocalized. Most of us have never heard professional lamenting women, but these women gave us some of that experience. Their voices blended with the voices of the violated girls and bereaved mothers of the book of Lamentations itself. As the stones began to disappear, the women's voices grow louder. The last of

---

* Originally published in a slightly different form in *The Hebrew Priestess* by Jill Hammer and Holly Taya Shere (Teaneck, NJ: Ben Yehuda Press, 2013). Reprinted with permission.

the stones were taken away, the reading ended and the center of the room was empty.

Nearly 24 hours later, we re-gathered for a ceremony to end Tisha B'Av. The center of the room was still empty. A single stone was at the center of the empty floor. We began a chant:

> What is gone
> We build upon
> Stone by stone
> Tear by tear
> We release
> And create right here.[2]

As we sang, the community came forward to replace their stones. Priestesses began to arrange the stones in spirals and vine shapes: a new pattern, not the old. The mourning women watched and slowly removed the shawls from their heads. Some of us began to weep. We were seeing the rebuilding of Jerusalem, of the world, of our own hearts. Later, we broke our fast together.

The mourning woman is the keeper of grief and also the bringer of comfort. She acknowledges the seasons of loss and prepares us for what will come. Mourning priestesses give voice to the love we have for what once was, and allow us to take that love into the future.

The Biblical Period
As the Babylonian empire grows and the exile of Judea looms, Jeremiah instructs the women of Israel: "Call the mourning women [mekonenot], and let them come; send for the wise women, and let them come: let them set up a wailing over us, so that our eyes run with water . . . let them teach their daughters weeping, and their companions lamentation . . ."[3] A *mekonenet* is a professional wailing woman at a funeral. She is a ritual expert at grief.

Lamentation is a ritual performed by mourning women from Korea to Egypt to New Orleans. The biblical book of Lamentations speaks of women weeping for the lost Jerusalem, and weeping for their own lost spouses and children. Some believe this ancient book was written or spoken at least partly by women, who had a tradition of performing grief poems after a death.[4] Men also recited mourning songs and poems in ancient Israel; King David's lament over Jonathan is only one example. II Chronicles 35:25 reports that *hasharim vehasharot*, male and female singers, recited laments for King Josiah, and these laments became a fixed custom.

In the book of Judges, there is a ritual involving the ritual grief of young women. In the story of Jepthah's daughter, a chieftain named Jephthah was about to go into battle. He made the foolhardy vow that, if God granted him victory, he would sacrifice the first creature to come toward him out of the door of his house. This was lethal stupidity, as we know from the rest of the Bible that *mevasrot*, female dancers, frequently came out of towns and cities to welcome returning warriors. Jephthah's daughter came out to greet him, and his response was to blame her for causing his suffering: he now had to sacrifice her to God.

> When Jephthah arrived at his home in Mizpah, there was his daughter coming out to meet him with timbrel and dance. She was his only child; he had no other son or daughter. On seeing her, he rent his clothes and said: "Woe, daughter! You have brought me low, you have become a trouble to me. For I have made a vow and I cannot retract."
>
> She said, "Father, do to me as you have vowed . . . Let this be done for me: leave me alone for two months, and I will go down upon the hills and weep for my maidenhood, I and my companions". He said: "'Go." He sent her away for two months, and she and her companions went and wept for her maidenhood on the mountains. After two months, she returned to her father and he did to her as he had vowed. She had never known a man.
>
> It became a law in Israel: every year, for four days of the year, the maidens of Israel went to sing mourning songs for Jephthah's daughter.[5]

Jephthah's daughter asked permission to "bewail her virginity" or "her maidenhood" before her father killed her as a sacrifice. She did this among other young woman, though the nature of the lamentation they performed is unclear. After the grisly deed occurred, it became an annual ritual for girls to go into the mountains and ritually grieve (*letanot*) for Jephthah's daughter.

The ritual of mourning may predate the story of Jephthah's daughter. An annual ritual of mourning may have been a seasonal lamentation for a dying and reborn god or goddess. The story of the maiden sacrificed by her father might be a later tale, meant to provide a "legitimate" explanation for the ritual. The phrase "they went down upon the hills" is strange—"they went up upon the hills" would be the usual phrase. This might indicate some sort of cave/underworld descent ritual similar to the one performed as part of the Eleusinian rituals for Demeter and Persephone. The girls who enacted these rites would have been lay priestesses of a sort, similar to the girls who did the annual dances at Shiloh.

In the Bible, there is no cycle of mythic life and death, no dying goddess or resurrected Osiris. Yet there does seem to be a relationship between some Israelite women and the God Tammuz, a dying and resurrected god of ancient Canaan. Tammuz, or Dumuzi, was the Sumerian/Babylonian Shepherd God, husband of Inanna. In the myth known as The Descent of Inanna, Dumuzi was condemned to live in the underworld. His devoted sister, Geshtinanna, volunteered to substitute for him half of every year. Like Persephone, Tammuz returned to the underworld at a specific time each year, and there was ritual mourning for him. The prophet Ezekiel complained that women were ritually weeping for the God Tammuz in the Temple itself:

> Next he brought me to the entrance of the north gate of the house of the Lord, and there sat the women wailing for Tammuz. He said to me: what have you seen, mortal? You will see even greater abominations than these.[6]

This text suggests that the prophet knew of Jewish women who were mourning, not only for humans, but for deities; they may have been priestesses of Tammuz, or they may simply have been part of an annual festival observance. Their weeping would have served to honor the spirit of the grain, and the sunlight that grows and diminishes. Like the tears of Geshtinanna, the women's tears assured that Dumuzi would return to the world in his proper season. Demeter, Cybele, Isis and other weeping goddesses in other myths also played this role.

The prophet Jeremiah also alluded to the ritual weeping of women and goddesses. Jeremiah invoked the spirit of Rachel, wife of Jacob, the matriarch who died in childbirth and was buried by the road near Bethlehem. Jeremiah transformed Rachel into a mythic figure weeping for Jewish exiles:

> A voice is heard in Ramah, lamentation and bitter weeping, Rachel weeping for her children, refusing to be comforted for her children, for they are not. Thus says God, Refrain your voice from weeping and your eyes from tears, for there is a reward for your labor. There is hope for your future, God says, and your children will return to their borders.[7]

Jeremiah, well aware of the myths in which mothers weep for their suffering offspring, depicts Rachel as an eternally compassionate mother, praying for the return of the people. Justin Lewis has suggested that Jeremiah was telling the people of Israel that they had a Spirit Mother (just as they did in the land of Israel, in the form of the Goddess Asherah). This Spirit Mother pleaded for them before the angry god, and her compassion rescued them from exile.

In the Second Temple period and beyond, there continued to be figures of women mourning. In II Maccabees, as Syrian-Greek soldiers defiled the Second Temple, Jewish women tied sackcloth around their breasts, and raised their hands toward heaven. This was an act of mourning and a prayer to God to help the people. The Christian depiction of Mary grieving for Jesus, accompanied by female companions, also is very much in the tradition of the mourning woman.

The Mythic Mourning Woman in the Post-Temple Period

By the rabbinic period, Shekhinah, the numinous Divine Presence, began to appear in the role of God's estranged wife. She took a particularly strong role as a mourning woman, grieving for the Temple's destruction. Shekhinah's "husband" was the transcendent aspect of the Divine, who had withdrawn into the heavens in anger. As enemies destroyed the Temple—the home of Shekhinah—she wept and reluctantly fled from Jerusalem:

> When the Shekhinah went forth from the Temple, she returned and hugged and kissed its walls and pillars and wept, and said: "Goodbye [shalom], my Temple, goodbye, my royal dwelling, goodbye, my beloved house! From now on, let there be peace!"[8]

In this *midrash* (story) the word *shalom*, which means both "goodbye" and "peace," expresses the Shekhinah's suffering and hope in a single breath. Another *midrash* tells how Jeremiah meets Mother Zion on a mountain near Jerusalem. In this *midrash*, the Jewish people are depicted as a mourning woman:

> Jeremiah said: When I went up to Jerusalem, I saw a woman sitting on the mountain top, dressed in black with disheveled hair, and she was weeping and wailing: "Who will comfort me?" I approached her and said to her: "If you are a woman, speak to me, and if you are a spirit, flee before me." She said to me: "I am your mother Zion." I said to her: "In time to come I will build you up."[9]

Much later, the Kabbalists integrated the weeping Shekhinah into their vision of God. They imagined exile as a cosmic disaster that affected all of creation. For the Kabbalists, the passage in Jeremiah where Rachel wept became a depiction of Shekhinah mourning her children's exile. Her grief was so great that it shook the entire world. Her mourning nearly turned the universe back into chaos and void:

> R. Yose then discoursed on the verse: "A voice is heard in Ramah, lamentation and bitter weeping; Rachel weeping for her children, for they are not." He said: "We have learned that on the day that the Sanctuary on earth was laid waste . . . Israel went into captivity with millstones on their necks and their hands bound behind them, and the Shekhinah was banished from the house of her Husband to follow them . . ."
>
> She said: "I will weep for my home and my children and my Husband." When she came down and saw her home devastated and the blood of saints spilled in its midst and the holy shrine and temple burnt, She lifted up her voice, and the higher and lower angels quaked and fell. The voice ascended to the place of the King, and the King wanted to turn the world into chaos again. Many armies and hosts of angels went down to meet her, but she would not accept consolation . . . She went all around the land of Israel and then into the wilderness . . . [10]

The weeping Shekhinah, like the weeping goddesses of the ancient Near East, is not only a lamenter. She is a healer. Her tears inspire God's mercy. So too, the grief of lamenting women was a way to ask God to console and heal mourners—mourners of individuals, mourners of community disasters and mourners for the brokenness of God.

The Talmud, the Middle Ages and the Modern Era

The Mishnah (the first written version of the Torah, from roughly the 2nd century CE) mentions mourning women as a standard part of Jewish funerals. We learn about mourning women because the Mishnah mentions they were restricted from performing certain kinds of laments at funerals that took place on minor holidays.

> On the new moon, on Chanukah and on Purim, women may cry out and pound their hands [in grief]. They may not wail

(mekonenot). Once the deceased is buried, they may not cry out or pound their hands. What is "crying out?" When they all sing together as one. What is "wailing?" When one speaks and they all answer after her.[11]

The Talmud notes that it was the custom of women to walk before the funeral bier with their heads covered,[12] and suggests that this is because "women brought death into the world" (because of the sin of Eve); however, the real reason may be that women were the chief lamenters of the community. The procession of women before a funeral bier may be a continuation of the customs of mourning women from the biblical period, as well as indicating the continuing sense of women's power in the realm of death. Women, who birth human beings into the world, also have the role of escorting them out of the world again.

Maimonides, the 10th century Jewish philosopher of Cairo, wrote in a similar vein to the Talmud:

> During [the intermediate days of Passover] women cry out, but they may not pound their hands on each other in grief or ritually mourn. Once the corpse is buried, they may not lament. On Rosh Chodesh, Chanukah and Purim, they may cry out and pound their hands on each other in grief before the corpse is buried, but they may not wail. What is meant by crying out? That they all lament in unison. What is meant by wailing? That one recites [a dirge] and the others respond in unison.[13]

This passage shows that, from 2nd century Israel to 11th century Cairo, Jewish women served as sacred mourners, singers and poets, giving vent to the feelings of mourners by expressing grief in sound and gesture. This was probably one of the only ways women could be public ritualists in that time period. We know of a variety of their techniques because of these texts: call-and-response poetry, pounding of the hands, and vocalizing or singing in unison. While women did not say Kaddish (traditional Jewish mourning prayer) for the dead, they were intimately involved in the mourning process—particularly those professional women who specialized in grief ritual. A 16th century Yiddish manuscript, called *Many Pious Women*, describes mourning women who sew shrouds while wailing, wearing special mourners' headdresses. "They stare out from their mourners' headdresses like owls, they bawl and cry for the deceased so sorrowfully, and stir up pity beyond telling."[14]

However, some Jewish sources discourage women's involvement in mourning. In the Zohar, women are described as a danger at a funeral because "the Angel of Death dances before them,"[15] and says that men and women should not walk near one another at a funeral lest harm come to the men. Other texts claim that a spirit of uncleanness clings to women at a funeral. The folklorist, Joshua Trachtenberg, reports that in Worms "men turn their faces to the wall when the women walk by" on their way home from a funeral.[16] These sources indicate a growing desire to take the public rituals of mourning away from women. However, many women retained their own customs around death: Sephardic women had a tradition of mourning songs, and Ashkenazi women recited *tekhines* (women's prayers) at graves.[17]

After the 14th century, women became involved in the chevra kadisha: the burial society, with its washing and garbing ceremonies. This secret society maintained elaborate traditions and customs, and every community had one. In Jewish law, only women are allowed to prepare a female for burial, and so this practice was and remains open to women, though women were not considered full members of the burial society until the modern period.[18]

By the 17th century, a few women were reciting Kaddish, but women continued to be barred from most public mourning practices.[19] The refusal, even in 20th century America, to allow women to say Kaddish was a major catalyst for Jewish feminism in the seventies and eighties; women like Letty Cottin Pogrebin and Susannah Heschel were galvanized by their mourning experiences. In liberal Jewish communities around the world, women have claimed the right to say Kaddish and publically mourn, and women rabbis and cantors lead funerals; even modern Orthodox Jews have released some of the strictures around women's mourning. In contrast, contemporary ultra-Orthodox practice forbids women from attending burials, saying Kaddish or performing many other kinds of mourning practices. There has been recent controversy in Israel because some rabbis are forbidding women from giving eulogies, even if that is their family custom. Millennia after Jeremiah reported the first lamenting women, the role of women in mourning practices remains controversial.

Mourning-Woman/Priestess Incarnations
Amy is a practicing Jew, a DJ and a promoter of Rastafarian music. An initiate of the Kohenet Institute, Amy identifies as a Mourning Priestess. She has lost many relatives in her life: her father died when she was eleven, and in recent years she has lost her mother and aunts. Amy is devoted to the memories of her loved ones, honoring their death-dates and saying Kaddish for them all.

Every time we do a *mitzvah*, every time we say a blessing or give charity, we are participating in *aliyat neshamah*, the rising of a beloved deceased person's soul. Everything we do can be dedicated to those we love on the other side.

When asked to define the Mourning Woman, Amy replies:

She is the priestess who is grieving, and because of her own personal experience with grief, she is there for those in mourning. Because of whatever loss she has experienced, she's been altered, and that alteration defines her. You lose a part of yourself; there's a sadness.

My personal experience enables me to comfort others. There's something so wonderful about Shechinah goddess energy—nurturer, healer, tender—the gift of life. Whatever life-cycle event is going on, the rituals we [priestesses] create are there to strengthen them, acknowledge whatever has occurred and pray for the future.

Kohenet graduate Ri J. Turner is studying for a certificate in Jewish sacred music. A composer of sacred chant, she understands the role of priestess as integrator of many kinds of experience, including sorrow.

She reports the following vision of the Mourning Woman:

In the moments between being awake and asleep, I saw all of us kohanot in a room, at a festive gathering, a new year's gathering. Then another woman entered the room—the New Year herself, embodied as a woman. She was clad half in black, half in white. She was veiled. There was the sense that she bore great grief, but she carried it sacredly. She was welcomed into the room by the kohanot, with great warmth and love, and she seemed comforted.

Grief herself is just another woman in need of our love, support, and welcome. In our circle, the love that we offer to each other, and to the Grieving One herself, makes it possible for grief to coincide with fullness, and for life to go on, for all of us together.

This vision is similar to visions of the weeping Shekhinah in ancient *midrash* and mystical sources, only this Shekhinah is surrounded by women who support and comfort her. At a Kohenet Institute retreat, Jess Schurtman created a papier-maché mask of Shekhinah weeping, with crystal tears dangling down her cheeks. Performing while wearing the mask, Shekhinah invited the audience to tell their sorrows so that she could mourn them. As we shared, she wailed out our grief in a loud voice. At morning prayer the next day, just before Kaddish, we passed around the mask, this time as a bowl full of blue ribbons. Everyone took a ribbon as a reminder of our mourning with Shekhinah. We recited the names of our loved ones and told their stories, bound together by the blue thread.

Spirit Journey: The Mourning Woman
You find yourself on a hill overlooking a ruin. It may be a building, or even a city. It looks as if the place is abandoned. You feel you are searching for something.

You wander the ruin. In an open space or clearing you find a tree. The tree has charred, cracked skin. Its limbs are burned away. It bears a single flower. Compelled by a strong impulse, you pluck this flower. As you do so, your heart is pierced with a great grief. You hear the weeping of a woman. You feel invisible arms embracing you, and you too begin to weep or express your grief in some way.

You look down at the blossom in your hands. As you watch, the blossom shrivels, dries up and blows away. In its place is a seed. You search for a place to plant this precious seed.

When you find the right place, dig a hole and plant the seed. Wait and see what grows. Perhaps the seed will grow a seedling, a temple, a baby or a fiery phoenix. Whatever grows, tend the new thing and interact with it. It will grow to maturity in a brief span of time. Notice what it feels like to do this work of tending, and what you learn from it.

As the new thing starts to grow and thrive, notice what happens to the ruin. It may completely transform as the new entity grows. See what unfolds. When you feel the process of growth and renewal is complete, depart the ruin (or whatever it has transformed itself into). Return up the hill and toward your waking self.

She Who Remembers and Releases: The Practice of Mourning as Transformation[*]

Yahrtzeit Practices

There are many Jewish practices of mourning, such as the seven-day ritual of *shiva*, the ritual of *shloshim* thirty days after a death, and yearly *yahrzeit* (year-time) observances marking the death anniversaries of loved ones. Traditional Jewish *yahrzeit* observance includes the recitation in synagogue of Mourner's Kaddish and the lighting at home of a 24-hour remembrance candle. It also may include a visit to the burial location.

If you are aware of the death dates of loved ones or those you are mourning, the *yahrtzeit* is a time to open to remembering. If you are mourning, remembering or honoring those whose death anniversary you do not know, or if you find yourself mourning even though it is not near

---

[*] © Holly Taya Shere, 2011. Originally published in a slightly different form in *The Hebrew Priestess* by Jill Hammer and Holly Taya Shere, (Teaneck, NJ: Ben Yehuda Press, 2013). Reprinted with permission.

a death anniversary, give yourself the gift of mourning ritual practice whenever it is needed.

Coming together in community—in worship space, in nature, or on a conference call—allows us to connect with the person who we are remembering. Recite Mourner's Kaddish. Share stories about your loved one. Share art or music or food that was loved by the person you are remembering. Open to celebrating that life and spirit.

Light an extended (24-hour) candle. Gather items of meaning and relevance around your candle. Recite prayers and poems. Sing sacred songs. Place pictures of your loved one around the candle or around your space. Bring natural elements onto your *yahrzeit* altar, such as a plant, a bowl of water or a feather.

Mourning as Pilgrimage

There is a Jewish custom of celebratory *hillula* (pilgrimage) on the death anniversary of *tzaddikim* (holy teachers, saints). A lesser known holiday, Lag B'Omer, is the *yahrzeit* of mystic Shimon Bar Yochai; pilgrims from around the world journey to celebrate at his grave. Among Moroccan Jews, pilgrimage has been and remains a primary practice of remembering. All over the world, Jews pilgrimage to the gravesites of *rebbes* and *tzaddikim* on the anniversaries of their deaths.

You might journey to the burial site of a loved one, or you might journey to a place that was one of their favorite spots, or somewhere you frequented together, when they were alive. For me, *yahrzeit* pilgrimages have included Shabbat morning flea markets to remember my Grandma, and to the Korean Spa to remember a priestess sister who loved spas.

Embracing Death

> *Death is an emergence, not an emergency.*
> *Death is ordinary and utterly acceptable and filled with awe.*
> —Susan Ariel Rainbow Kennedy

Years ago, as part of a seminar experience, I experienced an exercise designed to bring participants into awareness of how we perceive the process of dying. Seated in groups of ten or so, in family pods or circles scattered throughout the large room, we were told that "Death" would be coming into the room to select folks from each pod to join her, and that if she came for us or touched us, we had to respond. Death entered the room, robed and blindfolded, with attendants to help guide her. Her attendants steered her to each pod and then released her for her encounter with that circle.

Death came near some participants, and many people moved to avoid her touch. Others softened their bodies and relaxed their breath, closing their eyes. On occasion, she physically touched participants. More than one participant she touched struggled with her, resisting, eventually receiving support from others in the circle to willingly follow, yet often wailing along the way. Waves of wails among the family pods filled the room as their circle-mates were guided away from the circle.

Halfway through the exercise, a shift occurred. Death entered a circle, and rather than dodging, a woman in the circle held out her hands. As Death approached her, the woman linked arms with Death and began to dance. She whooped and hollered and let out calls of celebration and praise. The tension in her circle softened and her pod-mates joined her in ululations and cheers. One woman even began to softly stroke Death's hair.

Taking part in this exercise was the beginning of my personal exploration into the possibility of death as something other than something to fear, resist and avoid at all costs. Indigenous wisdom, earth-honoring wisdom and women's wisdom understand death as a natural process. Being aware of these perspectives is one thing, but encountering this in an actual dying is profound beyond words.

We in the Kohenet Institute community witnessed and supported our student/sister Yosefa as she priestessed her own dying from this place of presence and possibility. Yosefa committed to approaching dying as she had approached everything else in her life, with presence, humor, creativity and wild grace. In the final months of her life, she had at most a few hours of energy amidst severe pain each day. In the wee hours of each morning, she sat with the question, "What is the most important thing for me to do today?" She considered this question with much care, because even on a good day, there was generally only one thing she could do.

In August one day, she bought and sent chai to her sister for her birthday. Another day, she tattooed my hip. One day, she cooked mung beans and brown rice for her caregiver husband. Another day, she met with me about her funeral: "Make it a celebration. Make sure they know I was one of the luckiest people who ever lived." One day in November, she priestessed a funeral for a Jew in her recovery community. Another day, she exhibited new work in the Women's Tattoo Forum Art show. One day, she taught a workshop on "spirituality and kink" at a Leather/BDSM conference. The last day that month, the most important thing for her to do was to die.

In accordance with her wishes, some of her priestess sisters sat by bed serving as *shomrot*, guardians of her body in the hours after she died. Traditionally, this is a time of solemn recitation of psalms. We tried reciting them, but it wasn't what her spirit wanted. Yosefa wanted celebration. She lived free and she would die free. So we sung our hearts out and I swayed and prayed at the foot of her bed with fervor and a fierce joy that I never imagined belonged in a house of mourning. Yosefa was my teacher in the practice of becoming the Mourning Woman.

Further Reading

Anita Diamant, *Saying Kaddish: How to Comfort the Dying, Bury the Dead, and Mourn as a Jew* (NY: Schocken Books, 1999).

Karla McLaren, *Emotional Genius: Discovering the Deepest Language of the Soul.* (Columbia, CA: Laughing Tree Press. 2002). See particularly the section on grief.

Endnotes

1 The Kohenet Hebrew Priestess Institute (www.kohenet.org) is a community of women, guided by Jill Hammer, Holly Taya Shere and Shoshana Jedwab, dedicated to priestessing in a Jewish context. The Kohenet Hebrew Priestess Institute reclaims embodied, earth-based, goddess-oriented and feminist models of sacred service rooted in Jewish women's spiritual leadership roles throughout the centuries, from biblical prophetess-priestesses to

Talmudic healers and magicians to kabbalistic dream interpreters to modern feminist ritualists. The Kohenet training program uses prayer, ritual, text study and experiential learning to give women tools of spiritual leadership they can use in their own communities. The Institute meets at the Isabella Freedman Jewish Retreat Center, a spiritual retreat environment and center of Jewish farming and environmental activism in Falls Village, Connecticut.

2 © Holly Taya Shere, 2011.

3 Jeremiah 9:16

4 Nancy C. Lee, *The Singers of Lamentations: Cities Under Siege, from Ur to Jerusalem to Sarajevo* (Boston: Brill Publishers, 2002), chapters 1 and 3.

5 Judges 11:34–40.

6 Ezekiel 8:8.

7 Jeremiah 31:15–17.

8 Lamentations Rabbah, Petichta 25.

9 Pesikta deRav Kahana 166.

10 Zohar I, 203a.

11 Mishnah, Moed Katan 3:9.

12 Babylonian Talmud, Berachot 51a.

13 Maimonides, Mishneh Torah, Laws of Mourning.

14 Harry Fox and Justin Jaron Lewis, Many Pious Women: Edition and Translation (Boston: Degryter, 2011), 234.

15 Zohar, Vayakhel.

16 Joshua Trachtenberg, Jewish Magic and Superstition: A Study in Folk Religion (CreateSpace: 2012), 179.

17 Jennifer Breger, "Women at the Cemetery: Historical Notes," *The Orthodox Jewish Woman and Ritual: Options and Opportunities: Death and Mourning* (Jewish Orthodox Feminist Alliance), 12.

18 "A Short History of the Chevra Kadisha," *The Orthodox Jewish Woman and Ritual: Options and Opportunities: Death and Mourning* (Jewish Orthodox Feminist Alliance), 7.

19 Barbara Gaims-Spiegel, "Women and Kaddish," *The Orthodox Jewish Woman and Ritual: Options and Opportunities: Death and Mourning* (Jewish Orthodox Feminist Alliance), 9.

Shechinah*
By Geela Rayzel Raphael

Shechinah,
The Divine Feminine
Is a path, is energy, is a concept and symbol.
She is the Goddess, the primordial Mother giving birth to all that is,
    She is a force that binds and transcends, guides and connects
    And destroys.
    She is the force of life, the Source of Life,
    We have her in us, we see her around;
    She manifests in many different ways.
    She is the pulse felt in our bodies when the ecstatic music stops and we are left with the afterglow to breathe in—
    We can feel her, sense her, but can't quite grasp her.
    Shechinah traveled with the Israelites in the desert and showed Herself in many forms:
    She was the Pillar of Fire that guided us by night,
        The black flame of the burning bush,
        The indwelling presence of the Tabernacle and in our hearts.
    Her destiny is bound with Israel and she hovers today over the Kotel, the Holy Western Wall, like a dove in the cleft in the rocks.

---

* From *The Hebrew Priestess* by Jill Hammer and Holly Taya Shere (Teaneck, NJ: Ben Yehuda Press, 2013).

We also welcome Her as our beloved on Friday night.

Shechinah is the power in a circle of people speaking the truth from their hearts with compassion.

She is the process that transforms wheat into bread.
She is the love in a bowl of soup when we are sick.

   She is the Divine justice among three judges

   Yet She calls us to rejoice in community

   And rests Herself under the Tree of Life in the Garden of Eden.
I serve her in Joy.

Temple Weaving: Jewish Weaver-Priestesses and the Creation of the Cosmos*

By Jill Hammer

Modern Judaism and Christianity are still shaped by the fact that the Second Temple in Jerusalem had a male clergy. Male and female lay worshippers could participate in temple rites, but only male priests could make offerings and conduct rituals. However, according to a number of sources, women had one temple role assigned exclusively to them: female weavers wove the sacred curtain that hung over the Holy of Holies. These women were not called priests or priestesses, but the texts available to us suggest that these weavers had a priestly aura attached to them: they may have been the closest thing temple ritual had to priestesses. Their tradition provides us with an alternative model for the meaning of priestly service, one based in female work and female-bodied images of creation, and offers thoughts about connections between world myths of women weaver goddesses, the holy women weavers of the Second Temple period and the weaver-priestesses of our own day.

Biblical Women Weavers

Exodus texts describing the design and construction of the tabernacle (the *mishkan* or portable dwelling-place for the Divine) are elaborate and detailed. Women played a significant role in bringing the materials for the tabernacle, and in working with the thread to make the tapestries for the tabernacle walls. In Exodus 35:22, we learn that "they came, men and women, all who were generous of heart, bringing brooches, earrings, rings, and pendants, gold objects of every kind." Later on, we hear that

---

* Originally published in a slightly different form in *The Hebrew Priestess* by Jill Hammer and Holly Taya Shere (Teaneck, NJ: Ben Yehuda Press, 2013). Reprinted with permission.

"All the wise-hearted women spun with their hands, and brought the spinning: blue, purple, scarlet, and fine linen. And all the women whose hearts lifted them up in wisdom spun the goats' hair."[1]

The inclusion of "wise-hearted" women in the preparation of the sanctuary materials is notable given that biblical text does not often comment on women's participation in communal ritual life.[2] This may be an indication that Israelites understood women's spinning and weaving work to be an important contribution to the community's cultic centers.

In the book of Kings, women receive specific mention as weavers of cult objects for Asherah, the Mother Goddess of the region. We read that for a significant portion of the first temple's existence, objects representing the Goddess, Asherah, stood within the sacred compound.[3] The Bible relates that during the Josianic reform, these objects were removed from the temple and destroyed. Batim, houses or shrines woven for Asherah, were among the things destroyed.

> He brought out the Asherah from the House of Adonai to the Wadi of Kidron outside Jerusalem, and burned her in the Wadi of Kidron, and ground her to dust, and scattered her dust over the burial ground of the people. He tore down the houses of the *kedeishim* (holy people; priests) that were in the House of Adonai, for the women "wove houses there" [*orgot batim sham*] for Asherah.[4]

The word *sham* (there) in the text indicates that the weaving was done within the temple. The weavers, specifically mentioned as *orgot* or women weavers, may have been dedicated to Asherah, or may simply have been employees. However, their presence in the temple supports the theory that they were sacred weavers of some kind, much as the *ergastinai* of Athens were sacred weavers. *Kedeishim* would probably have been priests (or priests and priestesses, as a masculine verb could be applied to a mixed group) of Asherah.[5] *Beit*, house, is a common biblical word for shrine, and *batim* may have been sacred fabric shrines or canopies. Or, the *batim* could have been garments or draperies for the Asherah itself.

Asherah may or may not be Goddess of Weaving; scholar Susan Ackerman argues that she is, based on a small and ambiguous amount of textual evidence.[6] However, we know for certain that Asherah is goddess of creation. She is called *qaniyatu 'ilim* or *qnyt 'ilim*, "creatrix of the gods," and also "mother of all."[7] The weaving of these women may suggest that the weaving is performed in the temple as a parallel for Asherah's creative power.

There is a clear biblical tradition of sacred women weavers, one that spanned "normative" women who wove for the tabernacle, and "non-normative" priestesses who wove for Asherah. It is likely that both of these categories of weavers would have been normative in ancient Israel before the monotheistic reforms of the Deuteronomist. They might even have been the same women.

The Second Temple Period: Evidence from the Rabbinic World
Texts of the late Second Temple and Rabbinic Period suggest that there were women temple weavers during the Second Temple era as well. The Mishnah, a 2nd century Jewish law code, remembered, reconstructed or perhaps invented rituals that took place in the Second Temple. The Tosefta is a more or less contemporaneous supplement containing material not recorded in the Mishnah. We read of weavers in the Tosefta, which noted which temple workers were paid from the *trumat halishkah* (the census fund collected for the temple from every citizen).

> The women who wove the curtain,
> The house of Garmo who baked the showbread,
> The house of Avtinas who made the incense,
> Were all paid from the trumat halishkah.[8]

The House of Garmo and the House of Avtinas were houses of priests who specialized in the production of temple bread and temple incense. In this text, the women who wove the curtain for the Holy of Holies were equal to those who baked the bread and made the incense. The baking and incense-making was done on the temple grounds, which suggests that the weaving might have been, as well.[9] The women weavers may have been daughters or wives of priestly families who specialized in this work, though there might have been other ways to become a temple weaver, too.

The Mishnah seems to have censored this tradition, recording both the name of the priest who oversaw the weaving of the curtain (Elazar), and the name of the priest who oversaw the weaving and keeping of garments (Pinchas); but we read of no women.[10] Researcher Tal Ilan notes that the Mishnah may have been erasing the tradition of women weavers deliberately, because of its embarrassment at finding a mention of women as part of the temple cult.[11]

Ilan warns that the tradition from the Tosefta may be ahistorical: the ancient writers might have assumed there were women to weave the curtain, since throughout the ancient world women did sacred weaving work for temples, and since weaving was "women's work." Still, the general discomfort with women in the sancta might make it less likely that such a text would have been invented by rabbinic tradition.[12] There were, in fact, male weavers in Talmudic times, so it would not be implausible to say that male priests wove the curtains, if the tradition had wanted to say so.[13]

There is also a *baraita* (a tradition of the Mishnaic period not included in the Mishnah) about the women weavers. This *baraita*, which appears in different forms in different manuscripts, was later introduced into the Mishnah:

> Rabban Shimon ben Gamliel said in the name of Rabbi Shimon ben haSegan: the curtain (*parochet*) was a handbreadth thick and was woven in seventy-two batches. Every batch consisted of twenty-four threads. It was made of eighty-two times ten thousand (*ribo*) [alternate text: eighty-two maidens/rivot). They made two every year, and three-hundred priests would immerse it.[14]

The text in which 82 maidens make the curtain for the Holy of Holies is from the Munich manuscript of the Jerusalem Talmud. The reading found in all other manuscripts (82 times 10,000) makes no sense. The word "maidens" (*rivot*) was probably altered later by redactors who did not understand the text. Those redactors had forgotten, or perhaps wished to erase, the presence of women in the temple cult.[15]

The text seems to support the existence of women temple weavers, and indicates that the weavers were unmarried girls, just as the weavers of Athena's robe in Athens were unmarried girls. While virginity was not emphasized as a holy state in Jewish sources, there were other reasons why girls may have been preferred. Firstly, if the weaving had to be done within the temple or near it, a woman with a family could not have taken on the work. Secondly, the temple cult had a tremendous concern for ritual and sexual purity, and it is possible that the *rivot* were pre-menstrual girls. This *baraita* adds to the evidence for the historicity of the temple weavers as an institution.

Temple Virgins: Extra-Rabbinic Sources

The Apocalypse of Baruch, a Syriac text composed around the time of the Mishnah,[16] mentions the temple weavers as part of its narration of the temple's destruction. The text, in alignment with the *baraita* that refers to the temple weavers as "maidens," describes the holy weavers as "virgins."

> You priests, take the keys of the sanctuary
> and cast them to the highest heaven
> and give them to the Lord
> and say: "Guard your house yourself,
> because, behold, we have been found to be false stewards,"
>   and you virgins who spin fine linen
>   and silk with gold of Ophir,
>   make haste and take all things and cast them into the fire
>   so that it may carry them to Him who made them
>   and the flames send them to Him who created them.[17]

Like the priests, the temple weavers lived in the temple and were caught in the siege. Like the priests, they protected the sacred things. The priests cast the keys back to heaven, and the young women who wove the curtains cast their tapestries into the fire. The male priests and the female temple weavers were placed opposite one another in a dual-gendered portrayal of priestly devotion. For the Apocalypse of Baruch, these young women were not only craftswomen: they were guardians who preserved the sanctity of the holy vessels, just as the priests did.

A Christian text from the Rabbinic Period, the *Protoevangelium of James*, confirms some of the details of the Apocalypse of Baruch, and adds others. The *Protoevangelium of James* depicts Mary as a temple weaver, one of seven young girls of the house of David who were chosen for that work. Their duties (which colors they would weave) were assigned by lot.

> Then they brought them [the virgins] into the temple of the Lord, and the priest said: "Cast me lots, who shall weave the gold, the white, the linen, the silk, the hyacinth-blue, the scarlet and the pure purple." And to Mary fell the lot of the pure purple and scarlet. And she took them and worked them in her house.[18]

According to the *Protoevangelium*, Mary had been living in the temple since the age of three as a devotee (much as Samuel was given to the Tabernacle at an early age). When Mary was twelve, she was given to Joseph as a ward, and the priests assigned her sacred weaving to do in her home.

This is a legendary telling of Mary's life, in which many details were invented to support Christian theology. The idea that the virgins had to be of Davidic lineage fit with the Christian doctrine that Mary was of the house of David, and is therefore questionable (though it is possible that girls/women of aristocratic descent were chosen as temple weavers). However, the author seems to have been making use of existing traditions about temple weavers, such as that they were young virgins, and that they were regarded as holy. Some of these traditions may have been reflected in actual practice.

The assigning of color by lot is particularly notable. The Mishnah[19] indicates that priestly duties were assigned by lot at the beginning of each day. In ancient Greece and Rome, priesthood generally was assigned in one of two ways: by heredity, or by lot.[20] The assignment of a task by lot indicated its sacred nature and the need to "let God decide" who would serve and in what ways. In this text, we see women weavers treated as quasi-priestesses who participated in divinatory ritual and in the making of sacred things.

The Weaving-Stone

Both the biblical temple weavers and the Second Temple weavers appear in these texts without any legend or mythology about what they were doing. However, later Jewish myths offered meaning to sacred weaving. According to the Jerusalem Talmud: "Women are accustomed not to prepare or attach warp threads to a weaving loom, from the new moon of Av until the ninth of Av (when the Temple fell), because during the month of Av the Weaving-stone (*even hashetiyah*) was destroyed."[21]

Many rabbinic and mystical texts refer to the "weaving stone" (the *even hashtiyah*).[22] This stone is more commonly referred to in English as the "foundation stone" because of the *root shet*, or foundation. This stone was said to lie at the entrance to, or beneath, the Holy of Holies. It was regarded as a kind of navel of the world, and also as a real object related to the temple cult. According to the Mishnah, the high priest rested the incense pan on this stone during the Yom Kippur ritual that took place in the Holy of Holies.

> After the Ark was taken away [i.e. after the time of the First Temple], a stone was there [in the Holy of Holies] from the time of the earliest prophets, and it was called *even hashtiyah*. It was three fingers above the ground, and on it the high priest would place the incense.[23]

Later legends relate:

> The land of Israel is the navel of the world, being placed at its center. Jerusalem, is the center of the land of Israel. The temple is at the center of Jerusalem. The Holy of Holies is at the center of the Temple. The Ark is at the center of the Holy of Holies. And in front of the Holy of Holies is the foundation stone on

which the world was founded [or: the weaving stone of which the world was woven].²⁴

And also:

> The fish showed [Jonah] . . . the paths of the Sea of Reeds on which the Israelites traveled. It showed him the pillars of the foundations of the earth . . . and it showed him the nethermost She'ol . . . It showed him the underside of the Temple . . . and he saw there the foundation stone.²⁵

The word *shet* also refers to the laying of the warp of a loom: *shetiyah* means "weaving" in Aramaic. In a typical word play, the Talmud attributes the destruction of the weaving stone (the *even hashetiyah*) to **not** weaving.

Supporting this idea, the legends around the stone suggest a connection between the stone and the weaving of creation:

> The sacred shrine is considered to be like the world, and also like the making of the human, which is a small world. How so? When the Holy One began to create the world, the Holy One made it as a child grows within its mother. Just as the fetus in its mother's womb starts at the navel and spreads out this way and that way to the four sides, so too the Holy One made the world, making the foundation stone first and from it spreading out the world. It is called the foundation stone for from it the Holy One began to create the world.²⁶

These texts connect the "navel" of the world to the navel of an infant. Here, we have an image of God as mother and weaver. Contrary to biblical myth, God organically wove the world, like a fetus. If the Holy of Holies was the first point at which God began to weave creation, then the curtain of the Holy of Holies may have represented the weaving of the world. It is possible that the Jewish women's custom of not weaving on the anniversary of the temple's destruction arose in memory of the temple curtain as a symbol of cosmic creation, and as a statement that the temple's destruction was a kind of unweaving of the world.

This interpretation of the curtain of the Holy of Holies as a symbol of creation has support from a number of ancient sources contemporaneous with the last years of the Second Temple. Josephus, who saw the actual temple, wrote the following:

> It was a Babylonian curtain, embroidered with blue, and fine linen, and scarlet, and purple, and of a texture that was truly wonderful. Nor was this mixture of colors without its mystical interpretation, but was a kind of image of the universe; for by the scarlet there seemed to be enigmatically signified fire, by the fine flax the earth, by the blue the air, and by the purple the sea . . . This curtain also had embroidered upon it all that was mystical in the heavens.[27]

Note the words "a kind of image of the universe" and the reference to the four elements. In many indigenous cultures, the combination of the four elements together represents sacred space or the center of the world. In Josephus' writing of the *parochet*, the curtain of the Holy of Holies represented the world: The *parochet* was seen as a symbol of the creation, and its reweaving might have signified a renewal of that creation.

From Philo, the Jewish philosopher whose life spanned the 1st century BCE and the 1st century CE, we learn something similar regarding the *parochet* and the four elements: "The covering and the veil were stitched in various colors, with blue and purple and scarlet and linen . . . for purple comes from water, linen from earth, blue being dark is like air, as scarlet is like fire."[28]

In general, Philo's writing refers to weaving as a metaphor for the making of the universe. According to David T. Runia: "Philo . . . applies the image of weaving to the intricate structure of the cosmos, chiefly inspired by the biblical image of the speckled sheep, the curtains of the Tabernacle, and the high priestly robes."[29] For Philo, as for Josephus, the *parochet* and the forces of creation were intimately connected.

The apocryphal book of Enoch, written in the 1st century BCE and preserved by Ethiopian Jews and Christians, goes even deeper in connecting the *parochet* to the weaving of time and space. In the book of Enoch, the biblical personage Enoch received a tour of heaven, during which the angel Metatron showed him the heavenly *parochet*: "Metatron said to me: come, I will show you the veil of the All Present One, which is spread before the Holy One Blessed Be He, and on which are printed all the generations of the world and all their deeds, whether done or yet to be done, until the last generation."[30] Here, we see the *parochet* as the cosmic weaving of history, just as the Fates of Greek mythology and the Norns of Norse mythology wove all the world's events into their tapestry. This depiction of the holy curtain comes closest to naming it as a metaphysical cloth, holding all of the past and future within its images.

The New Testament names Jesus as an embodiment of the *parochet*: "His flesh was the veil of the temple."[31] The New Testament reports that when Jesus was crucified, the *parochet* "tore from top to bottom."[32] If Jesus was deity embodied in the world, it makes sense that the holy curtain, which embodied the veil between the world and the hidden realms, would come to represent his body.

Jews of the Roman period (as well as many other cultures around the Mediterranean) sometimes buried their dead with spindle whorls, and this burial practice might have been connected to the idea that spinning and weaving constituted creation and re-creation.[33] This would support the idea that holy women weavers were world-creators on a mythic level.

Thus, the holy women weavers of the Bible and later times may have been human embodiments of the divine fate-weaver sitting at the cosmic loom. If so, their work would have been a way that women participated in the priestly work of ordering and sustaining the universe. Their service might have provided at least one female-centered model for the meaning of the temple cult.

Holy Weavers in Cross-Cultural Perspective

The women who did sacred weaving work in the First and Second Temples paralleled other sacred weaver-women. In Athens, for example, *arrephoroi*, or weaver-priestesses, supervised the threading of the sacred loom.³⁴ Then, women known as *ergastinai* wove the *peplos*, or garment, for Athena's statue anew each year. This weaving represented the recreation of the social compact with the Goddess, as well as the recreation of the world and society as a whole. In Pausanias, we read of a similar ritual from Olympia in which priestesses of Hera wove a new robe for the Goddess every fourth year, in connection with the Heraean Games (a women's athletic event that preceded the Olympic Games).³⁵ Pausanias also recorded a ritual from Amyclae in which women wove a tunic for Apollo.³⁶ The annual weaving of the garment for a deity suggests renewal and rebirth of that deity, through the creative activity of women.

The weaving Norns of Teutonic myth were accompanied by real human women called *volvas* who were prophets of fate and were summoned to births to tell the fate of a child:

> Twas night in the dwelling,
> and Norns there came,
> Who shaped the life
> of the lofty one;
> They bade him most famed
> of fighters all
> And best of princes
> ever to be.
> Mightily wove they
> the web of fate . . .
> And there the golden
> threads they wove,
> And in the moon's hall
> fast they made them.³⁷

In Hopi culture, Grandmother Spider or Spider Woman created human beings at the direction of the primordial male deity:

> So Spider Woman gathered earth, this time of four colors, yellow, red, white, and black . . . molded them, and covered them with her white-substance cape which was creative wisdom

itself . . . and when she uncovered them these forms were human beings in the image of Sotuknang. Then she created four other beings after her own form. They were *wuti*, female partners for the first four male beings.[38]

Women's household weaving thus took on a decidedly mystical cast, and all the more so when the weaving was done in a sacred context. In many myths, the woman weaving at the loom merges in myth with the universe weaving creation and guiding its fate. This is true across cultures, from the Fates of Greece and Rome to *Iya Moopo* of the Yoruba (Goddess of Pottery, who forms creation). These theological images of women weaving arose out of real cultural and biological experience: women weaving essential household goods, women sending life from their wombs with a red thread attached. In many cultures (including Jewish culture of the Second Temple and Talmudic times), both women and men were weavers, yet it is usually women who are associated with mythic weaving: weaving that made the world.

Like other cultures around the world, Judaism has always had sacred women weavers in its midst. These weavers have not only been providers of goods, but representatives of the creative powers of the universe. While we cannot know the experience of the temple weavers, since no record exists to tell us, we can imagine that the sanctity of the work must have meant something to them. If the holy curtain represented the cosmos, the women weaving it were weaving the world, just as sacred women wove the world in legends around the globe.

It seems clear that, after the Temple's destruction, Jewish tradition largely forgot about the cosmic loom and its workers. Yet Jewish women continued to do sacred weaving and to make curtains and adornments for sacred space. Jewish women of past generations wove or embroidered a *parochet* for the Ark, or a Torah mantle on the occasion of a birth or wedding, or in memory of a relative. In some countries, Jewish women embroidered a *wimple* (Torah binder) and donated it to the synagogue in gratitude for the birth of a healthy child.[39] In Italy, a special blessing was chanted every Sabbath for the women who had done weaving or other fabric work to benefit the synagogue. While these images were human and not mythic, it is interesting that often the gift of weaving related to a death or a birth, as if a cosmic weaver lurked behind the gifts of a craftswoman.

Contemporary Weaver-Priestesses

The weaver-priestesses of the temple have inspired many contemporary Jewish priestesses. At the Kohenet Hebrew Priestess Institute, in a training program for Jewish women seeking to reclaim the priestess tradition, the weaver is a central image. One of the ritual items at Kohenet retreats is an "umbilical cord," a woven cord that hangs down from the ceiling to the center of the ritual altar space, attached to the round yurt walls by yarn spokes. A Kohenet graduate, Sarah Esther Richards, created the ritual umbilical cord. She remembers:

> At first during the *davvening* (meditation) it was just there.
> I asked the women what this thing was.
> They said: A web.
> Yes, I said, it's similar but that is not its main intention.
> I let the coiled middle cord down into the altar space, to the center of the altar.
> Ellie said: It's an umbilical cord!
> I invited the women to pass the end around the circle, so each woman could place it on their navel or otherwise interact with it.
> I invited them to imagine that they were not receiving their oxygen from the room but from the umblilical cord, as if they were getting it from the Goddess [40]

The umbilical cord, which, like the ancient curtain, represents the weaving of the cosmos, is now frequently used during important rituals as a tangible connection to God/dess.

Another Kohenet graduate, Ketzirah Lesser, makes fabric art, ranging from cloth mezuzah covers to curtains for the Torah ark. She has written:

> Weaving creates change. Change is scary. It's scary for the weaver and the woven ones. You have to trust in your skills. You

have to be willing to tear it all apart and start over. You have to be ready for the natural resistance to change and know when to slow down or when to speed up. You have to be ready for the moment when the fibers break and leave you with a hole to fix. You have to believe that either you are the fiber and G!d is the weaver or you are the weaver and G!d is the fiber. Sometimes you have to be able to believe both are possible.[41]

Jewish women weave wonders. We weave communities and we weave dough to create *challah*. We weave cultures old and new to create modern Judaism. I weave words, but I am part of a long line of weavers whose stories have never been told. My way of life is not new. It's what our grandmothers did when they reached the shores of America and had to create new lives for their families while still retaining tradition.

Rachel May Koppelman, an initiate of the Kohenet tradition, is an energetic healer, trained in reiki and other modalities. She sees her work as weaving work:

> The experience of the Weaver is an experience of fluidity: being able to channel whatever is appropriate or necessary or whatever can best serve the higher good. It's about sitting back and letting something come through. I often think of my life experience as a kaleidoscope. That image visually describes how I experience things. There are different individual things that need to be focused on, but that's all in service to the bigger picture. That's how I see the Weaver—as tying together different things in service to the whole.[42]

Rachel extends this image of the weaver to her understanding of the Divine, imagining deity as the integration function of the universe—the living force that binds everything together.

> The Weaver is divine intelligence that takes the individual strands and disparate things and makes this synergistic new thing. The weaving is a process that happens infinitely across

time and space. Think of the fractal. A fractal looks the same in microcosm and macrocosm. The pattern happens on the tiniest infinitesimal level, and what's happening at that level affects the big picture. Nothing is too small, nothing is insignificant to the larger perspective.[43]

Rabbi Lynn Gottlieb tells a story of her visit to a synagogue several decades ago, when she was one of the first women rabbis. She was seated on the *bimah*. Although she was the rabbi's invited guest, two male synagogue leaders accosted her and demanded she leave the *bimah* because she was a woman. When she refused, they grabbed her arms and attempted to remove her from the *bimah*. The *shul* erupted in argument, and the service stopped. After extended conversation, one woman pointed to the curtain over the Ark and announced: "I embroidered that curtain myself, and if she goes, it goes!" This was the end of the argument: the service went on, and Rabbi Lynn stayed on the *bimah*.[44]

Such is the power of the Weaver.

Endnotes

1 Exodus 35:22, 35:25–262.

2 Women are also singled out for mention in another mysterious text, Exodus 38:8, where women called *tzovot* (serving-women or ministering-women) donated their mirrors for the making of the priestly *laver*. These women are also mentioned in I Sam. 2:22–23, and may have constituted a class of sacred women workers, though there is no evidence of what they did. Mirrors frequently appeared in the ancient Near East as divination tools and as symbols of the feminine.

3 II Kings 23.

4 II Kings 23:6–7.

5 The Elijah stories suggest that priests of Asherah functioned in Judea as part of the royal cult (supported by Ahab and Jezebel). These priests may not all have been male.

6 Susan Ackerman, "Asherah, the West Semitic Goddess of Spinning and

Weaving?" *Journal of Near Eastern Studies*, vol. 67, no. 1: 1–30.76 Tosefta Shekalim 2:6.

7 G.R. Driver, Canaanite Myths and Legends (Edinburgh: T and T Clark, 1971).

8 Tosefta Shekalim 2:6.

9 Mishnah Middot 1:1.

10 The names here are somewhat suspicious. Elazar and Pinchas are names of Aaron's son and grandson. The other names in the passage tend to have patronymics attached and are more redolent of the Mishnaic time period (Ben Achiyah, Matityah ben Shmuel, Hugros ben Levi and so on). One wonders if the biblical names were tacked on here to an existing text.

11 Tal Ilan, *Mine and Yours Are Hers: Retrieving Women's History from Rabbinic Literature* (Boston: Brill, 1997), 139–140.

12 Ibid., 139.

13 Josephus, *Wars of the Jews*, Book 18, Chapter 9.

14 Mishnah Shekalim 8:5.

15 Ibid..

16 Tal Ilan, *Mine and Yours Are Hers: Retrieving Women's History from Rabbinic Literature* (Boston: Brill, 1997), 139–140.

17 Apocalypse of Baruch.

18 Protoevangelium of James 10:2.

19 Yoma 2:1–4.

20 Ross Shepard Kraemer, *Her Share of the Blessings: Women's Religions Among Pagans, Jews, and Christians in the Greco-Roman World* (London: Oxford University Press, 1992), 81.

21 Jerusalem Talmud, Pesachim 4:1.

22 *Shtiyah* means both "foundation" and "weaving," because the "foundation" of a loom is the setting of the warp.

23 Mishnah Yoma 5:2.

24 Midrash Tanhuma Buber, Kedoshim 10.

25 Pirkei deRabbi Eliezer 20.

26 Midrash Tanhuma, Shemot Pekudei 3.

27 Josephus, Wars of the Jews, Book V, Chapter V.

28 Philo, De Vita Moysis II, 87–88.

29 David T. Runia, *Philo of Alexandria and the Timaeus of Plato* (Boston: Brill, 1997), 255.
30 3 Enoch 45.
31 Epistle to the Hebrews 10:20.
32 Matthew 27:50–51.
33 Miriam Peskowitz, *Spinning Fantasies: Rabbis, Gender, and History* (Berkeley: University of California Press, 1997), 164–166.
34 Joan Breton Connelly, *Portrait of a Priestess; Women and Ritual in Ancient Greece* (Princeton, NJ: Princeton University Press, 2007), 32, 61, 202.
35 Mary R. Lefkowitz and Maureen B. Fant, *Women's Life in Greece and Rome: A Source Book in Translation* (Baltimore, MD: Johns Hopkins University Press, 1982), 277.
36 Ibid., 301.
37 Helgakvi Hundingsbana I.
38 Frank Waters, *Book of the Hopi* (New York: Viking Press, 1963).
39 Elisheva Baumgarten, *Mothers and Children: Jewish Family Life in Medieval Europe* (Princeton, NJ: Princeton University Press, 2004); Hayim Schauss, *The Lifetime of a Jew Throughout the Ages of Jewish History* (New York: URJ Press,1950), 79.
40 Sarah Esther Richards, Kohenet Institute, personal communication.
41 Ketzirah Lesser, Kohenet Institute, personal communication.
42 Rachel May Koppelman, Kohenet Institute, personal communication.
43 Ibid.
44 Rabbi Lynn Gottlieb, Kohenet Institute, personal communication.

House of the Vestals
By Janine Canan

Although the Vestals are covered now
in bubble and wrapping paper,
ready to be portered to some far museum—
one stone Virgin still stands tall,
head and shoulder gracefully draped,

the stump of her arm pointing in mid-day sun
past Caesar and Mussolini's plaza,
plastic crackling in the breeze that stirs
round her feet—here where Vesta Herself
once fluttered in her golden flame.

Now motionless the vulva pool,
stuffed thick with lily pads and edged
with ruffly pink roses, reminds of that entrance
where all arrive and soon depart—even we,
living priestesses of her Creation.

The Dream of the Snake Priestess
By Le'ema Kathleen Graham

The water and the customs and the white mud
are beneath me far below[1]
I stand high on a mountain top
I have climbed here at dusk
In my bare priestess feet
Have walked up the rocky crested butte
To take my stance
My snakes have guided the way
through infra-red/feeling vision
Though I stood *in the blind water*
My two snakes have uncoiled
Have risen to bite me again and again
      Ida Nadi
      Pingala Nadi
I breathe the twin serpents up my shushumna channel
The core of my body
My spine
Reverberates with copper and gold
Glows the sun itself setting
Gleaming inside me
Poised in my seven-chakra tiered skirt
Bare-breasted heart
Leopard on my head crowned with roses
I stand
Offering my two snakes

to the sky
The flutter of Seraphim
Winged angelic serpents
Come
And I am lifted up
By the *light, the pressure of nameless fingertips*
Carry me into the no-moon night
Where I meet my starry sisters
The Pleiades
At the head of the Medusa
Where all the veils are lifted
And we circle
In the Spiral of the Serpent

Endnote

1 From Pablo Neruda's "The Ruined Street" translated by Robert Bly. From *Neruda and Vallejo: Selected Poems* (Boston: Beacon Press, 1993), 45–47.

Yoginis of Ancient India
By Jalaja Bonheim

The day I stepped into India's heat, colors, sounds and smells, I instantly felt a profound sense of homecoming. It was 1981, and even though I had come to learn classical Indian temple dance, I would spend the next seven years of my life studying Hindu mythology and religion, mantra and chant, Tantric ritual and meditation.

Although many Westerners think of Tantra primarily as a sexual practice, it is in fact a demanding spiritual path that includes meditation, yoga, dance and elaborate circle rituals that evoke the ecstatic experience of union with the divine in and through the physical body. Through the practice of Indian dance, I was initiated into an ancient lineage of Tantric priestesses, and I was privileged to be blessed by one of the last living temple priestesses in India.

In my book *Aphrodite's Daughters*, I described how the ancient Indian foremothers appeared to me in dreams and meditations, asking me to share their wisdom with the women of my own day and age.[1] Today, I know I am not alone: Many women have told me of similar dreams and visions, and of their own sense of connection with this ancient lineage.

I'd like to tell you about a unique and unusual group of Indian foremothers who are reaching out to connect with us across the centuries: the 64 yoginis of Hirapur. A small village in eastern India, Hirapur, is a few miles from the city of Bhubaneswar. Its temple is a quiet, isolated sanctuary surrounded by paddy fields. Built in the ninth century, it is perfectly round, quite small—about thirty feet in diameter—and has no roof, a feature typical of yogini temples throughout India.

STEPPING INTO OURSELVES

As you enter, you see 64 stone niches carved into the circular wall. Originally, each one was graced with an exquisitely carved yogini, and all but one remains intact. Some look like typical Hindu goddesses with full breasts, a proud gait and a powerful presence. Some have animal heads or stand on animals. Some are emaciated old women, and some carry bows and arrows, or play drums. Shamanism is not a tradition we normally associate with Hinduism, yet it is impossible to deny the distinctly shamanic presence that pervades the ancient sanctuary.

Who are these strange beings? Hindu mythology describes them as attendants of Kali, also known as Durga, the powerful Warrior Goddess. Fierce and often fear-inspiring, she drinks blood, rides lions and tigers and is associated with the colors red, for passion, and black, for death.

Ancient myths credit Durga with saving the planet at a time when dark forces such as hatred, fear and greed threatened to destroy it. In her form as planet-saver, Durga is sometimes shown with a thousand hands holding a thousand weapons, symbols of the skillful means by which she transform injustice, cruelty and violence into peace, compassion and joy.

She is beautiful—so beautiful, in fact, that, according to Hindu myths, the demons were terribly distracted by her presence on the battlefield, and could not take their eyes off her. Wielding her sharp sword, she liberated them from the illusions in which they had become trapped and set them free to rejoin the ecstatic dance of the cosmos.

In her battle against the demons, Durga's greatest challenge came from a demon called Raktabija, who possessed a special power: whenever a drop of his blood touched the ground, a host of new demons would spring up. The 64 yoginis celebrated in the temple of Hirapur were expressly created to help Durga overcome Raktabija. Endowed with the power of flight, they surrounded him and lapped up his blood before it could hit the ground and multiply.

I had never heard of the yoginis of Hirapur until last year, but from the minute I first saw their images, I was fascinated. I knew that the Jewish and Palestinian women for whom I lead circles in Israel would intuitively identify with them and understand their meaning. Nobody has to explain to them how one act of bloodshed can multiply and trigger a hundred more. Moreover, they know that, to prevent such escalation, we must acknowledge, feel and transform the pain from which acts of violence are born, just as the yoginis transform darkness into light by drinking the demon's blood.

For weeks, the yoginis kept haunting my dreams and tugging at the edges of my consciousness, until finally I realized I needed to give them my undivided attention. And so, one windy day in late fall, I sat down with pen and paper and silenced my thoughts.

"Who are you?" I asked. They responded instantly, as if they had been impatiently waiting for my attention:

> *We are your foremothers. We are yoginis in the original sense of the word: women who are inextricably, eternally yoked to the divine. We are lovers of God, embodiments of the Goddess and priestesses dedicated with union to the divine. If the erotic charge we exude makes some people nervous, ask them why they would forbid the Goddess from making love, when all of her creation does so? Besides making love, we perform rituals and sit at the bedsides of the dying. We study, teach and celebrate the spirit of beauty. We practice yoga, music, dance, art, herbalism, midwifery and philosophy. We live in and are guardians of sacred space.*
>
> *Many people are afraid of us. Talk to the villagers around here, and they will tell you stories of ritually beheaded corpses and of ceremonies that break all religious taboos. Yet we are expressions of pure love, and our intent is not to harm but to heal. Our Goddess, Kali, is black, not because she is evil, but because she is unknowable, vast, eternal and uncompromising. As a sharp knife becomes an instrument of healing in the hands of a skilled surgeon, so our destructive powers serve the cause of life.*
>
> *We have contacted you because we want to impart our courage to you and your sisters. We want to help you cut through the fear that holds you back from giving yourself over to love, and to life. See how we stand naked, vulnerable, yet unafraid! If you hope to birth a new world, you too must have the courage to embrace the vulnerability so abhorrent to your ego.*

STEPPING INTO OURSELVES

Many women in your society are terrified of their own power, a fear that has been instilled into them for centuries. You must shed that fear now; for otherwise, you will remain helpless to overcome the dark forces in your world. The practice of yoga awakens power within you and teaches you to channel it in service of goodness. Remember that the greatest power is that of love, which dissolves the ego and allows you to realize your oneness with all beings. Serve the cause of love, and you will become invincible.

I paused in my writing, listening to the wind howling around the house. My mind was so full of questions I hardly knew where to begin. "Why do some of you have the heads of horses, lions, rabbits and elephants?" I asked. I sensed the yoginis laughing among themselves. Then, they said:

We have animal heads because we have animal powers. You too have the ability to merge with the consciousness of animals, trees, rivers and mountains. You must remember this if you hope to heal the planet. Open to the subtle grace of the leopard, the big-hearted wisdom of the gorilla and the soaring vision of the falcon. Sit with the rose and rest in the stillness of a rock. Free yourself from the tyranny of the busy human mind, and let your yoga incorporate not just physical but also inner stillness. When you practice the Corpse Pose, give yourself to the earth like a child to the mother. Let go of thought, and rest in silence.

You face challenges we never did. In our world, earth, air and water were pure and clean. Global warfare and terrorism were unknown. While we cannot solve your problems, we can tell you with certainty that you will not find the solutions you seek unless you align yourselves with the powers of nature, honoring them as gateways to the mystery beyond name and form.

Since I lead circles, and train women in circle leadership, I was especially intrigued to learn that the yoginis supposedly always form a circle when they touch ground. When I asked them to talk about this, they responded:

> *We stand in a circle because we are sisters. Though each one of us is different and unique, we are equal and united. On your own, each one of you can do only so much. But together, your power is immense. Together, you represent the many faces and forms of the Divine Mother.*
>
> *Claim the power of your sisterhood! Stop treating one another as rivals and competitors, and recognize your sisters as mirrors that reflect both your own face, and the face of the Divine Mother who lives within you. Remember that there is no greater channel of sacred healing energy than a circle of spiritually dedicated people.*
>
> *To us, circle gatherings are a basic element of spiritual practice. Though we value solitude, we cannot imagine a spiritual life that does not also include circle gatherings. Circles amplify our power and help us reach the state of union that is the ultimate goal of yoga.*

Finally, I asked the yoginis whether they had a special message for the yoginis of this day and age. I heard them say:

> *We want to speak especially to the young girls among you. Granddaughters, mothers of the future, you are beautiful and perfect, just as you are. Your bodies are worthy of love, reverence and worship. Relish the softness of your bodies. Be proud of who you are, and stop judging your beauty by the standards of others. When you realize that the Goddess lives within you, your standards will change entirely.*
>
> *Never forget that the true source of authority lies within. Honor your teachers, but listen within, and make your own decisions. You, too, are servants of the Goddess. Value yourselves, and do not keep company with people who treat you with disrespect. To protect the planet, you must dare to become visible.*

STEPPING INTO OURSELVES

Knowing your own worth will empower you to step forth with confidence to speak your truth in the world

"Thank you," I said to the yoginis. "Is there anything else?" There was a moment's silence before they answered.

Tell your sisters that we love them. Tell them to call on us. Tell them we are here to help.

Talking to the Yogini
If you have a question about your life that you would like the yoginis to help you with, try this:

- Sit down in a quiet place with paper and pen and write your question.
- Close your eyes and calm your mind, giving yourself permission to relax and sit in silence. Reassure yourself that right now there is nothing you need to think about or figure out. Let yourself go into an oasis of peace.
- After a few minutes, mentally reach out to the yoginis. Let them know you want to connect with them. Approach them with respect, humility and receptivity. Be open to the possibility that they might want to speak to you.
- When you feel ready, open your eyes and write down the words: Dear (your name) . . .
- Now simply listen with all your heart, body and soul, and write down whatever presents itself. Try not to let your inner critic get in your way. Keep the channel as wide open as you can, and record whatever comes without judgment, in a spirit of light-hearted curiosity. Don't edit, censor or question anything—just write it down.
- When you feel complete, thank the yoginis, set aside your journal and spend another few minutes resting quietly.

Endnote

1 Jalaja Bonheim, *Aphrodite's Daughters: Women's Sexual Stories and the Journey of the Soul* (New York: Touchstone Publishers, 1997).

Invocation
By Andrea Goodman

You, who hover
thousands of years
inside the King's Chamber in the Great Pyramid,
who recognize my song and sing with me,
you, who remember what all have forgotten,
who wait and listen for the pilgrims' return,

take me into your heart of hearts,
keep me safe in your stone arms,
help me to live with the song always
on my lips as it is on yours,
the spell of renewal
chanting itself through me.

Teach me again
the alphabet of beauty,
the traces of time
buried and unburied,
where great birds
sweep the sky
and wings protect
the wanderer.

STEPPING INTO OURSELVES

I ask you to mention
my name in your council,
to reach for me often
through channels of filament
so I will remember myself
as I entered your perfect space
where I know myself wholly, holy.

The Stuff of Life:
Clay, Figurines and Priestesses in Mesoamerica*
By Anne Key

The female figure is present throughout the thousands of years of Mesoamerican history, spanning its many cultures and encompassing various media, whether formed from clay, carved into stone or drawn on paper or pottery. Viewing these artifacts with the eye of a researcher and a priestess, I perceive many of these pieces as ritual implements. The evidence seems abundant that women were a dynamic force in the spiritual sphere.

However, from decades of studying these pieces, I have noticed a distinct gap between what I view *in situ* and in museums, and what I read in the academic research. While there seems to be a great deal of physical evidence of women, there is little research into women's roles and even less into women's part in the encompassing spiritual life of the Mesoamericans.[1] This winding road takes us through seeing women as artists, and then regarding their creations as ritual tools. With those two in mind, it is possible to envision women as priestesses and leaders.

There is evidence that women were the artisans of clay figurines in the earliest eras of Mesoamerican culture. In her research, Carolyn Tate shows that women were both potters and paper-makers in the Maya civilization. It was only after the Spanish introduced the potter's wheel that men became potters. She points out that, "The activities of hand-building pottery emulate grinding corn, forming corn dough, and cooking it, as the mythical First Mother of the Popul Vuh formed the human race of corn

---

* Originally published in a slightly different form in *She is Everywhere! An Anthology of Writing in Womanist/Feminist Spirituality*, ed. Mary Saracino and Mary Beth Moser (Berkeley, CA: Belladonna, 2005). Reprinted with permission.

dough."² Women, associated with the earth and the water, were the ones that formed the shapes from clay.

On a different tack, Joyce Marcus has also concluded that women were the original clay artists.³ In her examination of Formative Era female figurines from the Oaxaca area, she identified their extravagant hairstyles as markers for social status. When considering the gender of the artist of these clay figurines, she consulted modern hairstylists to see if the maker of the figurine would have to know how to create the hairstyle to achieve such realistic results. The hairstylists agreed that hairstyles of the Formative Era were depicted in such realistic detail that whoever made the figurines must also have known how to produce the hairstyle depicted. As it is highly unlikely that men styled women's hair in Formative Era Mesoamerica, it seems logical that both the hair styles and the figurines were produced by women.

Women as clay artisans persist to contemporary times. Women in Chiapas still model small figurines from clay and fire them in the cooking fires. These small painted figures are whimsical, representing daily life and sold to tourists for only a few *centavos*. In Michoacán, making clay figurines is still today considered women's work, as it has been traditionally.⁴

But, does the gender of the artisan matter? When we study the female figurines, does it make a difference if they were formed by women or men? If we view the figurines in relation to culture, as opposed to looking at the figurines solely in an isolated context, then the gender of the artist is certainly relevant.

When the figurines are regarded as a cultural artifact, the gender of the artists tells us about social formation of society; when the figurines are regarded as ritual tools, the gender of the artisan tells us about gender-specific spiritual practices. Female figurines crafted by women reflect the spiritual practice of women. What were their rituals like? What was their unique cosmovision? How were the figurines used and why did women make them?

Most ritual tools are also works of art. A link exists between art and ritual tools; both media are used to express what can and cannot be seen, uniting and giving form to thought. Further, ritual tools bring the formless into form. One example of this is using a feather to symbolize air. The feather, while not being air, brings some of the qualities of air, such as being insubstantial yet strong. Feathers also move air effectively and, when in their original state on birds, are in constant contact with air, using air to do the seemingly impossible—keep aloft a weight in a weightless atmosphere. Art and ritual tools bring multivalent meaning to a single concrete form.

From a physical perspective, creating art unites both sides of the brain, the left for the skill and the right for the inspiration and vision. The creation of art for sacred purpose brings the spiritual realm into the concrete. When viewed in this light, studying clay figurines as ritual tools allows us, in this century, to see how the women of previous times manifested their relationship to the Divine.

There have been numerous methods of categorizing Mesoamerican clay figurines, the most notable being the system authored by Valliant and based on physical features.[5] Methods of categorization that rely solely on physical (aesthetic) qualities diminish the possibilities for using these figurines, as well as the possibility that we will look at them as ritual tools. It sets them firmly in the category of something to be viewed rather than used.

There is certainly a difference between a clay figurine that a woman makes to sell in the marketplace and a clay figurine that a woman makes as a ritual tool. Both may look the same, and both may be evaluated by the same guidelines whether regarded as a piece of art or as a cultural artifact. However, both of these pieces are not the same, for the intent of their manufacture is completely different. This is especially applicable to objects with a numinous quality. At this point, there is not a recognizable metric for establishing the degree, or even existence, of numinous qualities. Yet, this is exactly the quality that separates an object made solely for aesthetic purposes or commerce from an object made with sacred intent. But, simply because we do not have the metrics for something, simply because we have not devised with a way to measure and quantify the unquantifiable, does not mean that the unquantifiable does not exist or is not intrinsic to the meaning of the object.

One of the reasons we can view these clay figurines as ritual tools—

objects created with sacred intent—is that they are often funerary objects. Objects that accompany a body in burial, and may presumably accompany that person into her next life, are important. Most Mesoamerican objects in museums and collections had funerary functions. As Coe has observed, there is a

> ... tremendous difference between ordinary artifacts and funerary material. ... I would, therefore, conclude from this that most of what one finds in art museums is not the stuff of ordinary life but, rather, is another form of scarce goods which have been taken out of circulation for this cult of the dead.[6]

While these goods can be used as offerings for a "cult of the dead" these scarce goods can also be viewed as ritual tools.

It should be remembered that the most spectacular pieces—the pieces we study, the pieces that hold the most meaning—are most often associated with ritual. It is no wonder that the artisans put the greatest effort and intent into creating these pieces. In contrast, there are relatively few ritual tools used in modern Euro-American culture. This can be attributed to the fact that spiritual practice in our culture is highly centralized; most ritual tools reside in churches. In a home-based spiritual practice, such as was common in Mesoamerica, ritual tools would be abundant. Again, in modern Euro-American culture, much of our most spectacular art is created for viewing and sale, not for use in ritual. It is no wonder that we overlook the ritual qualities of so much of the art of Mesoamerica.

For people, one of the most intimately known and powerful figures is the human form. Humans anthropomorphize the un-embodied or unknowable into something knowable by using the human form. Images of deities are often shown in human form.

The making of human figurines that become the first people is told in the creation story of the Aztec from the Leyenda de los Soles. Cihuacoatl (woman snake) grounds bones gathered by Quetzalcoatl from the underworld. She grounds them into flour, put the flour in a womb-like container and the gods bled their penises in a ritual of autosacrifice. In four days a boy was born, and four days later a girl was born. In the Mayan Popul

Vuh, the "maker-modeler" (the mother-father of life, the midwife-matchmaker) ground corn and mixed it with water to form humans.[7] The forming of human figures out of a substance, be it corn, clay or ground bones, is the act of creation.

The human form can also be a metaphor. *Milagros*, tiny metal figures for sale in front of cathedrals in Mexico, are often in the form of the human body, or parts of a body. They can symbolize the need for healing for a certain part, say a leg, or act as a metaphor:

> The milagro of the arm might represent an arm itself, and some condition associated with it, such as an injury, or, say, an arthritic condition. It might also represent one's strength, one's ability to work—and hence one's job—or some related concept. It might represent an embrace, and physical demonstrations of affection that involve embracing. Any part of the arm might be the focus of the prayers or the magic, such as the hand, for instance.[8]

In general, concrete objects, especially familiar figures, make the intangible tangible and manifest multiple meanings simultaneously in a single object.[9]

The female figure represents creation, fecundity. As the gender that gives birth, women are the repository of life. As a symbol, a female figure represents creation, and the ability for humans to create, which is, in itself, a divine act.

As a material, clay possesses many miraculous properties that make it a staple world wide. Its plasticity and strength make it easy to work with, and it is readily available. It hardens on its own and fires easily. Clay also has medicinal properties. It is used externally to absorb toxins from the skin while simultaneously exfoliating and improving skin circulation. Ingested, clay is an anti-diarrheal medication that relieves nausea and provides calcium. For these reasons, it is especially helpful for pregnant women.[10] Clay and female figurines combined create powerful multivalent symbols. Used in ritual, these figurines would have multiple applications.

Female figurines are some of the oldest known works of art. By regarding these figurines as ritual tools—works of art made to perform a sacred function—we open the possibility of glimpsing the oldest rituals performed by women. This, indeed, is an exciting prospect. By researching, unearthing and discovering women's rituals, we expand our perspective on women and their roles.

Regarding the Paleolithic and Neolithic female figurines from Europe and Mesoamerica, which stylistically shared many similar characteristics, the standing interpretation has been that these were fertility objects, possibly used to glorify, request or to reflect one's own fertility.

The ideas of fertility and a "cult of fertility" bring to mind many images. There is a vital reason that fertility is the basis of many religions, for there is no life without it. Fertility is the sustenance and rejuvenation of life on this earth. However, when one speaks of a cult of fertility, especially in the context of modern American culture steeped in Abrahamic religious values, the idea of a fertility cult is devalued, associated solely with sex or procreation or considered a component of primitive religions as opposed to more "advanced" religions. So at the same time that one regards the obvious fertility aspect of these figurines, it is necessary to define or redefine the concept of fertility to include all life and the moral philosophy that underlies the continuance of life, the endurance of fecundity.

There continues to be speculation that these figurines were "stone-age, sexual fetish" pieces.[11] This perspective presumes a male artist and sees the female model as faceless. It also traps women, again, in the male gaze, solely as objects of fertility and procreation, leading some experts to believe that prehistoric males (the artists) viewed females solely as reproductive mechanisms.[12]

Marija Gimbutas' research into Paleolithic and Neolithic Europe began a much needed re-visioning of these figures. Of her many contributions, two most heavily impact our view of female figurines and this study. The first is her interpretation of the symbols on figurines and pottery of the Neolithic. These symbols were commonly regarded as decoration, not as language. In *Language of the Goddess*, Gimbutas convincingly categorizes the repeating symbols, presenting them as purposeful ideographs laden with meaning.[13] This has been crucial to broadening the discussion around these figurines, to moving beyond their descriptive and aesthetic qualities and on to their possible meaning, uses and function. By finding meaning in what was previously considered decorative (that is, having only minimal symbolic significance and high aesthetic significance), Gimbutas began decoding the symbolic language of the artifact. She paved the way for the interpretation of meaning.

The second of Gimbutas' contributions with impacts on this study is her idea of goddess-based religion prevalent across many thousands of years throughout Old Europe,[14] with many of these figurines seen as images of a Great Goddess. Her work brought to the forefront an overwhelming amount of evidence that, in Old Europe, a female deity was honored.

Barbara Tedlock provides another perspective on these Old European figurines, linking them with shamans.[15] Many of the figurines feature dress characteristic of shamans who practiced midwifery. This link to shamanism adds another layer of meaning, connecting the figurines with real women performing real functions. It certainly moves beyond the idea of woman as mere model, passively procreating, to woman as illustrious figure, immortalized in sculpture.

Mesoamerican figurines have had a similar array of meanings attached to them. Bernal assigns the female figurines as fertility cult items, intimately tied to harvest and deity propitiation: ". . . .we see that the groups in the Valley of Mexico practised a fertility cult, related to natural phenomena and fecundity, for which female figurines were modeled in clay with a view to propitiating gods who controlled the harvest."[16]

Peterson links their development to the post-classical Mesoamerican cosmovision: "The clay women probably represent earth or vegetation goddesses made in connection with agricultural ceremonies. This was an important step in the development of one of the greatest magico-religious cultures in the world."[17] Kocyba directly compares the European Neolithic female images with those found in Archaic and Formative Era Mesoamerica; he attributes the decline in both cultures to the institutionalization of religion.[18] Román Padilla R. and Araceli Jaffer G. broaden the possibilities of the functions of female clay figurines to include:

providing magical protection, serving as amulets, votive offerings, toys, death offerings, or offerings to structures, or elements associated with fertility or represent deities.[19]

Marcus proposes that small, predominantly female figurines from Early and Middle Formative Oaxaca (1800–500 BCE) were used in ancestor worship rituals. She speculates that women created clay figurines of their "recent ancestors," female family members who had died, to be used in ceremonies honoring these ancestors.[20]

In a myriad of ways, female clay figurines can be seen as ritual tools. But what of the women who made them and most likely used them? Why are they not seen as spiritual leaders?

Viewing these figurines as ritual tools requires that we understand the underlying spiritual philosophy of those who used them. The set of beliefs termed "shamanism" accurately describes the spiritual philosophy of the Mesoamericans.

A comprehensive definition of shamanism is put forth by Barbara Tedlock based on both her academic work as an anthropologist and her personal work training with Mayan and other shamans. In her definition, shamans share these traits: the conviction that all entities (animate or otherwise) re-imbued with a life force participate in the life energy that holds the world together; the belief that all things are interdependent and interconnected; the vision that the world is constructed of a series of levels connected by a central axis in the form of a world tree or mountain; the belief that societies designate individuals to take on the role of shaman for their group; and the recognition that extraordinary forces, entities and beings affect individuals and events in our ordinary world and that rituals performed in ordinary reality can lead to effects in the alternative sphere.[21] To Tedlock's definition, I would add an observation from Sasakia, a specialist in Japanese shamanism: "the role of the shaman is related to the maintenance of the cosmology of the society."[22]

However, there has been an ongoing controversy over the use of the word "shamanism" in the academy. Numerous accusations of overreaching or even "sloppy" uses of this word[23] have led to calls for a strict definition. Though definitions such as the one quoted earlier by Tedlock have been proffered, there remains resistance to their usage.[24]

This recent backlash against the use of the word "shamanism" could be due to a number of factors, including an anti-spiritual bias in academia, based on the general idea that spiritual practice is non-rational (I mean this, of course, in a pejorative fashion) in contrast to the rational basis of academic work. The resistance to viewing spiritual practices in terms of shamanism reflects on the resistance to seeing clay figurines as tools in ritual practice.

Even when shamanic ritual practices are recognized, why are women not often seen in the role of shaman, as spiritual leaders, or as the ones who maintain the cosmology of their society? Part of this may be due to data on tribal societies collected by foreign men who did not have access to women. Part of this may also be due to the unfortunate fact that many people turn to Mircea Eliade's work when discussing shamanism. Eliade is widely quoted because he explores unifying concepts applying to many religious expressions. However, his work is hampered by multiple factors, including the fact that his work on shamanism is based solely on anthropological records as opposed to *in situ* observation, which often leaves the stories of women untold. Tedlock and others[25] have performed an excellent service to further the study of shamanism by clearly rebutting many of the tenets Eliade proposed. The unfortunate fallout of Eliade's popularity as a reference for shamanism is that women as shamans, and women's rituals overall, are, at best, overlooked and, at the most egregious, devalued. If we move from an androcentric idea of men as the prominent shamans and embrace the idea of women as shamans and leaders, we begin to view what we find in their graves, and in their homes, as ritual tools.

The study of ancient spiritual practice is hugely important. By researching spiritual practices in different contexts and searching for the common and uncommon threads, we are able to see more clearly the self-imposed paradigms of our modern spiritual practice; and when the paradigms of our modern religions are found to be less than "historic" or "natural," the gravitas they have accumulated dissipates, and ground fertile for new growth opens to the sun.

This is particularly important for women's place in religion. Certainly in the last 2,000 years in many parts of the world, women's leadership roles in socio-politically powerful religions have been incredibly diminished. When faced with the paradigm that women have not "historically" been spiritual leaders, we must understand the limits of the word "historic" as well as who was writing the history. If the idea of historic is expanded to the pre-historic, which is far, far longer than the historic, then we certainly see a more comprehensive view; we see women in a far greater, juicier context, not hemmed in by the present paradigm.

The figurines from the long and artistically productive Mesoamerican culture were multivalent and with multiple utilizations. Seeing them not only as dolls and votives but also as ritual tools enhances our scope for understanding the spiritual practices of the artists. Seeing them as created by women, for use in rituals led by women, opens new vistas for our understanding of women's roles in the spiritual lives of Mesoamericans.

Pieces that have been labeled as "pretty ladies" and children's toys might be viewed as numinous objects and ritual tools. Women grinding corn to feed their families and making whimsical toys for their children can be seen as women grinding corn to prepare offering tamales and crafting powerful objects of veneration. Women once considered the silent objects of the male gaze can be reconsidered—and regarded as spiritual leaders.

Endnotes

1 Notable exceptions are Carolyn Tate, "Writing on the Face of the Moon: Women's Products, Archetypes, and Power in Ancient Maya Civilization," in *Manifesting Power: Gender and the Interpretation of Power in Archaeology*, ed. Tracy L. Sweely (New York: Routledge, 1999); and Joyce Marcus, *Women's Ritual in Formative Oaxaca: Figurine-making, Divination, Death, and the Ancestors* (Ann Arbor: University of Michigan Press, 1998).
2 Carolyn Tate, "Writing on the Face of the Moon: Women's Products, Archetypes, and Power in Ancient Maya Civilization" *Manifesting Power: Gender and the Interpretation of Power in Archaeology*, ed. by Tracy L. Sweely (New York: Routledge, 1999), 86.
3 Joyce Marcus, *Women's Ritual in Formative Oaxaca: Figurine-making,*

Divination, Death, and the Ancestors (Ann Arbor: University of Michigan Press, 1998).

4 Claudia B. Isaac, "Witchcraft, Cooperatives, and Gendered Competition in a P'urepecha Community," *Frontiers: A Journal of Women's Studies* 16, no. 2/3 (1996): 161–189.

5 G.G. Vaillant, *Aztecs of Mexico* (Baltimore, MD: Penguin, 1965).

6 Michael Coe, "Closing Remarks," *Death and the Afterlife in Pre-Columbian America* (Cambridge, MA: Dumbarton Oaks Research Library, 1975), 194.

7 Today, the act of making tamales is considered sacred. The corn is the flesh, the meat is the muscle and the sauce is the blood.

8 For more on milagros, see www.faustosgallery.com/milagros

9 A figurine is also thought to be a form that "traps" spirit, making it controllable. For a look at Yoruba use of human figures, see Norma H. Wolff, "The Use of Human Images in Yoruba Medicines." *Ethnology* 39, no. 3 (Summer 2000): 205–224.

10 See Wiley and Katz, "Geophagy in Pregnancy: A Test of a Hypothesis." *Current Anthropology* 39, no. 4 (Aug–Oct. 1998): 532–545.

11 Though these sorts of interpretations are usually designated to an older, androcentric time in academia (see particularly Desmond Collins 1978), a relatively new general audience book, *The Prehistory of Sex: Four Million Years of Human Sexual Culture* (New York: Bantam, 1997) by British archaeologist Timothy L. Taylor, proposes some equally androcentric views of female figurines.

12 See Patricia Rice "Prehistoric Venuses: Symbols of Motherhood or Womanhood?" *from Journal of Anthropological Research* 37, no. 4. (Winter 1981), 402–414, for an excellent, though dated, review of female Paleolithic figurines and their possible symbolic meaning.

13 Marija Gimbutas, *Language of the Goddess* (New York: Thames and Hudson, 2001).

14 See especially *Civilization of the Goddess* (1994) and *The Goddesses and Gods of Old Europe 6500–3500 BC: Myths and Cult Images* (1982). When the latter was first published in 1974, though the figurines in the book were predominantly female, her publishers insisted that the title be *The Gods and Goddesses of Old Europe.*

15 Barbara Tedlock, *The Woman in the Shaman's Body: Reclaiming the Feminine in Religion and Medicine* (New York: Bantam Dell, 2005).

16 Ignacio Bernal, *A History of Mexican Archaeology: The Vanished Civilizations of Middle America* (London: Thames and Hudson, 1980), 36.

17 Peterson, Frederic, *Ancient Mexico* (New York: G.P. Putnam's Sons, 1959), 36.

18 Henryk Karol Kocyba, "La formación de las religiones insitucionalizadas y el surgimiento de las sociedades jerarquizadas en Europa centro-oriental y en el área maya," *Historia comparativa de las religions*, ed. Henryk Karol Kocyba. (Mexico DF: Instituto Nacional de Antropologia e Historia, 1998), 41–68.

19 Roman R. Padilla and Jaffer G. Araceli, "Las figuras preclasicas de Temamatla, Estado de Mexico," *Homenaje a la doctora Beatriz Barba de Pina Chan* (Mexico, DF: Instituto Nacional de Antropologia e Historia, 1997), 157–176.

20 Joyce Marcus, *Women's Ritual in Formative Oaxaca: Figurine-making, Divination, Death, and the Ancestors* (Ann Arbor: University of Michigan Press, 1998).

21 Barbara Tedlock, *The Woman in the Shaman's Body: Reclaiming the Feminine in Religion and Medicine* (New York: Bantam Dell, 2005), 20–21.

22 Nakanishi, F. "Possession: A Form of Shamanism?" *Magic, Ritual, and Witchcraft* 1, no. 2 (Winter 2006): 236.

23 From Klein, *Current Anthropology*, 43, no. 3 (June 2002): "It is our position that many of these writers, regardless of their disciplinary base, are using shamanism to provide predictable, easy, and ultimately inadequate answers to what are often very complex questions about the relationship of art to religion, medicine, and politics in pre-Hispanic Mesoamerica" (383).

24 For repartee on shamanism, *see Magic, Ritual and Witchcraft*, 1, no. 2 (Winter 2006) and *Current Anthropology*, 43, no.3 (June 2002), as well as *Current Anthropology*, 46, no. 1 (February 2005), F127. For a view of shamanism and modern paganism, see Graham Harvey, *Contemporary Paganism: Listening People, Speaking Earth* (New York: New York UP, 2000), 107–125.

25 Tedlock gives a comprehensive rebuttal of Eliade's scholarship on shamanism (see especially pages 64–65 and 72–75). Other rebukes of Eliade's

work include: Carol Christ, *Rebirth of the Goddess* (1997), especially 80–86; Ruth-Inge Heinze, *Shamans in the 20th Century* (1991); and Alice Beck Kehoe, *Shamans and Religion: An Anthropological Exploration in Critical Thinking* (2000). For a friendly view of Eliade, see Bryan S. Rennie, *Reconstructing Eliade: Making Sense of Religion* (1996).

My Family's Lineage of Priestesses
By Carmen Roman

My family of origin is of indigenous immigrants who moved from a small village to the city of Guadalajara in Mexico. They pray at Catholic Church, and venerate saints at home. However, letting a male priest influence the family is foreign to our customs. Instead, a council of elders led by a woman makes vital decisions that affect us all. In my family, women serve as priestesses for family and community. I know about the ideas, behaviors and rituals of these priestesses, how they managed their power—or did not—and their relationships to men. Those priestesses are my maternal grandma, Kila, my mom, Paula and my Aunt Chuy.

My grandma, Mama Kila, was the main inspiration for my personal growth and well-being. She was married at the age of 36 to a 17-year-old boy. During the four years of her marriage, she gave birth to two girls and a boy. Her son died in a home accident at the age of two, and my grandfather left home a year later. My grandmother raised her daughters by selling homemade tortillas and chocolate to residents of their small village. I saw my grandma as a healthy, loving and peaceful woman.

As a child, I knew little about her history and the pain she'd experienced in her past. At age twelve, Mama Kila was kidnapped, held captive, raped and tortured by an adult man in her community. The community did not rescue her, maybe because an older man stealing a young woman was a tolerated practice at that time, and frankly probably still is in small villages. This was the case particularly for girls who had no fathers to protect their "honor," like Mama Kila. After a few months, she managed to escape and return home. Instead of being comforted after such a traumatic experience, she was blamed. Her mother asked her to leave because she was not a "pure woman" and was a social shame. Mama Kila then made her living in whatever way she could.

Far from being resentful or bitter, Mama Kila was serene and calm. Her body was truly sacred for her; she was always careful about eating a healthy diet, going for walks and getting plenty of rest. Mama Kila put water to heat in the sun all day so she could take a shower in the afternoon. She took a long time to dry her skin and comb her hair in the sunlight. She considered cooking, cleaning and taking care of the home as sacred practices. Her modest, daily attire was a homemade dress and simple shoes; she only wore a store-made dress to go to church on Sundays. She never wore makeup or jewelry.

She lived in our home until her death, and my parents always respected her opinions. The best relationship Mama Kila ever had was with her son-in-law, my father; she was always concerned for his well-being and vice versa. She had a great relationship with her brother, who functioned also as a father for her daughters. I got to experience her relationship with my father on an everyday basis. It was a relationship of respect and mutual compassion; it seems that at some point she deliberately eliminated relationships with violent or harmful men.

Mama Kila taught me how to read and write as well as to knit and sew. She shared her philosophy of life and told stories about the Mexican revolution, which she had witnessed. At age 84, she seemed healthy but complained about a stomach ache and stayed in bed for two days in a row. I was only fourteen years old when she asked me for a private meeting in the last minutes of her life. She talked to me about her concern for her daughters and grandchildren and their safety after her death. Then she said, "I am going to die today." She gave me instructions about her funeral. It was sad to see her go, but also beautiful to witness the death of a priestess. Her teachings are not words but wonderful shared moments that I keep in my soul.

Paula, my mom, is the oldest daughter of her family. Her priestess-hood is about serving the community. At her home, which is her temple, Paula ensures that every person who visits has a delightful meal and someone to talk to. Some have adopted her as a mom. We, the blood daughters, are well known in the community as Paulita's daughters.

Paula held the highest level of education (fourth grade of elementary school) on both sides of my family until my dad went back to school in his late fifties. Due to the lack of certified teachers in the village, she taught elementary courses from the age of twelve. Later, she became a clerk at the local pharmacy; now, people entrust her with both their emotional and physical problems.

Because of her herbal remedies, healing abilities and therapeutic talks, visitors come back often with all kinds of emotional and physical complains. She prescribes beverages to sick children, and hugs and blesses anybody willing to accept her love. She talks to women and men who are having marital problems and older women who are being victimized by men. Paula does not have a title of a psychologist or social worker, but she functions like one for the community.

For many years, Paula baked bread in a domed stone oven that my father had made. I remember that she and my father used to bake for several hours on Saturdays, producing enough bread to feed our community. Other times, we sold tamales that she made. Even now, whatever she cooks, people love to eat it and consider it a fantastic excuse to sit and talk to her for long periods of time.

The way she honors her family is by cooking, gardening, cleaning and taking care of their immediate needs. Her spiritual practices include praying, singing, and doing art crafts, such as sewing her own clothing. Paula also knows how to take care of herself. Her most sacred practices are taking the time for a nap every afternoon and going for long walks around the neighborhood where she stops to greet people. As Paula's daughter, I learned about forming loving relationships with all people despite their age, academic background or skin color.

Paula is now in her seventies and has been married to my dad for 44 years. In contrast to the women of her lineage, she has been blessed with a husband who adores her and takes good care of her. Although they had seven pregnancies, three boys and one girl died before or shortly after birth. Her personal life is a combination of personal challenges and blessings. She suffered with severe asthma for fifteen years, until she had a near-death experience in her late forties. Despite their poverty, health problems and lack of formal education, she and my dad have made a terrific partnership to help the community and they have a fabulous life together.

Aunt Chuy, my dad's sister, was the priestess who led the council of the family for forty years after the death of her mother. I considered her my second mom because she babysat me for long periods. Aunt Chuy's favorite rituals were praying, singing church songs and reading the Bible. She also cooked for parties and family gatherings. She traveled more than anyone else in the family and brought us little presents along with new stories. I began traveling with her when I was four. Like my mother and grandmother, she dedicated her life to her priestesshood and promoted cooperation and sacred rituals in the family. She made new babies or partners feel they were part of the family. She wanted us to be as passionate about religious activities as she was. She called us early in the morning to sing us a birthday song every year. She was always ready for rituals or parties. I admired her courage to speak up anytime or anywhere she saw an injustice.

Aunt Chuy got married at the age of fifty for the first time, and her husband happily took a supportive role in her life. He had good listening skills and a sweet way of talking to us. Aunt Chuy's rule, on the other hand, was somewhat different: she was right all the time and always quick to argue. Thus, every time we did something contrary to her beliefs, we got a private lecture, which included examples of our immoral behavior. I did not like being scolded as a "sinner child of God" as she used to call us. Most of the family members hated her methods, but she was loved and obeyed by almost all of them. We knew Aunt Chuy cared deeply about us, although she had a hard time relating in a kind and loving manner.

When I was in my early thirties, Aunt Chuy unexpectedly announced her retirement from the leadership position of the family council. She improvised paper crowns and named Maria, a cousin, as her successor to lead the older generations. She appointed me as her successor for those my age and younger. Maria and I were upgraded from assistants to priestesses without much of an announcement or instruction. We declined the roles until her death, but agreed to help actively in the council. I expressed my concern about our different leadership styles, since I did not want to lecture the family or provide such a traditional education. Aunt Chuy reluctantly agreed to keep her position.

For the last seven years of her life, after she was widowed, Aunt Chuy looked lonely and sad despite the frequent visits of her two brothers and the big party the family put together for her eightieth birthday; other family members did not visit her or listen to her point of view anymore, but instead contacted Maria or me. She passed away at the age of 83. She spent the last month of her life in a coma in a cold room at the hospital. She was warmly attended around the clock by family members, who later reported how upset she looked. During her burial, I conducted a goodbye ritual with the open casket. After reminiscing about her tough life and her wise leadership, I asked people to express what they had learned from her. It was amazing to hear how most of the family members were moved by her teachings. Most of them concluded that family unity was the greatest legacy she gave us. It is sad that her difficult character did not allow us to show her our love.

I consider myself a priestess for myself, my family and my community. I have been in the role of spiritual guide for my peers and for people of different ages. I perform rituals when needed. In the past few years, I have closed the eyes of people who have died and visited newborn babies in our family, visited family members and neighbors who were in emotional need, and attended special meetings at the family council when conflicts have arisen. Both being psychologist and having shamanic training have helped me to develop self-awareness. I am as grateful for the influence of other loving and caring priestesses I encounter in my life as I am thankful that I had access to a formal education.

Aloha Priestess Path
By Leilani Birely

Pupukahi i holomua
Unite to move forward[1]

Aloha! I open with a *pule* (prayer) blessing for all those who take on the *kuleana* (responsibility) role of priestess. As a Native Hawaiian woman, I have been taught since before I can remember to honor the *aina* (land), the *kupuna* (elders) and to ask permission in all the work I do as a Hawaiian daughter, *kahuna*, and High Priestess.

> *Aloha Akua Wahine* (Goddess)
> Please let your Daughters walk lightly on this Earth.
> Allow them to live in *pono* (balance) and right action with one another,
> to have peace in their hearts for the rituals, the women and the students they work with.
> Allow them to always ask permission for those cultures they would like to celebrate.

I founded the Daughters of the Goddess Women's Temple on Summer Solstice 1996 to foster the culture and spirit of Aloha handed down to me through my Hawaiian heritage. In the Hawaiian language, Aloha means affection, peace, compassion and mercy. It is my wish that each sister who enters this temple be imbued with Hawaiian cultural etiquette and protocol and the Aloha spirit. In this way we all become "ambassadors of Aloha," reversing what cultures have done to oppress our indigenous ways and spirit.

Transformation and healing through the spirit of Aloha is part of the gift and mission of Daughters of the Goddess. Through preservation and perpetuation of Aloha and of women's magical and mysterious traditions, we dance together to create a beautiful story. I want the women I work with to experience what it means to be touched by the spirit of the land of Hawai'i Nei, the expression of the Hawaiian essence.

Part of being a priestess is listening to women's stories. Sitting for hours listening to the stories told by my Grandma Chong in Hawai'i has helped to form my priestessing in many ways. I learned how important it is to share my story as well as to listen. In rituals, we make space for women to share a piece of their story before the ritual begins. In this way, the art of oral storytelling and sharing from the indigenous traditions is passed on. For those who have grown up in an environment without story sharing, it can be challenging to learn to sit, listen, hear and remember the herstories of our female lineage; but time and time again, participants have remarked how much this means to them and how much they learn and grow from being in the position of storyteller or listener.

A lot of Aloha teaching is about mending and transforming racism and cultural appropriation; we gather women of many diverse cultures around the altar. Teaching can be in a formalized structure; it's more important that the lessons come through listening, being present, attending ritual and ceremony, and being patient while the stories unfold.

I learned from my *kumu* (teachers), *kupuna* (elders), aunties and uncles "how to act," as we say in Hawai'i. I model the values, customs and behavior of Hawai'i, of my family and of our people. Many of the sisters I teach and with whom I circle are not of Hawaiian blood, but they uphold this mission of passing on the Aloha spirit. As I pass these customs to my sisters, the *mana* (spiritual power) I carry within me from the Hawaiian Islands and from my ancestors is passed on to each woman in the circle. In this way, we foster together in harmony the Aloha spirit, which is felt by all.

It is delightful to hear women chant beautifully in Hawaiian once they have learned the depth and meaning of the chant. I recall a European elder in the Women's Spirituality movement instructing me not to bother teaching white women to chant in Hawaiian, because they "wouldn't get it." Thankfully, this has not been true at all.

I see how deeply the Aloha spirit opens hearts and souls to the Goddess. I share Aloha through a hug, a *hula*, a chant and making *leis*. Through Aloha, hearts open, healing happens, unconditional love manifests and we tap into womanpower in its purest and rawest form.

In Hawaiian culture, unconditional giving, hospitality and community spirit are primary. For example, a Hawaiian child is taught to take off her shoes before entering a home. This is a way of honoring our *hale* (home), a way of leaving the negative and physical energies we collect on our shoes outside of homes and creating the sacred gateway between the outer world and the inner sanctuary. Ground space in the home is sacred and is often used for sleeping. There is no need to have beds for our house guests; as long as there is a pillow and blanket, there is plenty of room for visitors. All who are invited into a Hawaiian *hale* (home) are welcomed with open arms, a hug and a kiss on the cheek. Food and drink are always offered and shared, no matter how long or short the visit, or whether the visit is planned or spontaneous. All who enter the Hawaiian *hale* feel the warm embrace of the Aloha spirit.

In Hawaiian culture, we prize sharing and cooperation between *ohana* (family/group) as high-status social behavior, while we look with disdain upon territorialism, stinginess, over-attachment to material possessions, and putting individual needs above the *ohana*. The values we prize above all else are respect for our elders, our teachers, our leaders and our *kupunas*. We believe in the preservation and perpetuation of the continuous cycle of traditions and lineage of culture. We reflect on the past with great reverence and share this past with our beloved *mo'opunas* (youngsters). In the Hawaiian oral tradition, we share our history and beliefs through storytelling, *hula*, chants and praises.

As Hawaiians, we know the knowledge and interconnection of the *aina*, animals and plants. We have a deep reverence and respect for the delicate and intricate dance among all life forms. We understand the truth and importance of the spirit that lives and dwells within each plant, animal, human and the *aina*. We know that the depth and scope of knowledge spans far beyond those things that we can actually see with our eyes or touch with our hands.

Huna is what we call the hidden knowledge, the mystery, the unseen realm. Whenever we dance *hula* or create ceremony, we call on the ancestors or the Great Mystery to open us up so that we may receive spiritual guidance from our *ike*. Hawaiians see life and spirituality as interconnected; a separation between the two is not of our mindset. Spirituality is filled with life and it is spirit that gives form to life.

All I have learned from the classes, my teachers, my culture and my ancestors moves me to share the forgotten and lost knowledge that is so powerful that it can become a vehicle for women to move together in sisterhood. Our foremothers left legacies and it is our right and blessing to join together to reclaim, preserve and perpetuate the traditions and ceremonies of our ancestors. As a priestess of the Goddess, I provide community, the Aloha spirit and a space for Women's Mysteries to continue as our legacy, honor and birthright.

Endnote

1 "By working together we make progress." This Hawaiian proverb emerges from the Hawaiian culture as paddlers pulled together on command in order to make the canoe move quickly forward.

Centuries
By Janine Canan

In memory of Marija Gimbutas

O Century, my Century, whence did you come?
Sheep and cows once blissfully grazed on Mother's
millennial mounds. Rivers chatted, berries bounded
past the pistachios and fat red apples. Grasses fed
the ovens with bread. Villages gathered round her temple.
Vessels rose in bright array. Naked priestesses danced
in gold, and coaxed their lyres into grateful song.

Then, O fearful one, six thousand years ago
horsemen swarmed from barren steppes upon that
loved and fertile Land, swinging daggers and swords.
Inventors of weapons and slavery who worshipped the Sun,
wearing strings of teeth they raped and raided, razed and smashed.
Crushing the laws of Nature, they built a law of Terror—
the patriarch took his own family to the tomb.

Twentieth Century? No, you were never a century
of Christ, divine child of the Mother who taught
the sweet sovereignty of Love. Iron men nailed his body
to the cross and crucified his teaching—surrender
succumbed to dominance, compassion to violence.
Generosity was devoured by greed, innocence twisted
into guilt, and beauty mocked to shame.

Are you, my maddened Century, to be the last?
Bully rides tank, sub, plane with annihilating ammunitions,
inseminating land, sea and sky with numberless poisons.
What does he not violate? Tribes, women, children,
animals, plants. Even atoms hemorrhage radiation.
On skyscraper throne, in weapons temple, at money altar,
adoring his power, he gnaws on the heart of God.

O my battered Queen, once voluptuously green,
do you remember those dark wet caves where
hundreds of centuries past a Birth began? Wandering
through salted pillars, we entered a womb of Wonder.
We lit our fires, and on her crystal flesh we rang our
bellowing chimes. Fine-footed, large-bellied creatures romped
across her surging walls to bring forth ecstatic Life.

O Century, laborious Century! Drop by drop, your bloody
columns thicken. But our ancient fire glows still.
Now is the time to strike our truest chord! Her vast heart
pounds. Her waters splash. And moaning, praying
She pushes us down the narrowing canal against
the burning door. Lips open to Light. The moment arches.
Red petals flutter. Into the garden, a lark descending.

Three Times a Priestess
By Jade River

In 1978, I was called to priestess. At this time, I didn't know any priestesses or what a priestess did; I only knew that a resolve filled me to create a religious structure that afforded the privileges of traditional religion to the women's spiritual community. In 1984, Lynnie Levy and I founded the Re-formed Congregation of the Goddess, International (RCG-I) the first legally incorporated tax-exempt feminist women's religion in the United States. RCG-I still continues and I remain one of its priestesses. This is my story.

Hallows Night 1976
We laid a fire and cast a circle on a wooded hilltop to pledge ourselves to the Goddess. All of us were new to the Craft, but were drawn to commit ourselves to her. We lit the fire and began stating our intention to work for the empowerment of women with magic. As we spoke, the fire began to burn in earnest. Our circle was too small for the rising blaze. We stepped back trying to escape its intensity. We believed we should not break the bounds of the circle, so we moved to its very edge. The fire, however, would not relent. It danced higher and hotter but none of us stepped away. We stood resolutely despite our discomfort and made our promises.

With relief, we fled to a nearby park shelter. In the shelter's dim light, we saw each of us had a small, red, star-like mark. One of the women touched my neck where the Goddess had marked me as her own. My life would never be the same.

Candlemas 1977

Although we had made a commitment to do magic for the empowerment of women, none of us knew where to start. "Feminist witches" in Louisville, Kentucky did not identify as such because of a spiritual connection. It was, instead, a political identification with women's raw power. Undaunted, I continued to question them. Finally, they admitted they knew "real witches" in Cincinnati.

Many of us who had been on the hill at Hallows traveled to Cincinnati, and for the first time I stood in a coven circle. I had anticipated women well versed in the Craft, but found instead a well-meaning group of neophytes with a copy of Z Budapest's book, *The Feminist Book of Lights and Shadows*. We read the book together and tried to figure out what to do. Eventually, we had a ritual planned. This group became my first coven.

Spring Equinox 1978

There was an upcoming conference featuring Z Budapest called Witches and Amazons. We traveled to Ohio in a panel van with beanbags for seats. During the presentations, I heard a whisper on the edge of my perception: "Bring them together. No one need be alone." A hint of being called to do the Goddess's work glimmered in my consciousness. Crawling back into the van, I announced I wanted to organize for the Goddess. The women scoffed. I told them I was serious and if I had a little money I knew what to do.

The phone was ringing when I arrived home. It was my Mother calling to tell me that my grandmother (whom I loved, but with whom I had a tremendous values conflict) had just died and left me a 2.5-carat diamond ring, a mink stole and some nuclear power plant stock. The glimmer I had experienced washed over me in fullness. I was called to organize for Goddess.

Candlemas 1979

Being "called" by the Goddess was perplexing. I felt like I was stepping into something, but I didn't know what. Her message left me believing I needed to bring feminist witches together. This seemed like a form of leadership. Leadership in Dianic Wicca is called "priestessing;" Z was the only priestess I knew, and she was a ritualist. Although I had learned to efficiently do ritual, I did not believe this was what "Bring them together" meant. If one was not "called" to do ritual, was one a priestess?

I wanted to define what I was. Having no resources in feminist craft, I looked to traditional religions. Although they performed other duties, most clergy's primary responsibility was ritual. I worked with a woman who attended the Presbyterian seminary. She spoke about her interactions with the administrators of the denomination's headquarters who were allied with the seminary. All of these staff were called ministers. One day, as I drove past the Presbyterian headquarters, I had a flash of insight. The job of this institution was to bring people together. Its primary responsibility was to encourage interaction between people of faith. These administrators were acknowledged as ministers. I decided the work I was called to do was a kind of priestessing.

But how did one become a priestess? It seemed that being acknowledged as a priestess required both internal acceptance and community assent. In Dianic Wicca, the time for initiation is Candlemas. I extrapolated that, if one was to be recognized as a priestess, it should be on this same holiday. So on Candlemas 1979, I declared to my coven my intent to priestess. In feminist witchcraft, many things are done for a year and a day. If something can only occur on a specific holiday, it means a year and a day becomes two years. My coven agreed to consider my request to priestess on Candlemas of 1981. If, in the intervening time, they believed I had acted like a priestess, the group would acknowledge me as one.

Winter Solstice 1980
Choosing to live as a lesbian or a witch at this time in Kentucky meant being willing to risk everything. My friends and I were losing jobs, houses and children. The holidays were a difficult time, but despite this, we circled. Every year, my gift to my sisters was to rent a cabin high on the bluffs overlooking the Ohio River; it was a respite for a beleaguered group of women fighting for the right to practice magic and love whom they chose. Women came and went as their schedules allowed, but for several hours I was alone.

I thought about these women who were willing to brave the challenges of being a witch. Words came and I wanted to write them down. The document that emerged was *The Affirmation of Women's Spirituality*. Even though my hand penned it, I've always felt some sacred source brought me the words. The Affirmation was later to become the foundational document for the newspaper *Of a Like Mind* and the Re-formed Congregation of the Goddess, International (RCG-I).

Candlemas 1981
I was nervous as Candlemas approached. To get the coven to agree on what to have for lunch was a challenge. On this Candlemas, to be acknowledged as a priestess, I needed sixteen women to agree that I'd been "acting like a priestess." They created a ceremony in which each woman was asked to speak about my request to be considered a priestess.

The coven had been filled with struggle and I cannot say I was not involved; I had tried to provide support and kindness, but I was not certain it would be enough. Yet as women commented one by one on my fitness to be named priestess, I was amazed to hear even those women with whom I'd had conflict declare that, despite our differences, I had behaved as a priestess to our community. They draped a cloak around my shoulders and declared me a Dianic priestess.

Candlemas 1982
With my grandmother's estate settled. I did not think I could organize in Kentucky, so I began to investigate more tolerant places. I learned Wisconsin was the only state where being a lesbian was protected by law. My ex-husband expedited my decision when he found he could gain custody of our nine-year-old son because of my lesbianism. My ex was not a kind man. I believed that for him to raise our son would be a travesty. I fled with my son to Madison, Wisconsin. We bought winter coats and prepared to live in a lesbian-friendly northern environment.

It was time to start organizing. I'd heard a quote by Gandhi: "If you want to build a movement, you have to have a press." I thought a newspaper would be an excellent start and I began looking for women who could help: one who knew about printing, one who knew about writing and one who knew about photography. Soon I met Lynnie Levy—who had a degree in printing, a degree in photography and had attended graduate school in English literature. Lynnie readily agreed to work on the newspaper.

Hallows 1983

We named the newspaper *Of a Like Mind* and published the first issue in October of 1983. At that time, it was only one of two publications about women's spirituality in North America and it became a networking resource. Women read *Of a Like Mind* and found each other.

This was the priestessing work I was called to do.

Spring Equinox 1984

Lynnie and I started working on incorporation papers for a legal women's religion. In my day job as a nonprofit administrator, I had learned about tax-exempt organizations. I believed it was possible to be a nonprofit while still honoring the anarchistic nature of women's spirituality. Lynnie and I began to create the foundation for a women's religion.

I found one of the accepted religious structures in the United States was "congregational." A congregational model supposes members have enough in common to be considered a religion; however, individuals and groups within that organization have autonomy. Thankful for the religious dissenters who fled to this country and allowed this system to be recognized, we decided "congregation" was the correct name for a group of anarchistic feminists. Eventually, we chose the "Reformed Congregation of the Goddess, International" as the name for this new organization. Our early information described the reasoning behind the name: "Our name acknowledges this is not the first time women have recognized the need to express their spiritual selves in a supportive structure with other women. We are not beginning to find each other for the first time, but are re-membering and re-forming the ancient congregations of the Goddess."

In 1984, the Congregation became a legal entity in the State of Wisconsin.

Summer Solstice 1984

It has always seemed ironic to me that the Internal Revenue Service (IRS) determines if a group qualifies as a religion. In filling out their application, Lynnie and I found it required a list of the organization's clergy. In order to be considered for tax-exempt status, we would have to be priestesses of this new religion. So on Summer Solstice 1984, Lynnie heard my ordination vows, and I hers. Although this was a matter of expedience, being an ordained priestess of the first legally incorporated women's religion felt powerful. We now held the rights of lawful clergy in Wisconsin.

Fall Equinox 1985

Our application for tax exemption took months to complete. When it was done, we mailed it off to the IRS with some trepidation. But in September of 1985, RCG-I became the first women's religion with tax-exempt status and, in fact, one of the earliest Pagan organizations in the United States to be tax-exempt.

Fall Equinox 1986

Z had written *The Feminist Book of Lights and Shadows,* and feminist witches carried it home and began their practice. Most Dianics had little contact with each other. One evening, I asked Lynnie what she believed other Dianics thought. Without pause, she answered, "Why don't we ask them?" In that moment, the Defining Dianic Wicca Conferences were born. These conferences were organized as colloquia. We selected sixteen topics to be discussed in two conferences in 1986 and 1987.

Women from across the country came to these gatherings. We brought them together and, for the first time, we collectively shared our perceptions of feminist religion. These gatherings continued for another five years. From them, some of the foundational beliefs of Dianics emerged.

Fall Equinox 1987

During the Defining Dianic Wicca Conferences, there had been hot debate about what constituted "priestessing." There were women who believed a priestess was solely a ritualist; they contended that any spiritual activities other than ritual were peripheral to the core of the tradition. But other women held different views: Would we not also look to priestesses for healing, inspiration and spiritual guidance?

The dialogue was intense, and women who were not ritualists became disheartened as their work was discounted. The debate reminded me of my quandary about priestessing. In the early Women's Spirituality Movement, there were few learning opportunities. But in the previous twenty years, we had developed an extensive body of knowledge. There was, however, no format for sharing this knowledge and no form for recognizing those who had expertise.

I was considering going back to school to get my Master's degree, but I doubted I would learn what I wanted in traditional education, so I decided to create a priestess training for myself. It included comparative religion, magic, goddesses, the environment and a myriad of other topics. Following this plan, an interesting thing happened. My friends would ask, "Do you want to go to brunch Sunday?" I'd answer, "Thanks, but I'm going to the Friends (Quaker) meeting." Some of these women would then ask, "Can I come?" I found others were interested in spiritual studies and, from what began as personal scholarship, the curricula for the Women's Thealogical Institute (WTI) developed.

Near Fall Equinox 1987, WTI enrolled its first participants. The six-year self-directed program has led many women to a deeper commitment to their spirituality. WTI acknowledges women as priestesses, healers, scholars/teachers, earthwalkers, creatrixes, ritualists, mediators, guardians, crones and, of course, organizers.

Winter Solstice 2012

It is now Winter Solstice of 2012, 35 years from when the Goddess called me to organize. Over 3,200 women have found that the Affirmation of Women's Spirituality reflects their spiritual beliefs, and have become members of RCG-I. Almost 100 women have graduated from WTI, and forty of these have been ordained as priestesses by the Congregation.

In 2000, my priestessing came full circle. I was acknowledged by Z Budapest as a Dianic Elder Priestess for the work I had done and the organization I had helped create. I grew into priestessing with few models for how one priestesses. Despite this, Lynnie and I created an organization that trains and ordains priestesses.

I have found being a priestess is not static. My priestessing has changed, and continues to transform over time. I am a priestess once by her call. I am a priestess once for expedience. I am a priestess once by recognition. The voice still whispers to me. "Bring them together, Jade." No one need be alone. I have done the Goddess's work with passion and diligence. I have cut a path through uncharted territory. I hope that now, when others hear her call, there will be a path to follow.

Answering the Call of Service: Dianic Tradition and Women's Mysteries*
By Ruth Barrett

There are physical and psychological experiences and rites of passage common to all women's lives, crossing the boundaries of age, class, culture, race, sexual orientation and religion. For over thirty years, my work as a High Priestess, whose focus has been on creating and facilitating rituals, has been based in the assertion that women, as the physical embodiment of the Goddess (she who is the life force present in all things), are sacred, and our rites of passage are sacred occasions worthy of ritualizing.

From earliest times and across cultures, women have created, facilitated and participated in ceremonies and rituals that are gender based and separate from men's. The practice of female-only and female-centered ritual was not sourced from a rejection of males, but rather from an understanding and honoring of women's unique biological rites of passage and the ways in which our bodies inform our diverse life experiences. The interest in goddess- and female-centered rituals by second-wave feminists of the seventies provided a transformational vehicle for countering centuries of misogyny with a healing paradigm shift in consciousness. I was one of those women whose life was changed forever by the emerging Feminist Spirituality Movement.

My first teacher of goddess spirituality was Shekhinah Mountainwater, of blessed memory, a founding mother of the Goddess Movement and author of *Ariadne's Thread*. I met Shekhinah in 1972 and studied with her weekly in 1975 and 1976. When my studies formally began,

---

* Originally published in a slightly different form in *Women's Rites, Women's Mysteries: Intuitive Ritual Creation* (Woodbury, MN: Llewellyn Worldwide, 2007).

there were few feminist- or goddess-centered spirituality books in print. In 1976, Zsuzsanna Budapest, widely considered the mother of contemporary Dianic Wiccan tradition, published *The Feminist Book of Lights and Shadows*. This early work was incorporated into *The Holy Book of Women's Mysteries*, and included ancient women's festivals rediscovered by the research of Jane Harrison. This pioneering book drew many women, including myself, to feminist- and goddess-centered Witchcraft. I met Z that same year, and was eventually initiated into her coven, the Susan B. Anthony Coven #1.

Four years later, at Hallowmas 1980, Z ordained me as a high priestess and passed her Los Angeles ministry to me. For the next twenty years, I served as the High Priestess of the local Dianic community, teaching and facilitating ritual. I eventually co-founded the Circle of Aradia, which remains the largest and longest-lived Dianic community in the United States. I was the second woman Z ordained as a high priestess, the first being visionary musician, Kay Gardner, of blessed memory.

Being 25 years old at the time of my ordination, the responsibility of taking on Z Budapest's ministry felt enormous. How was I to build on Z's teachings and her largely improvisational approach to ritual? It was apparent to me early on that a majority of the women coming to the Craft through the feminist movement lacked a common magical foundation. I was concerned that this lack would compromise our ability to be as magically effective as we could be, despite our great passion to make changes in our lives and in the world. I began to develop and build a sound, consistent magical foundation and ritual practice that I could teach my students and local community, who could then pass on their knowledge and skills to future generations of Dianic Witches. To accomplish this, I explored both within and outside of the Goddess Spirituality Movement, seeking knowledge from other Wiccan and Craft family traditions. I began to incorporate and apply these magical practices in a Dianic context. I also brought my own contributions to the content of the tradition through my music, creativity, sensibilities and inspiration from the Goddess, as I was empowered to do. Through the rituals created and shared over decades with thousands of women and girls, together we entered the Mysteries of the Sacred Female with wonder and awe, challenging external and internal oppression and expanding the possibilities for deeper meaning in the daily sacredness of being alive.

The heart of the feminist Dianic Wiccan tradition honors Women's Mysteries: the five blood mysteries of our birth, menarche, giving birth/lactation, menopause and death. These rites include the essential physical, emotional and psychic passages that only women and girls can experience by being born female in a patriarchal culture and becoming conscious about how growing up in that culture affects our daily lives and female identity. Dianic rituals celebrate the mythic cycle of the Goddess in the earth's seasonal cycles of birth, death and regeneration. Those cycles correspond and overlap with female lifecycle transitions, and Dianics honor the Goddess in every woman through seasonal rituals. Our rites mark life passages and celebrate the female ability to create and sustain life, and to return to the Goddess in death. Dianic seasonal themes are not based on an exclusively heterosexual fertility cycle, as other Wiccan traditions are, and therefore are inclusive of all female-born women and girls. From the beginning of its contemporary practice, the Dianic Wiccan tradition has also inspired rituals that are intended to help women heal from, and counter the effects of, misogynistic, patriarchal social institutions and religions.

Dianic Wiccan tradition is distinguished by its exclusively female-born and -raised women's and girl's rituals, and its exclusive focus on the Goddess in its cosmology and its magical and ritual practice. Feminist consciousness, values and visions are often interwoven into the ritual content. The spiritual focus and ritual practices of Dianic tradition are practiced with, for and about women's experience of living, and the many ways that our female bodies inform our life experiences. Dianic tradition's goddess-centered cosmology, ethics, eclectic practices and rituals are primarily shaped and inspired by fragments of ancient goddess worship, folklore, the legacy of our feminist foremothers, our ancient and contemporary oracular heritage of divination and some adaptations from other Wiccan traditions. Dianic tradition's female-only rites herald back to ancient times, in which priestesses chose to dedicate themselves exclusively to a specific goddess and to serve women through that devotion. Women choosing a female- and goddess-focused ritual practice are actually reclaiming an ancient custom of their foremothers.

Unlike other religious and spiritual traditions, where religious experience focuses on an externalized source (a deity who exists outside of human experience), Dianic rites center on ritualizing the female body, where healing and revelatory experiences are made possible through the unification of the body, mind and spirit. Intuitive movement, dancing, chanting, drumming and sounding as part of ritual practice can achieve great meaning and facilitate healing at a deep level, especially when they are utilized with a clear understanding of a ritual's purpose. "Meaning is not in the world; it is not out there waiting to be found. Meaning is created in the interaction between the self and the other, the one and the many, the group and the natural world."[1] When the spiritual experience is embodied in the women who are participating in a ritual, a fundamental intention of Dianic tradition can be realized: to re-sanctify the female body as a manifestation of the Goddess, the source from which all things emerge and to which all things return. Lesbians and bisexual women , who may need to heal from internalized homophobia as well as the other aspects of misogyny, can experience positive transformation within a spiritual tradition that says the body of a woman who loves women is holy. Through the embodied spiritual experience of the Goddess, heterosexual women can heal from internalized misogyny and homophobia, reaching greater depths of self-love and love and appreciation for all women, as well as compassion and personal power.

When women empower themselves to ritualize passages that they deem significant, and to which they can ascribe their own meaning, they shed their old skins like snakes and emerge into a new reality—a new conscious awareness. The mundane world of the previous moment becomes transformed, and they are brought closer to greater understanding of the sacred. Women who create and participate in their own lifecycle rituals are saying that their lives are important, that their stories matter and that every human life is a gift to present and future generations.

Endnote

1 Karen McCarthy Brown, *Mama Lola: A Vodou Priestess in Brooklyn* (Berkeley: The University of California Press, 1992), 217.

Luck

By Susan Levitt

Paris was rotted. But Venice
was a mermaid's delight.
Rome was noble, magnificent and grand.
Cairo was magical. The streets
lined with secrets.

One such secret was revealed to me
by a tiny woman, so small
the physique of a child
that barely contained the energy of a giant
when she held my right hand, a coarse bloated mitt
clutching her elegant miniscule digits.
In a deliberate manner she pried back my fingers
as if peeling away the skin of an orange.
My heart line was long. "You love too deeply."
My head line was strong. "Quite the intellect, eh?"
My fate line was good, very good.
I must have lived many lives prior
to be so sure of my destiny now.
"One of the lucky ones," she said.
And I believed her.

Discovering The Priestess Within:
The Origins of a Thriving Women's Ministry*
By IONE

In the dream, Be-Be's face is luminous, her voice resonant and soft, exactly as it was when she was alive. My grandmother's words are simple, "Make a circle!"

With my dreams and intuition as my guides, I decided to launch a one-year training program in the intuitive and healing arts entitled Women's Mysteries: For Women Who Want to Go Deeper. The year was 1987 and I announced we were "women creating community with each other." I loved the term "community," in particular. It was an exciting and slightly daring concept for the times. Meditation, dream awareness and mythological studies, oracular forms, astrology, sound mysteries, ritual, ceremony and integration of dark and light were all a part of our investigations. At the end of a full year of being together, I planned to take the group to the sacred temples and tombs of Egypt. We would float on the ancient Nile River together, and I would share the wonder of what I had experienced there during several trips as a journalist on assignment.

Even so, I believed that what I was offering to women was simply a way of underlining ideas and achievements already in place, rather than breaking new ground. After all, we were supposed to have been liberated by then, weren't we? Feminism had taken hold since the seventies, and I had been a part of that big wave. We women were surer of ourselves, making headway in the corporate world, getting more assistance from our spouses at home and so on. We wore pants suits, jumpsuits and jeans,

---

* Originally published in a slightly different form in *Spell Breaking: Remembered Ways of Being. An Anthology of Women's Mysteries* (Kingston, NY: Ministry of Maat/Deep Listening Publications, 2013).

and used the new terminology of "Ms." Things really had changed, or so I thought. I was in for a surprise.

Every week, the women came to my loft in Lower Manhattan. Twelve of us, in all, arrived from very different locations in the city. Ranging in age from 18 to 45, most did not know each other at the beginning. A few were shy and others were quite outspoken. Some were married, some long divorced, some straight, some gay. Some were American, others Australian, some of African descent and others of European descent. All, as it turned out, were hungry for something they couldn't yet name.

I'd bring them up in the old elevator or—when it was not working, which was often the case—they'd climb the five flights without complaint. We sat on my well-worn cushions in a circle. We laughed and cried and sometimes we screamed in rage. It was good not having any close neighbors. We howled at the moon. We told our dreams. We were, we told ourselves, descending.

We were descending into a deep pit like Innana, the beleaguered heroine of the ancient Sumerian poem. Enki, the God of Wisdom, had blessed her. The blessing included the concepts of truth, descent into the underworld and ascent from the underworld.

We were ugly, angry, jealous, grieving. We thought and spoke the unacceptable, and we were, at last, not nice. Without travelling on planes, trains or buses, we had our own kind of space ships; we were inhabiting the other side of the moon, the dark side. There, we could behave as we liked, unseen and unjudged by spouses, friends, lovers, mothers or fathers.

In her ancient story, Inanna hears the moans of her sister, Ereshkigal, Queen of the Underworld. Bedecked with her special jewels, Inanna travels down, down, down, losing her garments and gems along the way. Upon her arrival, she must spend a period of time hung up on a meat hook before eventually being allowed to ascend, emerging as the shining Queen of Heaven and Earth, a whole and resplendent being.

We could certainly relate to Inanna's plight. We all knew what it felt like to be down there in the depths. We reminded ourselves with knowing looks when some thorny issue came up: "Yes, it's the 'meat hook'!"

Yet it was what happened next to Inanna that intrigued us even more—the mystery in the dark at the bottom of the pit that allows Inanna not only to survive, but to emerge in triumph.

Our circles were, it turned out, our own place of alchemical transformation. I would also label our process "spell-breaking," for we too would emerge, having broken old spells that had long held us in their grip. We were experiencing the living process of "creating community" and it looked and felt like nothing we might have imagined. It was wild, empowering and supportive in a deeply satisfying way. It would carry us through the year and on to the splendor of initiation in Egypt.

I would hear my grandmother's voice again at the Temple of Hatshepsut. There, in a secluded corner dedicated to the lovely Goddess Hathor, while standing at the center of a circle of Women's Mysteries initiates, I'd whisper aloud to her timeless spirit: "I've done it, Be-Be. We're doing it!"

Our experiences would prove to be a matrix for hundreds of subsequent Women's Mysteries students, fulfilling an undiminished need for a women's spiritual community. Wondrously, some 25 years later, we would understand what happened that first year as the foundation for an international ministry comprising 31 priestesses, each sharing the fruits of her unique healing with the world.

The Art of Disappearance
By Lorraine Schein

In their mountain hermitages
the Taoist women adepts
received esoteric instructions on rainmaking,
entering the water without leaving a ripple,
learned how to "fly to heaven."

Immortal Sisters,
they had left their bewildered husbands
to live in the wild.

In the fourth century,
Wang Gan set off for the mountains
to find his wife.

But she had already
soared into the clouds—
leaving only a pair of scarlet slippers
under the window.

For Aphrodite at the Water Wheel
By Rachel Koenig

Aphrodite
What do You ask of this
Priestess?
I have served You
in every season of
my lifetimes
And now,
as one desiring
  sleep
You
Awaken me!
And with Your
Wet fire
Tear open my heart door
this rough storm, meant only
for me.
My house clamors in
The chaos of
Your bliss
Now, not even
needing
The man.

Ecstasy, hidden,
sweetly revealed herself
in the ancient, undulating river where
I stood gazing upon You,
shuddering
while the fragrant wine of linden blossoms
filled me, and then the summer air.

Oh, Lady, Ourania
Contriver
Why
have You brought one
  so
deliciously near
this threshold,
my body?
How am I
to wind apart
the tight thread
of terror
that binds
his youthful limbs?
  Within Your veil,
by woven touch,
and whispers of
I know I know I know
  as Mysteries,
  Only You,
Limitlessly saturate.

Why do I call this
longing?
I, who have served You
lifetime after lifetime

must know
these hot tears
are but
illusion.

Yet, well on
in years, yes,
advancing,

I
hardly
recognize
The union of
the partings . . .

Thus far, I know:
It is
You who gave to me
this
Body
Of Water, of Fire
Of absolute
Evolution.
And if I am drawn deeper

It is
that like one
drowning
in
Your vastness
it is only inside the deepest waters
nearest death
do I recall
the teaching.

Great Goddess
Ignite
the emptiness!
Pour the Great
Bliss through Your faithful
While time obeys
Your laws only
So that now we part
Now we unite
All
longing
shattered.

Sacred Mother,
You shaped
this vase
graced it with
curves, Your moon-like
Breasts
Your dark, magnetic Delta.

Goddess!
if You bring one
to lie
near
Remember me
in the Temple of
Your arms
Stir me as Your
Vltava
swept up
in brief revolution
upon Your ancient wheel.
Return me, then
to the River of

STEPPING INTO OURSELVES

Your
ever-deepening depths
Move me
secretly
through
Your quiet lovers
who sleep through dawn
as I caress
who dream
as I live
Your dream.

Roles of the Priestess

Roles of the Priestess

A lament for what has been lost with the disappearance of the lineage of priestesses opens this section:

> The bees say to me: your answers lie buried on these heights
> They say: learn, from these remnants of the Mysteries,
> That history is a sibyl prophesying the loss of her sight.
> —Lorraine Schein, "Questions for the Oracle"

> We might ask, "Who is she? Where did she go for so long?" and more importantly, 'Why is the priestess needed now?' It is clear that she is calling women to hear her, to wake up from not noticing her long absence, to claim her for us in all the myriad of forms where she can be an intermediary and serve life.
> —ALisa Starkweather, "Walking the Priestess Path"

Reclaiming and creating the multi-faceted roles of the priestess today is one of the ways of resurrecting this lineage. Works in this section present expansive and sometimes contradictory views of the roles of the priestess which reveal the intricacies and complexities of priestessing in the present day. These views include clashes with modern feminism, geopolitics, religious heritage, and gender roles, combined with the diverse needs of the community. Priestesses have found inspiration in Hinduism which gives us living archetypes of the priestess, through ecstasy and service, and contemporary saints such as Ammachi show how women are the conduit of divine love. Priestesses in rural and urban settings discuss the ways that they have found to introduce the sacred into a world which does not often recognize numinosity and rarely recognizes female spiritual leadership

Roles of the priestess today include that of ritualist, leader, shaman, diviner, role model, coach, wild woman, warrior, witch, dreamweaver, or sensual sister. Her duties extend from scraping candle wax from the floor of the rented hall to carefully maneuvering group dynamics to being the one who creates and keeps open

> A channel between the seen and seldom seen realms in which we live, in relationship and in service to a community.... creating a doorway between the worlds that is wide enough for others to join her there and those people, by joining, expand the opening still further so that the flow of power is strong and transformative for all present.
> —Deidre Arthen, "I am the Earth: The Priestess in Service to Community"

Of the many facets of priestessing, a single thread winds and binds the seemingly disparate fragments.

> She who is priestess experiences the calling to hold the whole of the cosmos in reverence, to observe the tides and seasons and to immerse in marking the life of the cosmos through spiritual celebration. What others may call mundane, the priestess may call sacred. What others may call profane, the priestess may call an opportunity to engage in the evolution of cosmological design, for she who is priestess realizes she is no more and no less than the holy cosmos itself engaged in the act of its own imaginal becoming.
> —Pamela Eakins, "Priestess: Born Unto Herself"

Questions for the Oracle
By Lorraine Schein

Damn Apollo and Athena, those glare-loving Greek icons,
Why are they worshipped everywhere here at their white,
Broken-toothed temples under this too-bright sun?

And Delphi—broken marble of wisdom's site.
Why is the air above these ruins
Stacked light above light above light?

Our guide from Alexandria (sunglass-sheathed, Apollonian),
Points to an ancient inscription, giving one well-paying Greek city,
Rights to ask the first question.

The Germans and Japanese arrive next to sightsee,
Speaking in their harsh languages that intrude with the rest
On the silence of this shattered temple, on each tour's itinerary.

My gods are Artemis, and Hermes, my ruler. They're the wiliest—
Too fast to be prayed to, unmappable blurs,
Moon-bordered huntress, untempled, light-fingered bicyclist.

Just like then, we must still pay to get answers.
But why do I keep hearing bees in flight?
How many more steps to the priestesses' underground chamber?

The bees say to me: your answers lie buried on these heights.
They say: learn, from these remnants of the Mysteries,
That history is a sibyl prophesying the loss of her sight.

Walking the Priestess Path
By ALisa Starkweather

Walk when you feel your body leaning towards the fire. Meet the energy as your own. Remember you too are fire. Her body sways with the rhythm of the drums as the women form a semicircle around the hot coals and sing.

> *I walk on fire*
> *It's like walking on the stars*
> *I walk with my sisters*
> *with love and peace inside.*

She knows this firewalk will unbury the priestess archetype within her. She has consented to the experience, yet it has come sooner than she had expected.

"Am I ready for this?" she silently wonders. "But, oh, how something has been calling me to my own power and I know the time is now." Still, in this flickering moment, she doesn't know if she has what it takes to walk barefoot across the bed of coals estimated at twelve-hundred degrees Fahrenheit. The embers loom before her like a runway on her chosen path. "What is your deepest prayer for life? What do you walk for? Set your intentions!" says the one who is leading this ceremony.

In the night under the small crescent moon that lit the way in the dark for centuries of women's ceremonies, the coals glow like a galaxy set before her feet. With a burning in her heart to meet *the mystery of the Great Unknown, the Mother of Life, some old chain of fear releases like a shackle from her mind and, almost without thinking, she leans her body into the heat and walks slowly and with purpose across the orange embers straight into her sister's arms. She has crossed this threshold on her priestess path. Her "yes" causes a radical shift of perceptions that instantly questions years of limitations that she unknowingly placed on her own ideas of self. "If this is where this path begins, where do we go from here?" "Why did I wait so long to come home to myself?" are the silent inquires rumbling in her mind. The moon, the darkness, the fire, the women, the drums and the heat of the starbed have awakened in her an ancient memory and she knows that she is not turning back. She is here to come home to herself and to serve. Her lessons on her spiritual path in these woman's ways have begun.*

This glimpse into our firewalk ceremony is like looking into a tiny keyhole in order to see the vast sacred landscapes where women are unearthing the archetype of the priestess buried in our psyches. There is so much that is unexplainable yet it is becoming more and more important to bring her into visibility to see the rich history of women's spiritual lives. This work sought me, haunted me, dreamed ceremonies into my being until I consented to be the adventure tour guide and midwife of this mystical odyssey—a Women's Mystery school called Priestess Path.

Perhaps you remember a moment when you wanted your life to be of service with such a passion that, on bended knee and with humbled heart, you prayed. This is how it came to be for me. For many years, in all sincerity, I begged this beautiful universe to make use of my gifts, my love, my desire for a better world. In 1995, with hawks circling above my head in the sacred grove where my mentor, twenty years my senior, had trained me to work with women, a request came from the intuitional sound waves within (affectionately known as the little voice that talks to me) to begin a priestess training.

What did I do? For three years, I thought there was some mistake in these instructions, as if they were contained in a letter addressed to the wrong person. Though ardent in my request, I did not feel worthy for this task; but at last, when the same answer came repeatedly to me, I relented. It is a relief to see how much faster women are answering the call now. Without a track before me, it would mean that I was in for some serious bushwhacking with the Goddess. When opening the portals of this Women's Mystery school, I did not even know until the first weekend that this would not be about vocationally training women in the job of priestess; rather, it would be about the midwifery of birthing this archetype in each person so that she could source it for herself in many life situations as a strong woman on her spirit path. As Jalaja Bonheim writes in the "Path of the Priest and the Priestess:"

> Like small, powerful generators, archetypes may lie dormant until time is ripe for their resurgence. Today our inner priests and priestesses are knocking loudly on the doors of our psyche, demanding to be recognized, integrated into our spiritual life. If we listen, they will show us the way towards a new yet ancient form of spirituality, one that is world- affirming and joyful, that does not depend on the structures of organized religions and does not fragment our lives and ourselves. Today as in ancient times, they are the gatekeepers to other worlds, and the guardians of this one.[1]

Wild woman, old one, maiden-queen/warrior-witch did not simply knock but took the whole house down and settled herself in as a permanent resident on the sacred land she claimed for me. Shaman, mystic, dreamweaver, sensual sister pried away old rusty locks placed to protect my heart so she could live where I had been uninhabited. She slipped into my night visions, and in the day, when I walked the earth, she floated seductively near me with her perfume scenting the wind, insisting that I not only recognize her but initiate other women to be a part of her long-awaited homecoming and continuous lineage. She, in turn, welcomed me by magically opening portals within me, changing my very concepts of what is real and what is possible. My "yes" to her swelled my heart with the tidal wave of old grief made from the tears of women bereft for eons who silently endured the painful, too-long-forgotten separation.

With her own eyes revealing a sorrow so deep that you think you see in them the memories of the massacre of ancient ways, she looks upon me tenderly and with compassion. I weep aloud, unabashedly: "I needed you. Where have you been?" Like a mother with a child whom she commits to bring to maturation, she gathers me to her and my life forever changes in the binding of our cores. Sometimes, when women look into my eyes, they see her, ancient and strong, returned to us. She has claimed me to be one of her own daughters, sisters, lovers and mothers. As one of her conspirators, visionaries and revolutionaries, I wholeheartedly cry "yes!" She calls you, too, and is waiting for you to remember her sacred place in your life. She is the part of you that can buck the system, hold down the fort, speak with authority, open to Source. Any woman who takes her on will grow in her ability to be formidable, because she fills us with life the way the rivers fill the ocean. New life follows. With her presence, spiritual life awakens, and our path to our truest power begins.

More than a hundred women pour through the gateway to enter the grieving ritual being held in the back meadow next to the forest at the Daughters of the Earth Gathering. We are deep enough in the wilderness that our collective wails can be expressed without fear of disturbing the peace. Who are we, you wonder. We are ordinary women: nurses, scientists, wait staff, teachers, ministers, artists, activists, herbalists and more. We are all ages and of all beliefs. We are holding space together for our tears to be shed, our betrayals known, our wounds healed, our numb places felt. We are not hiding, nor are we wallowing. We are allowing ourselves to feel, even to fall on the earth if we choose. Our loud keens are nestled against the background of our sisters vibrantly singing to us. We lift each other up and call our sisters back from life's devastating losses, back from the grief and sadness into the promise of what is still to live. Being together, we are fortified not to give up or lose hope. We suddenly understand that we are not alone. As we perceive permission to be this raw and authentic, the places where we had been scared to show our sadness begin to surface, making room for our deeper love.

The first step of empowerment is the healing of old wounds and all the places where we quietly gave up on our own ability to change the world. The grieving ritual brings to life the priestess in action, both with women who come together to help create and hold ceremony, and with those who discover her when they open their hearts in trust to what is being offered.

Women who are facilitating may not say aloud, "I am a priestess," yet each knows this moment requires the holding of humanity's broken hearts in ways that will not further traumatize or inflict harm. For this we need skill, commitment and devotion. Transformational work teaches us to step from behind our ego and pride, put aside our agendas and be deeply humbled in the unfolding of the brave work of spiritual transformation. None of us is without wounds and, because of this, compassion pours its elixir into all of our scar tissue, allowing regenerative collective healing to occur. Without her role, the community could not go as deep, would not feel as protected. The surrounding guardians of this ceremony are the solid ground, the safety, the prayer-makers, the holders of sacred space between the worlds. Those holding are able to do so because they have planned and prepared the way and called in the energy and intentions for ceremonial space.

These women guided others to know what was expected of them and to watch for and embrace an awareness of each and every woman because trust is sacred in this emotional descent. If you ask them, they also feel supported because they are rooted in the steadfastness inherent in the ritual itself. For many who are new to ritual and ceremony with such transformative intent, there is something familiar in these places, even when it is something they have never seen before. There is recognition that the women holding the ceremony are the living template of the ceremonialist. As we take our spiritual power back, we know the role of the priestess is, in part, to be of service in the community.

As the world turns ever more to diversity and to challenges fraught with our differences, we need the knowing ways of the priestess to keep us together in love and with a vision of wholeness. We need mothers to hold us, grandmothers to guide us, medicine women to teach us and young women to passionately dream what is next for us.

We might ask, "Who is she? Where did she go for so long?" And more importantly, "Why is the priestess needed now?" It is clear that she is calling women to hear her, to wake up from not noticing her long absence, to claim her for us in all the myriad of forms where she can be an intermediary and serve life, if not save lives.

For centuries, women's power, on multiple levels, has endured oppression from violence and annihilation. To keep us safe, our mother's mother's mothers adopted beliefs that anchored internal oppression as a way of not stepping out to be seen, judged or harmed. This severely limited our ideas of self. Though there are still living legacies of existing priestess societies with ancient practices, the priestesses' powerful role, once pivotal in historical cultures, was obliterated in many areas where even the concept of her can seem foreign, if not mythical, to many modern women. One might be equally as shocked to hear history told anew with facts you never heard tell of in regards to the roles women took in shaping history.[2]

Imagine a time when the Goddess Ishtar, Inanna or Mother with a Thousand Names was worshipped for thousands of years. Temples to gods and goddesses were erected with such stability that some ruins remain today. Bulls, horses, cows, oxen, sheep were brought daily for offerings; the role of the priestess was vital in daily rituals. The priestess was a conduit between the spirit world and the physical. Her position was so powerful that kings and queens sought her counsel and wisdom. Her training brought out unique gifts, whether as seer, midwife, artist, healer, dancer or vessel of the Goddess in all acts of pleasure. In what became monotheism—a father god, a holy son, a virgin birth—spiritual tradition arose that excluded women and obliterated older stories where women were known as divine. This patriarchal view of a father godhead excluded not only women's roles in leadership but even women being seen as a part of God in worship, leaving the priestess in many ways destroyed and forgotten. The Goddess was largely erased in many dominant cultures, and women's spiritual authority was debased.

In more recent times, artifacts have surfaced in archeological digs, revealing female icons estimated as old as 35,000 years. There is now a resurgence of the Divine Feminine in our awareness. The core of these old teachings is the wheel of the Triple Spiral Goddess, seen as mother/crone/maiden or life/death/rebirth or creation/preservation/destruction-rebirth. This beautiful wheel explains how life cycles on earth. When a woman embraces these components without disowning what they mean or who she is becoming, she opens herself to a life that is more accepting of the continual changes and cycles in which we live, without needing to hang on to only one of the three. The archetype of the priestess can be found in any of these stages and can help those who are in the death cycles to remember that rebirth will come again. Ceremonies honor each stage, allowing a woman to own the power of each gift in the never-ending wheel of life.

> With three ropes laid carefully on the floor, a trio of spirals forms, each taking hold by connecting in the center and coiling out individually to symbolically establish three separate portals. One represents creation, the second preservation, and the third, destruction into rebirth. The woman blinks her eyes because she can hardly believe what she is seeing. What is ancient has crossed the threshold into the present world and this room is transformed into a temple of antiquity. Women with colorful veils and breasts revealed are dancing, singing and praying on the periphery of the triple spirals. Some are tending the hearth, and others the feast that will follow. Serpentessa, the High Priestess of this ceremony, smiles and tilts her head slightly in a bow that acknowledges this sacred moment. Assessing the initiate's nervousness and finding her willing, the priestess gently asks, "Have you shed what no longer serves you?" "I have," the initiate answers. "Are you ready?" her elder asks. "I am" she answers. Carefully, she walks each spiral, representing maiden, mother and crone. Stanzas of songs come to her in fragments:
>
> > She walks with snakes,
> > She stands on the moon,
> > Life, death, rebirth again and again.
>
> She feels the weight of the serpent around her shoulders writhing and moving as she steps. A mirror is held for her in the

center circle. She gazes into the eyes of her reflection and sees a newfound strength that is her own.

Now, in a time where women fight for leadership and to have more say in the laws of our lands, women are stirring en masse like bees in a hive. Women are asking the priestess within to rise again and take her rightful place, with her innate gifts, to reclaim her essential role in human society where women's leadership, spirituality and ability to assist in humanity's labor for the birth of new consciousness is essential.

Leading ceremony, building community, healing, taking leadership roles and being a vessel that can envision new paradigms are important skills in our ailing world. Something important is emerging from our intuition that deserves our rapt attention. It is time to unravel the key of life, death and rebirth, and anchor that understanding in this time when we are experiencing an exodus of life as we know it, with the fate of animals, plants and even human life hanging in the balance. Our intelligence alone cannot be our guide. Learning how to enter a trance state and dive into deep transformational territory can enable us to draw on our spiritual resources and human potential. Our ability to build community—particularly communities of women who are learning to bring people together with meaning and purpose—will strengthen us as a society.

There is a correlation between the return of the priestess and the decisions of so many women to stand up, know our value, trust our intuition and assume leadership roles in the caring of our communities, while also staying connected to our hearts, our purpose and the deeper meaning of our lives. Language can be so limiting but, if you are feeling these things, you are likely experiencing your inner priestess. With this understanding, let's talk about the limitation of words and the shadow of roles in a time where we are still emerging from long years of patriarchal domination.

There is a need for trained priestesses and for a history of modern priestessing. To those of you who have taken on priestessing as a vocation, thank you for your dedicated service and every effort you've undertaken to know your craft. To the larger population of women who are new to the idea of priestessing, I have some words of tender wisdom. The priestess archetype is an ancient blueprint available to all of us. Without it, we may be tempted to create titles that heighten our sense of value, authority and self-worth, but that really function as masks behind which to hide our feelings of inadequacy. I want to suggest that we may not need these words to define us. Roles can be a mask that keep us separate by our inability to be transparent with what it actually means to be human. If we wear the title priestess as a mask of authority, then we are in danger of creating a hierarchy where there is a judgment of who is trained and who is not and who is officially something and who is not. This hierarchy can separate us from what it means to be human. In losing transparency, we can also lose ground instead of gaining it in this magnificent time when women are needed to bring all sorts of original gifts forward.

Having seen people sometimes cling to their titles of "shaman" or "healer," I caution against doing the same with "priestess." I am not saying we should not have trained priestesses, as this has important vocational value, but rather that we should not become so attached to training and hierarchy that we fail to see the abundant place where we can tap into the priestess archetype and find her bubbling up in many guises. She is the ineffable life, cracking the cement of outworn ideas and sprouting between the hard places because she can no longer tolerate what is too small for her lifeforce. Allow yourself to embody her, draw from her and utilize her in your everyday life as a woman. And if you are trained, allow yourself to honor and respect her presence even in those who will never walk your specific path but who still embody the priestess. This is her time of return and she is dancing in the memories encoded in our cells.

> *It was an icy day when she drove from New York to Massachusetts. She had never been inside a Red Tent temple and did not know what to expect when she arrived to the round yurt building. On entry, she was welcomed by a woman who helped her let go of her long drive and her worries so she could enter unfettered. She could not believe how beautiful and healing this moment was when she entered this sacred womb-like*

space. Women were resting or quietly writing in their journals. One older woman was massaging another's feet, another telling a story in the chair. It seemed so natural, as if this had always been true. She'd heard of the grassroots movement of women supporting each other in Red Tent temples, but she'd never seen anything like this. A well of grief rose from her heart and, though she barely knew anyone, she began to sob aloud. Immediately, the women knew what to do: they embraced her and let her cry it out. Together, they were dreaming—together, we are dreaming— of a new world where womanhood is honored and the archetype of the priestess is coming home.

I have been facilitating women's empowerment and bringing forward visions that help us to reclaim our power for nearly 30 years, and I am filled with memories of untold beauty. As you read these stories, if you find yourself wondering about what you were taught to think from the dominant culture, questions may arise such as: "Is this real?" "What is this about?" "Is this a cult?" Then let us look deeper. The firewalk taught women to move past fear and see possibility in the impossible. The grieving ritual became a place where women could finally collectively voice their sadness about what the world has come to be and to support one another to keep the faith. The remaking of the temple restores a woman's sacred space where, even in such a busy world, we can remember the things that mean the most to us together with those we love.

The priestess archetype belongs to us as much as do hundreds of others: mother, queen, goddess, healer, warrior, lover. When we discover her, we give ourselves permission as women to access our birthright. Our pathways to these archetypes are not as random as you might first suspect, but are a spiritual landscape of women's leadership with the potential to heal our human world while staying connected to our souls and nature. The woman who trains herself to be with the unknown—who trains herself to take risks and have faith in the rebirth that inevitably follows destruction—will enable herself to be a wise and grounded guide for others. Though she may be hidden from your view, the priestess is showing up for the greatest job of our time. If she is talking to you in your dreams, take her up on her offer: you will be stronger for it. She is the potent lost part of woman just waiting to be found.

Endnote

1 This essay, titled "The Path of Priestess and Priest: Initiation into an Ancient Tradition," can be found in this anthology, *Stepping Into Ourselves*, on page 175.

2 In the three decades of her life's work with the Suppressed Histories Archives, Max Dashu gave us the opportunity to know a different story. If you are ever curious to see more of the power of women's courage and commitment through new eyes, you can find more of Max's work at www.suppressedhistories.net.

The Role of the Priestess*
By Delphyne Platner

What does it mean to be a priestess in a patriarchal world? Because our culture does not recognize the feminine counterpart to "priest," and, with few exceptions, initiation into priesthood is not an option for women in mainstream religions, even the word "priestess" needs defining. Contemporary priestesses of many different spiritual paths continue to carry on the legacy of their ancestral foremothers throughout history and pre-history, women whose "specialties we would say today fell under such varied pursuits as religion, philosophy, prophecy, ethics, writing, dance, temple construction and maintenance, ritual, fund raising, tourism, social work, and medicine."[1] Often the priestesses among us go unrecognized, as we lack a common terminology and understanding of their existence.

Contemporary priestesses are diverse in their background, training and devotion to spirit. Some have received formal initiations and taken vows within a traditional or organized forum, whereas others have created their own vows and initiations. While many different practices and traditions co-exist under the umbrella of women's spirituality, there are essential similarities between them. Women's spirituality is a way of perceiving and interacting with the world, not merely a philosophy, a doctrine or something learned from a book. There are multiple ways of gaining knowledge and accessing the Divine.

Embodied knowledge is highly valued and may manifest itself in a variety of ways including, but not limited to, visual, auditory and sensory

---

* Originally published in a slightly different form as "Conjuring the Priestess to Heal and Empower Young Women," in *She is Everywhere: An Anthology of Writings in Womanist/Feminist Spirituality*, ed. Lucia Birnbaum (Berkeley: Belladonna, 2005), 295–296.

perception. Often this knowledge appears in the form of a dream, or is activated by other forms of sacred arts such as meditation, yoga, dance or ritual. Despite apparent differences of geography, race, language, lineage, socio-economic status and religion, the essence of the rituals performed by priestesses is very much the same. Ritual can be understood cross-culturally because it taps into the mytho-cosmological reality of human experience. A fundamental tenet of women's spirituality is that anyone can have direct and deeply meaningful contact with the Divine.

This matristic worldview understands time as cyclical, or spiral, rather than linear, honoring the seasons, cycles and the process of transformation. The only thing promised to us in life is transformation, divinely symbolized by the Goddess in all her (actual and symbolic) guises: life, death and rebirth. Embracing women's spirituality means consecrating women's cycles with their connections to the cycles of the moon, the tides and the seasons. Of course, men have cycles too. All living beings do. Perhaps if our 21st century fathers, brothers, lovers and friends were able to embrace, celebrate, consecrate and honor their own cycles, they would recognize their interconnectedness to all life, instead of standing outside of nature and attempting to control it.

A priestess deeply venerates this interconnectedness and is dedicated to healing herself, others and the planet. She knows all things have a purpose, and thus reveres all that patriarchal religions have dichotomized as sacred and profane. She strives to balance light and dark, both within and without, for failing to recognize one without the other has sent the world spinning out of kilter. A priestess draws much of her strength from the underworld, domain of the Dark Goddess. She realizes that, although the chthonic realm has been demonized, suppressed or neglected by most religions, the Dark Goddess holds the power to bestow many gifts, including treasures such as creativity, passion, sacred sexuality, protection, ferocity, courage and death of the ego.

The priestess communes with spirit and the ancestors, performing rituals and divining for herself and others. "The High Priestess is the original Sybil, whose ability to enter the trance state and divine the future made her the mouthpiece of the Goddess."[2] She may consult the oracle through reading Tarot, throwing coconut or cowry shells, swinging a pendulum, inducing trance states, doing dream work, reading palms, studying numerology, astrology or the I Ching, scrying or reading coffee grounds, tea leaves or eggs. While there are countless methods of divination originating in various cultures, their intent is usually the same: a quest for divine guidance. The priestess listens with her entire being—to herself, to the Divine, to the earth, to her devotees.

In *Voices of the Goddess*, Caitlin Matthews articulates the role and responsibility of the contemporary priestess: "Fundamentally speaking, a priestess is one who mediates Goddess by making her power available to all creation. A priestess guards the mysteries of the Mother and helps initiate other travelers on the road to the spiritual home. A priestess changes things, concepts, people."[3]

A priestess navigates the space between the worlds, accepting her fate as a portal or doorway to the Divine. She is a resource for knowledge, information and healing in her community. She knows how to dance with the forces of the ancestors, gods and goddesses, spirits and natural elements. She resists the urge to believe she is the power, while trusting herself to be a vessel.

Endnotes

1 Norma Lorre Goodrich, *Priestesses* (New York: Perennial/HarperCollins, 1989), 1.
2 Vicki Noble, *Motherpeace: A Way to the Goddess Through Myth, Art, and Tarot* (San Francisco: Harper San Francisco, 1983), 36.
3 Caitlin Matthews, ed. *Voices of the Goddess: A Chorus of Sibyls* (Northamptonshire, England: The Aquarian Press, 1990), 15.

The Path of Priestess and Priest: Initiation into an Ancient Tradition

By Jalaja Bonheim

What is a priest? What is a priestess? Images of men in stiff robes in church on Sundays, and exotically clad women making offerings to their bizarre-looking gods suggest that priestsesses and priests inhabit a world other than our own and have little impact on our lives.

Nothing could be further from the truth. To understand the essence of "priest" and "priestess," we must look beyond the clichés to reconnect with our inner archetype: the vortex of power in the depths of our own psyche. Since the beginning of human history, this archetype has found expression in countless religious traditions. However, since archetypes are never static, contemporary priests and priestesses look nothing like their ancient Indian, Sumerian or Egyptian counterparts. As human society unfolds, so do archetypes, appearing in ever-evolving guises. In fact, priests and priestesses are everywhere in our midst; they just don't look the way we might expect. Rarely do they wear special robes, and many have no ties with organized religion, yet their contributions are crucial to our welfare and even our survival. Priests and priestesses serve the spiritual lives of their communities and hold open the lines of communication between the human and spirit worlds.

Over the years, I have worked with thousands of people in whom this archetype has been awakened, and I have formed my own understanding of what it means to be a priest or a priestess. I would like to share some of my thoughts and invite you to explore the personal meaning of this archetype for you. Let me start by telling the story of how the priestess awakened in my own life.

It began when I decided, one dreary night in Birmingham, England, to attend the performance of a young Indian dancer. Within no time, I had fallen in love. What affected me so powerfully were not just the brilliant silk brocade costumes, the exquisite grace of the dancer's movements and the raw power with which her bare feet stamped the ground as if playing a giant drum. There was something else, a compelling spiritual presence that radiated through the dance, endowing it with a luminosity that sparked a kindred light within my soul. By the time I stumbled out of the auditorium, I was determined to learn this art, and to do so in India.

On the face of it, going to India to study dance seemed insane. I was not a dancer, and had never studied dance. How could I reconcile this strange desire with my identity as an intellectual, or think of any sensible way to justify the journey I was about to embark on? Still, there it was—some infinitely stubborn, determined force insisted I must quit my job and go to India—not sometime in the future, but now! I had received a calling I could not ignore.

In June of 1981, I gave up my job at a British university and boarded a plane to India. I laugh to think that I saw it as a sabbatical of sorts. While I expected my life to be enriched, I did not anticipate its total and irreversible transformation. In fact, I was about to be initiated into a tradition so old that its origins are shrouded in mystery, maintained throughout the centuries by priestesses who passed their knowledge from generation to generation. At the time, however, I understood none of this. All I knew was that I was being dragged off to India by some force I couldn't explain.

After arriving in India, I happily immersed myself in the study of what today is called Bharatanatyam. I soon found that the gestures and poses catapulted me into states of consciousness that felt ancient, powerful, utterly natural and strangely familiar, as if I was remembering a language I once knew but had forgotten. As I pondered the amazing power of this dance within my own body, I began to understand why temple dance is known as a fifth Veda, or sacred scripture. Unlike the other four Vedas, which form a sort of Hindu Bible, this fifth Veda is recorded not in words but in the universal language of movement. Yet, like all true scripture, it communicates an awareness of unseen dimensions beyond the visible, tangible world.

Indian temple dance, I learned, is a relic of a complex, highly sophisticated, but extinct culture. In ancient India, every major temple supported a number of priestesses, who worshipped the deities through their ritual dances. These women were known as *devadāsīs*, a word meaning "female servants of God." As in many other places, these priestesses were the most highly educated of women. Besides dancing, they studied reading, writing, scripture, mythology, mantras, rituals, meditation, singing, music and healing.

Indian temple dance is one of the most beautiful fruits of the Tantric tradition. According to Tantric mythology, this universe is the loveplay of a divine being which split itself into male and female halves so that it might know the ecstasy of love. All men are splinters of this original God, and all women of the Goddess; through their lovemaking, God experiences the rapture of reunion. Revered as embodiments of the Goddess, the *devadāsīs* were highly skilled in the erotic arts, and men vied to make love to them, for to make love to a *devadāsī* was to re-enact the sacred ritual of creation.

In the ancient Indian temples, priests and priestesses lived and worked side by side, sometimes becoming lovers. However, in the rituals designed to celebrate God's lovemaking with the world, the priestess seems to have played a very different role than the priest. Joseph Campbell once said, "The male's job is to relate to life. The female's job is to become it." He also said "The man's function is to act. The woman's function is to be." A similar view seems to have prevailed in ancient India. Priests were defined by their actions: maintaining the rituals, the temple compound and so on. Priestesses were primarily defined by their female being and their knowledge of the triple mysteries of the physical body: birth, sex and death.

With the advent of patriarchy, the sexual customs of the priestesses contributed to their downfall. In a culture that valued female chastity and submissiveness, there was no place for these non-monogamous, proud, independent priestesses. Gradually, their tradition deteriorated, and the British eventually finalized its demise by cutting off financial support to the temples, defaming the priestesses as prostitutes and making their dances illegal, which they remained until India gained its independence in 1947. Current literature often refers to the sexual priestesses of ancient India and other cultures as "sacred prostitutes," an unfortunate misnomer that echoes the prude Victorian dismissal of "heathen" priestesses as prostitutes. In fact, the *devadāsīs* were not prostitutes but, as their name denotes, servants of divinity.

It soon became clear to me that going to India was the easy part. The greater challenge would be to integrate what I had learned into my life in the West. Shortly after my return from India, I started having dreams in which ancient priestesses demanded that I transmit their consciousness to a modern Western audience—a daunting task, considering how radically different our world is from theirs. In my bewilderment, I began dialoguing with these inner figures, hoping to gain a clearer understanding of their path. The following is an excerpt from their response to my question, "How will it benefit people to hear your voices?" Their words helped me understand that, to be a priest or a priestess, one does not need to have a temple, perform rituals, recite mantras or dance. The essence of the priest and the priestess lies less in what they do than in the attitude with which they do it; they teach us how to perceive the spiritual within the ordinary, and the sacred within the mundane. Here's what they said:

> *Many of you have forgotten how to listen to the soul, how to speak to it, how to give it the food it hungers for. Communities, too, have souls that must be nourished. Most of your communities are ravaged by spiritual famine. We want to remind you how to nourish your souls. Within you is a deep well of truth and peace and strength. We walk among you reminding you of that place, inspiring you to remember what you already know. We bring you the gift of sacred sight, so that you see the light that shines through all beings, animate and inanimate.*
>
> *We come from many places, many times, each one of us bearing her own special gifts. But there is one thing we all have in common. For thousands upon thousands of years, we have all joined in the one practice of performing ordinary worldly acts*

as worship. When we pull a baby into the light of the world, it is worship. When we cradle a dying man in our arms, guiding his spirit into the embrace of spirit, it is worship. When we sweep the floor, it is worship. It is worship when we dance, when we sing, when we light the candles. Weeding the herb garden, resolving disputes, cooking rice—all these things and a million more we have practiced, always searching for the light of the Beloved within each moment, always questioning, "Is it here?" Yes, it is. "And here?" Yes, here too . . . and here . . . and here . . . So that now, we can say to you, with complete assurance, that there is nowhere where Spirit is not to be found.

Now, as you know, is a time of danger, a time of crisis. Do you really believe your puny human consciousness can solve the problems you face? Do you really believe the solutions will come out of that fraction of your brain that you use? We don't. We feel concerned. We feel compassion. We feel urgency. We are here to teach you how to commune with Spirit in all its myriad forms, how to align yourself with the greater whole so that healing can occur on this exquisitely fragile blue-green planet.

As I continued to explore this path, I found that four essential elements define the path of the contemporary priest or priestess. These four elements are: ordinariness, ecstatic communion with the divine presence in the world, reverence for gender and sexuality, and commitment to community service.

Ordinariness

The *devadāsīs* were what you might call "spiritual professionals." Today, the demarcation between the "ordinary" man or woman and the professional priest or priestess has vanished. Of course, we still have our spiritual professionals, but most contemporary priests and priestesses are ordinary men and women who use laptop computers, wear well-tailored clothing and follow the stock market. Some have affiliations with organized religion, but many do not.

The bad news is that we are on our own, and since our culture provides little in the way of support and validation for priests and priestesses, many struggle to get by. The good news is that we are free—unbeholden to outer authorities in a way our ancestors never were. Nobody dictates to us what we are to believe, think or do. Instead of allowing outer authorities to disempower us, we have license to seek the source of authority within. And though the lack of social acknowledgment and support can be painful, it also helps prevent the arrogance that often arises when priests and priestesses form a special class of their own—a class, so to speak, of professional mystics. In our times, those who do the work of a priest or a priestess are rarely made to feel "special," and that is as it should be. Today, the privilege of expressing the priest/priestess archetype belongs to all of us.

Because the work of contemporary priests and priestesses is so interwoven with their daily lives, it is easy to overlook their presence and the value of their contributions. Often, the service and the spiritual nourishment they provide goes unnoticed and unappreciated. And yet, just as in former times, the priests and priestesses among us are the guardians and caretakers of our spiritual life. One gardener communes with plants, the other does not. One kindergarten teacher honors children as the wise spirits they are, another treats them as immature, imperfect adults. For one person, singing is a performance art, for another, it is a form of prayer. One of my clients never answers the phone without first reminding himself to mentally honor the caller as the Buddha, the Christ, the Holy Mother; another murmurs blessings into her soups and stews. Like a weaver brightens her cloth with strands of golden thread, so priests and priestesses weave small acts of devotion and prayerful remembrance into their daily lives.

Many women feel a natural sense of kinship with this path. Millennia of motherhood have guided the feminine path toward practices that could be done anywhere, at any time. If women wanted to lead a spiritual life, they usually had to find time to do so in the midst of changing diapers and comforting children. We all know women whose homes are oases of beauty and serenity. Intuitively, they sense the healing power of beauty, and know the sense of peace and well-being that an ordered, well-appointed environment can create. As the priestesses of ancient times offered flowers on the altar, purified the air with incense and prayed that all who enter the temple be blessed, so these contemporary women, too, are creators and guardians of sacred space.

Ecstatic Communion

As contemporary priests and priestesses, we are mystics and ecstatics who perceive the divine as an immanent power within the world—in mountains and rivers, animals and plants, and within ourselves. The notion of transcendence is alien to this path: Spirit surrounds us as the air we breathe and the ground we walk on. The song of a bird, the fragrance of a rose and the diamond glint of sunlight on fresh snow are love letters from the goddesses and the gods to us. If the Divine is right here, why transcend the world? Where would we go, and why?

Just as a *devadāsī* felt the Goddess moving and acting through her, so contemporary priests and priestesses honor themselves as embodiments of the divine. My Catholic clients often struggle with this idea; it seems heretical to them, even blasphemous. "I was raised to think of myself as a sinner," one woman objected. Yet as I reminded her, Jesus himself always emphasized each person's innate divinity. "Ye are gods," he said.[1] Connecting with our inner divinity is the deepest healing we can aspire to. Far from making us arrogant, any encounter with the divine utterly crushes our arrogance while also healing the wounds of low self-esteem and banishing the demons of self-doubt, judgment and shame.

This emphasis on God's immediate presence, and of God's desire to make love with us, infuses spiritual life with a great sense of tenderness, creative play and deep appreciation for all the sensuous pleasures life has to offer. Our path becomes one of ecstasy, born of intimacy with the divine.

Reverence for Gender and Sexuality

Just thirty years ago, this was a loaded subject to broach, especially for women, who had been called inferior to men for so long they were determined to prove themselves equal in every respect. Now that women have gained a certain degree of power, we can explore our differences without fearing they will be used to prove the supposed superiority of one gender over the other. We can let go of the unisex myth and acknowledge the obvious: we are different, yet equal. Once we accept this fact, we can get on with the exciting and joyous work of sharing our gifts with one another.

We have become strangely inured to the absence of priestesses in our churches. Yet in a balanced religion, the ordination of priests without priestesses, or vice versa, would be unthinkable, as would the worship of the divine in only male or only female form. When the divine assumes human form, the sacred couple appears—the One becoming two, male and female, who in their union celebrate their original oneness.

All priestesses and priests are lovers—lovers of the goddesses and gods, but also lovers of the world, and of men and women. Regardless of whether they choose to be sexually active, they celebrate the dance of life through their bodies. The priestess derives power from her female body, as the priest does from his male body, and both rejoice in the beauty and the perfection of what they are separately, and of what they can create jointly.

Priestesses are not female priests, any more than priests are male priestesses; rather, they follow two different but complementary paths. Simply put, they differ in the same way men and women differ and in the way God's masculine face differs from Goddess's feminine face. We are talking not about clear-cut, black-and-white polarities or clichés (such as that men are strong and women are nurturing), but about a spectrum of tendencies, within which each individual occupies their own unique place.

Serving our Community
Last but not least, priests and priestesses share a deep commitment to the welfare of their communities. They work to guard its soul so that its ears stay open to the song of spirit, its heart to the love of spirit and its eyes to the beauty of spirit.

One of the main ways we serve our communities is through our daily work. When we take a job, the inner priest is not interested in how much money it makes or how much prestige it carries. His concern is whether this work will nourish his soul and the soul of his community. If so, the doctor will feel awe for the mystery of the life he serves. The mother will know the value of her efforts and the cashier will sense that the thousand daily interactions he has with his customers matter, and have meaning.

My hairdresser, June, is an example of a woman who is very much in touch with her inner priestess and who performs her work as what can only be called an act of worship. She is quite aware of doing far more than just cutting hair. "I make people feel better about themselves," she tells me. "I help them feel beautiful and cared for." One might say that she merely caters to people's vanity, but June knows better. As a priestess, she knows that beauty is food for the soul, and she understands the healing power of gentle touch, caring attention and sympathetic listening.

In India, there is an annual festival day on which everyone blesses the instruments and tools they use for work. Dentists bless their drills, clerks bless their typewriters and tailors bless their sewing machines; on this day, my dance teacher would bless the wooden block and stick on which she beat out the rhythms for dance practice. In a wonderfully simple way, this ritual brings home the message that our work is a form of worship, prayer and spiritual practice. If the dentist can fill a cavity with as much devotion as a priest invoking the divine presence, then his work can bring him the same spiritual fulfillment.

After the publication of *Aphrodite's Daughters*, I received dozens of letters from readers who wrote about their own experiences with the priest/priestess within.[2] Like small, powerful generators, archetypes may lie dormant until the time is ripe for their resurgence. Today, our inner priests and priestesses are knocking loudly on the doors of our psyches, demanding to be recognized and integrated into our spiritual life. If we listen, they will show us the way to a new yet ancient kind of spirituality, one that is world-affirming and joyful, that does not depend on the structures of organized religion and does not fragment our lives and ourselves.

Today, as in ancient times, priests and priestesses are the gatekeepers to other worlds, and the guardians of this one.

Endnotes
1 See Psalms 82:6 and John 10:34–36.
2 Jalaja Bonheim, *Aphrodite's Daughters: Women's Sexual Stories and the Journey of the Soul* (New York: Touchstone, 1997).

Priestess of Kali
By Chandra Alexandre

I am a Priestess of Kali. With these few words, a whole cacophony of syllables arises in me. These are not the seed sounds of mantras turning on my tongue. Rather, they are the tones of language rushing to respond—some attempt to elucidate, to help the uninitiated understand what it means to occupy this space as a radical feminist and Western-born Hindu convert. The words come with memories of having endured the incredulous gazes of educated atheists in Indian households and meeting rooms, women and men who believe religion to be the downfall of humankind for all the injustice wrought in its name, particularly against females.

Some of the sounds move to simplify and articulate a position that is as straightforward as my breath, powerful and careful steps upon the planet. The words come with awareness that my footfalls are keeping time with the whispers and drumbeats of the witches, healers, sages and wise ones across traditions and history. They are in alignment with the teachings of my maternal grandmother, who had ready access to the unseen realm and taught me to believe in magic. Others seek to distance me from those who find the archetype of the terrible, devouring mother a convenient way to explain their theories and phobias. The words come to argue a larger vision, one spoken by great Hindu-Tantric mystics, those who see Kali clearly as both a birther of worlds and a devourer of them.

Finally, voices inside me move toward the challenges of what it means to be authentic, a lineage carrier and a female priest. The words come to claim space as I stand counter to the orthodoxy that recognizes only Brahmin men as her clergy and sees women's blood as impure.

They come to claim territory, as Kali worship has evolved to fit both new limitations (animal sacrifice, for example, is not welcomed in the Western world) and new freedoms afforded on American soil. They come because I have freely chosen an arduous path; on this path, I have received so many gifts, and I would love to share with others what I have learned on my journey.

Becoming Kali's priestess has meant that I have consciously invited the process of birthing my soul. And whether in Kolkata or San Francisco, this Goddess has both represented and simultaneously been more than personification, metaphor or archetype of my transformation. In 1992, Kali came to me in a dream. Larger than life, black and bloody, she invaded my New York apartment and asked me one pointed question: "Do you want to live or die?" With every cell of my body, I knew the answer and realized I was making some very bad choices if life was what I truly wanted.

Taking formal initiation in India six years later, I agreed to accept challenges both seen and unknown. The first of these involved rectifying my relationship with my body. Once addicted to perfection and suffering from anorexia nervosa, it was Kali's form as an emaciated goddess that brought me to my senses and helped me heal. When she is depicted as skeletal, her imagery offers us a glimpse at the paradox of Spirit incarnate. She is shown in this way because her life-generating aspect is so powerful that she is in a constant state of insatiable hunger and must be fed, but she can only be fed on her creation. She exists in the liminal at the same time that she is of this world, creating and decomposing the stuff of life to make life once again.

From the sufferings of my self-inflicted starvation to moments of spiritual awakening, Kali has inspired the work required in this body that I might experience some of the depths and heights of the human condition. Much like my original coming to Kali (or her coming to me), another dream recently offered me additional insight. In the dream, I held my young daughter in my arms. She had been taken and beaten by a group of people unknown to me, and had only just been returned to me. She lay quiet and comfortable in my embrace. As I held her, I knew she would heal and that what she needed most at that moment was my care and love. I reached over to take off her sneakers and socks. Pulling off the first sock, I saw the horror of her torment: her captors had broken every toe and twisted each around. When I awoke, I was shaking.

After the anguish of wrestling with that dream for days, I finally understood its truth: I am my daughter and the dream presented her dramatically in order to instruct me. She is unconditional love, such as that of a mother for her child, and she is the pain of living through the traumas of family- and culture-inflicted injuries. I realized, in holding this awareness, that I had been loving myself as broken all this time. Quiet and eventually comfortable with my brokenness after years of psycho-spiritual self-reflection, I had learned to kiss my wounds and go on, but I had not come to accept the whole of my being.

Just as I know my daughter is pure and perfect, regardless of all else, the same must be true of me. The dream's teaching was revealed: I need to own the beauty and essence of who I am, right in the imperfections of this physical birthing. The toes in the dream were a special message from my soles in touch with my soul. This, I have learned, is what it means to accept Kali's embrace: the birthing of the soul is the blossoming that happens when we are able to love ourselves completely.

To be aligned with the Goddess, Kali, for me, is to feel something within that could be mistaken for the will to live. I can only describe it as that philosophical sentiment the ancients refer to as a reflection of the Great Mystery—that which burns at the heart of one's being in profound resonance with the Divine as she exists beyond boundaries of time and space. But my lack of articulation here does not cloud what I know. She is not an agenda. She is not driven by imagination, theory or ego.

In one sense, she is merely the name I give to my awe at the wonder of the world through the lens of this incarnation. In another, birthed as I am from a particular marriage of energy and consciousness, she is the whole of biological evolution, at the same time that she is also the dancing of the stars at the limits of black holes. She is the innermost recesses of thought and the certain fabric of my existence. She is time and essence, space and reverberation. She is an unveiling of the folds and layers of breath that have gone and continue to go into life itself.

For over six months in 1998, I felt at home in the north and northeast of Bharat Mata (Mother India) as I did fieldwork of more than one kind, exploring my own assumptions, limitations and fears. I felt internal barriers crumble as I experienced the joy of being received without reservation by devotees of the Divine who cared not for my place of birth, only my sincerity. I felt other protections get stronger as I navigated alleyways and temples alike filled with decomposing fruit and flesh. My experiences hint at the beauty of Kali's teachings on non-duality, in which the elegance and horror of creation both become real.

This is reflected in much of Kali's iconography. She may appear with unbraided hair, for example, to denote sex or menstruation. To signify the bliss of egoless detachment, her snake-entwined arms may hold a severed human head in one hand and, in the other hand, at the level of her heart, a *kapala* (skull cap). My first visit to Tarapith, in West Bengal, provided a concrete example. There, I was welcomed after a grueling trip with abundant red flowers strung into fragrant garlands. Despite a glorious *darshan* (seeing of the Goddess, Tara) at the temple, the day ended disappointingly when the door to my pilgrim's guest house room opened to reveal a fresh pile of excrement on the bed. In India, the possibility for escaping the realities of life were, I was learning, greatly (and importantly for the spiritual seeker) diminished.

From the cosmic perspective, Kali is the sacrifice of spirit arising in the world. Following the whim of the Divine, she—the all-pervading and powerful force of conscious spirit—yearns, and then answers that yearning, becoming the yearning itself, as the limitless condenses into the world of matter and is created. In our bodies, we know pains of the flesh and the sufferings of the heart, yet we have only hints of the torment endured by the Divine. For the sake of knowing the taste of freedom and the scent of love, she is born. Many women's unadulterated experience of natural childbirth (my own included) offers one microcosmic expression of this reality; to say it another way, the rendering asunder is also a portal to unfathomable bliss.

Today, after annual pilgrimages to her homeland and over thirteen years of public *pujas* (rituals) offered in her name, I am much more comfortable with my role and responsibilities relative to her teachings in the flesh. The learning continues, of course, as I plunge more deeply with community into the realms she inhabits and seek to know more intimately the gateways she guards. Her gifts, sometimes even the passwords that open the gateways, have been largely earned on the path of practice and service.

In India, the person out in front initiating ritual by creating the container in which spirit can dance is called *purohit*. My Sanskrit teacher in America remarked once that I must claim that title and, in time, I have. I lead ritual and live an engaged spirituality, in part through the work of service in community. Every month, we gather, and Kali is loved through symbol and form, smile and sacrifice. Kali *puja* welcomes old and young, newcomers and initiates alike. We are family for that time of worship, no matter what our backgrounds or heritage, political preferences or beliefs. We each take responsibility for our worship, with my role being largely that of facilitator, and come to know her through our shared and unique experiences.

The worship is laden with verses from the *Rig Veda* and *Chandi*, ancient books of the gods and goddesses. We follow Hindu protocol in the temple and honor Kali in a traditional manner that includes incense, water, food, fan and fire. We honor her in a non-traditional manner as well, with sacred substances reflective of non-dualistic Tantric rites. These are intended to open us to the potentials for coming to the original soul that lies beneath the rubbish of our unquestioned assumptions, acculturated norms and internalized oppressions.

My own *sadhana* (spiritual discipline) has been a key to coming closer to original soul through the throwing off of various encumbrances. It is also what enables me to maintain the promise I made long ago to spread Mother-worship. From the lips of my first guru, Shyam Sundar Dash, to my ears and then to the shores of San Francisco, bringing Maa (Divine Mother) here was something with which I was charged. Certainly, I was not the first, and I did not have to accept responsibility for another iteration of Kali devotionalism in California (let alone America); however, at the time, it was the most meaningful thing I could imagine doing.

Since then, the promise has transformed, and the nature of spreading Mother-worship, and its meaning to me, has changed along with it. I have found myself speaking no longer of a promise but rather of a permeating vow. In 2003, I received another initiation in India by an Aghori Baba, this one at Kamakhya where the *yoni* of the Goddess resides in Assam. While the details of this are really another story, the point is that, with this particular initiation, I began to have embodied experiences of connection to Kali on a regular basis. The power of Shakti (the female force) became palpable, something I could feel and source in order to change outcomes. These arisings of energy necessitated my adherence to a regular set of spiritual disciplines, much in the way one's yearning to run a marathon or aspiration to pass a difficult exam requires strengthening through exercise and repetition in order to achieve the goal.

From there, the sense in me of priestessing Kali—of being both charged with and dedicated to being clergy—began to emerge. My commitment to her opened from breath to bone. I began a new chapter, one of realizing that the path of spirit is my way of life. This is the heart of my permeating vow and what it means to me to be her priestess: to live in engaged spirituality; to cultivate discernment in thought, speech, action and presence; and to actively disentangle myself from emotional entrapments, thereby allowing greater possibilities for love and liberation to emerge.

For your own work and practice, I offer you this, Kali's prayer, to be recited as you feel called by crisis or by spirit to the work of blossoming your own original soul: *"Om Krim Kalyai Namah."* I would translate it like this: "I bow to you, Kali, from your manifestations in the flesh to your revelation as the vibrations of the universe." With this, may Kali's gifts be yours to share.

Ammachi: In the Lap of the Mother*
By Linda Johnsen

Worldly love is not constant. Its rhythm fluctuates; it comes and goes. The beginning is always beautiful and enthusiastic, but slowly it gets less beautiful and less exciting. In most cases it ends up finally in upset, hatred and deep sorrow.

Spiritual love is different. The beginning is beautiful and peaceful. Then comes the agony of longing. This pain of love will prevail until it leads to unity with the beloved. This unity in love remains forever and ever, always alive, both within and without, and each moment you live in love. It will swallow you completely until there is no "you." There is only love.

The speaker knows what she's talking about. She is Amritanandamayi Ma, a diminutive, semi-literate South Indian from a small fishing village by the Arabian Sea. She grew up in abject poverty (even the sari she wore had been loaned to her), the victim of years of physical and psychological abuse. Sudhamani (Pure Jewel, her birth name) attended school through the fourth grade, when her mother's illness forced her to remain home to attend to the household. The work load was enormous for a nine-year-old, but Sudhamani's mind was absorbed in Lord Krishna. If she suddenly realized she had taken several steps without remembering Krishna, she would run back and walk those steps again, repeating the Lord's name. Sudhamani's unconventional ways were particularly

---

* Originally published in a slightly different form in *Daughters of the Goddess: The Women Saints of India* (St. Paul, MN: Yes International Publishers, 1994), 95–110. Reprinted with permission.

irritating to her brother, who was so enraged by her refusal to marry and her adamant insistence that she would take up the spiritual life, that at one point he actually attacked her with a knife. Throughout this harrowing childhood she practiced karma yoga, deliberately surrendering every thought and action to God.

Later in her girlhood, Sudhamani felt the call of the Goddess. She would walk to the seashore at night and, like a drop merging with the ocean, merge her heart in the fullness of the Divine Mother. Villagers would find her apparently unconscious on the beach, totally absorbed in the Goddess. While this makes for an inspiring story in retrospect, it had a less salutary effect on her family at the time, who had little patience for these "fits," and less for the coterie of devotees who began to gather around her. Sudhamani reached adulthood before her family finally grasped that they had a bona fide saint on their hands, and that the crowds gathering at their doorstep were not going to get any smaller.

In the past decade, millions have come for a glimpse of the holy woman from Kerala. When Ammachi (Darling Mother, as the Indians affectionately call her) appears in public, thousands stream out of their villages to receive her blessing. She is what the Indians call a *mahatma*, a great soul—the embodiment of absolute, unconditional love.

When I saw Amritanandamayi Ma in India, she was surrounded by over 20,000 devotees. Having just completed a program of devotional singing, she was taking time to greet her devotees personally. All of them. The evening passed, then the night, then the morning. There was not a trace of strain or fatigue on her face, and only 5,000 devotees left to go. Beaming her blessings at the enormous crowd, she touched every person who came to her, was completely present with each one, and pressed *vibhuti* (sacred ash) into their palms.

Is this for real? I wondered as I limped away from the tumult, my legs aching from sitting so long on the hard ground. The experience left me with a much deeper appreciation for the quality control standards Indians apply in gauging their *mahatmas*.

In the past seven years, hundreds of thousands of Americans and Europeans (and lately, Russians) have joined me in marveling at this forty-year-old woman, since Ammachi has been travelling from Zurich to Tokyo to Chicago, offering her gift of inspiration to all who attend her free programs of song and prayer.

To those of us yoga aficionados who have heard it all, Ammachi has nothing to say: speaking no English, she doesn't talk at all: she just is what she is. She speaks through her eyes, reaching out to embrace each astonished American or Australian or Swede who shuffles forward, rubbing our backs and slipping us chocolate Kisses. For many Westerners, this unlikely meeting is galvanizing.

The balding gentleman sitting across from me in the large San Francisco church where Ammachi is greeting visitors has been weeping for hours. Later he confesses, "My God, I haven't cried like that since I was five years old. When Ammachi lifted my face and looked in my eyes, and I saw that perfect, pure love, I just lost it. I didn't know such love existed."

Since Swami Vivekananda's arrival in the United States 100 years ago, most spiritual teachers from India have been lecturers and have stressed the practice of yogic techniques. The God-intoxicated mystics, like Vivekananda's guru Ramakrishna, tended to stay at home. Ammachis mission does not seem to be to reiterate that, through concerted practice, we can reach *sahaja samadhi* (the state of continual absorption in divine consciousness), but rather to show us what that state actually is.

Ammachi's tactic of refusing to deal with Westerners on a verbal level is brilliant: it forces us to come to her as she comes to us, from the heart. It strips us bare of our manipulative strategies; we are inarticulate children again, at the feet of our mother. Maternal and solicitous, radiant in her simple white sari, Ammachi wipes away the tears that flow spontaneously from many who have come here to meet her. Accepting an infant offered by a young father, Ammachi bounces the baby on her lap, laughing and teasing it affectionately. Everyone here is her child. She has the widest lap in the world.

Although Ammachi never got as far as the fifth grade, today scholars sit at her feet. Like India's recent sages, Ramakrishna and Anandamayi Ma, who were also barely literate, Ammachi speaks from the depths of her own spiritual experience. For a woman with no guru and no formal religious training, her understanding of Vedanta, Tantra and the intricacies of yoga is prodigious.

Fortunately, many of her conversations with devotees have been recorded, and translations of her teachings are now available in English. One pilgrim who crossed the backwaters of southern India's verdant tropical forests to reach Ammachi's ashram, hidden by coconut and palm trees from the sea some yards away, asked her what path of yoga is most appropriate for Westerners. After demurring that each individual is different and should be guided directly by his or her own teacher, Ammachi offered a general answer:

The path of devotion is the best for Western children. In the West, society is such that people, even from early childhood, take an intellectual approach to everything. Their analytical minds are well developed, but their hearts are dry.

"What can we do about this dryness?" wailed the pilgrim who, like me, understood all too well what Ammachi was getting at. Ammachi responded:

First, develop one-pointed love toward God. When that love becomes the center of your life, and as the devotional practices become more and more intense, your vision changes. You come to understand that God dwells as pure consciousness in all beings, including you. As this experience becomes stronger and stronger, the love in you also grows until at last, you become that. The love within you expands and embraces the entire universe with all its beings. You become the personification of love. This love removes all dryness from you. It is the best cure for all emotional blocks and negative feelings.

Reasoning is necessary, but we should not let it swallow the faith in us. We should not allow the intellect to eat up our heart. Too much knowledge means nothing but a big ego. The ego is a burden, and a big ego is a big burden.

Haven't you seen people who stand as guards for somebody

else's property, like a paddy field or a wealthy man's estate? When these guards talk to someone, they will pose as if the whole thing belongs to them. Scholars are like that. The real owners are the ones who have realized the inner wealth through meditation.

While the Sanskrit language and traditional Hindu scriptures are taught at Ammachi's main ashram near Trivandrum, the value of book learning is kept in perspective:

Children! Can one live in a drawing of a house? Can you enjoy sweetness by licking a paper on which "molasses" has been written? If you see a billboard advertising a jewelry shop in Kanya Kumari, can you purchase gems from the billboard? Of course not! Dear ones, just so, you cannot experience bliss merely by reading the scriptures.

Devotion without knowledge cannot free us, but knowledge without devotion is like eating stones. On the path of devotion we can enjoy the fruit from the very beginning, experiencing bliss in every action. In other paths, this occurs only at the end. We can get fruit from the jackfruit tree by picking it at the base, but in the case of other trees we must climb to the top to reach the fruit.

The bliss that comes from higher states of awareness cultivated through years of rigorous penance is freely available at any moment to those who love God. We have only to open our hearts. But how can we ordinary mortals pry our self-centered hearts wide open enough to let God in? "Real love arises only when all attachments to individuals, objects and personal interests drop away. Then the battle, of life becomes a beautiful play. It becomes selfless service extended toward the entire human race out of compassion. In that battle it is not your ego that is fighting, but love that is consuming your ego and transforming you into love itself."

Many teachers emphasize the importance of love, but Ammachi's words have a particularly potent impact on so many who have met her because they see that she walks her talk. "Ammachi gives all the time,

24 hours a day," reports a devotee who has known Ma for six years. "She lavishes her love freely on everyone who comes to her. She may be firm with them, but she always radiates unconditional love. That's why people are so shaken after they meet her. She's a living example of what she teaches, of what all the scriptures teach. She sets an example for the rest of us. It's incredibly inspiring. No one believes that what she does is possible till they see her doing it."

"Ammachi doesn't just lecture on yoga; what she does is model for us the state of continual divine intoxication and overflowing compassion," a secretary from Marin agrees. Unlike many saints who recoil from contact with ordinary people, Ammachi embraces the masses. "Many thousands of people come to cry on her shoulder," a disciple explains, "and she hugs and consoles them. She says that of the thousands who have come to her, very few have had anything happy to say. She says the sorrow of the world is immense."

"There are many ashrams where they will teach you how to become enlightened," Ammachi says, but she herself prefers students who not only seek union with God, but are deeply committed to serving humanity. At the same time, Ammachi is a yogini after the old school: she demands strict discipline on the part of her close disciples. I myself find the program of *tapas* (spiritual austerity) that she prescribes for the *brahmacharins* (celibate disciples who live with her) quite intimidating. It stipulates eight hours of meditation daily in addition to constant social service activities. Ammachi herself does not sleep more than two hours per night, and her disciples hardly have time to rest either.

When asked if this routine was also expected of her lay followers, Ammachi responded:

> *Mother does not like to use the word tapas because it scares many Western children. They think tapas involves physical and mental torture. They are afraid that through tapas they will lose all their desires, and they do not want that to happen. They want to enjoy life. The only problem is they have a wrong idea of "enjoying life." Real enjoyment depends on relaxation, not on tension. Yet most people are very tense all the time. Men are*

not able to spend any peaceful moments with their wives and children. They are more worried about their work, their business, their status in society and about what others will think or say about them. They want a new house, a new car, a TV or a new relationship. The modern man is fed up and bored with old things. His mind is always set on what he does not have. He is always living either in the past or in the future, never in the present, and he runs after everything he craves. He has no time to enjoy, to relax and be in the present. Finally, he collapses.

But you can turn your home into a haven, an abode of happiness and bliss. There definitely is effort involved; it can be a kind of sadhana. It is all right if you want to call it tapas if that helps you think of it as a serious matter.

The present way of living will only end up in greater distress and sorrow. The problem is you. It's within you, not outside. If you really want to enjoy life, try this path of mental disciplining and see what happens.

A griham (house) is an ashram or hermitage. That is how the word grihasthashrami (householder) came into being. A griham can be converted into an ashram. An ashram is a place where people devote all their time and energy to the remembrance of God, doing selfless service and developing qualities like love, patience and respect for others. They do spiritual practices to help them see unity in diversity. First, they fill their own hearts with love, and then wherever they go, this love is expressed in all that they do. They see beauty and harmony everywhere. Family life can also be like this. That is why a householder devotee is known as a grihasthashrami, a person who leads an ashram life while remaining in his house. He or she is a person who tries hard to attain the supreme goal, bliss, even while living with their spouse and children. This is possible if you sincerely try.

Impressed by the quality of renunciation they see at Ammachi's ashrams, women sometimes come to her believing they must leave their husbands to take up spiritual life. "Mother tells them, 'Why are you throwing him away? Serve each other. In this age, it is not appropriate for everyone to renounce the world,'"a devotee reports. Ammachi teaches men to see their wives as the Divine Mother and women to see their husbands as the Lord of the World, and also to serve their families, the community and the world. Humility and service are her constant themes.

If she is to succeed in spiritual life, Ammachi specifies: *Some of the qualities of a man, like detachment and courage, should be assimilated by a woman. Ladies are not generally interested in renouncing worldly life to attain God. Who would keep creation going? But if their interest is kindled, then they can make even faster progress than men.*

Basking in Ammachi's love is a wonderful experience, but for students who want to continue the work of self-transformation, Ammachi highly recommends the practice of raja yoga: *The ancient masters thoroughly studied the human mind. They penetrated into it and understood its subtleties. It was only after such exhaustive study that they have written down all the disciplines that a spiritual aspirant should observe. Today everyone writes a book. But Mother wonders what study they have done about life and their mind.*

The rishis (seers) were not superficial. They spent days and nights foregoing food and sleep to study their mind. The result was the attainment of ultimate knowledge. They knew well the obstacles that a sadhaka will have to confront during his spiritual journey, because they themselves had faced them.

Nevertheless, she says: *However much we meditate and do japa, it is of no use if there is no love for God. A boat travelling against the current will inch its way along no matter how hard one rows, but if a sail is tied, the boat will pick up speed. Love for God is the sail which moves the boat forward.*

Yoga students who complain that they do not have time for the spiritual practices Ammachi prescribes—*dhyana* (meditation), *japa* (remembrance of God), *kirtan* (devotional singing) and *seva* (selfless service)—receive a blunt response: *If we want to be more honest and sincere with ourselves, it would be better if we were bold enough to admit, "I'm not interested in spiritual matters," rather than twisting the truth* by saying, *"I have no time."* When we really have the desire to do something, time and the proper conditions will be at our disposal. Time and circumstance follow desire.

I spent some time talking with Neal Rosner, Ammachi's first Western disciple. He had spent twelve years as a monk at the late Ramana Maharshi's ashram in Tiruvannamalai, when a friend persuaded him to visit the then little-known woman saint from Kerala. Ammachi advised him: *You have been treading the path of knowledge for a long time and still have not achieved what you set out to accomplish. Why do you not try crying to God? You may be able to succeed in that way.*

"How is it possible to cry without reason?" Neal equivocated.

Take a photo of your guru and, keeping it next to you, weep to him to reveal himself to you and rid you of all your sorrow. Just try it. It is not as impossible as you think.

After Ammachi left to visit a devotee on the other side of the island, Neal tried to eat, but each time he raised the spoon to his mouth, he would burst into tears. Ammachi's image was indelibly imprinted in his mind's eye. His friend Chandru was deeply alarmed; these emotional outbursts were entirely uncharacteristic of Neal. "It's taking her a long time to return. I'll sit outside and chant my mantra," Chandru said. "Wherever she is, she may hear me and return immediately."

Sometime later, Ammachi's mother came rushing in. "Ammachi is coming," she announced breathlessly. "We were on the other side of the backwaters and could not get a boat to take us across. Ammachi started to shout, 'Chandru is sitting there in the hot sun and Neal is weeping to see me. If you do not find a boat soon, I am going to swim across!'"

At that moment, Neal recalled, Ammachi walked into the room. *Crying?* she asked him, innocently.

I mentioned ruefully to Neal that, in this country, many seekers have had far less benign encounters with spiritual teachers, and feel leery of uncritically embracing any new teacher who arrives from India, no matter how loving they may initially appear. "One should observe the guru's conduct, their life, their history, their teachings to see whether their life is reflected in their teachings, and the other way around also,"

Neal thoughtfully responded. "In the West, people are very credulous and feel that if they're having so many experiences when they go to spiritual teachers, it means the teacher is great."

"With Mother, I find that the way she was when I met her twelve years ago when nobody at all knew her except the villagers, and the way she is today, is the same. Her total lack of worldliness is the same. If you had seen Mother fifteen years ago, before she had any contact with society, you would call her an *avadhuta*. An *avadhuta* means someone totally beyond this world, beyond the physical plane. You would say they're crazy. They have no standard of anything. You used to find Mother lying in the backwaters in Kerala, in the water and mud, or dancing under the trees at night. She would eat off the ground, whatever anyone would give her. She was dead to her physical existence. I've seen this with my own eyes. Many times, she'd be sitting out in the sun in *samadhi* and it would start raining—you know the tremendous monsoon rain—and she wouldn't move. If you're in an airplane, you don't feel like walking on the ground. That's Mother's condition."

"There was an *avadhuta* in another part of South India that we once visited, and he was most offensive. He was spitting on Mother and no one could understand what he said. He was really dirty. He used to sit in one corner, and that was his whole life. When we came out of the room we were so angry, we never wanted to see the fellow again. But Mother just kept sitting in there. Finally we got in the bus and she just smiled and said, *He's really in the supreme state*."

"Everybody in unison said, 'Oh! If that's the supreme state, I don't want anything to do with it!'" And then she said, *None of you can understand it, and I can't explain it, but when you're in his state you'll understand why he's like that.* That kind of sums up Mother's inner life. We can infer so many things, but unless we get in her state ourselves we can't understand what it is, really."

"Mother did not used to wash or brush her teeth or bow in the temples," *brahmacharin* Ramakrishna adds. "She was beyond those things. But then some of the devotees, who were not beyond them, began to imitate her. Only then, for the sake of setting an example, she changed her ways, and began following the social norms."

"You can see the rest of Mother's life right in front of you," Neal continues. "Whether it's a woman or a man or a child or a rich person or a poor person, they're all the same to her: she's the mother. Everybody's a three-year-old child before her. That's how she sees everybody. And that's not just words. She makes us feel what we really are. We really are children of the Divine Mother, but as we grow up our mind gets hard and we get angry and proud and jealous—we become adults. We lose our innocence. But Mother says that you have to become a child again if you want to realize God, if you really want to be happy. Christ said the same thing." Ammachi is from Kerala, which is a communist state. I ask Neal how the authorities have dealt having one of India's greatest living saints in their midst.

"They're changing a lot. All of Kerala is changing because of Mother. People had lost faith in God; they gave up their religious traditions, mostly because of communism. And now thousands and thousands of people are changing because they see Mother, and they're convinced that she's the Divine Mother. If she goes somewhere outside the village, you can be sure there will be 15,000, 20,000, 25,000 people who see her in each place. People have been craving for a real saint, and they see that's what Mother is."

Ammachi makes no claims to being a divine incarnation; she insists, instead, that she is "the servant of your servants." *I want people to worship God, not me*, she has repeatedly stated, yet throughout South India I met people absolutely convinced she is an *avatar* (a manifestation of a deity).

"They feel that she's more than a saint because she's been like this since she was a child," Neal explains. "They feel that she's an incarnation of the Divine Mother. Traditionally, it's told that you can tell a person is an *avatar* if, in their childhood, they realized God, they use their realization for the good of the world, they're born masters and they had no teacher. This is very rare."

The day Ammachi first set foot in Moscow (August 17, 1991), Soviet communism collapsed. The symbolism of this coincidence struck me very powerfully. There has long been a strong Catholic tradition that Russia would be liberated by the Divine Mother.

Interestingly, when *brahmacharin* Chaitanya frankly asked Ammachi, "Are you God?" the ashram reverberated with the peals of her laughter. Referring to herself, as usual, in the third person, she replied, *Amma is a crazy girl. The only reason Amma is sitting here now is because no one has put her behind bars. Amma does not ask anyone to believe in her. It is enough for you to believe in yourself.*

"There have been other inspirational teachers in the West who have offered unconditional love to their audiences," I said to Neal. "The last time I saw one of these he looked terrible, as if he were on the verge of collapse. I assume it was because giving and giving just burned out his nervous system. Yet Ammachi keeps giving, one on one, not just to hundreds of people but to tens of thousands at a time, and she always looks fresh and joyful. How does she do it?"

"She says she's equipped for that job. That's why she was born. She compares herself to a sweeper, a person who cleans up all the rubbish and then afterwards goes for a bath. She knows how to take a bath, not physically but in her own way. Not everybody knows how to do that; they know how to give but they may not know how to get rid of what they're taking."

"It's unbelievable. I mean, her batteries are not like our batteries. She goes and goes and goes and we collapse. If you live with her, you're exhausted all the time. Mother comes home at four in the morning and then she reads letters until five. Finally, she sort of dozes off and then may wake up an hour later and off she goes again."

"We lived in one hut together for the first two years of the ashram. There was Mother and me and Swamiji (Amritswarupananda). I could never do that again! That was the most difficult thing I've ever done, living in the same room with Mother for two years. The light was on all the time because she'd never sleep. And always people in there, always she's very boisterous and lively—she's so full of energy and life. That room was like a circus all the time—always *satsang* (spiritual fellowship). Fortunately we got a second hut."

"Years ago, I was sitting in the hut in Vallickavu with the other devotees, enjoying Mother's presence, when suddenly I noticed a terrible stench," relates another of the *brahmacharins*. "I turned around and saw a leper walk in, completely covered with oozing sores. You cannot imagine the smell. I almost vomited. Mother jumped up and ran to him, her face shining with joy as if a long lost child had just returned home. She embraced him and fussed over him and washed his wounds with her own hands." At this point, the story takes a more shocking turn—confirmed by several witnesses I spoke to who were with Ammachi during this period. "She asked him to come again regularly, and every time he came in, she would lick the pus out of his sores. Over the months, the leprosy disappeared. Only one small sore remained. When we asked Mother why she didn't heal the leprosy completely, she said, *As long as the disease remains, he cries to God. If the disease is completely removed, he may become complacent.*"

Miraculous stories are told of all India's myriad saints. I personally find these tales charming and inspirational although—I'll be candid—I don't take them literally. However, while it's easy to shrug off purported miracles by historical figures long dead, it's discomfiting to hear life-transforming personal experiences related by credible witnesses sitting across the table from me.

One young man related that Ammachi was talking with a group of devotees in Vallickavu when she abruptly turned and commanded him to return home immediately, even arranging for a car to speed his journey. He rushed home to find his mother weeping before Ammachi's picture on the family altar. "I was leaning over the oven when I felt an excruciating pain in my heart," his mother explained. "I knew that I was going to die. Suddenly I thought of you, and knowing that you were at the ashram, I prayed to the Holy Mother, 'Please send my son back to me so that I can see his face one last time.' I fell unconscious to the floor, but woke up some time later, astonished to be alive. I smelled Holy Mother's fragrance and, as I slowly opened my eyes, I saw her sitting next to me. She was holding my heart medication in her left hand. *Yes daughter, you took the medicine. Be at peace, you are all right*, she said. Then she vanished. I jumped up and searched for her everywhere but she had disappeared. Still her fragrance permeated every room in the house. I returned to the kitchen and the pill bottle—which I keep locked in my medicine cabinet—was lying on the floor."

Listening to the Indians earnestly relate many such impossible experiences with Ammachi, I was struck by how differently they view the universe. In our culture, the Goddess is a feminist symbol of self-empowerment, an icon with dramatic political and philosophical resonances. In India, however, the Goddess is real. From earliest childhood, these people have listened to scriptures like the Chandi, in which the Goddess promises that, whenever her children are threatened or go astray, she will incarnate to save them. The Divine Mother is not a concept to them; she walks their streets and abides on the altars they build for her in their homes. When they look at a *mahatma* like Amritanandamayi, they actually see the Mother of the Universe moving among them. I leave it to the psychologists to explain the psychosomatic mechanism that allows this kind of faith to create apparent miracles.

I had the opportunity to observe the ancient Tantric Kanya Kumari ceremony in a Hindu temple, in which a three-year-old girl was dressed and worshipped as the Goddess. My interest was originally anthropologic but, as the ritual progressed, I found myself falling powerfully under its archetypal spell. The rite is also often conducted with adolescent girls, as well as with very elderly women. The great 19th century saint Ramakrishna worshipped his wife Sarada in this manner.

I arrive at the Mata Amritanandamayi center near San Ramon, California, having heard that Ammachi will be conducting a similar rite, called the Devi Bhava. I find many people I know here today, devotees from the Sai Baba ashram, from Ananda, from Self Realization Fellowship and from the Siddha Yoga center. There are Christians and Buddhists and Jews, all sectarian loyalties laid aside to greet a saint whose embrace is universal. The huge auditorium is so full that last-minute arrivals cannot squeeze in the door.

When Ammachi enters the hall, many devotees bow before her, and instantly my "cult alert" sensors start to blink. Except, if this is a cult, why is no one pressing me to join the organization? (It turns out there is no organization to join.) Why is no one trying to convert me to their theology? (Before the worship begins, I am told to visualize whatever aspect of God I am most comfortable with, and if I don't believe in a personal God, to imagine the formless reality.) Most surprisingly, why is no one pressuring me for a donation? Abrahmacharin explains that Ammachi abhors the modern tendency to turn spirituality into business, and has forbidden her disciples to ask for money. There is, however, a booth at the back of the hall where cassettes of devotional music and exquisite Indian jewelry are being sold for the lowest prices I have seen in this country. One hundred percent of the proceeds are used to support the orphanage, schools, medical clinics, vocational training institutes, hospices and homes for widows and battered women that Ammachi maintains in India.

In the next moment, Ammachi is on all fours, pressing her forehead to the floor. For a full minute, she bows to the divinity in us. I am caught completely off guard: I personally find it distasteful to bow to anyone else, and here this world-renowned saint is bowing to me! This reminds me that, in India, the significance of prostrating is to show respect to one another's divine nature, not subservience.

The program begins with Devi Puja, an ancient South Asian rite in which the Goddess is propitiated for the benefit of all beings. Waving spoons of flaming camphor and chanting *Om Parashaktyai Namaha* ("homage to the supreme primordial consciousness/energy"), we follow Ammachi's instructions as she speaks through Swami Amritswarupananda. "Mother says the masculine principle has overtaken the world and that is what is causing many of the problems today," he translates. "We must bring the nurturing energy of the feminine back into the world. That is why we are worshiping the Goddess today." We offer flower petals symbolizing all our hopes and fears, one by one, to Parashakti, the Great Mother.

After a vegetarian dinner, the Devi Bhava itself begins. The curtain is drawn back across the stage, revealing Ammachi as we have not seen her before. She is draped in a stunning sari, decked with jewels and wearing a silver crown. To Westerners, unfamiliar with this type of rite, she explains:

> *Children, when we see the dress of a postman, we are reminded of letters. Likewise, Mother's dress is to remind you of the Supreme. The world respects only the dress. The visual appearance of Mother in Devi Bhava is to release us from a limited perception of our Self and remind us of the Supreme which is our true nature.*

She is in *samadhi*, a state of intense meditative concentration. Like the Kanya Kumari rite, this ceremony allows us to symbolically enact the experience of being in the presence of the Mother of the Universe. This ceremony is so radically different from anything most of us have experienced in our own culture that I am frankly astonished no one walks out. Instead, people line up to approach "the Goddess," to make physical contact with the Divine. For many of the individuals here, that moment leaning across the Goddess's lap to receive her blessing is one they will cherish their entire lives.

"It's something instinctively felt by the people, in spite of the cultural difference they see there," Neal Rosner comments. "It's not on a mental level that they feel it at all. It's entirely intuitive. It's something they can't put their finger on, but it's so true and it's so deep in them. People love it so much because it's coming from the core of reality."

I cling to my cynicism. It is both my sword and my shield. From my teen years investigating paranormal phenomena, to my adulthood exploring various spiritual paths, again and again I have been impressed by our immense capacity to delude ourselves. We are credulous creatures; we want to believe, we want life to be magical, to be spiritually meaningful. Too often, we confuse our interpretation of events with the events themselves. Then when something untoward occurs, like a sudden death, we are stunned. For an instant, we hover at the brink of that terrifying abyss of stark reality the Hindus call *kali*. Then immediately, we scramble to find meaning in the event, to make excuses for God's apparently capricious will.

I have always been attracted to saints and their inspiring teachings but, in "real life," I work at a major research university, and I am exposed daily to fresh neurophysiological data revealing that much of what we believe is psychic and sacred in ourselves is, in fact, biologically mediated. Yet standing in the presence of a phenomenon like Ammachi, I feel my well-ordered, thoroughly documented version of reality begin to crack. I find myself asking new, incredible questions. Is it possible yoga isn't just about stretching into a pose, or enhancing one's clarity and creativity? Is it possible that it actually can be a door to another dimension of being, one that expands out infinitely, not only beyond the intellect but beyond human imagination? Is it possible that love can be more than a comfort zone or a social palliative, that it might be a vehicle into the very heart of God? Burned out on the hype about gurus, I resist "surrendering" to spiritual authority figures, yet some part of me wonders if it might be true, as Ammachi suggests, that *The guru is the embodiment of pure consciousness. There is no person there. He simply is, and you benefit from his presence. If you really want to use the guru, then surrender to your own Self. It is the same as the guru's Self.*

I inch my way toward Ammachi's chair, where she sits blazing with love. One after another, 2,000 people are coming forward to lean into her lap and be embraced and blessed by this enigmatic peasant woman from India. At one point, I get up to check in back of the curtain behind Ammachi but, incredibly, there is no electric motor running there. Where, then, is the powerful, pulsating energy I feel coming from?

At last it is my turn. I kneel hesitantly before Ammachi. The total compassionate acceptance emanating from her completely disarms me. For once in my life, I lay down my sword and my shield. I plunge into Amma's lap, throwing my arms around her waist, burying my head beneath her ribs. I am pitched into blackness. I reach out to Amma with all of my heart and find in her—nothing. There is absolutely nothing there. And yet in this vast emptiness which seems to engulf me, I sense something . . . conscious. It feels as if the nothingness of all of space and time is smiling. I pull back, amazed, and look up in Amritanandamayi Ma's radiant eyes.

I understand that this is an untrustworthy emotional reaction, but for one moment I find myself believing that, yes, this is for real. The teachings of the yogis are true. There is a state of luminous clarity that transcends and permeates everything. By revealing the divinity in herself, Ammachi is showing us the heart of reality: our own divine essence.

Behind me the *brahmacharins* sing a traditional *Malalayam bhajan* to Devi, the Supreme Goddess:

> Who knows Thy greatness,
> O Thou who art the substratum
> Of this illusory world?
> Thousands and thousands of living beings
> Seek Thy divine, radiant smile!
> Who knows Thy greatness
> O Mother, who knows?

The Dream
By Abbi Spinner McBride

I n my dream, once, long ago . . .
There was a brilliant beam of sunlight streaming in through the window. I opened the window and walked out onto the beam of light, following along on it as one might walk on a balance beam, each step more sure than the last, walking the light-beam toward the sun. The steps went by quickly and I went higher and higher; the air got very warm, but I was not burned. At last, I went through a door in the sun. Inside there was a brilliant, yellow room, where a beautiful, strong, old woman was sitting. She stood and asked me what it was that I brought and what it was that I sought.

I replied, "I bring my willingness to serve, my loving heart, my open mind and the gifts of music, beauty, magic and faith. I seek to be of service, to manifest good in the world, to create beauty, healing and magic so that the Universe may be well pleased."

The old woman smiled and nodded, and said: "It is so. I bless you with the gifts of a priestess. You will always know the right words at the right time and you will know when to speak and when to remain silent. I bless you with the gift of music, of melodies that sing themselves in your ear and rhythms that play themselves through your hands. I bless you with the knowledge of the power of listening and witnessing, that you may know how deeply healing these gifts are. Finally, I bless you with a glad heart and a willing spirit, so that you may go back into the world and share these gifts with those you encounter. Walk in Light and never forget who you are."

And with these words, the beam of light re-appeared under my feet and I danced back down to my room.

Priestess: Born Unto Herself*
By Pamela Eakins

I was not drawn toward entering into structured religion for the purposes of furthering the goals of that particular institution. Rather, I entered structured religion to find a position in society from which I could celebrate the sacred, but the religion, itself, was a means by which to celebrate; it could never be, for me, an unexamined temple of righteous. Religion has been a springboard of ideas for me, ideas that might have the potential to catapult me ever deeper into my own search for cosmological understanding. To this end, through time, I immersed in many religions, western, eastern, and indigenous, though this immersion, *per se*, did not make me a priestess. In fact, at various times, I worried about becoming trapped in a cage of internally, self-consistent religious teachings. However, there were moments when being inside a particular religion and under the protection of that religion was the only way to continue to practice—or to serve in a public manner. As I saw it, this is how a priest serves—cradled in the bounded realm of the religious paradigm.

I became a full-fledged priest, a fully-ordained minister in an interfaith and non-denominational church, in order to enter into a socially sanctioned profession that might fulfill my desire to serve as a priestess. In this profession, as a minister, I officiated seasonal changes and the seasons of human life. Being engaged in this profession and in this role in society made me a priest and honored my sense of myself as a priestess, but this affiliation did not make me a priestess. Being a priestess was

---

* A longer version of this article appears in Pamela Eakins, *Priestess: 3000 BCE to The Future* (CreateSpace, 2013). Originally published as *Priestess: Woman as Sacred Celebrant* by Weiser Books, 1996.

my deep inborn calling, a calling which may lead one into the priesthood, or may not. In fact, when I was ordained as a minister I sewed secret garnets and charms into the sacred stole which was laid upon my shoulders at the climax of my ordination. The garnets were to remind me that my womanness, my womanblood, my woman's sensibilities, would always take precedence over my duties to any religious organization. The charms were to remind me that, in my own consciousness, all religions lead to the same place: cosmic love and eternal reverence. I served in the priesthood for 25 years, but, during all those years upholding my values as a priestess was what mattered.

Being a priestess, to me, was not about politics, not about who was archbishop, not about how much to charge for a wedding, not about the clash of religion against religion. Being a priestess was about finding my own way to remain alive and astonished as a cosmologically oriented human being existing on a planet two-thirds of the way out on one of the spiral arms of the Milky Way Galaxy. As a priestess, I saw myself moving about the planet that moved about in the solar system that moved about in the galaxy that "traveled" with thirty sister galaxies through a universe filled with untold billions upon billions of galaxies, each one extraordinarily unique. I did not know in the beginning, perhaps five millennia ago—which is my earliest memory, to date—but I came to understand, that I, too, am a universe, born of cosmos, no more and no less than a star. I came to understand, through time and deep delving within and without, that the universe is not "out there somewhere." Rather, the universe is living its sacred life as me and through me right now. I came to understand that I am state-of-the-art cosmos at the cutting edge of its own development. My thoughts are the thoughts of cosmos. My actions are cosmic actions. I am universe unfolding—in each and every moment. It took me a long time to arrive at these sensibilities, which were not part of the teachings of the seminary in the 20th century when I was studying for the priesthood.

For me, being a priestess came to be about understanding that, for those who have ears to hear, every place one steps is holy ground. I came to value the whole of the universe as sacred. This was the path that opened to me from the inside out and from the outside in—throughout the millennia of experiencing what it means to inhabit our human consciousness. If I am sacred, all are sacred. If I am at the cutting edge of universal development, all are at the cutting edge of universal development—all that is in existence, right now. The now is the cutting edge of existence. You and I are breathing the same air in this very moment—at the very edge of existence. Our hearts are pounding out a universal rhythm in the core of our bodies—in the very center of existence. This is not a contradiction. We are edge and center perceiving this very moment in this very moment. We are the living universe with the ability to reflect upon its own nature. We can reflect and, on the basis of our reflections, alter our course. We stand at the cutting edge of universal consciousness, armed with the power of choice.

Becoming able to exercise the power of choice is what being a priestess means to me. Being a priestess means being a woman of power, a woman with the ability to know and to express the truths that are ringing in her soul. Claiming and exercising the power of self-expression is realizing true liberation. In fact, self-expression is the ultimate measure of liberation. To be unable to express one's core truths and values is to be bound into a life not fully lived. That is why, having practiced as both a priest and a priestess, I define the two differently. That is why I sewed the garnets into my minister's stole—so I would remember not to become trapped by a paradigm (any paradigm) someone might try to force me to accept internally or to publically uphold.

Being a priestess, to me, is expressing and receiving, in equal measure, searching and learning and continually evolving—as a woman of power. A woman of power knows herself, not once and for all, but as an ongoing process. A woman of power recognizes she is cosmos on the path of its own discovery and creation. To develop her creativity, she becomes highly attuned to the longings of her heart, for are the longings of her own soul not the longings of the universe itself moving toward wholeness? A woman of power attunes to the callings of her body, her mind, her heart and her spirit and allows herself to be moved by what she feels. Thus, a woman of power changes as the internal and external universe shifts. This is a good thing. Moving with the cosmic flow of energies while being aware of, and acting upon, the feelings in one's own heart is the key to becoming an active participant in the evolution of the universe. It is being an active participant in the universal adventure, which, ultimately, creates a deep and unassailable sense of meaning, purpose and fulfillment.

Being a priestess is about following the heart, and meeting and engaging with the Beloved—in whatever form the Beloved may appear. Thereby is the future conceived. Thereby does the priestess become the creatrix of that which shall be. The Beloved may appear as a person, a place, or an object; in any form at all. Being aware that one has encountered one's Beloved, and not being afraid to follow that truth, is what it means, to me, to be a priestess—she who is a woman of power.

Honoring that physical, mental, emotional and spiritual nudge—that deeply intuitive call—is what being a priestess means to me. Of course, there is not time in a lifetime to act upon all issues; thus, again, a priestess must enter into the power of choice. We cannot choose all, and by making a choice to enter into one engagement and not another, we must sacrifice many possibilities in favor of our highest calling. A priestess—a woman of power—knows this, and she chooses anyway. She makes a choice to do one thing and not another because she understands herself. She understands her deepest calling and she understands what it means to engage the Beloved. By taking action she realizes, fully and completely, that she belongs.

She was meant to be here. It took over thirteen billion years for our universe to evolve to bring her forth in her singular nature—just as she is right now—and now she realizes she is a key participant. She understands that what she chooses matters.

A priestess knows herself, which means she not only learns how to act proactively but how to navigate challenges. She teaches herself how to move through narrow physical, mental, emotional and spiritual straits. Like the archetypal priestess in Tarot of the Spirit—a Tarot deck created by my mother and me—she learns how to travel through the desert like a camel.[1] She might have to go for long stretches without water, thus she learns how to conserve. She learns how to fill herself, and ultimately, how to keep the endless channel of cosmic fulfillment open. She learns how to replenish herself at will. Striving to do this becomes one of her spiritual practices. As she learns the nature of self-fulfillment, she may become a water-bearer, she who not only fulfills herself but who offers sustenance into the cosmos.

A priestess is on the spiritual path. She realizes she is cosmos coming to know its own existence, and that is something she celebrates. She learns to discover joy in the greening of a field, the tumbling of a wave, the formation of a cloud and the chirping of a migrating goldfinch. The priestess has a deeply spiritual approach to life—or at least, that is my experience.

A priestess is not made by memorizing intellectual systems and practicing rote rituals. A priestess is an archetypal seeker ensconced in universal wonder. She is born unto herself as a celebrant of the Sacred. Her rituals are never rote and her knowledge is never static.

How does a priestess define the Sacred? For those who have eyes to see, all the cosmos can be held as sacred. She who is priestess experiences the calling to hold the whole of the cosmos in reverence, to observe the tides and seasons and to immerse in marking the life of the cosmos through spiritual celebration. What others may call mundane, the priestess may call sacred. What others may call profane, the priestess may call an opportunity to engage in the evolution of cosmological design. For she who is priestess realizes she is no more and no less than the holy cosmos itself engaged in the act of its own imaginal becoming.

Endnote

1 Pamela Eakins, *Tarot of the Spirit* (Red Wheel/Weiser: Newburyport, MA, 1992).

Garden-ing*

By Andrea Goodman

Listening to bird songs,
layered, the close chickadee chirp
over the distant seagull laughter,
with a gentle wind's hiss-whisper,
carrying the rose and milkweed perfume,
as my eyes thrill to the pink, purple and gold
of rose, campanula, rudbeckia
and borage blue, daisy white,
I am once again planted
in my garden,
grateful.

I ask,
How can I share this beauty,
as it fills me, spills over
my heart's cup?
Why am I so blessed
by flowers beyond counting, around me
in fragrant, vigorous embrace?
What purpose calls for my pleasure,
peaceful hours in solitude?

---

* From *Spell Breaking: Remembering Ways of Being An Anthology of Women's Mysteries*, ed. IONE (New York: Deep Listening Publications, 2013).

STEPPING INTO OURSELVES

I hear the answer:
Begin with your "solitude."
Remember that you are
intricately interwoven, circuitry
connected, lines open
at all times, whether or not
you are listening, sensing or aware
that you are simultaneously receiving,
giving, receiving a flow
of vibration forming constellations,
subtle as air or perfume,
magical as that hummingbird now at a blossom,
nourishing as salad,
inspiring as wise words,
multidimensional as your labyrinth.

As the breeze meets the tree branches,
it is altered into whispering sound
and fluttering dance.

As the beans and summer-squash meet
your body, they become
fresh cells, renewed strength.

As the beauty meets you,
it becomes a radiance
of gratitude and joy.

You are simply a star, radiating light
and warmth, like the Sun.

STEPPING INTO OURSELVES

Let there be no doubt
or doubt is what would radiate.

Allow your receptors their deepest
breaths, exhaling infinite song.

I am the Earth: The Priestess in Service to Community
By Deidre Pulgram Arthen

In a clearing in the woods, a woman squats on the earth inside a circle of 200 women, men and children, all bent low, listening with eyes closed, foreheads touching the ground, hands pressed into new springtime grass. A slow drum beat begins and, at first, her singing is barely audible.

I am the Earth . . . the drum beats in the pause. Then a little louder: *I am the Earth* . . With each repetition, the volume grows and people begin to join in the chant: *I am the Earth* . . . soon the whole circle is singing, each person opening themselves to a knowing greater than the words. Slowly, the priestess rises in the center of the circle and calls. The chant becomes a response:

> "The Earth is a healer."
> *I am the Earth.*
> "The Earth is a mother."
> *I am the Earth.*
> "The Earth shares her bounty."
> *I am the Earth.*
> "The Earth is a fountain."
> *I am the Earth.*
> "The Earth is in sorrow."
> *I am the Earth.*
> "The Earth is in joy."
> *I am the Earth.*
> "The Earth, she is crying."
> *I am the Earth.*

"The Earth has a song to sing."
I am the Earth.
"I am a blackbird."
I am the Earth.
"I am a river."
I am the Earth.
"I am a healer."
I am the Earth.
"I am a mother."
I am the Earth.
"What is the Earth?"
I am the Earth.
"Who is the Earth?"
I am the Earth.
"We are the Earth."
I am the Earth.
"I am the Earth."
I am the Earth.[1]

The chanting fades slowly and the circle throbs with power, with love, with knowing that we are not only connected to the Earth and to all of creation, but that we are the embodiment of each one of us, all of us together. We can feel it in our bodies and in our hearts.

The work of a priestess is to create and keep open a channel between the seen and seldom-seen realms in which we live, in relationship and in service to a community. It is not enough for the priestess to be able to contact spirit and travel in that dimension herself: a trained and experienced priestess can create a doorway between the worlds that is wide enough for others to join her there; and those people, by joining, expand the opening still further, so that the flow of power is strong and transformative for all present.

In order to serve in the role of priestess, a woman must first spend time deepening her own spiritual practice. She must know how to find the doorway herself before she can help others see it and she must be comfortable standing in the mystery before she takes on the responsibility of leading anyone else there.

There is no one particular path that leads to a connection with the essence of the sacred, to intimate knowledge of that seldom-seen realm lying just beyond our everyday perception. Many traditions and teachings can take us there. The crucial elements in the making of a priestess are commitment and depth of practice. Often, it takes years of daily discipline, meditation, chanting, ritual and trance work to build a reliable passage between the worlds.

Beyond that, becoming a priestess takes more than just being an accomplished individual practitioner: you need another set of skills. It is important to learn how to be sensitive to the energy of a group, to timing, and to how to structure and lead ritual. Because this is a path of service, you have to learn how to let go of self-importance and the desire to be the center of attention so you can meet the needs of the community you are working for. While there is a wide range of information in books, these skills are best gained through direct experience working with seasoned priestesses and also on your own as you find your voice.

For me, the term "priestess" implies that a woman has already spent years in training or deep practice and finds herself in a position of leadership in a community. By accepting that role in relation to a group, whether large or small, she has made a commitment to work for the benefit of that community as a whole, for individuals within it, for the spirits she is in connection with and for the land itself. It is a responsibility not lightly taken and, once embarked upon, it can be challenging, since the bulk of the work is not about herself alone, but intimately includes others.

In my way of working, a priestess's primary job is not to intercede for people or communicate messages she has received (although she may do these things, at times); nor is it to devote herself to a particular deity. Rather, a priestess's job is to use her abilities to help others in her community to have their own mystical or deeply spiritual experiences. Anyone can stand in the center of a circle of people, raise her voice and speak sacred names or sing out to call upon the ancestors but, without deep, internal, spiritual connection, these actions are, at best, dramatic; at worst, they fall flat and are just boring to those participating. A strong priestess holds the misty places open and bring us in with her.

I believe that ritual is an essential tool that a priestess can use to define the opening of a channel between the worlds, and to provide a doorway for those entering in. Ritual is the repetitive use of symbols, actions and language to create a meaningful experience, deepen focus and direct power toward a goal. It is a way to draw a group together, whether with one other individual, a small intimate circle, a longstanding community or a disparate collection of people.

Using the metaphor of a doorway, a priestess knows that there is a door, she knows where it leads and she wants to show other people how they can go through it. Ritual is a way to identify where the doorway is, to create decorations around the door so that others can find it and go in. However, if, in the ritual planning, the priestess focuses primarily on how fancy to make the door, she may lose sight of the fact that it is only a door. It is important to remember that the door itself is not the ultimate destination, but a means to enter into something else. Though some degree of theatre can be an effective aspect of ritual, a ritual is not a performance. Ornate effects, settings, choreography and language can often detract more than they add. Everything needs to remain in service of the ultimate purpose entering into a spiritual dimension.

Especially when working with a big group, it is important to find a balance between creating a doorway fancy enough that the less experienced in the group can see it, but not so intricately designed that it prevents the more experienced from actually being able to enter. Some participants may have never even attempted to do anything like this, so the priestess should provide material explicit and evocative enough to give them a sense of where they are going. At the same time, the priestess must recognize if there are people in her group who are spiritually adept and can enter into their own connection with the mystery without any external trappings or ritual ornamentation that might impede their experience.

In the ritual example at the beginning of this chapter, the priestess was in the middle of the circle and was a focal point for the group herself—or at least her voice was. That need not be the case, and in creating ritual a priestess often works unseen, because she does not need to be at the center of the ritual in order for her skill and expertise to make a difference. In community ritual, it is not the experience of the priestess or her presence that is most important, but what the experience of the group will be.

Group ritual helps us recognize the web of connection among us as human beings, as well as the connections we have with everything else. Something powerful happens when a group enters into a sacred space together, something different than what happens during solitary practice. A priestess can shape a ritual to consciously include that aspect of human connection into the experience.

I have been leading large and small rituals for over thirty years now and, in my experience, a successful ritual is usually well planned in advance, but does not always go exactly according to plan. This is because the plans have been flexible enough for the experience itself to guide the proceedings. This does not mean things are left "sloppy," but that there is room for the priestess to "feel" where the group is and what it needs at any given moment, and shift plans to align with that perception.

To be effective, even the simplest group ritual will accomplish certain key things. It will:

- Create a separation from ordinary space, using a gateway, ritual clothing, symbols, evocative surroundings, scents, colors or sounds.
- Acknowledge the land, ancestors, spirits—whatever the priestess works with.
- Establish a clear shared intention for the group.
- Include everyone present in active ways as much as possible.
- Use shared symbolism and language to create a focus for an intention altar, images and spoken or chanted liturgy.
- Create a connection within the group and a separation from ordinary awareness using tools like chanting, breath, movement and trance induction.
- Guide the group to and through the door.

- Direct power toward the intention, using some of the same tools as described above, or others.
- Acknowledge the group, the land and the spirit, with gratitude.
- Provide a sense of closure and completion.

One tool I have used in every step on this list is chant. In my years as a priestess, ritual has been my home and chant has been my ally. In my work with the EarthSpirit Community over three decades, I have used chant to help bring the community together and establish a rooted culture, and also to help carry us all deeper in our spiritual work, both individually and together. After such a long time, our primary chants are understood without explanation; children grow up with them and they are handed down through generations in families. Our chants evoke instant responses in us because of their association with particular rituals or actions or times of year. We have used chants so consciously over the years that they are now embedded in us and have become part of our culture. They are keys to a door; people can carry the keys with them and enter the door at any time.

Five hundred people are singing, dancing and drumming as they toss small balls of string and yarn in the air, weaving a giant web around the maypole in the ritual field at Rites of Spring. They sing:

Weavers, weavers
Weavers, weavers
We are weaving the web of life.
Spirit weaver, bone weaver, breath weaver, stone weaver
We are weaving the web of life.[2]

We have sung this song and woven this web for more than twenty years. We carry infants into the center of the web to add their tiny hands to the weaving. People take turns holding the spokes that tie together the web of community. Teenagers make way for elders to come in and add their strands to the web. We are connected with each other and with all of creation.

Once someone has participated in the tactile experience of this ritual—has sung the chant many, many times, walked through the door it opens and felt the power in coming together and planting the web in the earth—that particular place between seen and seldom-seen remains accessible to them. The chant becomes a key. And if, six months later, at a fire circle on the other side of the country, someone begins to sing "Weavers," then—while most of the people may be finding the chant enjoyable and evocative—the person who was at Rites of Spring will find themselves turning the key and opening the door to a powerful connection with community and spirit, a connection that goes beyond immediate time and place. A priestess knows where she is going in a ritual. She finds the doorway, opens the channel and helps those present go through it together in the context of their community.

Once the ritual in the woods is completed, the priestess grasps the hand of the person next to her and leads the group in a dance that spirals in and around so that each person passes every other one there. We are changed and we acknowledge each other, seeing in the faces we pass the experience we have shared and the wonder in the world around us.

In the circle of Earth and Sky
My heart flies to yours
We gather
We remember
And the pattern endures.[3]

Endnotes

1 Deirdre Pulgram Arthen, "I am the Earth" (©1982).
2 Deirdre Pulgram Arthen, "Weavers" (©1994).
3 Deirdre Pulgram Arthen, "In the Circle of Earth and Sky" (© 2002). Many chants and songs of the EarthSpirit Community, including the ones in this chapter, are recorded by MotherTongue on *Weaving the Web of Life*, available on www.cdbaby.com or at our website: www.earthspirit.com

Wisdom of Elders*
By Patricia Monaghan

the thin thirsty
tree croaks for
water

as it does
a duck flies
into view—

a fish leaps
into the duck's
mouth, becomes

a water tree, glossy
bark stream
ing branches—

yes, birds and
fish spawn forests,
rivers—the trees

wish to speak in
the constant silver
of streams,

---

* From *Seasons of the Witch: Poetry and Songs to the Goddess* (Cottage Grove, WI: Creatrix Books, 2004).

STEPPING INTO OURSELVES

not just stand to be
spoken through—
the trees wish me

to tell you this

On Becoming a Tree Priestess
By Kathryn Ravenwood

I never thought I would become a Tree Priestess. As I child I loved to play in the roots of trees and climb in them, but they never hinted about a future time when I would be their priestess. I didn't even know what a priestess was. I lived a conservative middle-class life in Wyoming that revolved around family, school, church and friends. I thought after high school graduation I would attend college and become a high school English teacher. But Spirit had other plans for me.

In 1970, I spent a short, magical time camping out in Big Sur, California. Getting there was truly an act of Spirit calling me. College life at a large university had turned out to be nothing like I expected. I did not feel like I belonged there or that my previous plan to become a teacher related to me anymore. Disenchanted and depressed, I dropped out and went back home, only to discover that home no longer felt right either. I was restless, feeling that something was missing. I no longer fit in with anyone I knew or with what my life had been up to that point. What was going on? Why wasn't I happy?

Spirit dropped a big hint via Johnny Rivers and his album *Realization*. The song, "Going Back to Big Sur" kept haunting me. I had never been to Big Sur and only knew it was "just south of Monterey," somewhere on Highway One, where there were redwood trees and you could go there to "straighten out your head." It sounded like a great place to me. I decided I would go there.

So I left home with only a small backpack, my dad's old World War II sleeping bag and complete naïveté. Spending most of my meager savings on an airplane ticket, I flew to Los Angeles. With almost no money left, no experience in traveling and no idea what I was doing, I followed that strange urge to change, grow and explore. I put out my thumb and started hitchhiking up the coast.

I realized later I had put myself in a very dangerous position, but Spirit was looking out for me and kept me safe. As I went from catching the next ride to walking long stretches alone, I thought, when I "got there," I would camp out alone by the ocean under a tree and somehow the meaning of my life would be revealed.

As I got closer to Big Sur, my excitement rose. The beauty of the coast highway and the unending view of the ocean opened my heart. I was meeting some very interesting people now who gave me rides: young people like me, out for adventure and new experiences, exploring the expansive mindset of the alternative life style of 1970. We were all searching for something: peace, love, purpose. The last ride dropped me off in front of the Big Sur General Store, which seemed to be the hangout place. Unbeknownst to me, Big Sur was a hub of hippies and other free-spirited souls camping out illegally amongst the trees. So much for spending time alone! But the "freaks" I met there weren't the main attraction for me: It was the trees that completely captivated my attention.

I had never seen redwood trees before and immediately fell deeply in love with them. Lying on my back, looking up at them towering over me as they vaulted into the sky above opened something inside me. I had entered into their temple of perfect, eternal beauty. I felt God through them. Looking back later, I realized it was a true spiritual awakening in its nascent form.

One day while hanging out at the General Store, I noticed a biker by a tree just off the parking lot. He was a big guy and didn't look at all friendly. Horrified, I watched as he threw his large knife into the redwood, extracted it, backed up and threw it again. Sap was oozing from the tree like fresh blood. Tree pain and sadness overwhelmed me. It was as if the knife was being thrown into my own flesh. I ran to the tree, getting between it and the biker's knife, my back against the trunk, facing the biker, my arms thrown open wide to shield the tree. "Stop it! Stop throwing that knife! Can't you see you are making this tree bleed? If you throw that knife again you will have to throw it into me. You will have to kill me first."

The biker stopped and stared at me. Our eyes met. I was scared but determined to protect that tree. I stepped forward to stand as close to him as possible. The twenty-year-old skinny hippy-girl and the big biker dude squared off.

"You come and apologize to this tree," I demanded. "You have hurt her and made her bleed." The biker didn't move. I stood my ground. Tension mounted. Then, something shifted. Putting his knife back into its sheath on his belt, he slowly walked up to the redwood. I went to stand next to him, gently took his hand and placed it on the wound his knife had caused. Quietly, I said, "See what your knife did?" His other hand went onto the tree as well, touching the bark, feeling the oozing sap. He looked up into the lofty branches as if he had never really seen a tree before. "Sorry, tree," he muttered. But the moment passed. He took away his hands and wiped them on his leather pants, and then turned, went back to his bike and roared away.

I sat down next to the tree, offering my love and comfort as a mother would soothe her injured child. From out of the blue afternoon sky, a black-and-yellow swallowtail butterfly drifted toward me and lit on my arm, walking up and down from hand to shoulder and back. It stayed with me for perhaps thirty minutes, gently gracing me with its peaceful beauty.

It was an initiation: a sign of transformation. But I didn't know that then.

My life evolved, as lives do, with joys, sorrows and experiences. As I grew older, I continued to seek a more spiritual path. I moved to Seattle and became involved in a women's circle, where I was learning about ceremony. At one point, Starfeather, the leader of our circle, held one of her Medicine Shield Retreats at La Push on the Quileute Reservation lands on the forested coast of the Olympic Peninsula. I decided to go and was looking forward to a weekend in a cozy ocean-side cottage, sharing Spirit time with my women friends.

A section of the road to La Push hugs beautiful Lake Crescent with its many old, big trees standing guard as if to discourage driving too fast. As I drove along, enjoying the ride, a late spring snow was lightly falling, making the road a soft white ribbon. To the left, tall trees clung to the side of the mountain. Endless clusters of rich green ferns feathered the ground beneath them. To the right, the deep, blue waters of the lake rose almost to roadside. No other drivers were out. I had this incredible place of beauty all to myself. I felt so blessed to be there at that moment.

And then Spirit spoke to me. "Turn off the music."

I turned off the CD I was playing. Deep silence and a sense of anticipation came over me. Driving slowly, I rounded the last lakeside curve of the road, leaving the soft beauty of the water and forest behind me. The road was now running straight through the complete and utter devastation of a clear-cut area. All the trees had been hacked down and partially hauled away for the lumber mills. For as far as I could see, the great forest had been decimated. It looked like a battlefield and the trees had definitely lost. It was heartbreaking.

And then, out of my mouth, a haunting chant emerged, a series of simple syllables intoned over and over in a minor key: "Hey ya, hey ya, hey ya-a; hey ya, hey ya, hey ya-hey."

Over and over, the chant poured out of me. It was a lament for the trees, perhaps coming through me from the ancient grandmothers who had once lived on this land. This was why Spirit had told me to turn off the music: so they could give me this sacred gift. As soon as I could safely pull off the road, I did, stepping out of the car into the cold, damp air. I reached into the back seat for my drum and walked out into the clear-cut, stepping over mounds of forest death, getting wet from the light misting rain. I found a place that felt right, and began beating the drum in rhythm to the lament. Facing each of the sacred directions, I beat the drum, chanted, cried and prayed for the trees. It was another initiation, but this time I recognized it for what it was. I thought, Thank you, Spirit, thank you.

In the weeks and months that followed, I shared the experience with my community. People started asking me to come and sing to their trees. Some were being cut down by municipalities to make room for new housing developments; some were diseased and had to be taken out; some were simply being honored and acknowledged by people who loved their woody neighbors. Before each of these tree blessings, I would pray that Spirit would guide me to be of help to the trees. I would dress in my best ceremonial clothes and show up with smudge and drum in hand. I would chant the lament to each tree, making offerings of tobacco, water, sage and crystals. Sometimes I would tie ribbons around their thick-barked bodies, as if dressing them for burial. The ceremony was never exactly the same. I let Spirit and the trees guide me. I held the great Standing People in my heart, honored them, wept for them and blessed them. I had become a Tree Priestess.

During this time, Starfeather put together a spiritual theater performance piece called "In Honor of Trees." We performed around the Seattle area, a stage full of tree priestesses telling stories and sharing memories of trees through spoken word and song. The spirit lament I had sung in the clear-cut was included in the script. One night on the way to a performance, I stopped at a grocery store to buy flowers for the altar on the stage. While deciding which lovely bunches to buy, I heard a song in my head. Singing along silently, I caught the tune. The words flowed in and, as soon as I got back to the car, I started writing them down. I thought I was remembering a song I had heard at a ceremony or on a recording, but I couldn't remember where I might have heard it before. When I met up with the other women, I sang it for them. Did anyone know it or know who might have written it? They laughed at me—silly girl! You wrote it! And so I had. Spirit had given me yet another blessing for the trees. I called it "There are Trees." Starfeather incorporated my singing of it into her performance: harmony in song, harmony among women, harmony for the Earth, harmony for the trees.

There are Trees

> There are trees in the mountains
> Growing on the edge of sky.
> And these trees in the mountains
> Sing to me as I go by.

STEPPING INTO OURSELVES

They sing to me of the old ones
Who once lived where I now stand.
They sing to me of the Mother
And the sacredness of land.

There are trees by the ocean
In mist and fog they grow so tall.
And these trees by the ocean
Are sending out their plaintive call.
They're calling us to remember
That we all must live as one.
They're asking us to surrender
Our deeds of greed and destruction.

There are trees in the city
Choking on smog and pollution.
And yet these trees in the city
Give their gifts to everyone.
They give us breath.
They give us beauty.
They shelter us from rain and sun.
We must honor and protect them
For the next generations.

There are trees in the moonlight
Their shadows cast upon the ground.
And from these trees in the moonlight
Our roots of peace can be found.
They hold the magic and the memory
And the hope of what's to come.
We walk their path of love and beauty
And a new world is begun.

There are trees. There are trees. There are trees.

Wings of Augury
By Lorraine Schein

My wings are driftwood,
For I have been a tree—
Wood that has dreamt in water
And emerges remembering, on the shore
As we dream, afloat in sleep's waters
Future drifting into past.

And I have been a hand
Holding high a sword,
Cutting hypnotic circles in a trance-smooth lake.

And I have been a black stone in the moonlight
And a dancer among black stones,
Dancing to black starlight.

A golden torque and vervain crown I wore then,
On the Druidess Isle of the White Maidens.

These things sacred to all priestesses:
Water, stone and tree.
The sea is an omen of the shell.
The shell augurs the sea.

STEPPING INTO OURSELVES

Fortunes can be read in fallen leaves
And in the white foam runes of the tide, where
Between their oracular duties and sweeping the sea floor
Begging for apples, the mermaids have often come ashore.

The Story of My First and Second Urban Street Trees
By Jennifer Jones

I live smack in the center of a large, old, East Coast city. In the midst of a lot of concrete and paving, hot summers and cold winters, planting a tree and keeping it alive is both a process and an adventure. My loving determination and commitment to protect her (the tree's) life are required, in addition to persistence in overcoming multiple obstacles. I had never thought of being a priestess, formally or informally, at the time of my first tree planting, but I had a fire in my belly to bring green to my block in the city. I had not yet associated the desire to spread greening with priestessing, urban or otherwise. I did learn from my first tree experience that others would emulate my greening behavior by planting their own street trees and putting up window planters.

On a largely unconscious level, at the time, I spurred the greening of my block. To me, this represents a way of bringing Her (the Goddess) forth in an urban environment. The greener setting gives residents, pedestrians, bicyclists, drivers and passengers, rollerbladers and skate boarders a chance to experience Her trees and flowers as they pass through our block, giving them a respite from the concrete and a visceral experience of planted life. I cannot help but hope that these experiences will enable people to value Her more.

In order to have a tree placed in front of my house for the first time, I had to contact the local civic association, where the greening committee was the only pathway for tree planting. Virginia, who was then the head of the committee, met me in front of my house to agree on where a tree pit could be cut into the sidewalk. It was a formal dance with the civic association toward my goal of a tree.

Sidewalks are complicated in the city, for many reasons, but in this instance we were looking for a block with no utility extrusions, like fire hydrants—or, as it turned out, bicycle racks. Virginia and I agreed that one concrete block had no extrusions—hooray!—and that I should be permitted a tree. After several conversations, we scheduled a tree planting. I was not allowed to pick my own tree type nor the actual tree, as such things can be highly controlled, so Virginia did the picking; but at least I would have a tree. The block of sidewalk would have to be removed as well, freeing up the earth, to which I always say "Yeah."

Imagine my surprise when I walked home from work the week before the arrival of the much-anticipated tree and found a bicycle rack bolted to the valuable extrusion-free cement block. I felt startled, mildly angry and momentarily helpless. Then I realized that I needed to get in touch with the folks behind the bike-rack project. If I was committed to greening my little area in the city, I would have to continue channeling my energy in this direction despite this new and unexpected obstacle. Why had they picked the one block without utility extrusions?

This was early in the downtown urban bicycle movement; the emphasis was only on the ability to lock bicycles safely and not yet on bicycle pathways on existing roads, and bicycle racks were being distributed throughout the city. I was able to get in touch the following day with a young man in the city working on the project and explain that I did not object to the bicycle rack but that this particular location in front of my house had just been designated for a street tree scheduled to be planted the following week. I suggested that the commercial sites in the near vicinity, mostly restaurants, might provide better locations for a bicycle rack than the front of my house. The young man listened and, blessed be, the rack was moved that week—a miraculously speedy timeframe in urban government endeavors.

The tree was planted the following week. I had successfully secured a human-modified pear tree, which never dropped pears but bloomed nicely in the spring for many years. I learned to love my tree, despite its having been modified from its original genetics (it felt a bit alien to me): the tiny pears could never grow into edible fruit, and the tree could never be fertile.

One day in a very wet spring, I noticed flat, flared-edged mushrooms growing out of the base of the tree on the south side. Though I removed the mushrooms, they ignored me and grew back. I removed them again and they grew back again. Realizing that there must be a more complicated situation occurring than just a wet spring, I did some research and discovered that there was probably root rot on the side of the tree with the mushrooms.

Unfortunately, if those roots were to give way, the tree would fall directly across the busy street and could reach the houses and cars parked on the other side, as well as folks in cars and on bikes riding in front of the house. I could not rest easily with that possibility. That sort of accident had occurred directly across the street from my house from the north side several years before when the local cable provider had cut the roots of a large healthy tree while installing cable down the street. My neighbors had actually come out and looked under the part of the tree touching my front porch, worried that I might have been entering my house at the time and been trapped. Sadly, but responsibly, I had my own street tree with the persistent flared-mushroom visitors removed in the fall, leaving the tree pit empty through the winter. The arborist who removed the tree was anxious to plant a replacement in the spring. I did not give him the chance.

A year passed and, as the next spring arrived, I was much further along my path to becoming a priestess than I had been with the first tree. Entering Her service has been a slow process for me, one I did not see coming but stepped into both sideways and backwards. When I started my study with Women's Thealogical Institute, I was not even concerned with the priestess path. I was only concerned with the chance to study about the Goddess. I have since realized that I am becoming a priestess, but I continue to wrestle to create my own definition of priestess, in particular a priestess who lives the majority of her time in an urban setting.

At least for the moment, I see my role in becoming/being an urban priestess in an urban setting as a way to help others open their eyes a little wider and experience Her in the city; to do what I can to protect Her animals, plants and ecosystems everywhere in the world; and to support other women as best I can in their creative efforts, their need for community and their economic well-being.

But back to my tree: For my second tree planting, although I should have planted a semi-mature approved type of tree (in keeping with civic association and city mores and rules), I rebelled (with my heart full of love for Her) and planted a young witch hazel, a tree native to this area and not genetically modified. I ordered her by mail, she came to my work and I carried her body home in my arms. To hide and protect her when she was planted, I changed the white plastic label to read "hazel" only, and not witch hazel. She knows what she is, I know what she is, tree experts and now all you readers know, but those who might react to the word "witch" need not see the original plastic label. However, she is an unusual choice for a street tree in the area, and many people look at her.

The tree is blessed with a round, wooden circle, about one inch in diameter, which I planted below her roots. The circle comes from our one-year Wheel of the Year study group with priestess Kim Duckett; I wrote "love" on the tiny piece of wood during a weekend session and saved it when I was not yet aware of its ultimate destination. I knew it needed to be placed at the base of the tree. It is both protecting and becoming a part of the tree as it composts, feeding it with love from below as well as my love from above. I have been working with words of power planted directly in the soil, swirled into sand or water, and this planting of the word "love" was an early effort.

I wanted to read a poem to the tree when I planted her and, after some research, I located the following poem translated from Portuguese. I read it to her the night of planting—just me, on the street, discreetly reading a poem to my new tree. I found a poem said to have been used in Portuguese forest preservation for more than 1,000 years:

Prayer of the Woods

> I am the heat of your hearth on the cold winter nights, the friendly shade screening you from the summer sun and my fruits are refreshing draughts quenching your thirst as you journey on.

> I am the beam that holds your house, the board of your table, the bed on which you lie, and the timber that builds your boat.

I am the handle of your hoe, the door of your homestead, the wood of your cradle and the shell of your coffin.

I am the bread of kindness and the flower of beauty.
"Ye who pass by, listen to my prayer: Harm me not."[1]

The tree is younger than is preferred for a street tree by various authorities; I have provided a pink piece of paper clipped to the metal screen surrounding her that reads,"Young street tree emerging—please be kind and gentle." I learned the value of composing words for a special sign to protect the tree from one of my life's teachers, a neighbor for whom I have great difficulty generating respect. But I had to respect that she had created a positive, fun, artistic sign that read "Good dogs go elsewhere"—meaning owners should direct their dogs to relieve themselves elsewhere—for her own tree and the plantings at its base. I respected her creating that sign and choosing those words, and I respected that the sign seemed to have worked. A priestess's teachers can often be women to whom they are not naturally or initially drawn, women they may not even personally like.

My own choice of magical protection words, "Young street tree emerging—please be kind and gentle" have worked, and my tree is flourishing. The rain washes the pink out of the paper periodically, and it becomes white. I then replace the paper so the surprise of the bright pinkness helps to protect her from those passing by on the sidewalk. As I have walked home, I have seen people move a little away from her while walking to accommodate others who stop, read and smile. I am learning to ask in writing that her life be protected and, in my asking, to gently direct people's attention to such a wonderful creation in the middle of an urban setting. I have come to understand that my asking passersby to be kind to the young witch hazel tree is an act of priestessing to them as well as to the young tree: I am offering them an invitation to slow down and acknowledge her, to respect her, and perhaps to take a moment to enjoy the survival and flourishing of a young witch hazel tree in a sea of concrete.

Endnote

1 "Tree Poems," North Carolina State University Cooperative Extension: www.ncsu.edu/project/treesofstrength/poems.htm

The Forest Rules

By Patricia Monaghan

Think of it as a kind of

speech: mushrooms shake
their heads when you stoop
to pick them. Berries drift
away on a sudden breeze. These
are not yet to be eaten. And the dead

disdainful tree is not yet
to be cut, no matter
how long it has stood easy
against the air, ready to

fall. And when it does, it may
still refuse you, until one day
it is ready, silent as fuel,
empty of the speech that filled
your eyes. Of course

none of this happens
but it does not happen
exactly like this.

---

* From *Seasons of the Witch: Poetry and Songs to the Goddess* (Cottage Grove, WI: Creatrix Books, 2004).

The Dianic Priestess*
By Ruth Barrett

With the resurgence of women's interest in ritual, Dianic Witchcraft and other female- and goddess-centered traditions, the role of the priestess is being revived. It is most often through attending rituals that women become attracted to the role of the priestess. With growing interest in ritual-making, and more women gaining experience in ritual facilitation, we must ask ourselves many questions: Where are the role models for contemporary women who are on the ritual priestess path? When you imagine yourself as a ritualist, a priestess or a ritual priestess, what are your expectations for yourself and others? What are your expectations based on? Do you have any models for spiritual leadership other than religious leadership models from patriarchal religions? "The role of the priestess awaits re-definition in the twenty-first century. Its keynote must be service, not power."[1]

There is a tendency to romanticize the ancient priestess, placing modern-day sensibilities or feminist values on what we imagine to be a glowing, utopian picture of the past. However, there were thousands of temple priestesses in Asia Minor, most taken from the lower social orders, who were relegated to simple or menial labor.[2] Daughters of poor families picked up the temple garbage, and that was all they could hope to attain.

High priestesses were given station by inheritance, "often born into royal families, thus priestesses by birth. They were also queens of the land as in Crete, Egypt, and Anatolia. Their ritual enactment of planting and harvest ceremonies ensured fertility and prosperity for all. They lived

---

* From *Women's Rites, Women's Mysteries: Intuitive Ritual Creation* (Woodbury, MN: Llewellyn Worldwide, 2007).

in both small and large cloistered communities. All were educated for religious duties, and separated by performance and aptitude."[3]

Ancient ritual priestesses were trained to embody the Goddess and thereby provide direct contact with her to the community they served. There was a religious and cultural understanding that individuals who were too weak personally, physically or intellectually to reach her by their own efforts could connect directly with her via their connection through the priestess.[4]

As contemporary women on the priestess path, our primary function is to create or to become a channel, a chalice, for an experience of the Goddess. In this way, we continue to function as the priestesses did in ancient times. Whether it is through ritual, writing, art, scholarship, dance, music or organizational skills, the 21st century priestess becomes the container that helps create sacred space wherein women can connect with the Goddess. Her work is to help others integrate life passages by providing facilitation services and energetic support at joyous events like births and cronings. She must also be prepared to escort the dying as they cross over, and then attend to those in mourning.

Many authors who have written over the past two decades on goddess spirituality in general, and the Craft specifically, use the word "priestess" to refer to any woman who facilitates in ritual. They make no distinction between the verb and noun forms of the word. I will endeavor to discern some important distinctions between uses of "priestess" as a verb or noun. "Priestess," the verb, as in "to priestess a ritual," describes the actions of a woman who takes responsibility for various parts of a ritual in a ritual circle setting or who facilitates her own ritual at her own altar. This woman is interested in magical skill development and perhaps does divination readings for her circle sisters and friends when asked. She facilitates or designs rituals when and as she feels like it. Her work is not a vocation but a hobby that is pleasurable and meaningful. Like a hobby, her service can be discarded when her interest wanes or too many conflicts arise. There are many, many contemporary practitioners who claim the title of priestess without the training or an understanding of the responsibilities of service. This confuses and undermines the role of the vocational priestess and her work in her coven or larger community.

The noun "priestess" is the title of a woman who has studied and trained, who has gained experience as a religious or spiritual leader, and who has grown adept in the propagation of her spiritual tradition or specialized area of ministry. This priestess can teach what she knows. She has trained rigorously and carved the many facets of her skill into a diamond of her own self. It is the journey of becoming a priestess that has shaped her. This woman has dedicated herself and has possibly been formally ordained as a priestess of her chosen vocation by the congregation, circle or community she serves.

The priestess is a woman who serves a community in a vocational capacity. If her central focus is ritual, she must excel in ritual-making, facilitation and the energetic skills required to execute those duties. If she is a Temple Priestess, she must have the skills and vision to create altars, ritual tools and an environment where women can experience a temple of the Goddess. If she is a Healer Priestess, she must know how to keep herself whole and centered as she serves her community, animals or plants that are ailing. Her most important tool is learning how to bring herself fully present in the moment. She is accountable and responsible for her service over the long haul. She experiences herself as an instrument of service to the Goddess and her women. She works consciously to be a living presence of the Goddess in her words and deeds.

The priestess is responsive to her commitments even when she doesn't always feel like it. This does not mean, however, that she sacrifices herself to her detriment, or becomes a doormat for others' needs. Self-care is essential in order to have the internal resources to offer service. To facilitate others, a woman must be able to come to them as a full vessel. It is difficult to flow when the well has run dry, when one's strength and energy are depleted due to lack of personal maintenance. A woman responsive to her commitments also knows her limitations and makes appropriate referrals when necessary.

On the other hand, one cannot control unexpected life events. There have been many times when I've been asked to serve when what I really needed was a few weeks of rest. At these times—such as after the sudden death of a community member's partner, parent or companion animal—I've just done what was needed and found the strength to be there. The

Goddess has never failed to give me strength and guide my service.

Too often, the complexity of the process a woman undergoes in becoming a priestess is minimized or misunderstood. A woman who is learning to become a priestess will undergo a process of self-transformation that is difficult to describe and can pose many challenges, while offering much enlightenment.

Endnotes

1 Naomi Ozaniec, *Daughter of the Goddess: The Sacred Priestess* (London: The Aquarian Press, 1993), 300.
2 Norma Lorre Goodrich, *Priestess* (New York: Harper Collins, 1989), 1.
3 Ibid., 11.
4 Ibid.

It's Easier to be a Priest than a Priestess*
By Nano Boye Nagle

The Beloved
moves across the room
like the caress of a forest fire
I lower my eyes
humbled by the radiance of her heart
She pulls me into a lovers' embrace
we fit with the familiarity of clay
Her breath tingles my neck
as she whispers in my ear
"I recognize you."
The Universe disappears
Ein Sof flickers
And for the memory of an instant
I understand[1]

—"Recognition," by Nano Boye Nagle/Ziji Salaam

Poetry, art and music are the sacraments of Queer Spirituality. They erode the defenses around our hearts. They reach in and pull us, through our longing, to stand side-by-side with truth. My passions for art, music and poetry find voice in my ministry. Ministry is the ideal job for me—writing, teaching, singing, making music, studying, praying, meditating, leading ritual and offering spiritual direction—everything I

---

* Originally published in a slightly different format as "Queer Spirituality" in *MatriFocus: Cross-Quarterly for the Goddess Woman*, Lammas 2003: www.matrifocus.com/LAM03/queerhtm

love. What other work would give me permission—in fact, require—that I do all the things I do best?

Minister derives from the Latin *ministerium*, meaning "servant." At first, I was uncomfortable with the idea of becoming a minister. It was not a vision compatible with my identity. I had forgotten my ten-year-old self who, when other kids were playing "house," set up a Catholic altar in my room, like the one they had at church. I performed mass alone, following an order of service stolen from the sanctuary, singing the priests' Latin chants, with no idea what they meant but aware they gave me access to power. It was a power I didn't understand, but it gave me permission and peace. By the time I was thirteen, I worked out that the Catholic God wouldn't hire me because I was a girl, and I gave up any ecclesiastic aspirations.

> I am a minister.
> A Minister!
> A f***ing MINISTER!

Ashok Bedi, MD and Jungian analyst, asked, "What is the last thing you can imagine yourself doing? What is hidden beneath your responsibilities, your 'shoulds,' 'cant's,' and the external expectations of your life?"[2] He believes knowing this is the key to finding one's right work. Until 1999, being a minister was the last thing I imagined myself doing. As a little tomboy, my heart was set on being a writer, an actor or a rock star. Through my twenties and thirties, responsibilities overshadowed my secret childhood dreams. In my forties each passing year took me further from that secret, into the arms of another. Ministry, like art, is a patient, seductive, demanding lover.

I have always hungered to be of service. As I grew spiritually, this hunger blossomed into an appetite for offering something sacred, a sacrament, an opening to the experience of the transcendent in the body of the moment. This hunger, this longing promises the possibility of holiness, whol-e-ness, of knowing ourselves as whole, knowing the Goddess in the whole of creation.

It's difficult to be a minister and deny any relationship to religion. Putting "Rev." before one's name is seen as a declaration of religious affiliation, most often assumed to be some form of Protestant Christianity. At the very least, "Rev." is a warning label: "This person has a belief in a Higher Power and is trained to use it."

Buddhism and Taoism make sense to me because they are compassionate and logical. They don't require belief in any gender-specific deity, or any deity at all for that matter. I have always felt and understood a force, a greater good running through my life, but couldn't relate to the idea of a goddess or god whose definition of what was good for me was anything I would want or be able to achieve. This began to change as I healed my relationship with my parents. They are, after all, our first experience of omnipotent beings, of the Divine Mother and the Divine Father.

At graduate school, I attended a lecture by Rev. Gina Rose Halpern, founder of The Chaplaincy Institute.[3] She told of her journey as a feminist artist, answering the call to ministry, eventually founding an interfaith seminary of the arts. By the time she was done, I was shaking. I rushed to the bathroom, sat in the stall, shaking, sweating, goose bumps up and down my arms. "Shit! Shit! Shit!" I cursed. "Girls like me don't go to seminary." This was definitely not part of my plan. The "call" to ministry engulfed me; it was undeniable. Although I had made peace with the G-word in either form, I was still estranged from religion. How could I be a minister without signing away my soul to an institution? The next day, my best friend confided in me that she was starting a two-year interfaith seminary training program run by my favorite professor. I had a long-time practice of "doing the next indicated thing." So despite my fears, and my resistance, I signed up.

At seminary, I was confronted with my attachment to my "otherness." My shaved head and black leather jacket bobbed alone in an ocean of classmates billowing white linen and flowing long hair. Their open hearts helped me realize the cause of my isolation was not external but inside me. As I came closer to ordination, the issue of my Irish-Catholic lineage took me by surprise. I started having dreams in which ancestors demanded to know how I could "go over to the other side." Was I becoming a Protestant? Did my ancestors give up their land for nothing? "Who do you think you are child?" It was bad enough that I was queer. Now, a mere woman, I was thinking about ministry. Didn't I know that we Catholics don't have ministers, we have priests? A woman priest would be an abomination. I avoided telling my parents about the ordination. Ironically, in my life it was more difficult to "come out" as a minister than it had been "coming out" as gay.

I tried on "Father Boye" for a while, but that didn't feel any better. Apart from being motivated by the proverbial "f-you," which didn't feel authentic any more, how could I align myself with that lineage of perpetrators, even if it was in name only? So, I settled into being an interfaith minister, becoming Reverend Boye.

"Minister" and "minstrel" are related words. As the ways of the Goddess were destroyed by the spread of Christianity across Europe, minstrels continued to travel between towns offering her sacraments in the form of myths, music and poetry. This was a decidedly queer form of worship. These minstrels told the old stories and sang songs to a Mysterious Lady, whose name was not spoken. Sufi mystics did the same thing, traveling the Middle East singing passionate, juicy poetry and chants to their god, "the Beloved."

My favorite definition of a Sufi is that the Sufi regards every thought, feeling and perception that she or he has (including sense of self) as a manifestation of the Beloved or as a particular view of the Beloved's face. It says in the Qur'an 2:15: "Wherever you turn, there is God's face." This means that every person and thing we encounter is also a manifestation of the Beloved and should be treated accordingly.

Prayers and practices opened my heart. I discovered the poetry of Rumi, Hafiz and Rabia. I drank them like vintage wine and passionate poetry flowed through me. I was drunk on the Beloved every day. I found myself fishing for mystical poetry: new teachings inspired songs or chants. Eventually, I surrendered and asked Murshida Rabia to initiate me. Staggering home, I hung up my black leather jacket and, blind drunk, stepped onto the path. I focused my ministerial studies on the Sufi message of love, harmony and beauty, and the scriptures of the dominant world religions, including the goddess traditions, looking for the places of unity between them and the universal truths they share.

By embracing Sufism and ministry, suddenly I had an identity beyond my sexuality. Being Queer is a cultural as well as a sexual identity. The Queer community had been the first culture to welcome and embrace all of me. As I moved into ministry, I thought for a while that I would have to "straighten-up," become respectable. After a valiant but short-lived attempt at passing, I accepted that I am very bad at being straight and genetically incapable of maintaining an inauthentic life. To deny our nature is to deny our divinity, so I decided I must be a Queer minister, inventing my own truth, my own version of Queer spirituality. Whether I am working in a church in the suburbs, leading non-violence trainings in the city, teaching ritual drumming or working as a spiritual director for women, I am practicing Queer ministry because I am a Queer minister.

These days, I find myself called more often to serve the Goddess. This requires reclaiming the religious aspect of my lesbian cultural heritage, which I abandoned in the eighties when I was told my queerness made me unacceptable to their goddess. More than once, I became the target of the radical, righteous morality of my lesbian separatist sisters. In my only experiences of being directly attacked for being myself, the perpetrators were separatist goddess women.

I came out in 1983 into a separatist, very PC London community. I could understand the intellectual and social justice-based politics, but I was not ready to tolerate the passion for the Goddess. I was an atheist; smart people didn't believe in God. As a butch, I put "goddess" in the same category as "princess": a "girlie thing" that had nothing to do with me. Even though I had always been woman-identified this was, practically speaking, an intellectual exercise. I was separate from the divine feminine and the girl hidden in my heart. We can only notice the faces of divinity we are willing to experience; I could not experience her and so denied myself the need for wholeness.

By claiming Queer spirituality, I hold a place for all aspects of myself and have a relationship with all aspects of the Goddess. Once I committed to a life lived from the heart, I began to notice the beauty and magic around me. In the rapture of falling in love with God, my heart had opened to the Goddess, for one could not exist separate from the other. "Ishq Allah Ma'bud Allah" is a Sufi prayer which means "God is love, lover and beloved," existing separate yet within the other. The Allah is the Divine, I am the Lover and Love is the connection between the two. For me, the Goddess has become the Beloved, and all that comes from her, including the God, has become the Lover. My work is to connect the two.

It took the sacrifice of my anger at "God, the Father" to know the touch of a divinity beyond gender. It took the sacrifice of my anger at my mother/women who did not embrace my version of being a woman as valid to experience the Goddess. Knowing the "Mother," I came to know myself as a woman and to open my heart wide enough to shine light on the maiden within.

As I look back, I suspect becoming a minister was, in part, a bid for legitimacy beyond my queerness. I thought being a minister came with a certain amount of privilege, entitlement and credibility. It took me a while to recognize that, whether I have letters before or after my name, queer/butch/dyke is what people see. If I want access to that power, it has to come from within.

In my unfolding relationship with the Goddess, because I experience the Mother in everything, the maiden within me is starting to express herself. I own a pink backpack and a "Hello Kitty" alarm clock. A couple of years after moving to Madison, I had my first "grown-up" job, working as part of a team doing psychotherapy with the families of severely emotionally disturbed children. I started growing my hair until I became aware that, if I had a professional meeting with a doctor, I was editing my butchness, attempting to soften my wardrobe. I realized this was a manifestation of internalized "butch phobia"; I had bought the messages I had been fighting against my whole life. I was doing to myself what my parents had done to me, denying the legitimacy of my expression of woman, my face of Goddess. Forgiving myself, I happily returned to shaving my head and buying my clothes in the young men's department. I haven't worn my leather jacket in years; it's not retired—more like on sabbatical. It has become safe, at least in personal ritual or with my lover, to occasionally embody the power of maidenhood. It was with grace and without resistance that I expanded my dyke-boy identity; I now experience the freedom that comes from living life as the biggest conversation possible.

Throughout this journey I have wondered if I have had other incarnations where I took holy orders of some kind, perhaps living a cloistered life. However, this time the ascetic life is not for me; it's clear I am to be in this world, even if I am not quite of it. Apart from that, I'm a "taurus" and I enjoy comfort far too much. To live the life I want, I must start to be self-supporting through my own contributions, no matter what my gender presentation. Oh, Mother! How many times must we die in the service of truth and an authentic life?

The more I experience my connection to the Divine Feminine, the inherited memories that all women share—the dangers of being a witch and a priestess—begin to surface. In response to the flickers of fear, I am developing some beautiful righteous passion, Kali-fired passion, carrying me until I am purified of all that separates me from my rightful experience of the Goddess in the world around me, carrying me until I can reach forgiveness. It is a path wrought with internal and external demons.

Going to seminary made me a kind of priest, although being a woman and interfaith I am considered low caste by dominant traditions. About five years ago, after leading drummers during a ritual, I was thanked as the Drum Priestess. It was the first time I'd been honored with that title, but it felt incongruous to me—priestess/princess have nowhere to land in my butch-girl psyche. More recently, I have claimed my position as Drumming Guardian, which feels right, as the drummers are the bowl to hold the light of the ritual. I am discovering that, despite my struggles, it is still easier to be a priest than a priestess. I now long for the time when I can stand up as a Guardian Priestess Witch and not mumble or drop my eyes when people ask, "So, what do you do?"

I don't understand why my heart responds to this call to service in these two paths, which on the surface seem polar opposites. There are many women who are both goddess women and Sufis, but I suspect queer goddess-identified Muslims are a rare breed.

I do understand the somatic experience of my heart opening when I hear someone sing the poetry of the Qur'an. I understand the radiance I feel after a day of retreat singing or chanting the ninety-nine names, radiance that inspired a lover to take one look at me and say, "You've been Sufied." I understand the recognition of my truth when I listen to a Sufi teacher share the esoteric wisdom of her path.

I do understand the magical moment when a group of individual women drummers slide into the groove and become one, the container for the ritual. I cherish the gift of watching a new drummer "get it," moving from head knowledge to heart wisdom—to knowing that drumming for public ritual is not about personal creative expression or spiritual experience, but about sacrificing their ecstatic encounter to serve the community.

I do understand that my looking as I do—queer/butch/dyke—allows me to reach and serve others who look like me. I offer them believable acceptance and appreciation for all aspects of their woman-ness. I bring them the tools of my personal practice to complement their Craft. I understand that I have accepted the assignment of bridge-builder. Like the two-spirited *berdaches* of some Native American tribes, I crisscross lines of gender, culture and religion. I accept that, at this point on my journey, I am more comfortable with priest than priestess. It is what is. I am both. I swim between them like I swim between genders, aspecting whichever would be of service in the moment. When I stand as leader of a Universal Worship Service, I am the priest.[4] The priestess creates and facilitates rituals to the Goddess for myself and other women. If I am allowed to lead the drumming in public rituals honoring the Turning of the Wheel, the Drum Guardian holds space.

In my Sufi lineage, we use the winged heart, the *tughraiInayati*, to represent the idea that the heart desires heaven. Inside the heart is a five-pointed star over a crescent moon. The star represents divine light and the moon represents the responsiveness of the heart. I was taught that this is to remind us that, in any given situation, I have the choice to be the star, bringing the light, or the moon, the receptive container and/or protector. I am the priestess and the guardian. We always have access to both. Both exist in us all.

I pray for the fire and the passion to stand true in my selves. I ask this for all the girls and queers to come, who need to see a priest and a priestess who looks like me. May I continue to flow with ease between these roles, knowing when to be the star and when to be the moon. May the world know her love, harmony and beauty, celebrate all her possibilities and honor all who live in her service.

May it be so.

Endnotes

1 *Ein Sof* is a term from the Kabbala, meaning the eternal force that existed before all ideas of deity existed. It is the primal creative force that created the universe and it continues to sustain all that is. It is at once immanent and transcendent, beyond gender, outside of time and disappears into description.

2 "Archetype of the Soul" is an analytical exploration of the guiding wisdom of our soul on the path to health, healing and wholeness. September 14 2002 at Aurora Psychiatric Hospital, Continuing Education Program, Milwaukee, WI: www.tulawellnessllc.com/index.php

3 For more on Rev. Gina Rose Halpern, see www.mysticalchemydesign.com/gina-rose-halpern-gallery.html. For more on the Chaplaincy Institute, see www.chaplaincyinstitute.org

4 See "Universal Worship is a Service, a Worship, a Training to Tolerate," at www.hazratinayatkhan.org/service.php

I Am a Priestess of Shechinah
By Geela Rayzel Raphael

I am a Priestess of Shechinah[1]
    in service to the Divine Feminine;
    Called to serve the Jewish people in this lifetime
    Through art, song, ritual, blessings and love.
Like Miriam the Prophetess, who led the women in dancing at the Red Sea after the Israelites crossed to safety;[2]
Like Devorah, the fiery torch woman who was judge, prophetess and warrior;[3]
Like Hannah who prayed and created weaning rituals;[4]
Like Sara, wise in years, who had the gift of the sight.[5]
I am kin to Rebecca, who knew how to inquire of the future through oracle;[6]
And as Leah, who knew the power of naming;[7]
And as the Daughters of Tzelophehad, who spoke truth to power to claim their rightful reward.[8]
I stand similar to the sisters of Bat Yiftach who wailed for four days in grief;[9]
and Hulda, the prophetess who knew her tradition and could discern the holy.[10]
I am reminiscent of Queen Esther, who used her power wisely;[11]
And of Ruth, who honored the bond of sisterhood.[12]

I plant myself in their shadows
Integrating their legacy

Grateful for their modeling
Glad they have left me hints of their action.

I too am called to dance and sing and pray and create ritual
And call women together to sit in circle
To challenge men to walk their highest path
And to tell ancient stories.

They call me rabbi
    Title earned after eight years of study—
    women only allowed in these last thirty years;
Yet it is through art and song and mediation I teach
I serve with the heart and I know I am Priestess.

Endnotes

1 Shechinah is the indwelling feminine divine in Jewish tradition.
2 Exodus 15:20.
3 Judges 4:4ff.
4 I Sam. 1.
5 Genesis 25:23.
6 Genesis 25:23.
7 Genesis 29:32.
8 Numbers 36:6.
9 Judges 11:40.
10 2 Kings 22:14.
11 See book of Esther.
12 See book of Ruth.

Reclaiming Adam and Eve:
The Work of a Priestess in Israel
By Hava Montauriano

I have always been ambivalent about my name: Eve (in Hebrew, Hava), named after my maternal great-grandmother and, of course, the first woman ever created, according to Jewish mythology. This name maintains within me a connection to the past, family, history and tradition. However, being a Pagan priestess at the present and feeling at odds with monotheistic religion for as long as I can remember, I have always felt this name was wrong for me. This is only one example of a larger dilemma I have as a Pagan of Jewish descent, and as an Israeli.

Israel is the birthplace of two large monotheistic religions: Judaism and Christianity. It is the homeland of the Jewish people, the place where the Hebrew tribes came together to form the Jewish nation, the place they have returned to after thousands of years of exile and persecution. It is also a country at war ever since its inception 64 years ago. Therefore, a lot of our identity as Israeli Jews is built on remembrance and on our ties to Jewish tradition and the ways of our fathers, and it is influenced by a common feeling of a society under siege. This feeling enforces solidarity and conservatism. All this is a heavy burden to carry when you are a Pagan priestess. With all the above weighing on my consciousness, how can I turn my back on tradition, especially when we, as Pagans, are taught to honor our ancestors?

As a Pagan, I believe monotheistic religion disconnects us from nature, from ourselves and our bodies, and from the concept of life as a cycle of life, death and rebirth, rather than a circle of punishment and domination. How do I reconcile these two aspects within me? How can we, as a Pagan community, reconcile them?[1]

There is no one way to be a priestess; each of us, as a unique individual with her unique connection to the Goddess, can bring her own vision into the role. The Goddess of many faces is enriched by priestesses with different understandings of their roles.

During my work as a priestess in the past ten or so years, and through my communication with the Goddess, I have come to realize that a priestess is not only what I do; it is who I am. It is both a private role (vis-à-vis the Goddess) and a public one. On a personal level, it means maintaining my connection to the Goddess, constantly revealing her various faces in my life and allowing her to teach me her lessons. On a public level, this means not focusing my practice only on my personal worship, but also taking on a community role, participating in public rituals and organizing rituals and teaching events. Furthermore, a priestess is naturally connected to her surroundings and influenced by them. It is her task to make a difference, to reclaim images of the Goddess that have been lost or distorted by thousands of years of patriarchy. I see it as my task, as a Pagan priestess and a witch, to turn the focus of our religious and spiritual experience from remembrance to sensation and action, to feeling and creating.

Jewish religion and Israeli culture have long been dominated by patriarchy and concepts of domination and control, rather than sharing and compassion. This is partly due to the constant state of pending war that makes militarism a very strong element in Israeli culture and society. But the ways of the Goddess are there to be rediscovered and reclaimed. This is one of our purposes as priestesses in this troubled land. Our task is to make this land truly a land of milk and honey, both symbols of the ever-giving, ever-nurturing face of the Goddess.

This work must be done without attracting attention to ourselves and to the Pagan community; although Israel is formally a democracy with freedom of religion a basic right in the Israeli legal system, the influence of the orthodox minority over legal issues and the public sphere reaches far beyond its percentage of the population. Therefore, like witches of the past, we must act in the shadow, we few, we happy few, we circle of sisters.

I see a special task for myself, as a priestess of the Goddess in Israel, in encouraging those who seek her to find her in our people's traditions, to uncover her from under the dark layers and lies of the Bible and its subsequent texts and legends.

As an example of this kind of work, I will describe a unique ritual I have facilitated, called "Reclaiming Adam and Eve."[2] The idea for this ritual was to return to the story of Adam and Eve in the Garden of Eden, a story that redefined the role of the Goddess and of women as inferior to God and man, thus setting the tone for an adversarial relationship between humankind and nature (personified by the serpent). The purpose of the ritual was to reclaim the ancient goddess of life and wisdom. Using the most basic myth of Judaism, this ritual was designed to re-imagine the Garden of Eden, with Eve as the Goddess and the two trees of life and wisdom her gifts. The Garden is the center of an all-encompassing, harmonic universe where the relationship between humanity and nature is that of union, not domination.

During the ritual, we invoked Eve as Goddess and the serpent as her consort. We set out to reinstate the Goddess to her place as giver of life, nourishment and wisdom, represented by the two trees in the garden: the tree of life and the tree of wisdom. The tree has long been a symbol of the Goddess; I consider the splitting of the tree into two to be one of many devices aimed at reducing the Goddess's all-encompassing unity into segregated territories. This was part of a process involving many more steps that devolved the Great Goddess into little more than a fertility symbol or sex icon.

In the context of this ritual, the serpent (as consort of the Goddess) was a symbol of the immediate and unmediated connection to nature that was lost in the years of monotheism. The image of the snake, as described in Genesis, engendered feelings of fear and distrust in nature, at the least, and justification for exploiting nature, at the worst. It then became necessary to discredit the snake, because the Israelites continued to think of the snake as a powerful healer well into the time of the first temple, and the snake was used as such even by the prophet Moses.

In order to make peace and heal our relationship with nature, we invited the snake to join our ritual by placing a beautiful clay image of a snake upon the altar. We then devoked the snake simply by passing it around widdershins (counter-clockwise) each of us saying goodbye to it in our own way. In my eyes, it was a beautiful reversal of the phrase ". . . and I will put enmity between thee and the woman, and between thy seed and her seed; it shall bruise thy head, and thou shalt bruise his heel."[3]

While in trance, we re-envisioned paradise as it might have been before the shift to monotheism changed our world from one based on communion with nature and partnership between the sexes, to one based on domination of nature and control of women. Finally, we graced ourselves with apples as an offering and a symbol of filling ourselves with the gifts of wisdom from the "forbidden tree" that the Goddess had shared with us. Eve was the one who introduced humanity to the mysteries of the Goddess using the fruit from the tree of life and wisdom, so the act of sharing the forbidden fruit is a small act of initiation. But this time, we are not being tempted; this time, we are actively choosing to eat the fruit the Goddess gave to us as a gift of knowledge. The wisdom is in knowing and appreciating our bodies as sacred, knowing the sacredness and interconnectedness of all nature and knowing the secret of living in communion with each other as man, woman, animal and green life.

An important part of the ritual was to share our thoughts and feelings regarding the myth of the Garden of Eden and, in this way, unravel its hidden meanings. We performed the ritual, naturally, in a sacred space—an inspiring and womb-like mud house. Discussing and sharing our thoughts in this sacred space allowed each participant to find his or her newly reclaimed images of Adam or Eve; this helped us reclaim our own unique masculinity and femininity and choose a more equal relationship between the two.

The Ritual
The story of Adam and Eve and the Garden of Eden is one of the founding myths in Western culture. So many of our most basic concepts about men, women, sexuality and the relationship between human life and nature are based upon what is described in this story, and thought of as holy truth. These concepts are entrenched deeply in our psyche; we are largely unaware of them. If we are to be free, we must first become aware of these basic concepts and of the roles they play in our lives, and then do our work as witches to change them.

Once we change our psyche, change in the real world will follow. I encourage you to read the outline of the ritual and perform the ritual yourself; this will enable you to discover for yourself how the story affects you personally, where and how it touches you, and which concepts you need to change for yourself.

Although I designed this ritual for a group, it can also be adapted to solitary practice. Choose a natural and pleasant location where you can perform the ritual privately. You will need a copy of the Bible, an image of the Goddess and an image of a snake or something to represent it (personally, I would avoid using snake skins that were extracted for the industry). You will also need bowls for cleansing, and water and apples for the offering.

Opening Statement

In this ritual, you will return to the story of Adam and Eve in the Garden of Eden. This story defined the role of the Goddess and of women as inferior to God and humanity, thus setting the tone for an adversarial relationship between humankind and nature, with nature personified by the serpent. To reclaim the ancient goddess of life and wisdom, you will re-imagine the Garden of Eden with Eve as the Goddess and the two trees of life and wisdom as her gifts. The Garden is the center of an all-encompassing harmonic universe where the relationship between humanity and nature is one of union, not domination and submission.

To purify the area of the ritual, use a clear glass bowl filled with water; sprinkle it around and see the water become clearer and more vibrant. To purify the self, use a clay bowl filled with water. Pass the bowl around the circle. Visualize all worries and aches, and whatever is not needed, and pour them into the bowl. When finished, remove this bowl from the circle.

Casting the Circle

Visualize yourself in a beautiful garden, filled with beautiful trees. There is a slight breeze, the air is clear and clean, the birds are singing pleasantly. You are at peace.

The garden is surrounded by four rivers of clear blue water coming from the center and flowing to each direction:

> To the east is the River Pishon.
> To the south is the River Gihon.
> To the west is the River Hiddekel.
> To the north is the River Euphrates.

As the rivers flow, they form a circle that holds us all together in a spirit of peace and good will as brothers and sisters. With this joint feeling, the circle is cast!

Invocations

Now invoke Eve as Goddess. You will reinstate her to her place as giver of life, nourishment and wisdom, she of the tree: the tree of life and wisdom. This tree has long been a symbol of the Goddess; call her as a symbol of unity of mind and body, and return to her, to a time and place before she was dissected and reduced.

Invocation to Eve

Place an image of the ancient goddess on the altar.

> *Tree of life,*
> *Blood of the birthing womb,*
> *Eve, our mother, mother of all life,*
> *You, who bring forth life,*
> *You, who are the source of wisdom,*
> *You, who walk besides us from birth to death,*
> *You, who were defiled and forgotten,*
> *You, whom we seek to reclaim,*
> *Eve, our mother, our teacher,*
> *Be welcome in our circle.*

Invocation to the Serpent [4]

Now invoke the Serpent, consort of the Goddess, a symbol of the immediate and unmediated connection to nature, the snake of healing and renewal. The image of the snake, as it is described in Genesis, engendered feelings of fear and distrust in nature, at the least, and justifications for exploitation, at the worst. The snake had to be discredited, because it was still being thought of as a powerful healer by the Israelites well into the time of the first temple, and was used as such even by the prophet Moses. Invoke the serpent and make peace with him in order to heal your relationship with nature. Invite the snake to join your ritual.

Place a clay image of a snake or something that can represent it on the altar, and say:

The Ssserpent,
Eternal, everlasting,
No end and no beginning,
The Ssserpent,
His silent glare alluring,
His sudden move can promise death
The Ssserpent,
Healer,
Consort,
Lover,
Priest
Beyond time,
Beyond space,
The Ssserpent . . .

Now, you are in this sacred space, with the presence of the Goddess and her consort, and your work begins. Read out loud the original story as it is written in Genesis 2:4–4:24, to remind everyone of the details and spirit of the story.

Now share your feelings and thoughts regarding the elements of the story: How does it make you feel?

If it is a mixed group, men and women can be separated into different groups to share, as the story contains different messages for men and women, and people may feel more comfortable sharing in a single-sex group. The purpose of the discussion is to bring to the surface the hidden agendas of the monotheistic religion and of patriarchy. Issues such as childbirth as a punishment to women, violence and control in a relationship, women as temptresses, the role of men and their relation to responsibility, our naked bodies as a source of shame and many more may be raised. Each person may find different verses or issues that speak to them, so allow ample time for sharing and discussion.

Next it is time for the work of transmutation to take place, the time for the magic to replace the distorted image of paradise with the feeling and knowledge of heaven on earth. This will be done in trance. Trance is a powerful tool to shift our consciousness. This is the "place" where you can connect with the deep self and with divinity—the place where magic happens.

The trance should be read aloud by one of the participants. If you are doing the ritual alone, read it and memorize it beforehand, and then visualize it step-by-step during the ritual.

The Trance [5]
Sit back or lie comfortably, letting your muscles relax, working from the crown of your head all the way down to your toes. Breathe deeply, letting air enter you deeper and deeper, letting it clean and refresh you. Your consciousness is expanding and you are feeling the fullness of your physical body, how well made and comfortable it is. It is expanding so you can feel your sisters and brothers around you, and you can feel the earth making up the solid ground on which you are lying. With the light winds, your consciousness is going out and pouring into the world around you. There are green growing plants everywhere, plants that can feed and heal you, trees that shade you from the warm sun, tiny and not-so-tiny animals living happily among the plants and within or on the ground. The buzz of insects and an occasional bird song fills the air. You are in paradise, and you were not even aware of this!

This beautiful place that sustains life, including your life, is the paradise you dream of, but it really is all around you. You walk in wonder among the paths, peek into corners and see your sisters and brothers walking in this garden, too. Everybody looks so serene and smiles. You make eye contact with them, smile back and embrace each other if you wish. Your clothes seem to drop away, and you find how good it feels when the sunlight, earth and wind touch your naked body.

Your random walk becomes focused and you are drawn to the center of the garden. You don't hear or see anything special, but you find yourself getting nearer to the center, where the shrubs and plants make room for a small clearing. Sunlight pours into this area and, in its midst, a very large woman is waiting for you. As you near her, you see she is part flesh and part tree bark, her arms are open to embrace you and her branches extend to shade you. You sit down at her feet, pressing against her body, her tree trunk. She caresses you and talks to you in murmurs and whispers. She says you are all her children, the whole world is filled with her children, and as she speaks you see each other as the children you used to be. She loves you, she is glad in your joy and happiness. She tells you your bodies are her design and gift, so you can live and enjoy the physical world.

You look at yourselves and each other and you are filled with joy and happiness; you are fully at peace. Listen carefully with all your senses, as she may have a special message for you. Her messages may appear in different forms.

After you have rested and filled yourself with this feeling of love and wonder, she tells you that you can go back to your adult body and your adult life, but she asks that you cherish and remember this feeling you have today and bring it back to your life, remember to view yourself and all others with love and trust, without shame or the will to dominate each other. She offers you each an apple from her branches, to nourish this knowledge within you.

You give her a hug and walk back through the clearing, passing through the garden until you see the place where you began your journey. You let your consciousness drift in and settle back in your resting body.

You slowly breath in and out, gently flexing and moving your muscles, starting from your feet and up through the body, until you open your eyes. You sit up carefully, and smile at each other. You are back, but you were never away. You are, as always, in her paradise.

You now grace yourselves with apples as an offering and as a symbol of filling yourselves with the gifts of wisdom from the tree that the Goddess has shared with you. Eve is the one who introduced humanity into the mysteries of the Goddess using the fruit of life and wisdom. The act of sharing the forbidden fruit is a small act of initiation. This time, though, you were not being tempted; this time, you were actively choosing to eat of the fruit that was given to you as a gift of knowledge from Goddess. This wisdom is in knowing and appreciating your body as sacred, knowing the sacredness and interconnectedness of all nature, knowing the secret of living in communion with each other as man, woman, animal and green life. With this act, you purposely and in free will embrace your newly reclaimed images of Adam or Eve, thus claiming your own unique masculinity and femininity and choosing a more equal relationship between the two.

At the time I performed this ritual, I was seven months pregnant, and I found it liberating to uproot a concept that was so deeply embedded in my psyche. The concept of childbirth as a punishment for Eve's sin is found in the phrase "in sorrow thou shalt bring forth children."[6] It is a completely different experience to approach the act of childbirth knowing that, with all the effort and pain involved, it is a blessing and a mystery, not a punishment. I am confident that this frame of mind has a lot to do with the way women in the Western world experience the act of childbirth.

Furthermore, I am a woman and, as such, I am an agent of initiation and my relationship to my "husband" is that of companionship and mutual desire—quite the opposite from the punishment set upon women in the Bible, where it says that "thy desire shall be to thy husband, and he shall rule over thee."[7]

Devocations

Devocation of the snake involves simply passing it around widdershins, with each person saying goodbye to it in their own way. In my eyes, this is a beautiful reversal of the phrase, "And I will put enmity between thee and the woman, and between thy seed and her seed; it shall bruise thy head, and thou shalt bruise his heel."[8]

Perform the devocation of the Goddess in front of her image on the altar and say:

Tree of life
Blood of the birthing womb,
Eve, our mother, mother of all life,
Eve, our mother, our teacher,
We thank you for the enlightenment you shared with us,
For the gifts of life, death and wisdom,
Thank you for gracing us with your presence in this ritual.

You may feel reluctant to open the circle and lose the feeling of harmony and peace that you now share. Take a moment to bask in that feeling, though eventually it will be time to open the circle. Call to mind again the image of the four rivers encircling you in the center of the circle, the light breeze and the singing of birds. Embrace the feeling of unity with your brothers and sisters and with all the life that surrounds you. Know that this paradise is here and is yours even after you open the circle. Allow that feeling to sink into your consciousness and release the circle. The circle is open.

Endnotes

1 The views and ideas expressed in this essay reflect my own thoughts, none other. The Israeli pagan community is small and encompasses many individual views regarding diverse issues like leadership, priestessing, thea/ology, community and Judaism. In this essay I share my personal views only.
2 This ritual, which I co-priestessed with another priest and priestess, was held during Mabon Festival in 2011.

3 Genesis 3:15.
4 My deepest gratitude to Or Ben Shabat, my life partner and co-priest in the ritual, for this inspiring aspecting-like invocation.
5 My deepest thanks to Dana Elias, my co-priestess in this ritual, for this text.
6 Genesis 3:16.
7 Ibid.
8 Genesis 3:15.

Flamekeeper: Priestess of Brighid
By Erin Lund Johnson

I am a Priestess of Brighid.[1] I am a flamekeeper in devotion to her, a path-walker of a spiritual tradition dedicated to her, a scholar in pursuit of knowledge dear to her and a Mother Priestess reviving a priestesshood and sisterhood in honor of her. This is my work and this is my way.

As a flamekeeper, I tend the Living Flame of Brighid every nineteen nights with other women tending in kind, and Brighid herself tending on the twentieth night. This stems from an Irish tradition kept by nuns dedicated to Saint Brighid, but many postulate that the practice derived from an earlier priestesshood and temple at the church site in Kildare. No longer solely a single flame tended in shifts on site, the flame has spread around the world as devotees have spiritually carried it via both lit and extinguished wicks to personal altars, where it is brought to life and faithfully renewed every 24 hours in a new location. This devotion has become a deeply meaningful practice for me.

Brighid made herself vividly known to me over ten years ago, in a flash of light, heat and imagery during a Reiki attunement, and flame-tending vigils have been opportunities to foster our relationship. I make prayers and offerings to her, sing songs to her and rest quietly within her light. I meditate and feel her healing energy, and in one meditation I began to travel with her in an otherwordly *immram*, an Irish word for spirit journey. We have built a special place together, which I now visit regularly in spirit, to commune with her and receive her guidance and wisdom. After each vigil I share my experiences with my sister flamekeepers, as do they after theirs, and through this sharing we build our own Well of Wisdom, from which we all may sip that we might grow together in Brighid's light. As a flame-keeper, I tend her healing well through stewardship of a portion of riverbank in my area, cleaning up debris, leaving offerings of food and song, and communing with the land goddess there. I consider Brighid to be my spiritual foster mother, in the Irish tradition, as she has led me to the cultural and polytheistic traditions of my Gaelic ancestors.

As a path-walker, I have developed a spiritual practice centered on her. It is designed to create meaningful moments of communion in sync with everyday living, and flows with daily, weekly, monthly and quarterly rhythms. Communing with Brighid every day has deepened my relationship with her, as it keeps me aware of her constant presence in my life. Each morning and evening, I invoke her blessings and protection with a short prayer and self-blessing, and I feel her energy and essence within me at these moments. I honor her daily at my hearth, the spiritual center of my home, where her heat, via electricity now, cooks my family's food and brings us together at mealtimes. I keep a corn dolly beside it as an icon for her, with a candle and a small cauldron in which to place offerings for her from our family dinners. I invoke her blessings upon the household in the morning when I turn on the stove to cook my breakfast, and I invoke her protection upon us in the evening as I lock up the house at night, leaving the light on over the stove. Once each week, I make a formal offering to her at the hearth, thanking for her many gifts. At new and full moons I make the *immram*, or spirit journey, to our special place, to drink from her cup of wisdom, and receive her *imbas*, or inspiration. And at each of the four Irish fire festivals, I honor one of her four fires with ritual and offerings: the fires of the head, hands, heart and hearth.

As a scholar, I pursue knowledge akin to what I feel traditional priestesses would have sought and valued: star lore, herb lore, Celtic lore and Women's Mysteries. I feel that traditional priestesses would have been a part of the druidic class and on par with the druid's stores of knowledge, if of a slightly different kind or obtained in a different manner; and I feel that flame-keepers today could be seen to be on par with modern druids, should they choose to pursue a spiritual tradition and a course of study as druids do.

As Mother Priestess, I developed all of these facets within the sisterhood of Nigheanan Brìghde (Gaelic for Brighid's Daughters), the Order of Brigidine Priestesses and Flamekeepers. As a flamekeeping order for the Goddess Brighid, it felt right to revive her priestesshood in modern dress so she might continue to guide us in our modern lives today. As a priestesshood would have shared a common spiritual tradition and course of study, so have I developed these offerings within the Order, in addition to the traditional devotion of flame-keeping and the unique service of well-tending. I initiated the practice of vigil-sharing after each shift to help us grow together as a sisterhood, rather than only as a collection of disparate individuals, and have grown closer to my sisters through it. I have also developed a group water-blessing ritual for the sisterhood to participate in collectively during Brighid's vigil, in which we sing over and bless bowls of water, which we then release into the land or our local waterways to spread their healing and blessings through the world. This enhances our connections to both Brighid and each other, strengthening our sisterhood and our collective healing intent through devotion to a goddess of healing.

As a devotee of Brighid, I am her priestess and spiritual foster daughter and, through nurturing my relationship with her, I have found my calling as Mother Priestess of an Order in honor of her, reviving her priestesshood for women today. I feel that a complete flamekeeper's priestess tradition has a place in this world and fills an important niche. It is the most prominent way in which I hold aloft the light of Brighid and keep it burning brightly as a beacon to all her daughters to see its glow and follow its flame, should Brighid call them to do so.

Endnote

1 Brìghid is spelled various ways (Brigid, Brigit, Brihde), but all refer to the same Irish saint and the Goddess who pre-dated her.

Holy Bite*

By Le'ema Kathleen Graham

The seventh snakebite, the worst I've ever received, was at a dance event on Samhain in 2007. I was asked to perform with my snake for the finale of the show and afterward lead a ritual spiral dance with the cast and the audience.

Two women had fought in the dressing room where my boa, Isis, was tucked in her basket in the corner. It seemed my sensitive snake had contracted the hostile energy in the space. When I came to gather her up for our dance and gently removed her covering, she jabbed her jaws into my left forearm and constricted tightly. I was taken aback and frightened. She wouldn't release her grip and I had to pull her off. This left a gaping wound that gushed blood. There were only two minutes before I had to go on stage, but the bite was serious and I needed help fast.

I motioned to a couple of dancers who were watching from the wings. One held my arm still, applying pressure above the wound, while the other cleaned it off quickly and applied antiseptic and a bandage. A third dancer standing nearby placed her snake bracelet over the bandage to hold it in place in an empowering gesture of sisterhood.

The music started. There is nothing like the ever-present now of being on stage that forces one to be completely in the moment. This time it was even more intense. I walked on stage in a composed manner, yet in an extremely altered and alert state: a goddess-embodied trance. I often choreographed my dances, but this time the serpent came through me, weaving the chaotic energies into reverence. Slow, dreamy music

---

* From *Dancing the Inner Serpent: Memoirs of a Suburban Snake Priestess* (Goddesswork: 2009, 2013).

soothed the audience and Isis calmed. The dance poured out of my body with surprising physical strength, from my legs, through my belly and out through my heart. No one noticed my injured arm.

The serpent's bite opened me to the fullness of my role as priestess. Ancient priestesses learned their particular function as part of the snakebite initiation. What the serpent chose to teach, the priestess learned to offer to others. I understood immediately that I was to hold soft, wise feminine energy and spread it throughout the group—smoothing the profane atmosphere into sacred space. To bring the people together in ceremony required this grounding and centering of the priestess.

We were now ready to invite our ancestors to join us. The voice of the snake came through me low, deep and strong:

> *Tonight is a special night. The veil between the worlds is thin, allowing us to make contact with our beloved dead. They are happy to be with us and want to help us fulfill the dream of the people. Touch the floor and speak their names. Ask them for help in your lives. Now we shall dance on the heads of our ancestors.*

Everyone touched the floor, calling in the ancestors. Then we flowed into a spiral dance while looking into each other's eyes, and sang:

> *Spiraling into the center, the center of the wheel, I am a weaver, I am the woven one, I am a dreamer, I am the dream.*

The bite was not easily healed. Since I was leaving for Egypt in five days, I saw my homeopath. She explained how to care for the wound and informed me that it was not an accident; it was a "holy act." It needed to happen before the trip to help me stand strong in the face of adversity. She gave me a new snake venom remedy: Viper!

After boarding the plane with my bandaged arm, I opened a book, *The Mysteries of Isis*, by DeTraci Regula. In it, she recounts the story of Ra, the Sun God, who has grown old and incompetent:

Isis decides that she cannot allow the destruction of the universe to occur and becomes determined to obtain the Secret Name of Ra, the supreme word of power, which will allow her to heal him and to also be able to rule in his place if necessary.[1]

She fashions a serpent out of the mud formed by the spittle of Ra. When the great serpent bites him, she offers to save his life if he will reveal his secret name, the source of his power. With the exchange in place, she chants his name to heal him so that he may continue his path through the heavens.

As the plane circled over the pyramids in the land of the Goddess Isis, I looked out the window and then at the wound on my arm, and realized that she even healed through the bite of the serpent. I wondered whether the bite on my arm was prophetic, reminding me, as a priestess, to make myself available for the personal transformation of others.

Endnote

1 DeTraci Regula, *The Mysteries of Isis* (Woodbury, MN: Llewelyn, 2002), 84.

The Unfolding One
By Jill Hammer

Tree of Life, you are seared stump
and seed. Weaver and stoneworker,

you spin the thread of life
and carve the channel through to death.

Womb of ice and sun, you scatter snow
and melt the fishponds.

Gate and boundary, you are a door to the stars
and a wall between atoms.

You are the dance floor and the eulogy,
From umbilical cord to umbilical cord, you are She.

You are the skin we wrap around our hollows,
and you are the marrows of our bones.

You are the infused oil of memory,
and the blood that forgets again, again, again.

You flow through us when we bathe the child and dip the bride
and wash the dead. In all the worlds we say your names.

The Priestess as Wedding Ceremonialist
By Josephine MacMillan

What business does a modern priestess have officiating a marriage? For hundreds of years, once a woman entered into the institution of matrimony, she had few legal rights. Not so long ago, a married woman lost everything from her name to her property in exchange for a man's simple promise to protect and provide for her and their children. It's hard to believe that, here in the United States, "land of the free," people were once forbidden to marry each other because of their skin color; yet today, in the same effort of control, most states deny couples their right to marry each other based on their gender. Moreover, women from most religious faiths continue to be banned from performing weddings. Why would a feminist devoted to serving the Goddess ever get into the wedding game, given its oppressive, sexist, racist, homophobic roots? As an American priestess in the business of performing weddings since 1992, I meditate on that question every time I'm asked to officiate one.

Marriage historically has been a survival strategy, a method for ensuring economic security and a stable environment for a couple and their offspring. It was originally a kind of cool-headed business agreement. It's only been in the last century that marriage became the romanticized tale of those who have found soul mates with whom they will happily live forever. Some people still hold on to this interpretation, but in more recent times marriage in Western society has emerged as the social, economic and political gold standard of relationships. Marriage is seen as a social decree that two people are making the "ultimate" commitment to one another (presumably they're pledging to live together, sleep only with one another, share debt and finances, and so on).

Marriage is becoming a kind of economic status symbol, as it's happening more in the upper classes and less in the lower. Marriage, precisely because it has a history of discrimination, has become a unique vehicle for addressing and correcting political, social and religious injustices.

Some of my reasons for performing weddings, I admit, are political, but I have other reasons, as well. Decades ago, a feminist fresh out of college, I began my profession as a ritual priestess, clairvoyant and spiritual healer. My first inclination was to reject my clients' requests that I perform their weddings, as I believed the custom was outdated. I was surprised when Spirit instructed me to officiate marriages despite my resistance, saying there were lessons to be learned and great healing to take place in this practice. Since then, I've stood in sacred groves, back yards and public gardens, tiny cottages and great halls, by magical springs and seaside, as the couples I wed imbued sacred meaning and profound beauty into the marriage tradition, and showed me how it can be made into a relevant custom and rewarding spiritual journey for many progressively minded people today.

For example, Daniel, a man whose wedding I performed years ago, recently told me that he, a self-described introverted and independent type, had thought that marriage would mean the loss of himself in exchange for a partnership. Instead, he found marriage to be an experience of expansion. He says: "I'm forced to include or say yes to things I would never have experienced if left to my own devices. Expansive. $1 + 1 = 10$. This is surprising." Daniel remembers that he and his wife stated one primary intention for their marriage: "To always return to openness, no matter what, and it's served us well." The marriage has inspired great spiritual growth for him. He explains, "This recognition that I am profoundly connected with another person has translated into a tacit experience of oneness with life itself . . . I'm working with life, not reacting against it. This is a fundamental shift. No longer a little ego being the effect of life, but a connected god-man . . . This shift can be traced back to the surrender of my 'separateness' with my wife. 'Is this my hot flash, or my wife's? What's the difference?' My little man-brain had to experience it in relationship with another, and then it shifted to my relationship to life."

Hearing the relationship stories of the couples I married long ago is the most fulfilling part of my job. I continue to be inspired by their exquisite journeys with love, long after they've left the altar.

Couples have hired me as a priestess to work with them in co-creating ceremonies that invoke the role of the Divine Feminine, the Goddess, into their wedding services and, they say, their relationships as well. People are hungry for the life-giving, forgiving, nurturing and fiercely loving presence of the Great Mother in their lives and present in their rituals. In performing wedding services, I learned that the priestess has an important voice in this ongoing controversial conversation on marriage. She has an active role envisioning a new story or perhaps reclaiming the original sacred meaning and mystery of marriage.

Over the years, the demand for priestess services has grown, but there have been few professionals in the field to respond, so, in 2002, I set out to change this equation. I decided to build a modern college of priestesses to perform weddings, as well as other rites, and founded Belladonna Sanctuary, a religious corporation dedicated to preserving women's spiritual traditions and exploring contemporary practice. Here we provide classes on the herstory of the Goddess, women's ancient and contemporary global spiritual traditions and eco-feminist theology. Belladonna trains people in the arts of seer-ship, trance-mediumship, subtle energetic healing and spiritual midwifery. We teach how to design wedding ceremonies and perform sacred rituals. Belladonna also offers courses about the legal rights and responsibilities of ordained priestesses, and offers tools for building a successful professional practice.

The act of becoming an ordained priestess is life-changing. Dawn, for years a minister in a church that referred to Creator as "he," transitioned to a path as an ordained priestess and began invoking the Goddess and referring to Source as "she." After ordination, she says, she experienced an immediate shift in consciousness and a palpable change in her physical being. She felt a sense of invigoration and began to dream of the Goddess. Most potent, she says, was that she noticed she became impossible to control or manipulate! In a variety of situations, men would invalidate her, insist she take orders from them or follow their lead and, if she didn't agree, she simply refused. This was completely different than how she used to behave in relationships with men. Standing with her title and crown as a priestess was like pushing the "on" switch to her personal power.

Do I need the government to sanction my title as priestess in order to be one? I believe the answer is no. Women will continue to reclaim all of the powers stolen from them, including those of the priestess, without certification or anyone's permission. However, the act of receiving recognition by the United States government that I function as a priestess and am joined in a force of many intensifies and legitimizes the power of the priestess on an institutional level; this legitimization then ripples out into the world and challenges those organizations that refuse to recognize women's spiritual authority.

Establishing an organization that the United States government recognizes and sanctions, as "an eco-feminist church serving all individuals interested in goddess traditions," has been deeply restorative to me, as I hope it is for all those traumatized by the violent oppression of earth-based belief systems and practices. Given the world history of persecution of spiritual women and the continuing violence against and resistance to women in roles of public leadership, it's deeply comforting and important to me that Belladonna Sanctuary legally protects its priestesses. With their California State license stating they are religious clergy, Belladonna's ordained priestesses may serve their communities as recognized spiritual leaders (without interference or inquisition) and legally perform services such as intuitive/psychic readings and spiritual counseling, spiritual healing through mediumship and the laying-on of hands, and officiate marriages. All of these acts by women were prohibited and punishable not long ago.

There are many types of priestesses. Their numbers flourished in ancient times and they are on the rise today. Here's a list of some of their most recognized roles and specializations: spiritual advisors and teachers; priestesses of sacred dance, art, music and song; healers and priestesses of sacred medicine; priestesses of sacred adornment and beautification; sexual priestesses; spiritual midwives of major transitions such as birth and death; seeresses, channels, mediums and oracles; and ritual priestesses who perform ceremony. A woman may focus on a single role or weave a multiple of these arts into her practice, shaping her unique style and service as a priestess.

Priestesses of goddess-and earth-based traditions are uniquely suited to provide wedding-related services that most religious organizations don't offer. For example, I have found that couples from diverse backgrounds are attracted to the Pagan tradition of handfasting, the custom of literally "tying the knot." In a handfasting, the wrists of a couple are tied with a single ribbon or rope and they declare their wish to enter into a union for a year and a day. At the end of this time period, they're free to announce their decision to either renew the relationship agreement or end it. I have had experiences in which couples have used a handfasting as an engagement ritual, used it instead of a legally registered marriage or used it as a tenet within their marriage ceremony.

When a goddess-honoring priestess facilitates a wedding, themes of the Divine Feminine, rituals of earth reverence and celebrations of the seasons are often woven into the ceremonies. Also common is the acknowledgment of children, community, ancestors, animals and nature spirits in the service. Recognition of the body, sexuality, sensuality and pleasure is highlighted. The choice of a priestess as ceremonialist is common for couples who wish their ceremonies to be outside in natural settings or inside non-traditional venues such as private homes, yurts, geodesic domes or caves. It's popular in today's weddings to have a priestess and priest co-officiate. The pair represents the balanced value of both male and female energies, divine mother and father, in the marriage.

In addition to performing nuptials, priestesses may facilitate divorce ceremonies. The act of dissolving a marriage contract is considered by some to be as important as its inception. The method of ending a sacred agreement, if handled with love and consciousness, is thought to impact a couple's karma and new relationships in the future.

Given the large number of people who officiate weddings in the name of a male god, I urge more priestesses to move out of the safety of their private women's circles and perform more rituals in public. The very act of a woman standing in front of a community consecrating a marriage shifts people's perception of female power on a deep and subconscious level. It can't help but shift our perception of God. It tickles our ancient genetic memory that firmly believed that God was a woman.

Once it's accepted (or remembered) that women can preside over religious functions, receive communication from spirit, connect to the divine and be conduits of this power, they are then on equal footing with men. On a very primal level, seeing women hold power in the public spiritual sphere stimulates people's belief and trust that women can therefore be authorities in other places, as in political office or corporations. The impact of the symbolic role of the priestess in public ritual reaches into our psyche; this is why it's important that priestesses be seen performing public rituals and openly invoking the Goddess. Men have long understood the dangers posed to them by women's spiritual leadership in public circles. This is why women have not only been banned from performing wedding rites, but have, for centuries and throughout the world, been branded as "witches" and systematically tortured and killed in order to imprint our cultural memory with the heated reminder never to return to this profession.

There is now a need for women to be seen once again as spiritual authorities advocating for the feminine divine, the female face of God, in large social and political spheres. In this sense, the priestess who performs weddings engages in a form of spiritual, social and political activism. The most extreme repression of women and girls is demonstrated by the great world religions' persistent rejection of the female as an aspect of the divine creator. To defy this religious propaganda and publicly reclaim the feminine divine is deeply and palpably restorative, not only to women, but men as well, as the Goddess resides in the hearts of all.

She Hexes Newscasters*
By Patricia Monaghan

What else could I do? For weeks
it had been one intolerable
word after another, war and
war and war again and it seemed

so easy. A word from me, and
songs sprayed from their mouths,
automatic carols: praise
for the caliber of clouds
and the blue shrapnel sky,
the bombardment of rain,
praise for the maneuvers
of finches and ravens, praise—

but it is not enough, even though
it is my strongest spell, making
beauty out of words. I repeat it,
I repeat it nightly, I burn
blue candles just to keep them
singing. Oh I want real power:

---

* From *Seasons of the Witch: Poetry and Songs to the Goddess* (Cottage Grove, WI: Creatrix Books, 2004)

that soldiers, aiming at men's
hearts, see into them and stop,
that presidents invoke old
powers—earth and wind and
all their deputies—that
generals sit before their maps
telling rapt stories of the dawn.

The Priestess's Toolkit

The Priestess's Tool Kit

A prayer from a priestess to her goddess opens this section:

> I am your vessel.
> She through whom you speak.
> The cup into which you pour yourself
> as you flow like wine.
>
> —Katie Anderson, "The Star Chalice"

As priestesses, we look to those who guide us, we gather the pieces, we recognize what is helpful to priestessing and we develop our own unique approaches to the task. This section provides some methods, skills and tools for those who assume the ancient title of priestess.

Priestessing requires one to have knowledge of a myriad of techniques. Included are a number of pieces on ritual design and facilitation, as this is primary work for many priestesses. Leading chants and harnessing the power of energy and rhythm are foundational skills for ritualists. The use of altars and incense add deepening layers to ritual, and techniques of performance enhance the experience, intensifying the impact for all.

Priestessing almost always involves groups and all groups have their inner dynamics. A priestess will be more effective if she recognizes those dynamics and responds to them in a constructive fashion. This is not easy, and nor does it come naturally to most people; in fact, this may be the most demanding and frustrating part of priestessing. Therefore, we have included a number of pieces addressing the complexities of groups.

Because a priestess holds the circle of adherents together, and beyond that opens the path for other women to become priestesses, this section encompasses practical and theoretical works on ordination and initiation.

"As within, so without" are key words to priestesses and priestessing. Integral to priestessing is the integrity of the priestess. Experience shows what works well, and what doesn't; several contributions address that topic. Because the role of priestess can be stressful, we need to develop and understand our internal processes and care for ourselves. We cannot care for others if we ourselves are frazzled, fragmented or fatigued. There are also pieces here to help with understanding internal processes, generating stillness within and connecting with the sacred.

At the end of the day we are all human, vested with the foibles and habits we were born with or have accrued in the process of living. It is the transformation of ourselves that is the magic:

> This that we have now
> is the crone's cauldron of changes.
> Together we season and stir,
> taste, season and stir some more
> until
> boiling, embroiling,
> bubbling and troubling,
> roiling and toiling,
> shifting and shaping
> the vital essence of our selves
> is changed
> into the elixir of holiness.
> —*Abbi Spinner McBride, "The Crone's Cauldron of Changes"*

Star Chalice

By Katie Anderson

Great Queen of the Heavens
I am your daughter.
I feel the pulse of your breath
upon my skin
And your hands upon my spine
that you hold, like two curtains
You are about to burst open and enter.

I am your vessel.
She through whom you speak.
The cup into which you pour yourself
as you flow like wine.

I am your daughter
And I wear your star.

Thin Places
By Breyn Marr

Ancient Celtic mystics said "thin places" are those places and spaces where the distance between heaven and earth—the sacred and the mundane—becomes ever-so-small. Thin places are most often talked about as physical places where the presence of the Divine can be felt differently, more fully, than in ordinary places. Your place of religious worship might be a thin place. The yoga studio you frequent or the altar space you have created in your home might be thin places. Your grandmother's kitchen during family gatherings or the women's healing circle you attend might be thin places. Within nature there are many thin places. And thin places can also be conjured up from deep within our own souls. Regardless of their physical "where-ness," or their source of origination, thin places always inspire in us a sense of awe or reverence. They create in us an urge to fall to our knees and surrender to that which is so much greater than us, and yet to which we are inextricably bound and of which we are part.

My question for priestesses—both as individuals and as a collective of modern-day mystics re-membering, re-vealing and re-birthing the feminine into our psyches and the world around us—is this: What if we lived our lives from the perspective that, everywhere we go, everything we do and everyone we meet is an opportunity to experience a thin place and be in communion with the Goddess, the Divine? What if we were to live as though heaven already exists on Earth? What if we were to approach daily chores as we would ritual or meditation? What if we, as priestesses, were to take it on as our sacred duty, our joyful burden, to guide others to see and experience their lives as thin and purposeful, as well?

STEPPING INTO OURSELVES

The truth about thin places, and about our contact and relationship with the Divine, is that it is not always easy, joyful or without challenges. We work on connecting and showing curiosity and compassion toward whatever questions, discomfort, negative reactions and difficult emotions arise as we move through our lives, because viewing these as thin places, too, is part of what we have been called to do in this life. This is where we deepen into ourselves and our priestesshood. This is where true learning and development of our inherent gifts occurs. This is where we experience alchemy—where our lead is turned into gold. I truly believe our work is to do all of this, but it is also bigger than this—much bigger.

The ability to always view the whole of our lives and all of our choices and interactions as thin places helps us lift our heads to see upward into our individual and collective dreams and visions for the way the world can be, the kind of relationship we can have with one another and the earth, and the kind of new reality we are co-creating for our world. But seeing is just a starting place.

Priestesshood is an ancient path of sacred leadership. Priestesshood is creating new ways of being, living, working and playing for the purpose of creating change. Priestesshood is action.

The priestess's path is about navigating between many worlds, accessing the heavens and embodying heaven on earth. Of course, we must be seers, but we must also be do-ers, be-ers, believers and change-makers. We must move toward fostering awe in others, fostering reverence and appreciation for both the mundane and the breathtaking, the shadow and the light. We must do this because we all see different parts of the dreams and visions, and we need everyone's parts to move toward the whole—toward bringing about new, peaceful and just paradigms.

The entire world is a thin place. We are thin places. The Divine already lives within us. We are walkers of an ancient path of sacred leadership. We are leaders. We are priestesses.

Hearing the Call of Service: The Priestess Path*
By Ruth Barrett

To be a leader, you must first learn to serve. The path to becoming a priestess begins with a calling; her voice speaking to your spirit, awakening you to the knowledge that your life has a specific purpose. You may experience the feeling of "coming home" that so many women describe upon awakening to the Goddess and her ways. Becoming a priestess is a deep and dedicated process of learning how to use and serve with this awareness. You may have the feeling that the Goddess is calling you and you must answer, but, ultimately, you alone must choose whether to serve.

Why is service integral to priestess work? What does it mean to serve others spiritually? In many ways, spiritual service is about empowering a community to identify and support its own needs. For me, serving women is serving the Goddess: I don't see any difference. When I am ministering to women, my challenge is to open my heart, mind and hands, allowing the Goddess to work through me. In many ways, being a good leader is also like being a good mother: listening, setting boundaries, helping others see how their behavior affects others, and being negotiable (with some bottom lines).

Loving the Goddess, and even having a personal relationship with a particular aspect of her, is basic to Dianic Witchcraft and its practitioners. Feeling that a particular goddess speaks to you is a part of the practice of witchcraft that can develop over time. Some women call themselves priestesses out of a desire to express love, commitment or devotion to a

---

* From *Women's Rites, Women's Mysteries: Intuitive Ritual Creation* (Woodbury, MN: Llewellyn Worldwide, 2007).

particular goddess. It must be understood, however, that the term "priestess" is relational not just to the Goddess or to oneself, but to those whom one serves.

The word "witch" can describe a woman who is completely self-defined, practicing alone or with others without performing acts of service to a community. It is not possible, however, for a priestess to be completely self-defined, as her coven or spiritual community must also recognize her as a resource in their service.

What is a community, especially a spiritual community? The Oxford Universal Dictionary's definition of community is "a body of people having common organization or interests or living in the same place under the same laws; common character; agreement; identity." Many women consider themselves involved in many communities. Thus, "community" may include the larger global sisterhood of women, the geographic area where one resides, special interest groups, and spiritual circles. All of these circles require various levels of participation and intimacy. A woman priestessing in a spiritual community must feel and consistently demonstrate her commitment to the growth and well-being of the women she serves. As a result, she may wear many hats: as teacher, mentor, friend and sister community member with her own needs.

Although it's a good beginning, loving the Goddess, in itself, does not make one a priestess, just as being a devout Jew or Christian does not automatically make one a rabbi, priest or minister. My initial reaction when a woman says that she wants to be a priestess is to howl inside like a maniacal coyote! "Why would she want to do that? Is she crazy?" It is, at times, so incredibly hard.

What is your motivation for leadership? The title of priestess sounds mystical and powerful, and conjures up fantasy images of flowing robes, crescent tiaras, charged magical tools at your fingertips and rooms full of chanting, awe-eyed devotees lingering on your every muse-inspired word. You dispense wisdom directly from the Goddess herself, channeled in perfection to the unquestioning multitudes that wait and depend on your guidance.

If that's your vision, get another hobby.

The reality is this: You will be the last one left in the rented hall, scraping candle-wax droppings off the floor with a razor blade.[1] Even though you try to delegate volunteers to help with the cleanup, when women slip through the cracks at the end of the night, it is your butt on the line because you rented the place. You will be blamed for everything and anything that goes wrong—not just in the ritual, but in the lives of the people who attend the event. You will become the archetypal "mother to the masses," with everyone's feelings and unfinished business with their parents, their bosses and the last lover who dumped them projected onto you. You will be sick of politics and held to a standard of personal conduct that no one can, or should, maintain. You will want to quit many times over, all the while knowing that the only path that exists is forward.

Why would you consider the priestess path? Do you want attention from your community? Do you think you will feel better about yourself? Do you want to feel extra special or important? If you say "yes" to any of these questions, look for another hobby. If your need to do this work is ego-driven, your expectations are based on a fantasy that will not sustain you when the hard reality sets in.

In considering the responsibility of becoming a priestess, ask the following questions: What does the title of "priestess" mean to you? Do you feel that there ought to be criteria and standards for priestesses that women can expect from someone who calls herself by that title? If you could set these standards, what would they be and why? What standards do you set for your own priestess work? How do you know that you have met your own standards? What expectations do you have of a woman who calls herself a priestess? Why do you think you are good priestess material? Do you have a loving and compassionate heart? Is it your passion to serve the Goddess by serving women and Mother Earth as a vocation? Do you have proven creativity and skills? Do you wish to offer them in service to others? Are you deepening your skills in order to help others? What experience do you have in taking on leadership responsibilities? Do you feel that you are, or would be, a good group facilitator? Do you have the ability to communicate well and connect compassionately with others? Have you acquired skills and practice in conflict resolution and group process? Are you willing to be accountable for your actions, say when you are wrong and apologize when it is due? Have you made a commitment to the ongoing process and journey of knowing yourself, accepting both your challenges and strengths?

Working to evolve beyond our patriarchal conditioning and build a truly feminist world is a challenging task, yet this personal commitment is essential for priestess work. What personal work have you done to examine any internalized racism you may have? What personal work have you done to examine issues of class, sexism and homophobia? A woman on the priestess path must understand that this examination, called "self-facing" in my community, can be extremely painful. How a woman communicates and uses and shares her energy is dependent on her vigilant awareness of herself and the unconscious tendencies and unexamined habits she has learned from her culture.

If you have the desire to empower and assist others in making their lives more meaningful, you might be on the right path. You will need great courage, will and discipline to develop yourself as a tool of spiritual service. Once you become a priestess, you have made a commitment for life.

In discussing what it is to be a priestess, I realize that every woman who takes on this mantle does not share my standards and expectations. I ask a lot from women who train and step up to serve, just as I continue to ask a lot from myself. I want only the best for women and therefore I want priestesses to be prepared to stand alone, if necessary, and work in partnership alongside their sisters in community. To serve a community as a priestess, a woman will ideally undergo specialized training and personal development. The process takes years and involves patience, personal sacrifice and dedication. It takes years of hard work to gain knowledge and experience, integrate it, practice it and understand how to serve with it. A woman on the priestess path learns that time is her friend. It gives her the accumulation of experiences that will enrich and transform her into someone who can serve her community effectively. The years of training, thinking, experiences, challenges and visioning contribute to the quality of her work in the world. If her training is deep, she will not be the same person who began the journey. Like the Goddess Inanna, she will descend through the seven gates to the underworld, hang dying on the hook of her fears and doubts, and rise again to the heavens. She will doubt and question everything. She will continue to question everything for the rest of her life.

Service is not servitude, as in placing yourself or others either above or below. To work effectively, there must be relationships of mutual honor between the priestess and the women she serves. Service becomes self-destructive or martyrdom when it becomes a harmful burden, a yoke, and is disconnected from its previous or original motivation. It is important for a priestess to set and keep a standard of self-care in which she models healthy living practices and healthy relationships. She must be able to receive support from her sisters. She must confront her own internalized misogyny, be self-respectful and present the consistent expectation that her community treat her with respect and love. It is imperative that she develop the skills of discernment and learn to gently diffuse challenging situations.

As women raised in a patriarchal society, we are all too skilled at participating in our own abuse. By the time a woman has reached the point where she feels resentful, she has long since crossed the line between service and self-victimization. When this happens—and it will—she should pause and ask a trusted elder or another priestess for feedback and help in order to regain her energy and perspective.

So why would anyone become a priestess? If it is what you are here to do, any negative experiences or fears cannot deter you from your passion to create and serve in this way. With the right attitude, challenges will only make you stronger, providing you with invaluable life experience, personal growth and the knowledge that you are contributing in a uniquely powerful way to the lives of others. As you work compassionately alongside your sisters to heal from your own internalized oppression, you will add strength to the evolution of human consciousness that the Goddess represents. You will be a part of the morphogenetic field that is growing to restore the Goddess and her teachings to her daughters.

Priestess Specialties
In the Dianic tradition, we do not have first, second and third degrees, as many other Wiccan traditions do. Instead, we have recognized

developmental stages of learning and skill that can evolve into expertise or into answering one's calling to become a priestess. These stages are called *initiate* (a woman who has studied the minimum of a year and a day and chooses to self-initiate or be formally initiated as a witch), *priestess* (a woman who has developed her ministry) and *high priestess* (a priestess with many specialties who can perpetuate her tradition and create and maintain community). Most often, the high priestess is also a *ritualist* who can facilitate the rites of our tradition and holds the center energetic in the rituals.

In the Dianic tradition, a priestess develops and then names her own ministerial specialty in her own words. For example, I have ordained, among others, women who named their priestess path as "Priestess of Morphogenesis" (meaning "form coming into being"), "Priestess of the Veil," "Priestess of Her Voice," "Priestess of the Signs and Symbols of Astrology," "Priestess of Her Mysteries," "Priestess of Visual Arts," "Priestess of Mothering," "Priestess of the Singing Spirit," "Priestess of the Guardian Path," "Ritual Priestess," "Priestess of Her Wisdom" and "Temple Priestess." Some of these ministries are highly individualized and personal, such as "Priestess of Her Voice." In the herstory of the Dianic tradition, very personalized ministries such as these were not expected to be taught to others, even though these women were expected to provide spiritual service through their specialty's naming. It is my hope that, as our tradition evolves, all priestess specialties will be encouraged, taught and mentored so that options for service may be visible to others who are called to the same work.

Thus far, ministries such as Ritual Priestess, Guardian Priestess, Drum Priestess, Temple Priestess and Priestess of the Veil have developed skill sets comprising bodies of work that can be taught to others drawn to the same calling. For the purpose of this book, however, I wish to discuss the priestess specialty with which I have the most experience.

The Ritual Priestess

In addition to being a High Priestess who teaches classes in the Dianic tradition, I am also a Ritual Priestess by calling and vocation. The ritual priestess is a facilitator whose spiritual service is to act as a creator and guide for the ritual experience. She must have knowledge and skills in all aspects of ritual-making, including designing rituals, creating invocations, using sacred tools and symbols, and understanding energetics. She must have the ability to monitor, sense, shape and direct the energy created by the group toward a focused purpose. She must also be equipped with skills in counseling, communication and organizing.

A ritual priestess must have a working knowledge of what is needed for each seasonal sabbat and lunar phase, with respect to both the physical needs of the ritual (someone has to remember the matches) and an intuitive sense of energetic needs. She must be capable of creating and facilitating rituals that link the cycles of the Goddess with Earth's seasonal cycles and the cycles of women's lives.

A ritual priestess is responsible for, and must be capable of, providing safe space for women in ritual. Her behavior and attitude deeply affect the experience of everyone present. If women are open during the ritual, as they should be, they are, in a very real sense, temporarily entrusting their psyches to the priestess's care. Ritual priestessing is not just about what you know, what you have read or what skills you can demonstrate in a ritual circle; it is also about how you are, and how able you are to be present with the women you serve or the groups you facilitate. A ritual priestess understands that her service does not end when the ritual is over; it includes preparation before the ritual begins, performing the ritual itself and supporting women through the days, weeks or months afterward when they are experiencing the transformational effects of the magic they have created. The ritual priestess may continue to provide guidance, support and containment for their experience throughout this process, and she must therefore be willing to see through to the end what she helped initiate. This is her sacred responsibility.

I believe that the most important skill the ritual priestess must learn is how to bring herself, fully centered, into the present time. This is critical because she must simultaneously embody the energy of the ritual space, be at one with the flow of the ritual and direct it as it evolves. She must develop impeccably clear personal boundaries, so that she can sense and experience the differences between her own energy and the energy of the individual she is guiding or the group she is facilitating.

This is fundamental to the ritual priestess's ability to serve effectively, both inside and outside the ritual space. Within a cast circle, she holds the center point, allowing the Goddess to work through her, listening to her voice while directing the intended work and flow of the rite. This means expanding herself energetically to hold and fill the larger container that comprises the ritual space, and improvising as the energy shifts among the participants—being flexible with the ritual structure while maintaining its essential intention.

When I am really working the energy in a ritual, I am completely centered and open. I must get out of my own way in order to be receptive and flexible. One part of my awareness tracks where the ritual is going and what is supposed to happen next, while another part remembers that I have a candle to light, as well as all a list of other things I have decided to include in the ritual. Meanwhile, I am monitoring the energy, sensing what is happening and anticipating what needs to happen next, while still supporting and maintaining the integrity of the cast circle. This fluid awareness can be developed by knowing the pathways of your own mind and the disciplined practice of moving rapidly through expanding and contracting states of consciousness.

The ritual priestess directs the ritual flow; she does not control it. She is like a maestro conducting an orchestra: with her baton, she directs the orchestra's pace and dynamics while being at one with the music; if she doesn't feel the music, the musicians will sense that she does not feel connected to their playing. There is a dynamic between the conductor and each member of the orchestra, an energy that leads to an inspired musical experience. So it is with the ritual priestess and the participants.

Advance ritual preparation is essential to embodying the ritual's intention, becoming fully present and serving the participants, but advance preparation differs with individual ritual priestesses. For some, preparation starts a week ahead; others take more time. Some priestesses may prepare by consciously slowing down, spending time in quiet contemplation, making things to adorn themselves with, "feeling into" the ritual theme, taking a pre-ritual bath, doing a self-blessing or singing and chanting. Others may sit at their altars and ask themselves questions such as, What am I feeling? What energies do I need to help me serve in this rite? Discovering how to best prepare oneself to serve is a wonderful opportunity for self-intimacy and personal empowerment.

When I serve as High Priestess in ritual, my primary function is to hold the center energetic. When a facilitator "holds center," she physically and energetically embodies the ritual theme to such an extent that the ritual's energy emanates from her entire being, evoking the same intention from the other women participating, so that together they fill the ritual space with their energy. If the facilitator is doing her job, others can actually feel this process happening, even though they may not consciously be aware of its source. Unless another woman is designated to do so, it is my responsibility to bring the presence of the Goddess as the Great Mother into the container of the cast circle. Although I may serve as the primary ritual facilitator, I am not to be the focus of the ritual—I am not a presence at the center of the ritual, as if I were starring in a play or show. My facilitating role is to appear and disappear as the ritual requires—to both embody the energetic flow of the ritual and contain the ritual, to both monitor the energy and guide the flow forward in accordance with the ritual's intention. My visible presence is only important inasmuch as it helps the group's energy to be a cohesive source of support for the women in doing their work. Holding the center energetic is an advanced and invaluable skill for women who facilitate rituals and are interested in ritual priestessing.

A ritual priestess must learn to embody the intention of the ritual, not the structure. The ritual's structure must be flexible enough to adapt to the situation or group of women, while the intention must be strong enough to remain the same. The ritual structure exists only to support the intention. If the form does not allow for the possibility of spontaneous creativity, the ritual will strangle from an inability to breathe. It will be boring, stagnant or uninspired. I listen to the voice of the Goddess singing through the ritual. I keep my eyes open for her arrival, and welcome her when she comes. Once, at a Spring Equinox ritual, a little girl was holding onto her mother's hand and dancing in place, clearly wanting to move freely. As a chant to the Maiden Goddess rose and the energy soared, I drew her forward into the center of the circle to dance the Goddess with my support.

Given breathing room, a ritual lives to address what is meaningful in that moment for that group and for that occasion. Words and gestures emerge as they are inspired from the heart and from the Goddess, not from a script. Be flexible. Dare to spread your wings and risk falling. If the only route you know to a given destination is on the highway and there is an accident slowing traffic to a snail's pace, you will be late or miss your purpose for the drive. If you are flexible and know alternate routes, you can get off the freeway, take other streets and get to your appointment more or less on time, accomplishing the task at hand.

Shekhinah Mountainwater uses the word "seasoned" to describe a priestess who has had years of experience in service. I also describe some priestesses as seasoned who demonstrate expertise in their specialty as adepts. Because a seasoned priestess aligns herself to the theme of the ritual, she speaks or acts out of her connection to the Goddess in service to the ritual's purpose. After years of experience in learning, practicing, preparing and honing her skills, when Shekhinah enters a ritual space, she simply opens herself to the Goddess and trusts her training. As one of my students put it: "Read the energy and do what's appropriate." As simple as this sounds, it only comes from experience gained over time, an ability to put creativity and intuition into service, a willingness to make mistakes and an ability to self-critique each ritual.

A ritual priestess's repertory contains all the skills and experiences she has internalized over the years, enabling her to jump into the unknown and think on her feet. Every ritual has its challenges; some are greater than others. For example, what would you do if a dear relative of the bride died suddenly a day before the wedding ceremony? As the facilitating clergy, how would you acknowledge that experience in the ceremony? If you don't, it will be there anyway, looming like an elephant in the living room. After preparing a wonderfully deep ritual, you might discover that you are working with a group of women who don't relate to anything you are saying and are looking at you like you have four heads. How might you be flexible in these various situations?

You have to be prepared to adjust to the environment, as well as to the level of understanding and experience of the women participating. Sometimes you have to change, adapt or even throw out the whole thing and create something else that will meet the needs of that group of women. What happens when you have been asked to facilitate an outdoor group ritual for 200 women and the microphone you are given is dead? What do you do when you arrive to facilitate an outdoor ritual at a festival, having planned to lead a free-form group dance, and you realize that the ritual site is pockmarked with gopher holes? Bear in mind that women come to rituals because they are interested and have a need for a meaningful spiritual experience. Ritual priestessing requires physical stamina, mental and emotional flexibility, and a huge sense of humor.

Ordination

When a woman is ready for ordination as a Dianic Priestess, she usually knows it. However, this knowing should not come from a desire to be publicly named a priestess. She must have moved past that mystique and ego gratification and be doing the work she is here to do, without fanfare. In doing her work—in being challenged by it, in growing, integrating and centering herself into the work, and the work into her—she becomes her service. It no longer matters what she is called: she knows who she is because she has become the work, the hand of the Goddess is upon her and others recognize her as living her work. At ordination, a woman begins a new cycle as priestess. Ordination does not commemorate the end of her service but formally begins her work anew. She steps out as girl-child again, in awe of the world, with gratitude that the Goddess has made it possible for her to serve as she has been called to do. With ordination comes formal and public responsibility for her work, her interactions with others, the ways she conducts herself and the ways she embodies the Goddess in the world on a daily basis.

Assisting women in identifying their own needs and supporting them in meeting those needs is at the core of a priestess's service. A priestess teaches women mostly by example. To do this authentically, she must be motivated by a desire to serve and enhance life for all. A priestess presents opportunities for women to access their personal power and experience themselves as sacred—as the Goddess. In order to encourage my students to be honest, vulnerable and open, I must do the same. In this way, power is equalized between student and teacher, while acknowledging differences with respect to experience and knowledge. To guide a student through deep transformational work, I must also have done my own inner work, and must continue to do it.

A priestess does not set herself apart from the community she serves but is deeply involved with its growth, with an open ear to feedback. She is especially open to constructive feedback, which equalizes power, encourages participation and stimulates growth; and she works to create a feeling of partnership with the person giving her the feedback. This is very different than seeing the person with the criticism as an enemy or as being in opposition. Taking the initial position that both are working for the greatest good allows for real communication and for joint solutions. Where there are very different positions being taken in a discussion, the priestess must be strong enough to speak her truth, especially in the face of opposition or opinions she disagrees with, while still being able to listen to and consider other points of view. A priestess must be open to the simple questions, the deep questions and even the unspoken questions behind the spoken one. She must learn to know when it is best to speak and when to keep silent and listen.

There is a difference between the call to service and the call to be ordained. In Western culture, most women are taught to serve others, but does that translate to an authentic call to serve the Goddess as a vocation? Because ordination often confers legal ministerial credentials, many women unconsciously revert to patriarchal-style thinking: What are the guidelines and rules in order to get my "stamp"? Ordination is not a diploma for completed classwork. Being a priestess is about what you are—what you become as a result of what you have done. Who you are can be a presentation. What you are is a totality of being. It is out of being a priestess that your spiritual service is sourced.

Ordination in the Dianic Tradition
In the Dianic tradition, a high priestess can only be ordained by another high priestess. This assures a continuity of lineage and some basic teachings, even though each high priestess will take what she knows and teach the tradition through her own perspective. The women who have been ordained as high priestesses by Z Budapest or me come from diverse

backgrounds and orientations. Most of them also have diverse backgrounds in their magical training. This diversity celebrates the evolution of the tradition and the gifts that diversity can bring. With a wide range of specialties, some of these high priestesses focus on assisting women with individual spiritual development, while others work more often with groups and hold center in larger communities.

Once she's been ordained by either another Dianic priestess or high priestess, a Dianic priestess can ordain other priestesses at her responsibility and discretion. If a priestess desires legal ministerial credentials, she may need to enroll in a priestess training program that offers credentials or is affiliated with a federally recognized Dianic or other Wiccan 501(c)(3) tax-exempt organization. Ministerial credentials allow a priestess to legally marry and bury, and provide access to visit a sick, injured or dying congregant in a hospital intensive-care ward without being immediate family. It may also allow her to offer healings and divination, and provide pastoral counseling to individuals; priestesses can enroll in specialized courses for ministers to learn pastoral counseling. At this time, Temple of Diana, Inc. is the only federally recognized Dianic temple offering a priestess training program and legal ministerial credentials specifically for Dianic priestesses in the Z Budapest lineage.

The traditional ceremony of Dianic ordination provides an energetic charge that empowers and nourishes the priestess throughout her ministry. Lori, a priestess I ordained who named her ministry "Priestess of the Singing Spirit," describes Dianic ordination this way:

> She (the priestess) sources her spiritual foundation through training that embodies the essential energetic context central to our tradition. This specific combination of Dianic education and the sacred rite of Dianic ordination ensures that every one of her priestesses enters through the same doorway of service to the Goddess and her women.[2]

As an Elder in my tradition and a High Priestess, I am often asked about how I evaluate a prospective priestess: what qualities do I look for in a candidate, and how do I identify those qualities? Things have changed since the seventies and eighties when, more often than not, a woman was ordained as a priestess based on her potential, not on an actualized, developed ministry. Today, when I consider ordaining a Dianic priestess, I use the following questions and criteria, based on my own years of spiritual service: Is this woman definitely working her spiritual path? Can she clearly identify and articulate her focus? Can I easily observe that she is doing her work? What makes her priestess work specifically Dianic, goddess-centered and woman-identified?

A woman who fulfills these criteria excels in many areas but has a consistent, identifiable focus that is obvious to the women of her community. If a woman cannot name her ministry or clearly demonstrate the nature of her spiritual service, she is not yet ready for ordination. The work of a priestess is not about potential but is actualized work in the world. The being and the doing are one. Is there a circle of women willing to accept this woman as a priestess? If there is not, I would seriously question her readiness for ordination, at least within her chosen specialty. To ordain her without community recognition would be to put the cart before the horse.

When a woman is truly walking the priestess path, she is passionate about her work; she is driven to do it and is also sustained by it. It is how she creates, and the work, however challenging, feeds her spirit. She wrestles with patriarchy and its limited concept of deity. She loves life and honors the Goddess by serving others, whether human, animal or green ones. She knows how to craft energy, hold power responsibly and value her own work. Such a woman demonstrates the ability and willingness to examine her own motivations and desires for service. She dares to dream. She dares to craft those dreams into reality. To endure and thrive on her path, she must be self-nurturing, self-sustaining, self-facing and patient.

I look for strong women who will not be deterred, although they may struggle. Priestess work is not for those who are easily distracted or discouraged. I look for women who can take responsibility for their not-so-perfectly-evolved selves, and thus can be compassionate with others as they are compassionate with themselves. I look for women who aren't perfect. Frankly, I am a bit mistrusting of "perfect" women, because priestesses are women who struggle in life like everybody else.

They aren't afraid to be human and a part of the world. It is a priestess's humanity that gives her the ability to empathize and hold compassion for herself and those around her.

I look for a woman who is inspired by life and by other women's creativity and accomplishments. I look for a woman who is not afraid to be a beginner and to learn from others, especially the students who are there to learn from her. This woman refuses to stay on the pedestal others may try to place her upon—or the hole that others may try to push her off the pedestal into!

I look for a woman who is in it for the long haul. Although the nature of her service may change over time, she is doing her work with each breath because she has become a channel for the Goddess in the world. She is a priestess because she is doing the work for the sake of the work. Being a priestess is not a phase, a fad or a cycle in life that she is passing through. The Goddess is guiding her, even as she knows that the day-to-day reality of being in her service is not always comfortable.

To live and work in spiritual service to women is to honor life's passages and transitions to the fullest. The priestess stands for the Goddess in the world, speaks for her and does her work by being her hands and heart. Being a priestess requires courage, stamina, patience, great love and an enduring sense of humor. The function and role of the priestess is needed again in the world as we return to creating and participating in women's rites. It is my hope that the role of the priestess continues to evolve, modeling power that comes from within, shared with her supportive sisters and helping to facilitate women's connection with themselves, each other and the Goddess.

Endnote

1 As part of the ordination ceremony, I now give an ice scraper for candle-wax droppings to women I ordain.

2 Personal communication.

Priestessing with Integrity
By Sylvia Brallier

Priestess . . . favored by the Goddess, wise woman, sage and a guide to others on the path. Being a priestess is a vocation that honors the sacredness we embody as women. We are fortunate to live in a time when the Goddess is returning and we can represent and support her work here in this world as priestesses. It's easy to make up romantic notions about what it is to be a priestess. Not to say that some of them aren't true, but it's a package deal that includes real challenges and great blessings. When the rubber meets the road, what does being a priestess really entail?

Whether initiated as a priestess within a tradition or by the challenges and blessings of life, certain responsibilities are part and parcel of the vocation. The job of priestess doesn't stop when you leave the circle. It is a life commitment to accountability and integrity, not only by performing your duties to the best of your ability but by walking in life as a living representative of enlightened behavior and speech. As a priestess, your behavior sets the bar. One of the greatest gifts you can give is to teach by example and live the teachings as fully as you can. Here are some guidelines for your consideration.

- **Use authority responsibly.** Just because you are a high mucky-muck now doesn't mean you should throw your weight around in an irresponsible way. As a representative of the Goddess, it's doubly important that you leave the dominator paradigm out of the mix and create new methods that honor the needs and rights of the whole rather than the privileged few. When people look up to you, your words already have a lot power, so you can effectively convey your meaning and get results with gentle skill and finesse to get results rather than using words like blunt instrument being wielded with brute force.

- **Stay grounded.** When interactions get hot, someone has to help them cool down; as a priestess, that someone is often you. You do not have the luxury of getting emotionally overheated; you need to sort out your own issues so you don't lead others into even more chaos. If you need to take some time to simmer down before speaking, do so. It's worth the wait.
- **Be vulnerable—carefully.** We all know it takes more strength to be vulnerable than to appear strong. However, if you are in a leadership role when you begin to feel control slipping away, be aware that you are taking everyone else along for the ride. Be strategic about when and how you let others see your guard down. Sometimes shedding a tear can be the perfect thing. Then get back on that horse and ride it home from a place of centered power. If you aren't there yet, work on it.
- **Seek guidance when you need it.** No matter how much you know or have experienced, there will always be times you need advice as well. Find a therapist or a circle of peers to talk to so that you can work on your issues outside of your priestessing responsibilities.
- **Say what you mean, and mean what you say.** If you want your words to have power, be sure you can follow through on any commitments. Do what you say you are going to do, or be accountable if you can't. When your word can't be trusted as fact, clear trust cannot be created. Trust is not hard to establish, but when you break trust, it can be hard to re-establish. This means it's important not to commit to something you can't follow through on. If you're not sure, say "maybe" or "I'll get back to you on that"; if on a rare occasion you can't do what you've said, be accountable.
- **Lead from your Heart and your Head.** Neither your heart nor your head will show you the one sure path. When you allow

wisdom and feeling combined to inform your choices, you are more likely to have success than if you rely on one or the other solely. The fact that we honor intuition in the Craft doesn't mean we toss out logic as an act of rebellion. Compassion is important, but some situations are better served by drawing a line in the sand than caving in because you care. Seek balance in all things.

- **Practice what you preach.** Hold yourself to the same standards you ask of others. Power does bring some privilege, but if you begin creating different rules for different "classes" of people, you will arrive back at the old dominator paradigm in no time.
- **Admit when you are wrong.** Most people have more respect for those who can admit they are wrong than for those who pretend they are always right. No matter how "sure" you are of something, there will always be gaps in your information—and any of those gaps might easily change something that seemed obviously right to something that is clearly wrong. Similarly, if you don't know the answer to the question or the solution to a problem, say so; nobody likes a know-it-all. Admitting faults, lapses and gaps in knowledge are essential to exhibiting strength through vulnerability. Pedestals are easy places to fall from—and the higher the pedestal, the farther the fall.
- **Take the high road.** In every group, there will be some who will try to "take you down"; this is especially true among Pagans who, as a whole, tend to rebel against authority. At some point, someone will project whatever unresolved issues they have with their parents or other authority figures onto you. Don't take it personally. Resist the temptation to lash out. Instead, try to resolve the issues with a compassionate perspective. Own whatever part in a disagreement is yours, no matter how small. People with strong defenses often push less when they feel more heard. This isn't to say you should take responsibility for other people's issues; just own what you can, no more, no less.
- **Don't encourage back-biting behavior.** You will, at times, hear people talk about others negatively when those others are not present, and it's easy to be seduced into participating. Remember

that it's your job to lead by example. Also keep in mind that, no matter how impeccably you try to behave, the target of back-biting might someday be you.

- **Don't think in "us" and "them" terms.** This mentality promotes another aspect of what we are trying to rise above from our culture of origin. Don't be silent when you see something wrong, but do try to deal with wrong-doing in the most enlightened way possible.
- **Curb your spiritual ego.** No matter how far along you are, you are still a baby. Think of yourself as a tightrope walker. On one side, you have full access to the powers of universe and the wisdom of the ages. On the other side, you are just a child wearing her mother's clothes, not even able to walk much less navigate a tightrope. Give equal awareness and attention to both sides of the tightrope. There is wisdom in knowing you are just a beginner. You can be humble without being self-effacing. Know that every person you interact with has a lesson for you, whether they mean to be a teacher or not.

Being a priestess is more than a sacred profession: it is a way of life that requires mindfulness in thoughts, actions and speech. While the path is narrow, the gains are great for those willing to walk it with courage, willingness, curiosity and compassion. Being a priestess is not a road for the faint of heart, but it is definitely a path for those who want to be the change they would like to see in the world. Blessings on your journey.

Priestesses I Have Known
By Calypso

I don't think of myself as a priestess. I create and lead ritual. I develop and teach classes on goddess spirituality and Paganism. Occasionally, I am asked for advice on relationships, spiritual matters or practical issues. I am in a small home-based group, a larger circle of women and an even larger circle of women and men. But I don't think of myself as a priestess.

Maybe the reluctance to think of myself as a priestess comes from my distaste for the professional clergy found in mainstream religions, who so often become stuck in dogma, focus on the pecuniary aspects of religious practice or even abuse those who look upon them as authority figures. Maybe it comes from a focus on egalitarianism in spiritual life. As a refugee from organized religion who has rejected the notion that humans need a "middleman" to experience the sacred, I don't want to be a "middlewoman." Thinking of myself as an ordinary woman with personality traits such as stubbornness and persistence, I don't feel authentic in claiming any special gifts, or of being "chosen" for the role of priestess, or having talents that others do not have. I think of myself as a seeker and learner, encountering the unfolding love and joy of the Goddess and being fortunate in having the company of others on this path. It is the company of these others I want to share, for I have been blessed in knowing women who do use the title "Priestess."

Sarasvati

At one time, I had the pleasure of being in many ritual circles with a talented musician, vocalist and composer who I will call Sarasvati. Tall, thin and graceful with a dancer's build and movements, and strikingly beautiful with long dark hair and piercing dark eyes, Sarasvati epitomized the qualities of priestess. One reason she seemed to have such great impact as a priestess was that her entire life had been a preparation for the role. She had been an entertainer, a singer, a dancer and a massage therapist. She was skilled in reiki and aromatherapy. These occupations and the skills they require had helped her develop sensitivity, empathy and compassion.

Sarasvati's highly developed sensitivity for others enabled her to speak almost intuitively to their needs. Her ability to read people enabled her to draw their best from them. When she turned her gaze on a person, it seemed as if she saw right into their core; no artifice was possible because it would be readily apparent. Some found this to be disconcerting.

She had an instinct for ritual and carefully observed those who participated in her circles to see if their energy or attention was waning or if they needed some assistance. If so, she stepped in with just the right words, songs, dances or actions to redirect the energy. Her rituals were dynamic: she experimented with new forms and incorporated just enough structure to maintain interest without inhibiting spontaneity, innovation or creativity. She was devoted to creating a space where magical experiences could happen and where one could experience the divine both within and without. She had strong convictions about the nature of her rituals, which translated into energetic and inspiring events——yet the very strength of her convictions could lead to bruised feelings when there were differences of opinion among the ritual planners.

Sarasvati taught me the value of preparation, engagement and the ability to confront. Preparing for the role of priestess is essential; no one who walks into it unprepared will do well. Even those gifted with intuition and compassion must learn techniques to help them express these gifts. Engagement requires total immersion in the activities of the priestess, regardless of what the activities are, as well as sensitivity to the dynamics and energies in those activities. The ability to confront means tackling difficult issues directly—always an unpleasant task and one I avoid if at all possible. However, issues, if continually avoided, not only continue, but become worse; sometimes the kindest thing you can do is confront individuals about the issues they bring. In the worst circumstances, your efforts will be ignored or resented and the individual will continue their destructive habits; in the best circumstances, the individual will then confront and address their issues for themselves.

Hera

Another priestess I encountered I shall call Hera. Hera owned a metaphysical shop that offered "free" Wicca classes. Intrigued, I enrolled, but soon learned that these "free" classes were not free at all. There was mandatory spell work that required one to purchase all materials (candles, parchment paper and so on) from the shop at greatly inflated prices. All spell work had to be performed three times, which added to the expense. In addition, there was a weekly fee for the altar flowers, a sabbat fee and a wood fee for the sabbat fire. There was also a Saturday evening fundraiser where attendance was required and an entry fee was charged; ritual attire was to be purchased from the store; and on and on.

There was also an elaborate hierarchy within this small community. Hera used a magical name referring to one of the mysterious figures of the Arthurian tales and her name always had to be prefaced with "Lady." Indeed, everyone was to refer to everyone else as "Lord" or "Lady," though that did not lead to an egalitarian system. There were four levels of hierarchy, beginning with those who had just begun classes and those with first-, second-and third-degree initiation. In fact, no one had third-degree initiation and it was rumored that Hera refused to grant it because it would make those individuals equal to her in authority. Those newly enrolled in classes wore different-colored ritual robes and had to curtsy, eyes down, to anyone of higher rank than them, and wait to be recognized. For the newcomer, practically everyone was of a higher rank.

Rituals were not held in the store itself but in a remote location where all participants were required to camp out overnight, which entailed an additional investment in camping equipment. Hera generally arrived later than the rest of us to a tent already erected by her minions and stocked with her favorite foods, especially smoked oysters and the ketchup she liked with them. One time, someone forgot the ketchup and all of us searched frantically for a bottle of ketchup that could be provided to Her Highness, terrified of her wrath. No one was to bother her whilst she rested in her tent until the three- or four-hour ritual began close to midnight, but the rest of us were to create the ritual circle, a physically demanding task that had to be performed precisely. She did not participate in the ritual itself, and indeed never led rituals, but made a grand entrance and then observed from a comfortable chair close to a warm fire and took note if anyone made a mistake. Mistakes were discussed and corrected, somewhat publicly and embarrassingly, at a later date.

Hera did not actually teach the classes. Those who had already had at least one initiation taught the weekly classes, for no pay of course. Classes were strictly run and demanding. The curriculum was formalized and no deviation was allowed. For someone new to Paganism or Wicca, the classes were informative and the discipline involved was good training. They were, however, all form and no substance: there was little to no attention paid to the spiritual aspect of Paganism. I learned the words and movements to rituals, but not the reasons behind them. Instead, there was so much hierarchy that I often thought I might as well have remained in a mainstream religion.

I learned from Hera the need to be personally involved in the activities of a group. Her distance from the classes and rituals led to a situation where the teachers abused their power over their students. The students tended to feel she was not engaged in the process and had no real concern for the progress, or lack of it, of the students. For those who looked for an alternative from mainstream hierarchical religion, the experience of this group was not a positive one and many did not complete the courses, or left after the first initiation. This led to a constant turnover in leadership and a basic instability in the group itself. The group never developed a self-identity or sense of camaraderie. Almost all involved at the same time I was have left, not wishing to remain affiliated with this priestess.

Because of my experience with Hera, I realized how difficult it is to finance a Pagan group or maintain a small business with a Pagan clientele, a valuable lesson for me since I had harbored a desire to open such a shop. In the years since I was involved with Hera, I have visited many metaphysical stores and always wondered how they managed to stay in business. Many Pagan groups are based in commercial stores simply because it is one way to finance them. Let's face it, most Pagans aren't wealthy, and Paganism, with its antipathy to organized religion, does not often generate followers who are willing or able to contribute a portion of their income weekly, or even monthly, to a circle or group. Survival for Pagan groups is often rooted in a commercial structure. The trick is not to let that structure overtake the spiritual nature of the endeavor; many Pagan businesses manage that balance nicely. Sadly, Hera's commercial emphases led many to conclude that profit was her only concern. Although she stayed in business, the commercial nature of her classes overwhelmed their spirituality.

Hathor

For a priestess to move into a community that is already formed is a challenging task that will either bring out the best or the worst in her. Hathor faced just such a task. For Hathor's first ritual, she wore a sensible sweater and skirt, and she had marvelous long curly hair that had a life of its own. She was clearly nervous, and I discovered later that she'd been full of misgivings and self-doubt. Her entry into this close-knit community was not easy. Many wanted the new priestess to replicate what had come before, but replication was just not Hathor's style, and nor should it have been. Hathor faced critical and sometimes vitriolic attacks from those who remained attached to the former priestess. She weathered this with grace and a common-sense, straight-forward approach, examining the criticism for relevance, making changes as she deemed appropriate and shrugging off what was clearly motivated by meanness.

Hathor changed the way things were done in this circle, in a way that expressed not just her personality but also her concern for the way the environment influenced the flow of energy. She created rituals from the heart and full of bristling energy. As she became more comfortable with her role, she experimented with ritual, pushing the limits of possibility. At several rituals, it seemed there was so much energy that we were all vibrating on a different level. Patricia Monaghan's description of the Goddess Hathor is also an excellent description of Priestess Hathor:

> . . . she was patron of bodily pleasures; the pleasures of sound, in music and song; the joys of the eye, in art, cosmetics, the weav-

ing of garlands; the delight of motion in dance and in love; and all the pleasures of touch. In her temples, priestesses danced and played their tinkling tambourines . . . [1]

While Hathor did not think of herself as a spiritual counselor or therapist, she had the knack of saying exactly what would make a person see the issue in a different light. One of her gifts to the community was to ask several of the women who were active at the temple to assist her as priestesses. This, in itself, was a daunting task, as each woman had a different personality and needs. It took a truly skilled priestess to draw out each woman's best talents, and minimize the conflicts that would inevitably occur. Together these priestesses created rituals of joyous synergy and depth.

I learned many important and valuable things from Hathor. Perhaps the most important was that each priestess, to be true to herself and the Goddess within her, must develop her own way of doing things. Each priestess calls to her those who hear the call of the Goddess within her, who respond to her particular energy. Hathor was sensitive to the nature and energy of the land and worked diligently to nurture and develop those energies. For the ritual fire, she preferred to use materials that had grown on the land and had died, but she first thanked them for their service and asked their permission to be burned in a sacred fire. Struggling plants were sung to on a regular basis. This care and sensitivity for the environment was touching to many and made us all more sensitive to how we related to our own environments. She was also adept at discerning what tasks each of us were most suited for, and was able to ask us to help out in a way that made helping out fun, and not a chore.

Baba Yaga

A priestess of a quite different type was someone I shall call Baba Yaga, after the Eastern European Goddess who lived in the deep woods. Baba Yaga was the epitome of the hedge witch, living far away from town, striding about on thin spindly legs, dressed almost always in ritual wear, with long, stringy, somewhat unkempt black hair. She cackled and smoked a cigar. She even had a wart on her nose. Upon first meeting her,

I felt that I had encountered the real thing: an authentic witch.

Baba Yaga conducted all the rituals herself and didn't insist upon any special treatment just because she was the priestess. In fact, she worked harder than the rest to create this special place of the Goddess. She led learning circles in which we all learned of the Goddess, from ourselves, from each other and from her. She introduced many to goddess spirituality, opening doors and pathways heretofore unknown. She introduced us to knowledge not found in books. Many came to her for counsel and advice, and she did the best she could to help them, although her advice was not always rooted in sound common sense. Her rituals were simple yet sincere. She was clearly motivated by her great love for and dedication to the Goddess, and tried to conduct herself as an instrument through which the Goddess worked.

Baba Yaga was by no means perfect but came with all the usual human failings. She had a tendency to play favorites, which created jealousies and the impression that there was an inside group and an outside group. I learned firsthand how devastating this could be. Baba Yaga would have a favorite to whom she would grant prominent roles in ritual or upon whom she would bestow gifts, and then suddenly, without warning or explanation, she would drop that individual and take another as her favorite, causing puzzlement and hurt feelings.

Despite this disconcerting habit, I learned much of what I know today about the Goddess from Baba Yaga, such as that the complexity or simplicity of a ritual is much less important than its sincerity. Even the simplest of rituals, if heartfelt, will touch participants and, I am sure, the Goddess. Baba Yaga's deep devotion to the Goddess and her fierce defense of her was a model to me of what a priestess should be.

Titania

Titania, named after the fairy queen referred to by Shakespeare in *A Midsummer Night's Dream*, was also called Queen Mab, as in *Romeo and Juliet*. These were both fitting names for her, as Queen Mab was a miniature creature who drove her chariot into the minds of sleeping people to help them experience wish fulfillment, while Titania was a tiny woman whose pixie-like appearance belied her strength, knowledge, experience and ability. Titania formed one of the largest and longest-lasting circles in the community, apparently without creating rancor, hard feelings, competitiveness or any of the other catastrophes that can plague Pagan or goddess groups.

Titania was adept at creating rituals that captivated the mind and the senses, stressing incense, music, drumming, dance and drama. This skill came from long years of practice as well as her experience in a variety of different groups and traditions. From her early career as a performer and entertainer, she learned techniques for engaging an audience.

Those who attended her rituals felt welcome, as if they were her special guests; her beautiful smile and words of welcome always warmed the heart. Her rituals were elaborate, carefully planned and skillfully developed, yet never stiff or stuffy, and attendees felt comfortable. Like Sarasvati, Titania's entire life was devoted to being a priestess, and her skills were finely tuned. She drew the best from those who developed rituals with her, and her experience and commitment were amply evidenced by the loyalty and love those in her community felt toward her and each other.

I learned from Titania that elaborate and complex rituals can also be sincere and open a channel to the Goddess. Her great attention to detail, including scents, sounds, costuming, lighting, music, motions and words, created a container in which an earnest seeker could experience the Divine. Her rituals were always different, always captivating and always new. What impressed me most, however, were the sincerity, love and joy that lit up her face as she greeted strangers and friends, planned a ritual or spoke of her work for the Goddess.

Demeter
In another situation, a priestess moved into an existing community. The new priestess was earnest and sincere, but had little experience of working with people, no experience with public ritual and no real preparation for the role. The other priestesses perhaps had unrealistic expectations of her and were too quick to criticize. They offered help, but the priestess

considered their ideas and offers of help to be criticism and felt insulted, which resulted in angry outbursts followed by tears.

Clearly this priestess, whom I'll call Demeter, felt threatened by the experience of the others and had a tendency to think of herself as a victim surrounded by conspirators. In a fairly short time, the entire structure collapsed; some of the priestesses left, and there were hard feelings all around. Those who remained tried to support Demeter, but she grew increasingly suspicious, accusing them of going "behind her back" if they had any dealings with the others in the group, or with other groups. She attempted to recruit more priestesses by offering training, but when they turned to others with more experience, she rejected them too. She was sincere and clearly devoted to the Goddess, and no one worked harder than she did. In fact, she took exquisite care of the ritual space and initiated several new programs. Because she had a compassionate heart, she had a habit of picking up strays, whether animal or human, and this sometimes, sadly, backfired on her, creating unpleasant dilemmas. She needed more confidence, experience, empathy, people skills, self-examination and a thicker skin.

The lessons I learned from Demeter were the most difficult; because of that, they were perhaps the most important ones as they dealt not so much with the external aspects of priestessing, but the internal qualities of a priestess. Since I have tendencies like hers, Demeter forced me to take a long, hard look at myself—and I didn't always like what I saw. I, too, have a tendency to feel hurt when none was intended; rather than either letting criticism flow off my back or addressing it directly, I hide, nursing my hurt feelings, feeling like a victim and letting the wound fester. With Demeter, I could see how this limited her ability to see the needs of others and of the community; thus, her ability to share her talents with the community and create an environment that would enable others to connect with the Goddess were diminished and her inner light was dulled. Because of my experience with Demeter, when I feel that I have been hurt, ignored, or insulted, I now try to examine my own emotions, and the circumstances, and move beyond my feelings. I am not always successful, but I am more sensitive now to my tendency to overreact and to run and hide.

After having experienced such a variety of ways of priestessing, I conclude that there are a number of pitfalls for priestesses. Pitfalls include traits and practices such as: creating a hierarchy; stressing form over substance; insisting on fancy titles without doing the work to earn them; distancing onself from one's students; stressing one's self-importance; playing favorites; having little or no preparation or experience; allowing one's ego to guide how one relates to the community; and yielding to both insensitivity and over-sensitivity. These can all lead to difficulties, but it's especially important to understand that there is a delicate balance between sensitivity, over-sensitivity and insensitivity. A priestess needs a thick skin because she is the one who will be criticized whether or not criticism is warranted. The trick is to be able to determine which criticisms are valid and which are not.

There are also distinct characteristics and practices that create a priestess who touches hearts and opens a channel for the Goddess. One of these is preparation, both in terms of years of education or experience, and in terms of each ritual and each time one is called upon for counsel and advice. Equally essential are compassion, intuition, practice, hard work, knowledge, discernment, the ability to differentiate between substantive issues and non-issues, a sense of humor and above all, devotion to the Goddess, the call of the Goddess and a commitment to serve the Goddess and her community.

I have been privileged to know many priestesses and to observe what has been successful and what has not. I have learned much from these women; some in a positive fashion as models of what a priestess ought to be, and some as models of what one should avoid. Either way, they have all been my teachers. I admire them all for having the courage to identify themselves as priestess, thereby inviting both criticism and praise. The Goddess has blessed me in allowing me to know all of them. She has led me along this path for a reason. It is with humility, fear, anticipation, pride and gratitude for my teachers, and knowing that this is not an ending but a beginning, that I step forward and reclaim the ancient title of priestess for myself.

Endnote

1 Patricia Monaghan, *The New Book of Goddesses & Heroines* (St. Paul, MN: Llewellyn Publications, 2000), 146.

The Hierosgamos of Hathor and Horus
By Normandi Ellis

Shake the sistrum.
Light the candle.
Before the shrine of Hathor
Annoint the brow, the heart, the womb.
The prophet and priestess come
to purify the temple and their land.
Hu, the sweet breath of life, fills their mouths.
Sia, Divine Mind sizzles and seizes them.
Heka, the magic eternal, inhabits their flesh
and fills their mouths and tongues.
Oh soul of Hathor,
Oh soul of Horus,
Hear me. Bless us this day.
Keep us safe.
Circle the temple.
Pour out the water.
Draw our protection with magical fire.
No gloom, no sorrow enters where
the god and goddess awake and live.
The Eye of Horus comes in peace.
The Eye of Horus crosses the horizon.
The fire is made to shine.
The temple is made to shine.
The bodies of the god and goddess shine.
Their light pleases Horus.

STEPPING INTO OURSELVES

Their perfume pleases Hathor.
May it be with us as it is with them.
May the gods live in us and we in them.
Shake the sistrum.
Raise the voice.
The door of the temple opens for Horus.
He bathes in the field of rushes.
He awakens in the living stream.
The door of the temple opens for Horus.
He bathes in the field of rushes.
He awakens the living stream.
The door of the temple opens for Horus.
He bathes in the field of rushes.
He awakens in the living stream.
O, Hathor, mother of Ihy, of happiness,
See how she dances,
She dances for love of her Heru.
O, Hathor, mother of Ihy's happiness,
See how she dances,
She dances for love of her Heru.
O, Hathor, mother of Ihy, of happiness,
See how she dances,
She dances for her love of Heru.
Without such love no worlds exist,
yet the river flows and emmer grows.
In her left hand, the white feather of Ma'at
In his right hand, the white feather of truth.
They dance as one.
One feather.
One breath.
One eye.
One love.
One soul
Two flames.
Light the fire within the cauldron.

Weave the spell of perfect peace.
Enact the Great Rite.
Celebrate with cakes and wine.
We thank our god and goddess
for entering their temples
in us and in their places.

The Circle of Theatre and Ritual
By Nan Brooks

I began studying to be a priestess—completely unwittingly—at age six with my first public performance. How the recitation of "Once There Was a Snowman" could be considered priestess training, even in disguise, is highly questionable. But because I was fascinated with the world of theatre performance, recognized an important truth about how energy is always circular, and, frankly, because I felt loved when the audience smiled at me and applauded, I determined to learn all I could about theatre. When, in my thirties, I discovered the Goddess and Women's Rituals, I also discovered that I knew quite a lot about how to create rituals. Training in theatre, it turns out, was a large part of my lifetime priestess training.

My training began with spoken word and dance, but I was soon required to know about the use and movement of energy, how to "read" an audience and how to incorporate rigorous discipline in my daily life. By the time I was a teenager, I had learned about "unity of style," the design principle that makes a stage production—and a ritual—feel cohesive. I had learned to consider how we use our senses and perceive our surroundings. I had been taught the practicalities and value of collaboration. I treasured even more the magical times when we come together, in the theatre or in ritual space, to sit together in the dark. Stepping between the worlds was familiar; watching and sensing the movement of energy became my way of being in the mundane world as well as in my art. Of course, I barely thought about all the knowledge I had been given by circumstances and some very generous teachers; I simply loved the collaboration and ever-surprising moments of discovery. Recognizing that I am a priestess brought it all into focus in a new way.

Not every woman who wishes to be a priestess, or discovers that she is one, is so fortunate. So, with thanks to all the collaborators and teachers from my theatre years, I offer these musings about the ways in which theatre can empower the priestess and help us become more accomplished ritualists.

It is a common misconception that actors are good liars, that they can fake emotion and disguise truth; the best actresses are the ones who let us see the emotion behind the words and read their minds and hearts. They reveal universal truths in highly personal situations. While the situation may not be real, the actress draws upon her innermost self to bring a role to life, and to serve both the play and the audience. I have heard actresses talk about getting "out of the way" to let the character and the play's message come through. The actress, then, is a vessel, much like the priestess who portrays or aspects a goddess when enacting a myth. I find it fascinating that many of the finest actresses in history, such as Eleanora Duse, Sara Siddons, Sara Bernhardt and Eva LaGallienne, were also mystics. Eva LaGalliene wrote about Duse:

> She saw theatre as a great force, capable of spreading beauty and understanding, whose function it was to quicken in the minds and hearts of the people an appreciation of the nobility of suffering, to awaken in them a sense of the sublime; to rouse them from their torpor and through a heightening of the emotions make them aware of the mystery and wonder of the human spirit.[1]

When acting students are asked to write honestly about the reasons they pursue the profession, most confess (with some embarrassment) that they experience the divine for themselves, and at the same time find a spiritual connection with an audience, when they do their best work. These same students are often surprised to learn that others in the class feel the same. So it is with the priestess, who seeks to establish a spiritual connection, within herself and with others, through ritual.

There are misconceptions about priestesses as well. The common image of a woman in flowing robes lifting her arms to the moon in ritual is a lovely picture, but not particularly accurate. For one thing, not every priestess is a ritualist. A woman's primary calling as priestess may be as healer, scholar, activist, musician, artist, administrator, naturalist—the list is long.[2] But every priestess must also be a skilled ritualist, no matter what her aptitude or even her interest in creating community rituals. A woman who wishes to lead ritual may not necessarily be ordained or identify herself as a priestess. For that reason, I use the word "priestess" as both noun and verb.

Creating ritual requires skills in storytelling, music, dance and movement, design, use of color, communication and the expression of emotional truth as a form of healing; these are the theatre arts as well. When a priestess combines these skills with her understanding of mythology and theology/thealogy, her compassion for others' journeys and her commitment to service, magical rituals result.

Theatre and ritual have long been connected. In many ancient cultures, public performances were a way to teach important myths to the young or to classes of people who were denied the education that was offered to the "priestly" *[sic]* class. So the earliest theatre was storytelling with sacred intent. In the circle of history, contemporary ritual has become a way to teach those same ancient myths. We enact them in sacred spaces and repeat them at certain seasons or holidays so that the narratives and meanings are restored in our group memory.

Many of those early plays were raucous, so as to capture the attention of a crowd in an outdoor marketplace, much like commercial entertainment today. Such entertainment may fulfill a need for distraction, but is not particularly meaningful. Effective theatre, like effective ritual, provides opportunity for communal experience, intellectual exploration and emotional release. A group of people, safe together in the dark, can share experiences that are at once universal and personal, leading to profound experiences that cannot be described easily.

When we willingly step between the worlds in ritual, we do so trusting that we will be safe, respected and empowered. We hope for connection with community and the Goddess, and the priestess is the one who makes that possible. Of course, she does not do that by herself: every ritual results from collaboration among those who plan and prepare it, those who attend and, most important, the unseen guides and divinities whose presence we request.

Another misconception is illustrated in the theatre saying that "the director is god *[sic]*." This is meant to enforce the understanding that she is responsible for all aspects of the play, that her word is the last word and that it is pointless to argue with her point of view. However, theatre is highly collaborative, as is ritual. No director—and no priestess—creates alone. Even a simple play requires designers and technicians to create the costumes, scenery, make-up, hair styles, props, lighting, sound amplification, music and sound effects, not to mention the theatre space itself with seats, heating and so on. Likewise, a simple community ritual usually calls for a team of collaborators to research, write, plan, provide music, drum, provide visual art for the altar and ritual space and fill various roles before, during and after the ritual, from setting up chairs to guarding the space with fire extinguishers and energetic protection.

Leadership is often an issue for women, both because we are inexperienced (still!) and we are creating new ways to lead. The ritual priestess is often an example of servant leadership; she holds her own because, without a center, the circle will not hold. At the same time, she collaborates and takes the needs of the community into account at every turn. Common misconceptions aside, how can principles and basic techniques from theatre support the ritual priestess?

Energy Follows Intention[3]

The priestess's preparation always begin with the setting of an intention. A stage director would not dare to begin any other work on a play until she has studied the script (usually for months) and knows exactly what meaning she believes the playwright intends. In ritual, the clearer and firmer the intention, the greater the energy. Intention is the foundation upon which ritual is built and will flow. Setting the intention can take time and it is tempting to rush on to more exciting things, like what color robe to wear or which chants to sing. But all those details need to express the intention, so it's best to build the foundation before decorating the house.

The ritual priestess may spend time studying, meditating or conversing with a planning group to arrive at a one-sentence statement of purpose that answers the question, "What do we want people to take away from the ritual?" It may be a commitment to act for justice, a sense of renewal or an appreciation for nature's cycles, for instance. One simple sentence can be repeated often as the preparations continue to inform the choices about many details. This will result in a ritual in which the energy is clear and active. Once the intention is set, the content and setting of the ritual will fall into place. I have seen planning groups take an hour or longer to ponder their intention and whittle it down to one brief sentence, and then plan the entire ritual in complete detail in less than twenty minutes.

Setting intention also involves deep and continuing self-examination by the priestess. We know celebrity is not artistry; we can tell when a performer is onstage to seek attention and applause because the energy is "off." The performance usually feels incomplete and tinged with desperation. It makes us uncomfortable in some way, though we may not be able to define it. The energy may seem to go only one way; rather than coming back to us in a circle, it leaves us a little tired. On the other hand, in the presence of an actress who is there to explore the human condition in our company, perhaps even to teach, the energy feels whole and strong; it moves in its natural circle and we feel comfortable with it, even when the emotion is difficult.

A priestess whose primary motivation is to be noticed and admired will create a very different ritual than a priestess who leads to serve the Goddess and her community. Although members of the circle may not be able to describe what they feel, the priestess's needs will affect the energy of the ritual. Even during the ritual itself, a priestess must be watchful lest she become enamored of the attention she is receiving and distracted from her role.

Everything Works Together
Good rituals touch all the senses—sight, hearing, touch, smell and often taste—and afterward, we use all our senses to communicate with one

another. I believe our senses are often the way the Goddess guides us. Setting and colors, music and spoken words, dances and processions, and the scents of oils and flowers all contribute to draw those present into full participation. In good theatre, the integration of these sensory elements is called "unity of style." The set and costumes are harmonious in color and from the same historical period. A play by Shakespeare doesn't have a rock-and-roll soundscape (unless it has been adapted to a setting in, say, the sixties). When the intention for a ritual is in place, unity of style happens naturally.

Similarly, ritual planners need to brainstorm what colors come to mind when the one-sentence ritual intention is repeated. Any idea is worth considering at this stage. What sounds come to the ear? What sort of movement comes to mind? Is the setting warm or cool, indoors or out? With imagination, a plan can develop in just a few minutes. Of course, the images for a deep winter re-enactment of the descent of Kore-Persephone (darkness, bare branches, solemnity, pomegranate seeds, mournful chants and eventually flowers and spring-time songs) will be quite different from those for the celebration of a girl-child's menses (bright colors, lots of red, cheerful songs, bells, a drummed heartbeat, stories from women in the circle). Once the images and sensations have been fully explored, it can all fit into an organized plan.

One Thing Leads to Another

Things happen in order. In theatre, everyone knows the script. Ritual, too, follows a basic order that we can find in worship services of many faiths. The beginning, middle and end of the ritual must be clear. It is just as important to know how the ritual will end as how it will begin; after all, the intention does not include leaving everyone confused. The basic stages include the following:

- **Create a sacred space.** Cleanse the space, light candles, decorate the altar and put everything into place.
- **Welcome the participants.** Explain what will happen using words that state the ritual's intention; have a procession into the space; bless each person who enters.

- **Dedicate the sacred space.** Cast the circle, call the elements and invoke the Goddess.
- **Raise the energy.** Use droning, chanting, drumming, dancing or all of them combined.
- **Prepare for transformation.** Allow time for quiet reflection, meditation (guided or otherwise) or listening to and pondering words of wisdom.
- **Perform the central act of magic at the heart of the ritual.** This is the moment of transformation, often the emotional peak. It is usually the moment when energy follows intention most clearly. It may be indescribable or take an unanticipated form, which is a sign that the Goddess is at work.
- **Give thanks.** Invite circle members to talk about their experiences of transformation or other reactions to the ritual. Encourage them to offer support to one another as an act of mutual gratitude. Follow up with drumming, dancing or feasting.
- **Ground the energy.** Prepare to return to the mundane world by quieting the drums, calming the chanting and settling the energy.
- **Give thanks.** Thank the divine, the spirits in attendance, the directions/elements and the participants. Thank collaborators; this is an important way for the priestess to honor her community.
- **Open the circle.** As you cast a circle in the beginning, now is the time to close it.

Memorization is Good

It is difficult to read a script in the dark (a fact that often takes priestesses by surprise), which is one good reason actresses learns their lines. Also, reading requires focus on the page, which diverts energy from the important work; and reading sends a message that the priestess doesn't really know what she is doing and/or that she doesn't care enough to take the work to heart by committing it to memory.

Plan Carefully; Then Let Go

The planned details are important, but magic happens in its own way and the priestess must "go with the flow," while at the same time keeping the ritual intact. Some of the most effective rituals I have attended have been those where something went "wrong," but the wrong turned out to be perfectly right. I believe that the unexpected is often a gift from the Goddesses we invoke. When we invite the element of air, we may be rewarded by the wind of unexpected change.

Whatever the surprise may be, the priestess, like the actress, works on more than one level of awareness at all times. She remembers what she has memorized: the order of the ritual and what she and others plan to say and do. She senses the energies among participants, speaking loudly enough to be heard in the circle, watching participants for signs of distress, maintaining safety around candle flames and more, while also guiding the energies of the ritual to further the intention. If she is fortunate, one or more of her colleagues serves as a guardian to help keep everyone safe and protect the flow of energy. Actresses develop such multiple skills with practice, and priestesses can do the same.

Practice, Practice, Practice
It can take years for a priestess to become comfortable in her own skin as a ritualist. Every planning meeting and ritual is an opportunity for creativity and growth. Sometimes a ritual doesn't go well, but I have yet to see the earth stop turning as a result. A sense of proportion and a sense of humor serve the priestess well.

Rehearsals are as good for ritual as for theatre. They can ease everyone's nervousness, help with memorization, provide time and space for creativity and generally help everyone feel more secure. Rehearsals can also be opportunities to integrate eager newcomers or teach skills to less experienced circle members.

I suggest that we offer a ritual whenever an opportunity appears. The mainstream culture offers little in the way of sacred celebration for the significant transitions in women's lives, and ritualizing the important moments keeps the sacred at the forefront in our daily lives. Rituals are important for Women's Blood Mysteries (such as menses, birthing and menopause). They are important for times of crisis (such as illness, dying and mourning). They foster healing and calm. And they celebrate successes and joys: new jobs, new homes, new children, accomplishments of all sorts and, of course, civil unions and weddings.

The basics from theatre can sustain the priestess just as they do the actress. Remember that energy follows intention, servant leadership is effective, collaboration is fertile, everything works together, one thing leads to another, memorization is good, it's important both to plan carefully and to let go, and it's essential to practice at every opportunity. As we create a world where women are empowered by celebrating the Goddess, may these principles serve you well.

Endnotes

1 Eva LaGalliene, *The Mystic in the Theatre* (New York, NY: Farrar, Straus and Giroux, 1966), 18.

2 The Women's Thealogical Institute of the Re-formed Congregation of the Goddess, International provides a program of study that supports the many ways a woman can serve as priestess. www.rcgi.org/study

3 I am indebted to Margarette Shelton for this profound statement, which has guided my work for many years.

Minoan Snake Priestess*
By Le'ema Kathleen Graham

The next day I took the fabric to Dhyanis. We put our hands on the material and blessed it, asking the Goddess to energize our work. I had recently been with Ammachi, where I received a mantra, so I chanted that secret word under my breath through the entire process of making the costume. The sound vibration filled every cut, every stitch and every action of sewing.

For hours and hours we worked to create the wondrous garment of the Minoan Snake Goddess. One by one I gathered all seven of the flounces, spacing the ruffles with my fingers. Dhyanis sewed them onto the bell-shaped underskirt made from sheer white organza.

Over the years, Dhyanis has made many costumes for me. She has the hands of a magician and always seems to bring forth the costumes of my visions. But this was the best one yet! After three days, we completed our labor of love. When I tried the garment on for the final fitting, we burst into tears and laughed delightedly at our accomplishment. I knew that when I wore it, I would appear as the Goddess. Dhyanis exclaimed, "You got the prize this year. I can't wait to see the dance!"

On the evening of the performance, Dyhanis ushered me into a private dressing room. Backstage, I was more nervous than usual as I warmed up while listening to the music with headphones from a portable CD player. I prayed for the creative force to pour through me and revitalize the lives of the community. I prayed for the ability to imbue the

---

* From *Dancing the Inner Serpent: Memoirs of a Suburban Snake Priestess* (Goddesswork: 2009, 2013).

Divine into the spatial configurations of the dance. And I prayed to be of service in my power.

The dance begins in the dark. I stand upstage with my back to the audience, facing the hand-painted silk backdrop of a palace temple on a hillside under a full moon mirrored upon the sparkling blue Aegean Sea. Stately and upright, poised and potent, full of raw electric energy, I can barely move—a chthonian portrayal of the Minoan Snake Goddess. I hold the snakes in my hands; their lithe bodies entwine my arms, which cross over my breasts. A mandolin accompanies the vocal overtone chanting of the singer in a plaintive introduction. My body sways and then spirals counterclockwise while my feet are planted firmly in place. Slowly, I turn my face to the audience, one side and then the other, with a soulful expression. Then I turn my body around—the statue coming to life. I circle forward in precise steps, returning to the present day—an ancient priestess in ceremonial posture in a formal rite.

There, in the very center, my breasts are revealed as I lower my arms down, out, around, ultimately rising into the Minoan Snake Goddess's provocative stance. I hold this posture for one full measure and then walk on the tips of my toes downstage, the snakes held high in the air. When I reach the edge of the stage, I lift the snakes to my third eye. Their forked tongues lick my face and ears as though whispering primeval secrets to me. My hypnotic state deepens. I lower the snakes to my breasts and holding them like suckling infants, I rock them in my arms and sway from side to side.

The serpent energy stimulates me, and I begin to glide in the infinity symbol, holding one snake high and one low, alternating sides. A series of grapevine steps leads me into a spinning crescendo; my face looks toward the heavens, the snakes outstretched from my hands. The flounces on the skirt create a whirling matrix of the chakras and I become the embodiment of our double-helix DNA. I am wide open, a vessel exuding love, blessing all who witness.

As I made my way off stage, I was overcome with emotion. Oh my, what have I done? What hath the Goddess wrought? In the beginning, I felt shy and vulnerable, wary of exposing myself as a vessel for the spirit of the Goddess. But in the costume we merged, and I grew to fit her. Transported, I forgot myself. My attunement was so complete that I stood transfixed, staring at myself in the dressing room mirror with honeyed eyes of mystic wisdom. A larger-than-life energy swirled around my body and shimmered in my aura.

It took a while to get back into present time. Once my snakes were put back into their basket, I removed the headdress, slipped out of the magical garment and looked at my naked body with wonder and gratitude. A prayer came to my lips. "Thank you, dear Goddess, for allowing me to be the vehicle for your radiant presence, for guiding and keeping me on this path of your sacred dance. This four-chambered mansion in my chest will forever be your dwelling place."

Raising the Sacred Fire:
How to Build and Move Energy in Ritual*

By Shauna Aura Knight

Together we are singing, moving, dancing, chanting and drumming around the fire in the center of the circle. The energy builds and slows, then rises up again. I move the drum beat, and the drum beat moves me. We draw closer; I look into the fire-lit eyes of people around me and we smile as we sing. We drop the chant down to a whisper, and then bring it back up again. Our song is a prayer for transformation, a prayer for our individual gifts to be transformed on Brigid's forge into their highest potential. I am singing for my gift and the gifts of everyone there. Our prayer is singing, movement, rhythm and our shared intention. The chant moves into a tone that rises and falls like a fire at the bellows until we hold the silence together.

Have you ever worked to build ecstatic energy in rituals? Raising energy in ritual can be a difficult function to facilitate. Many ritualists get a chant going only to find the group stops singing as soon as the ritualist pauses to take a breath. Despite the challenges, there are some skills, tools and processes you can use to help build potent, transformative energy in rituals.

Facilitating ecstatic energy requires the ability to sense energy and understand the logical energetic flow of any event. Having talent as a singer, drummer, musician or dancer can help, but it's perhaps more important to have a team of people that is engaged, excited and willing to model the energy as an example. Excitement is contagious; if you are

---

* Originally published in a slightly different form in *Circle Magazine: Celebrating Nature, Spirit, and Magic* 105 (Winter 2009): 17–19: www.circlesanctuary.org/circle Reprinted with permission.

invested in the energy, your participants will be more willing to commit their energy as well.

While some ritualists may be gifted with the ability to see auras and energy, I'm not among them. I sense energy more kinesthetically and I also work with energy less as a metaphysical thing and more as the life force cycled from our bodies. As we breathe in oxygen, there's a chemical reaction and we exhale carbon dioxide: chemical reactions release energy. I can also see energy through the physical reality of body language. So sensing energy is largely about being observant.

Think about the last meeting or class you attended. How were people sitting? Did they look interested, or bored and tired? How about the teacher or facilitator; did her voice drone on or was she excited? Now think about a concert or sports event. How did you know that people were excited? Were they standing up and cheering or dancing? When they applauded, what did you feel inside?

Notice the environment around you and how you can sense the energy level of the group. Energy comes across through body language, movements, actions, the way we talk and the look in our eyes. If I'm talking to someone and they're not looking at me, I don't feel like they're really interested in me. But if I go to a friend with a problem and they look deeply into my eyes, I feel they are present and connected to me.

Adding Elemental Energy
Here are some ways to add energy in ritual, broken down by element:

- **Earth—body, movement, dancing.** Whether you're a great dancer or you just sway back and forth to the rhythm of the chant, you add the energy of your body. When you move, your blood moves faster. As your body burns calories, it radiates heat and the energy of your physical life force.
- **Air—breath, speech, chanting, singing.** In ritual, you add air when you speak an intention aloud or lend your voice to the chant. When you sing together, you breathe together, harmonizing your breaths and pulses with others'. You don't need to be a good singer to make a sound and add the energy of your voice.

- **Fire—rhythm, percussion, drumming.** Drummers can add some of the intense sound and rhythm to the ritual. You can also add rhythm by clapping, stamping, snapping your fingers or by making rhythmic sounds through vocal percussion and with your mouth.
- **Water—connection, intention, emotion.** You can connect to the intention of the ritual within the depth of your heart, and to others in the ritual through deep, sustained eye contact or by touching hands. If you're emotionally invested in the community— if you're connecting to the Divine and to the Divine within yourself—you add your emotional energy to the ritual. Even if you are not physically able to move, if you're rhythmically challenged or if you're not comfortable singing, you can add energy by holding the intention in your heart.

Building Energetic Flow

Any ritual has an energetic flow and what happens in the first few minutes of the ritual will set the tone for later on. In the rituals I offer, which are in the ecstatic tradition taught through Reclaiming, Diana's Grove and other shamanic traditions, I work to get people engaged in the ritual and invite participation.

Here is a typical flow of a public ritual in the ecstatic, participatory style. Usually these rituals are facilitated by an ensemble team, so each piece may have more than one person leading it:

- **Market/promote the ritual.** Emails and flyers set the tone for the ritual theme and help build communal trust in the ritual team.
- **Greet participants.** As people arrive at the space, the ritual team greets them. Ideally, everything's already set up so you can welcome people to the space, since welcoming makes people feel safe, and more willing to risk singing and moving later. Having social time for at least a half hour before the ritual helps people transition from interacting with traffic into ritual space.
- **Allow time for a pre-ritual talk.** This session (fifteen minutes or less, to ensure you hold people's attention) addresses the

theme, intention and any ritual logistics. Give people a chance to speak, even if it's going around the circle with names, as that sets a tone of participation and helps the group move from strangers into a tribe. It's a good time to address basic group agreements of what's okay to do, and to teach any chants so people aren't stumbling to learn them later. You can also use the elemental model (above) to let people know how they can add their energy.

- **Gather the group.** Instead of beginning with smudging or similar purifications that involve a long line, Diana's Grove uses an energetic gathering. This is a purification using sound and rhythm to move people from individual mind into group mind. The idea is to begin at the energetic level of the group and take them to a more collective place. You can have the group sing a tone, or clap and move and sing to build up some energetic fuel for later in the ritual.
- **Ground the energy.** As much as the gathering is about group energy and group mind, grounding, in this context, is about connecting more deeply with themselves, becoming more present with the Divine and connecting to the theme of the work. A typical tree grounding can work just fine, or any meditation to facilitate participants going internal to get into a sacred mindset.
- **Cast a circle.** For the rituals I offer, casting a circle is less about creating an energetic barrier to keep negative energies out than defining an energetic boundary acknowledging that you are all in one place together. As grounding is internal, circle casting takes you out of yourselves to connect as a tribe. The circle is the edge of your tribe for the ritual, and it's important to establish connection and safety. This is the cauldron that will hold the soup. In ecstatic participatory ritual, one or two people facilitate the circle-casting, but the intention is for participants to add their energy to the process. The challenge is to cast the circle in an inclusive way and perform the invocation in two minutes or less to keep people engaged.
- **Invoke the elements.** Use the elemental invocations to invite participants to lend their voices, bodies, movements and

intentions, and deepen the theme of the ritual. In the rituals I work in, instead of facing each direction, the elemental invoker moves into the center and invites the whole group to invoke the element. An example: "Will you join me in welcoming Air? Will you take a breath together, will you make the sound that is the wind in the trees that blows the leaves to the ground, will you move as Air moves? Air is the breath of life; can you feel how the change in the air heralds the change in the seasons? Welcome, Air."

- **Center the circle.** I typically work with center as the gravity well that draws the community together. What is the reason that people came? This is another opportunity to connect the group together as a tribe, and to the center that holds you.
- **Invite deities, ancestors, allies.** Invite whichever deities or allies you'll be working with in as inclusive a way as possible. Inviting each person to participate, is more potent than letting them watch a ritualist do the work. Liturgy and poetry can be powerful, but if you want the group to add their energy later on, give them some way to participate in every piece, even if it's just closing their eyes and imagining the ancestors.
- **Include storytelling.** Often the working part of the ritual begins with storytelling or some piece to add context to what you're doing in the ritual. This piece can be longer than two minutes, provided you give people a chance to get comfortable.
- **Transition to a trance journey.** Use storytelling to transition into a trance journey that will move the theme from a story about gods and heroes to a story with which participants can personally interact. Storytelling and trance journeys help people take their energy within, but will require a transition if you want them to come out of trance and be active.
- **Get physical.** Offer experiences for multiple learning styles (visual, auditory, kinesthetic and so on). If the trance journey helped participants connected with the fire of their personal magic, you might make that intention physical by inviting people to choose a stone to represent their magic. Or you might

have them stand and go to an altar to offer their personal magic to Brigid's forge to be transformed. Physicalization helps integrate the ritual intention, and transitions people from internal to external so they are ready to participate in the energy.

- **Build energy.** Sustained energy fuels the magic. Start slow and build by layering chanting, movement, harmonies, vocal percussion, drumming and more. The ritual team should be fully engaged; if you aren't willing to stand up and sing, no one else will be. Allow the energy to rise to a peak of sound and rhythm, followed by a moment of silence. Eight to ten minutes is typical for this stage; fifteen minutes may be longer than many people can chant. The energy, and the ritual, should have a defined ending. People can drum and dance more after ritual.
- **Perform a benediction.** Let people know what the ritual was about; you could say, for example, "Brigid, thank you for helping us find our personal magic and transform it in your forge. May we support each other in community." This seals the deal on the work and leads to devoking the allies and elements. The benediction and opening of the circle provides a last chance for the group to connect as a tribe before the ritual ends.
- **Enjoy dessert or a feast.** Ecstatic participatory rituals tend to not include cakes and ale in the ceremony because of the energetic lag created by a long wait for food to be passed around. A post-ritual dessert or feasting offers intentional bonding time to grow community.

Bits and Pieces

Here are a few final points to consider:

- **Layer in voice, rhythm and movement to build and sustain energy.** As each layer builds, gently add another layer; this will feel quite natural to the group and they will be more likely to participate. Drummers should follow the group's energy rather than driving the group; if the drumming builds too fast, the group may "check out." If you find the energy is spiking too quickly, drop the chant down to a whisper and build it back up. Invite group participation through eye contact, by beckoning or by asking, "Will you join your movement and voice to this ritual?"

- **Have a team of people who are willing to sing and dance to model what behavior is okay.** Watch a ritual where one person starts to clap; if no one else does, they'll stop because they don't feel safe, but if a second or third person join in, others will, too. If you have some strong singers, use a chant with two parts or harmonies to add another layer of energy. A basket of rhythm instruments offers another opportunity for people to add sound.
- **Work the energy by finding a balance between letting the group drive how fast the chant builds and pushing the energy along.** The energy will plateau, and then rise again when you add a layer. At first, it will be hard to sense if the group is ready to finish or has just reached a natural plateau, where another layer will build the energy back up. Notice people's body language. Are they willing to stand up and sing? The kinds of energy you can build into ritual will depend on your team. Do you have drummers and singers? Do you have ten attendees, or 100? What chant are you using—is it cradling, or an energy-raiser?
- **Observe the rituals of different groups.** What happens to the energy when forty people smudge themselves or stand in line at an altar? How long do people speak? When is it boring? When are people invigorated, willing to sing or participate? When do they glaze over?

It takes time to build the skillset of creating ecstatic energy in ritual, but these tools should offer a way to frame ritual in terms of energy and help you begin to build techniques into your own rituals. With practice, you can raise the sacred fire of ecstatic energy in your rituals.

Priestessing Ritual*
By Ruth Barrett

Many women who are drawn to Dianic tradition, women's rituals and goddess traditions live in small communities and consider themselves fairly isolated. Women gathering in these communities are likely to share similar levels of experience, inspire one another and learn ritual skills through trial and error. There may not be any other groups practicing Dianic or goddess-centered ritual in their area; there may not be elders nearby to teach or train them in ritual and magical skills. The experience of these women will be different from those practicing in larger cities where they may have access to more resources and training. It takes a lot of courage and determination to self-educate, to dive into areas where you don't have guidance, to gain experience wherever you can get it and to fall on your face as a group when a ritual goes awry.

Unfortunately, many women have done a lot of reading about goddess traditions and believe that this has made them instant ritualists. Reading about rafting the Grand Canyon and actually having the skill, courage and experience to do it are very different. Although scholarship is important and can inform your ritual concepts and ideas, becoming an effective ritualist means integrating intellectual concepts and information with hands-on, energetic skills and an open heart. It takes time, experience and practice. This integration of skill and knowledge can create a ritual experience that is moving and transformational.

---

* Originally published in a slightly different form in *Women's Rites, Women's Mysteries: Intuitive Ritual Creation* (Woodbury, MN: Llewellyn Worldwide, 2007). Reprinted with permission.

Unless a specific woman establishes a ritual group with herself as the focus point or leader, most women's ritual circles work on a consensus model of decision-making. Groups sometimes form to practice ritual skills, and everyone usually starts out with the same level of experience, or lack of it. If you are part of a circle, or choose to form one, rotate responsibility to allow for all women to learn and be supported as they are learning.

Not every woman has a desire to serve in a priestess capacity. A woman should be encouraged and supported to take risks, but if she feels unprepared or unwilling to fulfill a facilitator role, respect her right to decline. Facilitation should be voluntary. Always offer each other the opportunity to stretch, rather than stress, your abilities. If a woman is nervous or self-conscious, other women in the group with more confidence can support her by honoring the skills she already has and making space for her to grow in her confidence with constructive feedback when she takes on new responsibilities. If your circle is a supportive environment for practicing skills and learning by trial and error, everyone will grow in their abilities and confidence in their own time. When a woman facilitates ritual, she gains valuable experience that could eventually move her toward becoming an ordained vocational priestess, should she desire it.

I believe that no ritual role or job is less or more rewarding than another when you learn to embody the Goddess and bring her through you in your service to women. Every woman in a group has something to offer. Identifying the abilities, skills and talents within a group can be fun, as well as eye-opening. My old Moon Birch Grove coven sister, Sylvia, had no interest in facilitating ritual; what she loved to do was cook! To the group's delight, she made seasonally inspired meals for each sabbat. This was Sylvia's gift, offered in service to the group. Given that honoring space, Sylvia later developed into a fine storyteller of goddess myths.

Ritual priestessing is not for the faint of heart or for those who are overly controlling. If you fear chaos, the unexpected or the unforeseen, choose another vocation. A ritual facilitator regularly finds herself in challenging situations that are not at all what she originally planned. The ability to be flexible is a must-have trait to cultivate. You will get lots of practice.

In order to facilitate others, you first need to know how to be a good participant. I don't believe it is possible for a woman to priestess/facilitate a ritual effectively until she first knows how to truly participate in one. What are our responsibilities as participants in a ritual? What can you learn from participating that can help you become a better ritual facilitator? When asked about their responsibilities as ritual participants, some of my students listed these points:

- Stay focused, centered and present.
- Lend energy when energy is required.
- Follow instructions given by facilitators.
- Respect any guidelines or safety requirements.
- Avoid side talk.
- Take care of yourself. Check in with yourself periodically during the ritual.
- Take responsibility for your own experience.

I more often use the term "ritual facilitator" than "ritual leader" or "priestess" when working with women who are learning ritual priestessing skills. Although a ritual priestess is a facilitator, a facilitator is not always a ritual priestess. Thus, the word "facilitator" more clearly describes the role of the woman taking responsibility for the ritual or an aspect of it.

A facilitator is a woman who makes the way easier; as an act of service, she assists in creating the experience of the participants. Like a guide on a journey, the facilitator's responsibility is to hold the vision and the purpose; to keep the compass, to know what the ultimate destination of the ritual journey is and to help everyone get there and back safely. If you were leading a group on a hike, you'd have to watch the trail and set a pace that matched the energy of the participants, or be prepared to motivate them to match yours. It would be your responsibility if someone got lost or wandered too near the edge of a cliff. Like the leader of the hiking group, as you gain experience in facilitation, even though you may not have hiked on a particular trail, you know the forest, have the feel of the pace needed, and can improvise as the weather changes or other factors arise. Always have a magical first-aid kit on hand for bruised egos or raw emotions.

When a woman first begins her ritual work, she may find herself memorizing lines, words or movements. Gradually, though, a change, a shift, happens: a glimmer, a revelation or a deepening as to what ritual facilitation is really about. This shift of awareness moves from simply following the ritual structure or form to being part of, and guiding the flow of, the ritual's purpose. Sensing and guiding the ritual's intention as a flow of energy that has a shape and direction is a skill gained from a deep understanding and practice of energetics. It means not only holding the ritual intention and shape but also being fully present in the moment-to-moment experience yourself. This is part of the transitional experience from being a ritual facilitator to becoming a ritual priestess.

In becoming a ritual priestess, you are able to craft energy within yourself as well as without. You learn to know when the ritual is working because it is like a light switch being turned on—a feeling of rightness, a physical experience of a perfect fit. A good metaphor would be learning to play a guitar. At first, your fingers struggle to remember chords and move in proper time. You are ever conscious in trying to remember where your hands need to be. Your fingers need to develop the strength to hold the strings against the frets. As you master the skill and the strength, you are no longer conscious of having to place your fingers on the right frets. Your brain and muscles remember automatically, and instead of thinking and struggling, the music comes through you.

The Technology of Rhythm
By Layne Redmond

My research into the history of the frame drum took me on a journey among women that stretched from the earliest known examples of human symbolic thought to the rise of Christianity at the beginning of the modern era. I discovered that, for thousands and thousands of years, people throughout the Mediterranean world worshiped forms of a nurturing Great Goddess. At the heart of this worship was the frame drum. With it, she regulated the rhythmic dance of the cosmos—the progression of seasons, the cycles of the moon, the growth and fruition of crops, the lives of her people.

Ancient sources tell us that the frame drum was not just a powerful symbol of spiritual presence; it was an important tool for many spiritual experiences. Priestesses of the Goddess were skilled technicians in its uses. They knew which rhythms quickened the life in freshly planted seeds; which facilitated childbirth; which induced the ecstatic trance of spiritual transcendence. Guided by drum beats, these sacred drummers could alter their consciousness at will, traveling through the three worlds of the Goddess: the heavens, the earth and the underworld.

Scientific research from astrophysics to biology tends to support the idea that rhythm is a fundamental force. Neurological studies into the way our brains function suggest that drumming and other spiritual practices of our ancestresses could indeed bring about a transformation of ordinary consciousness. By banning her drum, the patriarchal religions

---

* Originally published in a slightly different form in *When Drummers were Women: A Spiritual History of Rhythm* (New York: Three Rivers Press, 1997), 169–179. Though currently out of print, a new edition is in press. See www.layneredmond.com

that suppressed the Goddess cut off our access to significant parts of our own psyches. They destroyed psychological and spiritual techniques that had been used for many thousands of years.

Today, many people turn to science instead of religion to make sense of their world. One of our most popular origin myths is the Big Bang Theory of modern astrophysics. According to this theory, all the material of the universe was once compacted into a hot, dense ball. About fifteen to twenty billion years ago, there was a tremendous explosion. The shock waves of this primordial sound flung matter across space, where it eventually coalesced into the galaxies, solar systems and individual planets. Scientists still have no better way to describe this moment than as the "instant the universe was born."

A related concept in physics today is the Superstring Theory, which replaces the former idea of separate subatomic particles with an image of loops of vibrating strings. The frequency at which these strings vibrate, and the rhythmic patterns generated by their interplay, determine how they manifest.

The idea that the universe is, in essence, a symphony of vibrations emanating out of an enormous first beat suggests the science of music, and many scientists use musical analogies to describe their theories. Princeton physicist Edward Witten says, "In the case of the superstring, the different harmonics correspond to different elementary particles—electron, graviton, proton, neutrino and all the others, are different harmonics of a fundamental string, just as the different overtones of a violin string are different harmonics of one string."[1] Experiments performed by Hans Jenny, founder of cymatics, the study of wave forms, lend support to the theory that vibrations give form to the material world.[2] Jenny found that when sound waves were introduced to various material substances—water, alcohol, pastes, oils and so forth—they created symmetrical patterns with uniform characteristics. The undifferentiated substances were organized instantly into organic forms. Put simply, Jenny's research shows that rhythm shapes matter.

The Pulse of Life

To approach creation from another perspective, let's move from astrophysics to biology, from the birth of the cosmos to the birth of a single human being.

It is often said that the first sound we hear in the womb is our mother's heartbeat. Actually, the first sound to vibrate our newly developed hearing apparatus is the pulse of our mother's blood through her veins and arteries. We vibrate to that primordial rhythm even before we have ears to hear. Before we were conceived, we existed in part as an egg in our mother's ovary. All the eggs a woman will ever carry form in her ovaries while she is a four-month-old fetus in the womb of her mother. This means our cellular life as an egg begins in the womb of our grandmother. Each of us spent five months in our grandmother's womb, and she in turn was formed within the womb of her grandmother. We vibrate to the rhythms of our mother's blood before she herself is born. And this pulse is the thread of blood that runs all the way back through the grandmothers to the first mother. We all share the blood of the first mother—we are truly children of one blood.

As a tiny, pulsing egg, we experienced the birth of our mother, the growth of her body, her joys, her fears, her triumphs. For fourteen to forty years, we rocked as an egg to the rhythms of her body. Men cannot convey this continuity of cellular energy to their sperm. The father imparts not the imprint of a lifetime but only the fleeting energy of a few weeks. Man's nature is, in many metaphorical ways, a quick rise and fall—the vanishing and resurrecting energy reflected in so many of the ancient male gods.

At the fetal age of four weeks, our own heart starts to pulse. The auditory nerve begins to pick up vibrations from our environment about twenty weeks later. We begin to synchronize our movements not only to physical sounds but to the rhythms of voices, the vibrations of thoughts. Our mother's emotions create complex chemical interactions in her body, and their particular energies permeate the womb. Her dream cycles affect our sleep patterns. By the time we are born, we are already imprinted with the rhythms of the language, emotions, feelings and interactions around us. These rhythms will always seem the most familiar and natural to us, no matter how beneficial or detrimental they actually are.

Scientific studies have shown that our moods, emotions, thoughts and bodily processes are rhythms of chemical energy. The Puerto Ricans call this fundamental rhythm, which marks how we walk, talk and interact, *tumbao*. It is an expression of the totality of our personality.

As the body takes shape in the womb, consciousness begins. It can be detected as brainwaves—rhythmic vibrations emanating from the brain and nervous system. All through our lives, our state of consciousness is governed by the rate of these vibrations. Using electro-encephalographs, scientists can measure the number of energy waves per second pulsing through the brain. They have developed a system of classification differentiating states of consciousness.

As you read these words, your brain is probably vibrating at between fourteen and twenty-one cycles per second. These are called "beta waves." The state of awareness characterized by beta waves is associated with active, waking attention, focused on everyday external activities. Beta waves are also in evidence during states of anxiety, tension and fear.

"Alpha waves" vibrate at seven to fourteen waves per second. They indicate a relaxed internal focus and a sense of well-being. "Theta" waves vibrate at about four to seven cycles per second and indicate the drowsy, semi-conscious state usually experienced at the threshold of sleep.

The slowest frequency, from one to four cycles per second, is the "delta" level, the state of unconsciousness or deep sleep. The brains of fetuses emit delta waves.

Beta waves dominate in most humans past puberty. But the brain activity of other animals registers well within the alpha range, which also correlates to the electromagnetic field of the earth. So when the Tantric Yogi sought to bring herself into alignment with cosmic vibrations, she aspired to the alpha state, which is in fact the basic rhythm of nature.

Neurological studies indicate that the brain is divided into two hemispheres that share control of mental activity. In very young children they develop as one, but at about five years of age, each hemisphere begins to specialize. The right brain functions as the creative center. It is the seat of visual, aural and emotional memory, and processes information in holistic, intuitive terms, relying on pattern recognition. The left brain is the administrator, what we sometimes call the rational mind. It proceeds in logical, analytical, verbal and sequential fashion. Incoming information is identified, classified and explained.

If one hemisphere is damaged, the other one is able, within limits, to take over its functions. Normally, though, the memories, mental associations, ideas and processes of each hemisphere are somewhat inaccessible to the other. In ordinary consciousness, either the left or the right brain dominates in cycles lasting from thirty minutes to about three hours. We shift from one side to the other depending on which skills we require.

Not only do the two hemispheres of our brains operate in different modes, they also usually operate in different rhythms. The right brain may be generating alpha waves while the left brain is in a beta state. Or both hemispheres can also be generating the same type of brain waves, but remain out of sync with each other. But in states of intense creativity or deep meditation, or under the influence of rhythmic sound, both hemispheres may begin operating in the same synchronized rhythm. This state of unified whole-brain functioning is called "hemispheric synchronization."

As the rhythms of the two hemispheres synchronize, there is a sense of clarity and heightened awareness. Feelings of self-consciousness and separation fall away. The individual is able to draw on both the left and the right hemispheres simultaneously. Hemispheric synchronization on the alpha level can create feelings of euphoria, expanded mental powers and intense creativity. This may be the neurological basis of higher states of consciousness.

Many ancient religious practices seem to have originated in attempts to induce the transcendent experience of hemispheric synchronization. Chanting rhythmically while gazing at geometric figures, like the Tantric combination of mantra and yantra, facilitates synchronization by simultaneously engaging the verbal skills of one hemisphere and the visual skills of the other.

Because each hemisphere controls the motor skills of one-half of the body, rhythmic movement can also effect synchronization. Rhythmic dancing, accompanied by music and chanting, was an integral part of the pre-Christian religious experience, often bringing the dancer into a trance-like state of ecstasy.

Drumming is perhaps the most effective way to induce brain-wave synchronization. Musical comprehension has been found to be a joint function of left and right hemispheres. Andrew Neher conducted a series of well-known experiments showing that the rhythms of the drum act as an auditory driving mechanism, able to drive or entrain the subject's brain waves into alpha or theta states.

Our culture heavily values left-brain functions and has associated them with male characteristics; as a result, men have been educated to develop an asymmetrical specialization in left-brain functioning. The right-brain functions have been labeled "inferior" female characteristics, creating a splitting-off and devaluing of half of ourselves. In the drive to develop the left brain, we've neglected the potential of the right brain and also forgotten techniques for synchronizing both hemispheres.

Entrainment

Rhythm is catching. Mothers croon soft lullabies or rock their infants to lull them to sleep. Like Gilgamesh, military drummers still pound out martial beats to rouse patriotic fervor. As we interact with other people, our personal rhythms influence one another.

This ability of one rhythm to draw another into harmonic resonance is called "entrainment". The power of some people's rhythm—such as pop stars Michael Jackson and Tina Turner, civil rights leader Martin Luther King, Jr., and even Adolf Hitler—is such that thousands and perhaps millions of people can entrain with them.

Research by William S. Condon shows that language is structured rhythmically with body movement.[3] To communicate successfully, people must be able to adjust the tempos of their expression to one another. When people converse they interact in complex rhythms almost like a dance. The harmonious entrainment of their conversational rhythms allows each person to listen and respond at the right intervals, instead of overlapping or interrupting the other person or coming in too late. When a person's rhythm is continually disrupted or suppressed, the effect can be severe, leading to boredom, exhaustion, depression, anxiety, anger. Although everyone must learn to respond to the give-and-take of conversational and social rhythms to some extent, in our culture adjusting to the tempos of others is a skill particularly valued in women.

Sometimes we find ourselves naturally synchronized with another person. When a high level of effortless entrainment occurs, one's own rhythm is fully expressed. This is one of life's greatest pleasures. Falling in love is falling in rhythm with someone.

Major events like birth, marriage, pregnancy, illness, separation and death are stressful partly because they break familiar rhythms. People who are experiencing grief or depression seem to be painfully unable to create and maintain organized patterns of behavior. They have lost their personal rhythm. The need to replace broken rhythms often drives people unconsciously to try to re-create lost relationships.

In archaic communities, the shaman used the drum to entrain the consciousness of initiates with the divine rhythms of the earth. Practitioners of Nada Yoga used the entraining capacities of music to align their minds with the bibration supportion credation. Oracular priestesses, temple priestesses, *maenads* (female followers of Dionysis, literally translated as "raving ones"), were all skilled at drawing from the skin head of the drum rhythms that entrained the minds of worshipers, moving them inexorably toward a state of ecstatic union with the divine. Drumming was a necessary and respected skill among these holy women.

Nestled between the hemispheres of the brain, where the cerebral cortex, cerebellum and limbic system meet, is a small organ called the "pineal gland." Its function has long been a matter of scientific dispute. For a long time, scientists thought of it as a vestigial organ, perhaps used to sense light in our ancient biological past. Because its current function was unknown, it was assumed to have none.

Indian mystics sought to raise their *kundalini* (awareness or consciousness) to their spiritual center, the third eye. This third eye, like the *uraeus* (Hathor's divine cobra), rested in the center of the forehead, which is the location of the pineal gland. The same spot is also related to the sacred Egyptian eye symbol, which stood for light in all its forms—the light of the sun, the light of knowledge, the light of the spirit.

Contemporary research into the function of biological clocks suggests that the pineal gland is indeed a kind of light sensor. The sun—and, to a lesser extent, the moon—pour energy into the biological environment in the form of light. This penetrating energy affects our bodily rhythms through our nervous systems. The pathways and orchestration of light's influence are as yet unclear to modern scientists, but it appears that the pineal gland may be the jewel in our biological clockworks, keeping us in sync with environmental time and influencing the physiological and emotional rhythms of the body.

The study of biorhythms is a relatively new field and it is still unclear exactly how biological clocks function. What is known is that all life responds rhythmically to the cycles of nature. The 24-hour solar cycle, called the "circadian rhythm," appears to be the most basic.

Out of Sync

Through an enormous expenditure of effort and resources, modern science is coming to the same conclusions the ancients knew from immediate experience: that life is inexorably rhythmic. Rhythm drives the planets in their orbits and the fetus in its growth. Rhythm prompts the cycle of the earth and the cycles of our emotions.

This hard-won knowledge seems to have little practical effect on our contemporary culture. Biological research has demonstrated that patients' receptivity to drugs and medical treatment fluctuates in 24-hour cycles, and to a lesser extent in seasonal or yearly cycles. Traditional Chinese medicine has taken these cycles into account for centuries, but modern Western medicine ignores the concept of biorhythms.

It's becoming apparent that some of our major physiological and psychological ills may be a result of being out of sync with environmental time. "It is the tension between the internal clocks and the clock on the wall that causes so much of the stress in today's world," says anthropologist Edward T. Hall. "We have now constructed an entire complex system of schedules, manners, and expectations to which we are trying to adjust ourselves, when, in reality, it should be the other way around."[4]

Shutting ourselves away within our steel, concrete and glass prisons, insulated from rhythmic fluctuations in light and temperature, we block ourselves off from seasonally appropriate changes in physiology and behavior. We run the risk of damaging our biological cycles. Laboratory experiments in which human beings are isolated from environmental energies produce symptoms of lethargy, fatigue, irritability and boredom in their human subjects. The physical costs may be even more deadly. Studies conducted by John D. Palmer suggest that our biological clocks affect the functioning of every cell in our bodies, and cancerous cells may be cells that have lost this vital rhythmic regulation.[5]

In ancient cultures, the tempo of human life was synchronized with the rhythms of the earth. The priestess's frame drum was the thread that led back through countless millennia to that first beat that vibrated the world into being. People understood life as rhythm and woman's body as a reflection of that primordial truth. Her reproductive cycle expressed her intimate connection to the environment and was the basis for the earliest time-keeping systems. The Mediterranean cultures, as well as the Celts, the Germans and others, used a lunar calendar, with the new moon heralding the start of a new month.

The Romans imposed the Julian calendar we still use today on the Western world, but they were not the first to abandon the lunar model in favor of a man-made system. Lunar time caused problems for large-scale bureaucracies. First, the length of the lunar cycle is not constant. Second, the actual time of the rising of the new moon varied depending on the longitude and latitude of the observer. As early as 2500 BCE, the bureaucrats of Sumer came up with a new calendar in order to regulate tax collection. This change from calendars based on nature to calendars designed to serve the purposes of those in power was one of the earliest rejections of the truth of direct experience.

The ancients studied the stars and the earth with humility, motivated by a sense of awe and a desire to participate as fully as possible in the rhythms of the universe. Our division between objective and subjective truths—science and religion—didn't exist. Contemporary science, with its left-brain analytical bias, is skeptical of anything that smacks of the intuitive or mystical. The only experiences worthy of its interest are those that can be measured by machines or expressed as formulas.

Some scientific advances have greatly improved the lot of humankind, but when science attempts to define the nature of reality using only what are called "objective criteria," it denies the validity of the sacred.

If scientists are the new priesthood, they minister to a religion devoid of the Divine. Judaism, Christianity and Islam have stripped divinity of feminine qualities; science goes one step further, canceling the concept of divinity entirely. Religious experience is subjective; it is not rational; therefore, it cannot be validated. In this new religion, nothing is sacred but the dry truths of statistics.

To most people, the dogmas of science are incomprehensible. They must be accepted on faith. Yet we deny the validity of personal experience in service to this "objective" truth. Those who separate themselves from the natural world in order to study it lose the vital connection that makes sense of the whole. They have forgotten that consciousness itself is subjective. When a human being subtracts herself from the equation of the universe, her results are doomed to be incomplete.

Reclaiming Ourselves
Many scientists are using new information about the natural harmonies of life to great advantage. Biorhythmic studies have breathed new life into the ancient practice of music therapy.

When the shaman's knowledge of healing through sound fell into disrepute in the West, the discipline languished. Music was felt to have a calming effect on some nervous diseases, but that was thought too vague and subjective to be worthy of serious study.

In the last few decades, however, music therapy has become respectable. This may be due in part to the fact that music's influence on pulse, blood pressure, heartbeat and so forth can be measured on machines. These scientifically sanctioned tests reveal that music can, indeed, alter consciousness.

At the Marino Medical Center in Boston, in an informal setting, I participated in an experiment testing the effect of drumming on brainwave activity. A volunteer was hooked up to an EEG machine. As soon as I began to play my frame drum—without any time lapse—his brain waves entrained with the sound he was hearing. When I shifted rhythms, his brain waves shifted simultaneously.

The research and hypotheses mentioned in this chapter suggest that we are locked into an interactive system of personal, cultural and environmental rhythmic needs. Hall predicts that "rhythm will . . . soon be proved to be the ultimate dynamic building block in not only personality but also communication and health."[6]

Yet contemporary society has forgotten this need to be in rhythm with ourselves, one another and nature. Conventional wisdom preaches that we are entirely responsible as individuals for our own behavior. We need to find effective ways of reconnecting with the rhythms of our environment, our bodies and our deepest selves. For a growing number of women, drumming is once again becoming a sacred technology capable of restoring those patterns.

Endnotes

1 Edward Witten, P. C.W. Davies and J. Brown, *Superstrings: A Theory of Everything* (Cambridge, England: Cambridge University Press, 1988), 170.

2 Hans Jenny, *Cymatics* (Basel: Basilius Presse AG, 1974).

3 W. S. Condon and W. D. Ogston, "Speech and Body Motion Synchrony of Speaker-Hearer," Perception of Language, ed. D. L. Horton and J. J. Jenkins (Columbus, OH: Charles E. Merrill Press, 1971).

4 Edward T. Hall, *The Dance of Life: The Other Dimension of Time* (New York: Anchor Books, 1984).

5 John D. Palmer, *Introduction to Biological Rhythms* (New York: Academic Press, 1976).

6 Edward T. Hall, *The Dance of Life: The Other Dimension of Time* (New York: Anchor Books, 1984).

Ritual Design and Facilitation: Chanting that Works*
By Shauna Aura Knight

"How do you get people singing?" people ask me. "How can I get my groups at home to actually join in the chanting voluntarily? I start singing the chant and it stutters and dies horribly." I've been to rituals where everyone mumbles along with the chant; actually, a decade ago that was me, secretly praying the chant would end soon.

Getting people to sing is extremely challenging. Phaedra Bonewits put it succinctly in a sacred sound workshop she led at Chrysalis Moon Festival, that once people developed the art of recording, we stopped hearing musicians sing their "okay" versions of songs; now, we only hear the best take out of multiple tries and thus learn we shouldn't sing unless we can be perfect.

I am not a perfect singer. In grade school, I was the one the music teacher asked to sing more quietly because I was off key. When I started attending Reclaiming rituals, they encouraged me to sing anyway. Over time, I discovered that I could hit the right notes on the chants, I just had to sing them enough times to learn them. My voice got stronger. Eventually, I began leading rituals on my own and there was no one to teach the chant but me. I survived, and learned how to do it better.

Chanting Tips and Tricks
You don't need to be a musician to lead chants. Here are some of the tips and tricks I've used. I haven't ever taken a music lesson, nor do I read music, though I have learned from some trained musicians like Lucinda

---
* Originally published in a slightly different form in *Circle Magazine: Celebrating Nature, Spirit, and Magic*. www.circlesanctuary.org/circle. Reprinted with permission.

Sohn, a former choir director. Primarily, I'll use terms that you don't need to be a musician to understand.

Overcome Tone Deafness

What people usually mean by this is that they can hear that they are hitting the wrong notes, but can't make their voices sing the right ones. For most of these folks, the solution is pretty straightforward: sing more until you learn the song. Also, try singing the chant at a lower pitch; a lot of what I thought was me being tone deaf was just that I was trying to match my voice to notes too high for me to hit.

Learn the Chants

I sang along to chants alone so nobody would hear me singing off key. I found that I needed to sing a lot of times to really learn a chant, to learn the correct notes through muscle memory. I can't teach a chant that I don't know.

Warm Up Your Voice

Even after years of singing, my voice sounds terrible if I haven't warmed up. I need a half-hour to an hour of singing to get my voice properly warmed up. I often sing in the car to get ready to facilitate a ritual. I'll keep singing until I can hit and sustain the higher notes in my vocal range. When working with a group, I try to find ways to help a group begin to warm their voices up, such as by toning.

Find the Right Pitch

You can't teach a chant at a pitch the group can't sing, and you can't lead a chant if it's too high-pitched for your own voice. By pitch, I mean singing higher or lower. I don't know what key I am singing in, but I do know when someone is singing a chant too high for my voice. If I'm leading that chant, I start it on a lower note so that I can sustain singing it.

I've found that inexperienced singers are generally more comfortable singing chants pitched a little lower. People who are not used to singing will drop completely out of a chant that is started too high. I've heard an axiom that you must start chants higher because they drop in pitch, but what I've found is that chants drop in pitch because they are started too high. When I start a chant at a pitch most people can follow, the chant stays there.

Picking Chants
Two important points about choosing chants are to pick good chants, and to pick the right chant.

Pick Good Chants
Perhaps this is obvious, but there are really a lot of bad chants. A good chant is simple enough that people can easily learn it, and musically complex enough to be engaging.

Pick the Right Chant
Just because it's a good chant, doesn't mean it's the right chant. There are basically two kinds of chants; they either hold space or build energy. Some energetic chants may be hard to sustain for a long time, so they're not suited to holding space, but it would impossible to build energy with some droning chants. Generally chants in a minor key are easier to use for holding space, while it's easier to build energy with chants in a major key. Chants in three-quarter time (like a waltz) are easier to use for holding space, gently rocking and cradling; chants in four-quarter time are easier for building energy.

You might need to hold space in an extended healing ritual, or to hear oracular messages from a drawn-down deity; a slow chant keeps the group energy focused. An energy-building chant that will build a cone of power works better if it has more complicated layers; two-part chants tend to build energy more strongly, if you have a group that can sustain it.

Maintaining a Chant
Keeping a chant going can be more difficult than it seems. The following points should help you become a better chant leader.

Strengthen Your Voice and Lung Capacity
You may eventually want to take voice lessons. Singing while standing

and projecting from the diaphragm will give you more vocal power. You can work over time to build up your lung capacity by singing tones like *Om* over and over. I can sing a chant for forty seconds without breathing, if I'm careful. Keep in mind that singing notes at the higher end of your range takes more breath. Having strong breath control allows you to keep singing as other voices tire.

Be Loud, but Not Too Loud
To lead chants, you need to project. You not only need people to be able to hear you; you also need to give the chant vocal power because your loud voice will make participants more comfortable singing. The trick is to sing with just enough energy and enthusiasm to infect the group without overwhelming them; sometimes too much enthusiasm can turn the group off. You have to balance out your volume based on the group's energy level.

Soothe your throat with honey, lemon, cough drops and pickle juice. There are lots of remedies for soothing throats and removing phlegm. I spend an hour warming up my voice to get the roughness out of my voice, but Burt's Bees honey and lemon cough drops have helped. Some like tea. Pickle juice can clear your throat out, but it's rough on your throat over time. However you do it, make sure your voice is clear when you start singing.

Advanced Chanting
Like everything, chanting also has advanced skills. Here are some tips for helping people progress to advanced levels of chanting:

Give People Permission to "Suck"
People get nervous when they are singing and the chant sounds bad, so I let them know that it's okay if it doesn't sound great at first, that we're learning the chant and it'll take seven to ten repetitions to just get the melody. People feel less embarrassed and more willing to push through because I've given them permission to sound bad at first.

Address Off-Kilter Breathing

There are places where everyone breathes during a chant: *Oh, Mother* (breathe) *We are calling* (breathe) *Your children* (breathe) *We need healing* (breathe) *Power, Power* (breathe) *Our love is our power* (big breath).[1]

With my lung capacity, I'm able to sing through the entire verse and into the beginning of the next repetition without needing to breathe. Why bother? A big breath means a big silence. Singing through adds vocal interest and maintains energy. It helps to have multiple people trained to sing through the breathing parts, but one strong voice can do it. When participants aren't sold on singing, they're waiting for any excuse to stop. When the chant leader takes a breath, what goes through their minds is, "Maybe we're stopping."

If I sing through when everyone's breathing, it never enters their minds that we might stop. This keeps the positive intention. I'm smiling and looking into their eyes while I'm singing, projecting energy that says, "Let's sing this because we can bring the deep magic." Then I breathe after everyone has started singing the next line strongly. This is a difficult technique; I have to fight my body's urge to breathe when everyone else does, but it can be effective in getting people past the initial "hump" of the chant.

Smile and Show Charisma

When I'm chanting, I'm singing, not screaming or frowning. I'm putting my life force and energy into the chant. I'm engaging people in direct eye contact, inviting them with all of my energy to join me. I find the energy to do this by going forward and backward in time: forward to the moment when everyone is enjoying singing the chant and opening up to the divine, backward to the last time I sang a chant and the group connected to the magic. I use that energy to get people past the "hump." Your energy and positive intent is the fuel to engage the group.

Connect with the Group

Sometimes you may need to start slower. I have seen some ritualists with hyper, over-the-top energy who cause the group to recoil; it's too much, too fast, too showy. The trick is to meet the group at their level, entice and engage them. Remember that amazing energy you want to evoke. If you fall in love with that moment, with that divine connection, when everyone is singing and connected and whole and holy, you've found the fuel you need to bring into the chant you're singing. When I talk about authenticity in ritual, that's what I mean.

Develop other Chant Leaders

Helping others strengthen their voice and anchor chants will increase your ability to get a group of people singing; the more strong voices you have, the easier it will be.

Sing Harmonies

I learned to sing harmony by singing along with MP3's of chants; I sang the wrong notes until it sounded right. Harmonies almost always add something, though you need the group to have a solid grasp on the chant before you bring in a harmony line. It's better if you have designated chant anchors for melody and harmony. If you can only add one harmony, go for a lower harmony; this adds a "floor" to the sound, which makes it's vocally easier for most people to do. Someone with a higher voice can add a high harmony, which pops up the energy.

Add Drumming

Drumming can either really add to the chanting or completely collapse it. I've facilitated rituals where drummers with no rhythm joined in; once one of those drummers begins, it's pretty difficult to discretely ask them to stop. An off-kilter rhythm can really throw your chanting out of whack. Typically, I try to test out a chant with a drummer first or work with drummers I know; otherwise, I try to set up an agreement that drummers will drop out if I give them a hand sign. Skilled drummers can add depth to a space-holding chant and help build an energy-raising chant.

Invite Rhythm

People can snap, clap and stomp if you model that kind of rhythm-making, though it may take a few tries before people join in. Let the energy of the group tell you when they are ready for rhythm. If you start clapping and nobody follows, they aren't ready and you can try again in a minute. Having other ritualists who will join in and model what you are doing encourages others to participate. Adding rhythm and other layers keeps the chant from losing energy when it hits a plateau.

Practice, Practice, Practice

There are more chanting techniques, but these tips should help you get off to a good start. The single best tip I can offer is to practice. With time, you will get better at chanting.

Endnote

1 Chant by ALisa Starkweather: www.alisastarkweather.com

The Perfect Prayer: Incense and Scent Crafting
By Katlyn Breene

May the air clear my mind
May the water open my heart
May the earth support and nurture my body
May the fire purify my spirit
And the smoke, carry my prayers . . .

The burning of incense can be a perfect prayer. Gather the bounty of the earth, drink in its sweet fragrance, transmute the prayer with fire and watch it rise to heaven taking your heartsong with it. In solitary ritual, the sweet smoke rises and the priestess sits by the light of a single flame and a glowing censer, letting the aroma guide her back to center, letting it uplift her spirit, healing body and soul. A mental/spiritual bond is created between the scent and the feeling, so that as priestesses we may bring that connection to our community.

For a priestess who seeks to guide people to a common purpose and intent, the sacred smoke ascending to the sky can bring the focus of a group together and help them visualize their prayers being lifted and released.

As the sweet smoke rises, all in the circle share the blessing. The scent unifies the intent and the group heart to one purpose. There is magic in scent creation; it can change and enhance consciousness. The wisdom of the body and the senses recalls ancient memories of the sacred smoke used in every temple, every age and every place on earth.

Incense is a universal magickal tool, and a priestess is wise to understand its power. Incense transforms both ourselves and our environment.

It creates sacred space in a breath. It focuses and purifies in a breath. It is in-spiration, combining all the elements into a shared experience.

Scent is powerful. It is the sense that connects directly to the limbic system, our primal brain. Smell is not limited by our logic and inspires our passion. When we offer a gift of flowers, essential oils or incense to another, we are giving a deep and lasting scented memory. Scent is our path into the wild, the uncensored and the primitive, instinctual world.

Knowing what botanicals to burn and how to burn to them to greatest effect is knowledge worth exploring. There is an art to using incense and getting it to release its complete aroma. Here are a few ways for the priestess to effectively use and understand incense in ceremony and personal transformation. May this open a path of deeper appreciation and aid you in the work.

Ways to Effectively Use Incense
Olfactory connections enhance inner work, personal transformation and therapy. Create them and create a positive scent memory. Incense can be used very effectively during guided meditations. The scent can change the feel of the place to which you are leading your listeners in the meditation. It can also serve as a cue to return from their journey. For example, if your meditation begins "imagine that you are in a forest and the scents of cedar and pine waft over you," you might want to introduce the fragrances of cedar or pine. Blessings at rites of passage, such as handfasting, birth celebrations, passing over and memory, can be more beautiful and meaningful with the use of sacred smoke. Developing and making your own blends for special occasions is a gift of love.

I believe priestesses should not wear perfume into a ceremony but should have the ability to create magic by weaving carefully chosen scents though natural anointing oils, essential oil mists or incense; it's also a courtesy to those with sensitivities to synthetic perfume. Hydrosol mists or essential oils in an atomizer with water are excellent for those who might be smoke sensitive.

Frankincense, rose, lavender and white sage essential oils are all good basics for creating mist. Start with about five to ten drops per ounce of water and add more if desired. Remember to always shake the atomizer bottle well before use. Mists are cooling, grounding and easy to use in any situation.

There is magic in the smoke of the incense itself, so do not disregard it. Instead, use it effectively, even if the odor of the smoke is not sweet or pleasing. A veil of sacred smoke can banish and protect, acting as a vehicle for visions and consciousness. Smoke was also used for divination and scrying in many ancient cultures.

The aroma of the smoke will be diffused if you are outdoors. In that case, use more incense. Smudging herbs, bundles and resins on charcoal are best in an outdoor setting. The scent of a stick or a delicate blend can be lost on the wind, which is fine if your intent is to make an offering or a prayer, but not if you want the incense to affect your group ritual.

Indoors there are other many options for creating a light, pure-scented atmosphere. If anyone has smoke allergies, an electric heater allows all the fragrance and energy of the scent with very little smoke. While it is not ideal for ritual because the cord restricts movement, it is effective for setting a mood and intent in the home.

If you are using a mixture of leafy plants and herbs, perhaps following a traditional formula or recipe, consider adding a few drops of the essential oil of your chosen herb to help the scent come through when you use it as incense. Unfortunately, when most leafy plants and herbs are dried and burned, the smoke only smells like burning leaves; but these old blends have intent and tradition behind them, so using them wisely can enhance a blend.

There are many fine incense formularies available today, written by incense artisans and scent crafters to create synergistic blends that smell good and act as an olfactory invocation. You can tell when reading many older "spellbooks" that the writer might not have actually burned the blends they wrote about but put together a recipe from folklore and lists of correspondences.

As with wine, food and perfume, you get what you pay for. Inexpensive resins and other botanicals have most likely been ground up and stored in a warehouse until most of the scent has dissipated. It is well worth the time and effort to find a good source, or use trading or wildcrafting, to obtain incense materials. In wildcrafting, plants are harvested from their natural or "wild" habitat. Wildcrafting supports sustainable harvesting, where only the fruit, flowers, or branches form the plant are taken.

If you live in a desert climate and sage grows in your area, find someone to trade with, perhaps someone from a cooler climate who might trade for cedar. There is nothing better than consciously gathered fresh botanicals for priestess work. Store materials in an airtight container and keep them out of direct light or sun until ready to use. Resins that have not been ground or broken up have the longest shelf life.

When ready to use, break resins into smaller bits by placing the resin chunk in a freezer-weight plastic bag and striking it with a mallet until is the desired size; these bits will be easier to burn and will have better scent dispersion. If the resin is very sticky, like raw tree sap, it works well to freeze it before breaking it up.

A priestess might consider always having with her a "road kit" for use in ritual or when wildcrafting. It could contain a few types of incense that are easy to use and transport, such as smudge bundles, natural stick incense, a feather, a lighter, a small knife and a container dedicated to collecting tree resin and incense botanicals. Remember to always ask permission of the plant first and to give thanks to the plant teachers when wildcrafting.[1]

Censers and Charcoal

A censer is the container in which incense is safely burned, which can be anything from a ceramic pot or dish or a seashell to an ornate work of art. The censer should have a wide opening at the top to allow circulation; it should be made of fire-resistant material and should have an aesthetically pleasing appearance. Brass, bronze, stone and ceramic censers are most commonly used. Abalone shells are best used only for smudge bundles, as they get too hot to touch with charcoal.

Place some sand and white rice chaff ash in the bottom of the censer to help absorb the intense heat of the charcoal and protect the censer and the surface upon which it rests. Ash placed on top of the sand allows air under the charcoal so that it will burn well. The sand and ash can also hold stick incense. The sand can be earth, salt, aquarium, marine or volcanic sand; it's nice to use some kind of sacred earth such as from a favorite beach or desert location. Rice chaff ash can be found at fine incense suppliers or a Chinese market; it is made just for use with incense and has no scent of its own. I highly recommend using a censer with a wooden handle so you can move it without burning your fingers.

There are two types of incense charcoal: self-igniting and natural. The easiest to use is the self-igniting charcoal, which comes in disks that are inexpensive and work well outdoors. They contain potassium nitrate, also called vesta powder, as a burning agent that causes a sparkling effect when first lit; the downside is that this does give off a slight odor when being lit. The second type is a natural charcoal with no burning agents. This charcoal, usually made from willow or bamboo, is known as Japanese-style charcoal. This type takes longer to light but it is very clean burning, making it perfect for indoor use, and there is little odor when lit.

When preparing to perform a ritual, be sure to light the charcoal at least fifteen minutes before you plan to use it; this gives it enough time to light completely and to have a nice bed of white ash on top. The ash keeps the incense from scorching too quickly and allows for more scent. The coal can be extinguished if the incense is placed on it too soon.

To light any type of charcoal, use the flame of a candle or, if outdoors, use a wind-proof lighter. Using pinchers, charcoal tongs, chopsticks or your fingers (carefully), hold the tablet over the candle flame or lighter until the edge begins to glow. Place the coal in the prepared censer. Wait until the charcoal is covered with grayish-white ash, which will cushion the incense from the direct heat of the coal. This will take five to fifteen minutes. Fan or blow on the charcoal to help get the tablet started.

Make sure the charcoal has enough air flow so it doesn't go out. Sand alone won't allow the charcoal to breathe like ash will. Some censers come with a metal screen that fits over the bowl to hold the charcoal; these work well but some of your blend can fall through if you do not apply it carefully. Place your incense directly upon or next to the charcoal. Most charcoal will stay hot enough to burn incense for about thirty-five to forty-five minutes. I like to light one coal first and then place another near it (just touching) in the censer, ensuring you will have live coals for a longer time. Be sure to store your charcoal in an airtight container, tin foil or plastic bag when you are not using it, as moisture in the air can make the charcoal difficult to light.

Purification and Smudging
Purification is one of most well-known uses of incense for priestess work. You can use many different types of incense for this work, including white sage, frankincense, copal (*copal blanco* is my favorite), *breuzinho* (or *breu claro*), *palo santo*, dragon's blood, juniper and camphor.

Burning a smudge stick will clear a space or a person's energy. White sage (*Salvia apiana*) is a panacea of healing and clearing. The smell of fresh white sage is intensely therapeutic, and sage maintains it's potency when dried for long time. It will lose some scent over time but, compared to other herbs, it is very long-lasting. Store sage bundles (and all types of incense) in an airtight container.

To smudge a person or an object, burn the clippings of dried herbs or resin on charcoal, or use a sage bundle in an abalone shell or clay bowl. Rub your hands in the smoke and then gather the smoke and bring it into your body or rub it onto yourself, especially onto any area that you feel needs spiritual healing, focusing on your intent all the while. When completed, move on to smudge others. Use your hands, a feather or a fan to lightly wave the smoke over the person. Direct the smoke to the whole body, paying special attention to the heart and over the head. Look for shadows in a person's energy field and fan the smoke to these areas. This helps to heal the spirit and to "close up" any holes in their energy. If smudging a large group, try just making a clockwise spiral of smoke from the solar plexus over the head and to the heart. A single wing feather is my favorite smudging tool. You can feel the current of air and vitality as it moves around the person being smudged.

Smudging should be done with a constant feeling of love and humility, giving respect to the sage itself for sharing its medicine. It is such a beautiful ritual tradition and we should always be thankful to our plant teachers. For those who want to learn, participating in a purification ritual is a very good way to experience and to take the first steps on the path toward being a priestess.

To roll your own bundles of smudge, try using a bamboo sushi mat. I like to gather the boughs of fresh sage or other botanicals into a bundle of the size I desire and then bind the stems together at the base with a rubber band. Let the sage hang for a few days until limp (not dry) and then use the mat to roll the boughs tightly together, just like a sushi chef creates rolls. Then rubber band the mat closed and let them dry in a cool place out of direct light. When you open it, it will be firm and compact and ready to tie with cotton thread and thoroughly dry. Other herbs or boughs that have meaning to you, or are traditional, can be added, but pure sage bundles are best. Some botanicals are well suited for smudge bundles; these include cedar, rosemary, sweet grass, desert sage (sage-brush) and many types of artemisia and lavender.

Blessing and Protection
It is a wonderful idea to cense your whole home often. Use a censer with a wooden handle so you can move around freely. Light the incense and carry the censer from room to room. Focus on the energy you want the smoke to contain, for example, to banish negativity and blockage, worry and stress, and instead invite peace. Burning resins, precious woods and sage creates a lingering perfume that builds over time, so your home will soon acquire a lasting sacred scent.

It is a good idea to do a house blessing ceremony every year in your home, traditionally in the first part of February or after your spring cleaning. It is also a good way to clear a new home of unwanted "old stuff" and negative energy. Blessing your house as a family can bring together everyone's intentions for future happiness and help to release old patterns or presences.

Have all involved decide together upon the night to do the ceremony and agree upon what you want the ceremony to accomplish. You can do this alone or with family and friends. This work is good for almost any spiritual tradition, or just to do a general "house cleaning." Have your censer, lit charcoal, incense, smudge fan or feather and a single white candle ready before you begin. I recommend frankincense, white sage or a good purification blend.

After dark, gather together and take a moment to focus on your intention; it should be very clear in all your minds. Is it to cleanse and clear the house for the coming year? "Banish" some energy that does not feel right? Bless a new home to make it your own and cut any connections to the past occupants?

Now, room by room, turn off all the lights in the house until you are in the last illuminated room. Light the candle (or each person present could have lit a candle as well), then turn off the last light. Try to have the candle(s) in a holder that will catch the wax drips.

When everyone is ready, take a few moments for complete silence. This is the time to focus on calling in the Sacred to help you in this work or to picture in your mind what you want to accomplish.

Place a pinch of incense on the hot coal or light your sage bundle. Don't use too much all at once, just a little bit for each room. You don't want too much smoke.

Beginning with the room you are in, carry the light of the candle and the smoke of the incense to every corner of the room, and don't forget to open closets as well. Imagine the light and smoke completely ridding the space of all that is not desired. Let them act as the symbolic bringers of peace and tranquility.

Walk silently through every room in the house, letting the light and smoke do their sacred work. If one place feels extra "uneasy," spend some more time there until it feels clear. Salt and water can also be cast in these areas to ground and clear these spots. Do this until all rooms have been purified. Open a door or window to the outside at this point, picturing all negativity you "banished" rushing out of the house. Come back to the room where you started; you can turn the lights back on if you want. Blow out the candle while together saying out loud something like, "So be it!" or "It is done!" Take in and release a deep breath and know that it is completed. Give thanks for the unseen help you called to do this work and to the spirits of the medicine plants that aided you.

Group and Personal Work

When at a circle or gathering, try placing a censer of burning incense on the ground at the entrance. As each person enters, they step over the censer, allowing the sweet smoke to rise up and envelope them. Women can take a moment to let the smoke beneath their skirts and scent their veils.

A good piece of "ritual tech" for large gathering is a smudge gate. Have two people stand at the entrance to the sacred space or circle with censers of incense or smudge bundles representing the elements of fire and air. Everyone entering passes between them and is purified with sacred smoke. It creates a portal or threshold between the worlds and moves very quickly. You may also want two additional portal people to represent water and earth with rose water, or water and salt, to bless folks at the smudge gate.

There are times in gatherings when people need to speak from their heart, vent their emotions or talk things out. This sensitive time can be made sacred and the process eased by using incense as a purifying agent. When you, as a priestess, see that someone needs a safe space in which to speak, light the smudge bundle or incense and clear the area around them, bringing them clarity and gentle focused attention. This is an effective way to initiate a conscious transition and a thoughtful exchange.

When you build a sacred fire, place an offering of incense, resins, flower petals or spices on the earth before you lay the wood. You can do this artistically in a pattern or design that reflects your intent for the ceremony. At the fire, place flat stones close to the perimeter. When the stones get hot during the night, you will have a perfect way to burn your chosen incense as an offering without charcoal.

When you need to center and ground yourself for sacred work, let your sense of smell aid you. Choose to burn incense that is special to you when you seek inner peace; let it help you make that connection. For me, the scent of frankincense immediately uplifts my spirit and allows me to let go of stress and "get out of my head." After using a certain fragrance or botanical many times, you will form a link in your consciousness that will help take you to your desired mental and emotional state.

After many years of using all types of incense, there are a few things I recommend, especially for personal meditation. This is time you take for yourself and your inner well-being; you do not want a lot of strong scent and smoke. I find that fine Japanese incense sticks are the best for indoor meditation and quieting the mind. They are refined and beautiful, tiny thin sticks of pure precious woods, resins and herbs which can be very costly but worth the price. Consider finding a blend you like from a reputable Japanese company or supplier; most suppliers offer sample packs of their more precious sticks.

Incense Offerings
Throughout history, cultures and religions have used certain incenses to honor their deities. Incense is used to offer prayers because the smoke rises to the heavens, carrying the prayer from the physical to the spiritual plane. The ancients believed incense provided access to the gods.

In creating blends for deities and archetypes, think of the element the deity or archetype represents as well as botanicals from the region of the deity or archetype. Consider what grows in their country of origin, but also invoke your personal "scentual" experience and impressions. Go to the ancient texts and get a sense of what was used. In the process of creation, a great deal of magic and synchronicity can occur.

When going out into nature or any wild place to do sacred work, give offerings to *genus loci* (spirits of the land). Ask for their blessing and permission to work there. Incense or small bits of organic food can serve as an offering, something that will be assimilated and leave no trace. Remember to say "thank you" when your work is done.

Aarati is a Hindu devotional ritual that consists of burning camphor pellets or cakes held in a small censer or plate. The censer is waved in gentle circular movements before the image of a deity or honored person to symbolize devotion, blessing and the dissolution of the ego. This simple rite is amazingly powerful and beautiful; the dancing light playing upon the altar or beloved seems to bring all to life in a mystical way.

Camphor is highly purifying and very sacred, and is used to symbolically dissolve the ego since it burns completely without leaving any trace. When burned, it emits a sweet, strong fragrance, which symbolizes how we, too, should sacrifice ourselves to serve society, in the process spreading the perfume of love and happiness to all.

Aarati is a form of worship performed to purify the mind, express devotion and connect with the Divine. Burning camphor in ritual removes or burns away that which separates us from the Divine. *Aarati* can be used by all to purify and bless with light and scent.

Place several pellets of ceremonial camphor (not mothballs) in a heatproof bowl or censer, preferably one with a wooden handle; these are available from Indian markets or websites that supply *puja* (ceremonial devotion) tools. Light them with a match or lighter. They will flame for several minutes and then go out on their own. It is best to let them burn away completely; do not extinguish them. Pellets can also be floated while burning in a bowl of water. This creates "holy water" to be used in ceremony. Light the pellet and then pick it up with tongs or tweezers and place it gently on the surface of the water. It is a very beautiful sight as the flames dance upon the water.

This is a very brief overview of incense in the life and work of a priestess. Very few practices have such a timeless effect on ritual; I hope that women will take the time to learn to use incense and fragrance in their own work, explore its beauty and power and discover the secrets that fire brings forth.

When I place a tear of resin upon a white coal and smoke gently rises, I feel connected to the heart of a ceremony that unites all cultures. The sweet scent opens us to a celebration of life that transcends beliefs in a universal language.

See "A Guide to Incense Botanicals" located in the appendices of this volume for descriptions of useful incense botanicals.

Further Reading and Sources
Carl F. Neal, *Incense: Crafting and Use of Magickal Scents* (Woodbury, MN: Llewelyn, 2003) and *Incense Magick: Create Inspiring Aromatic Experiences for Your Craft* (Woodbury, MN: Llewelyn, 2012).

Carl has devoted his life to Pagan incense education and crafting.

Susanne Fischer-Rizzi, *The Complete Incense Book* (New York: Sterling Publishing, 1998).

    Susanne can provide information on regional, historical and indigenous types of incense.

Recommended sources for powdered wood, resins and botanicals used incense:

    Essence of the Ages: www.essenceoftheages.com

    Carries all types of incense from around the world, an important reliable source.

Scents of Earth: www.scents-of-earth.com

    Offers a wide selection of incense materials and hard-to-find resins.

Mermade Magickal Arts: www.mermadearts.com

    Provides the very best in natural incense.

Endnote

1 There are too many wonderful techniques for burning incense to mention here, but there are many great online sources. I recommend the non-profit website, www.making-incense.com. It covers a great variety of instructions on using and making your own incense. And please come visit me at Mermade Magickal Arts: www.mermadearts.com.

Priestess of the Doors
By Kathryn Ravenwood

The image of a priestess, for me, always includes an altar. The rest of the details fill in from a rich and endless source of possibility. The priestess is old or young, dressed in exquisite temple finery or simple robes. She may be barefooted, crowned with sparkling jewels or equipped with magic wands or amulets of power. She might recite from an ancient codex or utter a silent supplication. But she always stands before an altar.

Altars have always been with us. We know altars. We create them. We live with them. We serve at them. My house has an entire bedroom dedicated to being an altar room in honor of the sacred directions. It is my place marker, so to speak, of my priestess intention. Caught up in the world of working for a living, dealing with all of life's challenges and celebrations, it is easy to lose focus on being a priestess. Altars are a tangible way of holding that focus, whether to honor the ancestors, to make offerings to the goddesses and gods, to pray, sing, chant and drum, or to hold space in sacred silence. I adorn my altars with cloths, candles, statues, pictures, vessels of water, stones, dirt from ancient temples, crystals, feathers and even a sword of power. Over the many years of tending these altars, I have learned much about the commitment of being a priestess and the ongoing process of my own becoming.

Perhaps the most profound thing I have learned is that those altars are not just structures to hold my medicine tools and treasures: they are doorways leading to sacred portals. Learning to navigate what opens beyond those portals has forever changed me and continues to astound me. It is one thing to invoke the Guardians of the West, honoring them as holding that place in between the day and the night, the light and the dark, the place where we sift and separate that which is no longer needed. It is quite another thing to find that the Portal to the West has indeed opened, at your request, and to find yourself actually in that place of shadow, dealing with letting go of things or people or conditions that no longer serve you.

This is what it is to be a priestess, to know the doors and be prepared to honor and intentionally experience what they open into. It is why we study, prepare and pray, and why we build altars to honor and remember what we have learned and what is yet to know.

I do not want to go through a doorway, find myself in unknown territory and not know who I can call upon to protect and guide me. The doorways before which our altars stand exist whether we honor them or not, and they have a habit of swinging open when we least expect it. Perhaps you've just fallen madly in love, or the divorce papers ending you marriage have arrived in the mail. Perhaps you lost your job, found out you were pregnant or had a miscarriage. Maybe you are deep in a dreadful dark night of the soul that seems to never end, or your have just been diagnosed with a life-threatening illness. You've reconnected with a long lost friend, won the lottery, planted a garden, gained a new perspective, passed an exam or danced in the rain. There is not one event, one emotion, one experience you may have that does not exist in one of those directions our altars are built to honor.

When I first learned to create altars, I would sit before them, calling upon the Guardians of the Gateways to open and grant me passage into their sacred lands. Night after night, I would experience them and then return, offer my gratitude, blow out the candles and go to bed. It took me a while to understand that the door swings both ways. Not only do we cross those sacred thresholds, but our altars provide the access for the Guides to come and be with us. It is a bit like a cosmic student exchange program.

I also used to think that if my life was going well, I must be being a "good little priestess." If I said all the right prayers, invoked the right Guides, tended my altars and kept my priestess world in good order, I was walking the sacred path. What I came to learn is that life is messy and things just are not that simple—even for a priestess.

I had become very comfortable "hanging out" in two of the gateways. I embraced the teachings that came from those directions and became adept at many of the lessons. Life was good. I was content. But a Priestess of the Doors must learn to face each direction, tend each altar equally, and be willing to walk her path with a balanced viewpoint. And so the lessons shifted. I found myself experiencing things I was far less comfortable with. Spirit was pushing me, challenging me. I now faced a different gateway and it was wide open, streaming its opportunities for growth right at me, and those opportunities were exactly what I had been avoiding. It was time to change.

While this was a disrupting and fearful time for me, I had help. I knew from my nights of invoking and honoring the Guides exactly which doorway had opened. It shouldn't have been such a shock; after all, I had an altar for it. Recognizing the energies and patterns led me to that altar where the tools and teachings I needed lay waiting for me to help me meet the challenges. I was not thrilled with this change, but I knew I had to meet it and learn from it. It is part of the priestess training.

Life is not linear. We do not smoothly move from one gate to another in perfect order. Just when we think we have something mastered, the door can open again and we can find ourselves re-learning the same lessons or finding those lessons were just the primer in a vast book of knowing.

A priestess goes through what everyone else on the planet experiences. What is different for the priestess is knowledge: sacred knowledge passed on in rituals, books, Tarot cards, "fairy stories," dreams, moments of serendipity and epiphanies received from trees and snakes and spiders. The priestess uses this knowledge to intentionally build her altars, honor the teachings in her prayers and know she can face the world with an intrepid faith that, no matter what comes through any door, she can handle it.

It isn't always easy being a priestess, but I cannot imagine trying to navigate life any other way.

Priestess Me
By Heather Artemis

The vessel is on its side
Who will retrieve it?
Will it even be noticed
Lying there in the dust?

Ancient hands
Once honoring life itself
Poured out libations
For those with Great Spirit,
But those sweet ones aren't around
So how will we learn to read the signs?

Priestess me
Oh Fair One
I long
Desiring
to restore beauty and truth.
But I am fed only lies
The wine is poisoned
And divinity has scattered to the four winds
Or is parsed out in fifty minute sessions
And owing to the present economy
And the fact that there is no public
It takes a lot to support a priestess today.

Bid me now
And I'll carry what is put into my hands
May it be in the care of delicate creatures,
Dangerous but desperate?
Or should it be your wish
That I remain empty handed,
Set down and release everything I bring forth.

Your gifts are immense.
I doubt
one frail thing can play host
to you.
The benediction may be over
But I didn't get to touch anything.
And this spirit is known to me only in the flesh.

Gone are the temples,
which once housed immanence
And the playful celebrants
Teaching each other
Rituals of love and devotion.
But I do not forget.
I call to you now.
Priestess me.

Animal, Vegetable, Mineral Offerings*
By Anne Key

Though I would usually go to the temple in the morning and at sunset, most of the time the temple sits open, waiting and unattended. This is, I believe, a part of the magic and beauty of this temple—that it is open to anyone. It makes the temple a unique and extraordinary place. It also answers a very interesting but most likely unasked question: In a culture such as modern Protestant-leaning America, where giving offerings is an unusual act and places of religious worship are not usually open to the public, what do people do in a temple where there is no posted protocol for offerings and no one around to direct their actions?

People come, most often singly, and leave offerings. Every day, I find some assortment of candles, plastic flowers, fresh flowers, jewelry, sage wands, beer, art and photos carefully placed in the temple. Most often these items are left in front of a particular goddess, the intention clear. One day, I found a tiny silver pendant in the shape of a knife, the miniature handle curved and the blade straight, resting in the lap of Sekhmet, an offering honoring one of Sekhmet's many names, "Sekhmet of the Knives." I regularly found sage bundles in front of Madre del Mundo, offerings linked with her Native American roots.

What to do with all of these offerings? At first, I tried an administrative solution, meaning an across-the-board decree: all offerings would be either burned or buried at the turn of each season. But then, some offerings begged to have different outcomes. And so I moved from a blanket policy to a case-by-case process, with established precedents, of course.

---

* Originally published in a slightly different form in *Desert Priestess, a memoir* (Las Vegas, NV: Goddess Ink, 2011).[1]

Flowers were the easiest. Flowers are a traditional offering for deities, probably because they are beautiful, scented and, even when cut, they retain a spark of life. I left vases inside and there was usually a water bottle or two around to fill the vase. When the flowers passed their prime, I offered them in prayer in a ceremonial fire. I think fresh flowers are one of the best offerings because of their heady scent and vivacious colors. As they need to be replaced periodically, fresh flowers also show a continued devotion. And, when burned, they provided a final offering in the fire. They are probably the most traditional offering worldwide.

Plastic flowers are a different matter. Plastic flowers provide color and beauty not found in the desert landscape, and they are inexpensive, even available at the mini-mart in the gas station in Indian Springs, the closest town to the temple. Plastic flowers provide the gift of beauty and color, but they do not provide scent, or any sense of life, as an offering.

For my priestess duties, plastic flowers were a conundrum. They did not naturally disintegrate, nor did I think it wise to burn them, so when people left plastic flowers, I would take them out at the next turn of the season clearing and bury them alongside other non-burnable offerings.

Incense and candles were also popular offerings. These offerings, like flowers, follow ancient traditions. Incense burns and releases a sweet smoke that drifts skyward, making it a perfect offering for the deities. Candles hold the spark of life, the flame. Frankincense, myrrh and *kyphi* were popular incense scents left for Sekhmet as they had been used in Egypt, and rose incense was left in honor of La Virgen de Guadalupe. Many people brought candles to the temple, often beautiful tapers and votives. However, in the summer, when temperatures regularly soared above 100°F, and frequently over 110°F, candles would melt quickly and often drip all over the rocks on the floor, giving me something else to clean. I preferred that people bring tea lights or novena candles, as they were self-contained.

I was always so appreciative when people left incense and tea lights in the temple for others to use, because not everyone came to the temple prepared and, once inside, the urge to light candles and incense is instinctual.

Another traditional offering is food. All sorts of foods were left as offerings at the temple: apples, strawberries, cakes, honey, nuts, meat, to name only a few. I burned all the food offerings in the temple fire pit, usually after the mice and other critters had had their feast. One time, an offering of a dozen or so papayas became the center of a feast for the ravens. And what a feast it was! The ravens picked at the papaya and flung bits of it all around the temple, on the statues, everywhere. I was cleaning up bits of papaya for weeks. After that, I remembered not to let fruit sit too long in the temple.

Liquid offerings abounded, especially juice and beer. These I poured out at the feet of the Goddess in front of whom they had been left. Because of Sekhmet's association with beer, and most specifically red beer, I would often find six-packs of Killian's Red beer left for her. And every month or so, someone would come and leave a case or two of bottled water. I would pour out a bottle as an offering and then bring the remainder to the guest house.

Jewelry was another frequent offering. Rings and necklaces were left on the statues as adornments for the goddesses. After a certain time, I removed the offerings from the statues. Sometimes I buried them, and other times I took the whole piece of jewelry and kept it in a box for a special ritual when that particular goddess's statue would be adorned. If the jewelry was made of beads, I often restrung a few different offerings together to create a beautiful adornment for the statue. If the offering had glass or semi-precious stone beads, I might cut the string and mix the beads with the stones of the temple floor.

The offerings that couldn't be burned or poured were buried. Placing things within the earth is an act of nourishing the Earth, honoring her cycles, the continual nourishment of life-death-life. The Earth transmutes the energy of these offerings, bringing them into her cycles.

In the dry clay earth around the temple, it was no easy task to dig holes large enough to bury offerings. Fortunately, Ben was always willing to swing the pickax and dig a deep hole. One time I dug the hole for some offerings, so it was not very deep. I cut myself on a shard of pottery to be buried, and I bled on the offerings. Though I worked to cover them thoroughly, they were uncovered by some beast the following night. The second burial, executed by Ben, went as planned. The items stayed buried.

It was, in a way, ironic. While so often ceremonies are centered on the idea of infusing something with energy, my work with offerings at the temple focused on defusing and transmitting energy. Too many offerings, too many intentions, too many personal heart-felt prayers, too many tears began to add up in the relatively small temple space. I would cleanse the temple regularly, both physically and energetically, to keep the space open, willing and ready to receive the new.

One bright morning, I walked into the temple to find a photo in a large wooden frame with wrought-iron bars across the front. The photo seemed to be someone's promotional shot as an exotic dancer. It was accompanied by a note in which she explained that she was seeking the protection of the temple. The framed photo stayed in the temple by the west door and I burned a candle in front of it for her. After a few weeks, I buried it whole with the prayer that she would always be protected. I took her photo out of the frame so that she would not be imprisoned, but rather protected by the embrace of the land.

One of the largest offerings left was a painting on canvas and a manuscript for a book detailing the tragedies of the author's life. Her pain, horror and anguish emanated from the manuscript and the painting. After much contemplation, I decided to burn them both, seeking to release the artist from her past, and to release her mind from the idea that her anguish was the only and best fuel for her art.

Sometimes the offerings left me with my own sense of despair, anguish and responsibility. I tried to intuit the best possible course of action with each offering, wanting to honor the wishes of people I had never met. One particularly poignant offering was a dead lizard, wrapped neatly in a cloth and tucked in a shoebox. Inside the box along with the lizard were a T-shirt, the lizard's watering bottle and some food. This box was placed lovingly in front of the statue of Madre del Mundo. I cried when I found it. Ben dug a deep hole and we buried the lizard near the temple.

There were times when offerings needed to be broken. Some items held great strength and energy, and I felt that it was better for that energy to be released. When I broke an offering, I did it with the prayer that the energy infused in it would be released and would support the highest good. Breaking an item never meant I disregarded it. The most difficult offering I had to break was a candlestick in the shape of Sekhmet. It had very strong magic, very beautiful love magic woven into it. But it was the turn of the season, and this offering had already been in the temple one extra season, so it was time to move it along. I dug its own special hole, and as I placed it into the hole I prayed that its love would be released and nourish the earth. When my spade hit the candlestick and it broke, I could feel the waves of love move out.

Not long after I began my service as priestess, I encountered one offering that was particularly memorable; it had an immanent power but was also a little creepy. The offering was left on what we called the "moon rock," a boulder situated on the short path approaching the south entrance of the temple. Large and white, on full moon nights the moonlight illuminated the rock and gleamed brightly. There was a deep indentation on the top in which, just as Patricia had, I collected the rainwater that accumulated in the indentation when it rained on full moon nights, an extraordinary occurrence considering how little rain we received.

One morning, I went out to the temple and noticed some small, odd squiggly bits in the moon rock's indentation. I looked closer and was struck by their familiarity. Over the years, I have been the beneficiary of many gifts from cats, often left on the front porch, and these squiggly bits looked familiar, like rodent entrails. There was also blood on the rock. Not a lot, but some. I put my hand on the rock, nearby but not on the entrails (I am squeamish about these sorts of things). When my hand rested on the rock, my head instantly went fuzzy like a TV screen after the station has signed off. I knew I had to be careful with this offering.

In retrospect, I would have handled the situation differently, say smudging with palo santo and rinsing the rock with water from the spring. But at that time, only a few months after I had come to the temple, I relied on what I had learned from my grandmother about how to clean. I trotted back to the house to get my trusty magic rubber gloves, and called on the lessons of my grandmother and the smell of "clean" I learned from her: Clorox ® Bleach. With gloved hands, I removed and buried the entrails, and then set about cleaning the rock, hoping that was the right thing to do. I had the distinct feeling the offering was beneficial—powerful, with no ill intent. As I wiped the indention of the moon rock, I recognized the power and intention of the offering, honoring whoever had left this with palpable love and purpose.

My thoughts return to one dark and clear November night. Ben and I are wending our way home from an evening in Las Vegas and, as we come down Highway 95 and draw close to the temple, we can see light streaming from the doorways and beaming through the roof. Immediately fear and anger well up in my chest—is there an uncontrolled fire inside? No one is supposed to be in the temple after dark without calling me first. As we speed up the dirt road, I see there are no cars in the parking lot and my fear surges—has someone set fire to the temple and then left? Before the car stops, I jump out and sprint across the sand up to the temple.

I reach the doorway and stop in my tracks as I am met with a beautiful sight. The temple is steeped in light emanating from thirteen novena candles glowing in front of La Virgen de Guadalupe. A circle of salt rounds the fire pit, designating it as a sacred and protected area. I stand in the cold night air, breathing in the space, filled with passionate intent and galvanized by love. An ardent petitioner has been here. I begin chiding myself for the anger I had held earlier for the illicit visitor, and my heart swells to have come home to the temple filled with radiance and the magic of someone's ritual that now nourishes this sacred space.

Endnote

1 *Desert Priestess: a memoir* recounts the author's years as a priestess to the Temple of Goddess Spirituality Dedicated to Sekhmet, located in the Nevada desert.

Priestessing Yourself
By Ruth Barrett

Since a contemporary Dianic practitioner facilitates her own spiritual experience at her own altar and there is no intermediary between herself and the Goddess, every woman can learn to "priestess" herself. Facilitating yourself in solitary ritual is an excellent way to learn how to be both a participant and a facilitator. Solitary ritual can be a very powerful and intimate experience. And since responsibility for the ritual rests entirely on you, including all the preparation, enactments and outcome, there is even more flexibility and room for improvisation. The time actually spent in ritual can feel more fluid, like a moving meditation or a monologue.

You may find you need more time than you expected between the planning phase and enacting your ritual. This time between is not necessarily about avoiding the ritual, but time for your unconscious mind to integrate and process the ritual purpose. Be honest, and trust yourself: you will know when the time is right.

Even in solitary ritual, pre-ritual preparation is very important. It helps to ensure your deep surrender to the ritual's purpose. You may experience an intense degree of personal intimacy once your self-consciousness is alleviated through personal energetic preparation and purification of the ritual space.

A former student of mine, Barbara, facilitated herself in a ritual she designed several months following a miscarriage. She had previously performed rituals only in a group setting and was hesitant about

---

* Originally published in a slightly different form in *Women's Rites, Women's Mysteries: Intuitive Ritual Creation* (Woodbury, MN: Llewellyn Worldwide, 2007).

ritualizing this loss on her own. The purpose of her ritual was to let the spirit of the child go, to honor herself as a creator, to heal the pain of the loss and to open herself to life again. Creating and facilitating this ritual on her own allowed her to flow with her own intuitive timing, spending hours with herself in a space of loving compassion. She described her ritual experience as profound.

Generating Stillness: Creating Sacred Space*
By Kathy Jones

Generating stillness within—generating a loving, sacred space which emanates outwards to all who come into its presence—is an essential skill for a priestess. This stillness is not inertia; it is not the passivity of sleep or the empty house of death. It is an alert stillness, a deep pool of silence that will respond if a flower falls gently onto its surface, or if a stone dropped into it creates ripples that move across the surface as the depths remain still. It helps calm the racing minds and emotions of all who come into its presence. It is a loving stillness that emanates the soul, evoking an opening to soul energy in all those who come in contact with it. People become more relaxed in the presence of this stillness; they become calmer, less guarded, less defended, more open. They feel safe and able to express their feelings and show their human vulnerability, the source of true strength. Through a synchronous vibration, this stillness encourages people to feel the place of stillness within themselves, and to connect with their own soul's energy.

The only way to create stillness and generate sacred space is by becoming still; it's a truism many of us find hard to accept as we live our busy lives and with our active brains continually chattering. There are many meditative techniques designed to bring us to that place of stillness within; you may already be familiar with them. Here I would like to offer a goddess-centered approach.

Sit in front of your altar with your back straight and your legs in a comfortable position. Close your eyes. As you get used to sitting, bring

---

* From *Priestess of Avalon, Priestess of the Goddess: A Renewed Spiritual Path for the Twenty-first Century* (Glastonbury, England: Ariadne Publications, 2006), 320–322.

your consciousness into the present, recognizing where you are and what you are doing. Bring your attention to your breath; feel it and listen to it as it moves in and out of your mouth or nose, down into your lungs and out again. Feel your abdomen and breasts rising and falling with each breath. Become aware of oxygen entering your body from each breath in and stale carbon dioxide leaving as you breathe out. Notice how shallow or deep your breath is. Allow the breath to deepen. Count twenty breaths.

In your mind's eye, visualize the Goddess in a form that is familiar to you, as the Lady of Avalon, or Brigit, or Rhiannon. See her there in front of you in as much detail as you are able, seated or standing. See her form and the position of her limbs. See her clothing, her headdress, anything she carries in her hands. See her face and its expression. Feel the stillness she holds within her; even when her body is moving. When the image in your mind becomes stable, place it in your heart.

Feel her loving stillness entering your heart and filling your body so that your body and aura become a still, radiant center while life goes on all around you. Hold this feeling of stillness within for as long as you can. This is her sacred space.

As you hold this place of inner stillness, open your eyes and look around you. See if you can hold this still place with your eyes open. Continue to feel the spaciousness within. Slowly stand and begin to move. Again continue to feel the spaciousness within. Take the feeling of spaciousness with you into your everyday life, holding it for as long as you can.

Practice this visualization over weeks and months so that the feeling of inner stillness or sacred space becomes familiar to you. In time, you will be able to move into the place of stillness at will, whenever you want to, in ceremony as you priestess and hold space for others. As we become more able to find that place of stillness within ourselves, we consciously generate stillness or sacred space through our priestessing, so that others with whom we come into contact can feel that stillness too.

We create sacred space not through the ability to arrange an outer space—lighting candles and incense—but by generating sacred space within, which radiates outwards and is felt by others. We take time before each ceremony to generate stillness within and to connect to that inner space by becoming completely focused, as we arrange our temple space, light our candles, burn our incense and pray to the Lady.

As well as cultivating stillness within through spiritual practice, it is also important to cultivate emotional expression, so that emotions do not become dammed up, generating disease. The Goddess path is one of expression, rather than suppression, of emotions. We need to do this on a regular basis, whether through conversations with family, friends or skilled counselors; through the appropriate release of tears, anger, sadness and joy as we feel them; through artistic creativity of all forms; and through music, movement, song and dance. As we release our emotions, we empty out, creating psychic space within, in which her silence can find a peaceful home.

As we quiet within, we cultivate trust in her, for she has brought us to this place of peace. Our faith in her increases as we see the positive effects she is having in our lives. We find that we know certain things to be true that are unprovable by worldly measurement, but that come from a deep inner knowing that is true for us. All these things are benefits of finding stillness within.

The Crone's Cauldron of Changes
By Abbi Spinner McBride

This that we have now
is the crone's cauldron of changes.
Together we season and stir,
taste, season and stir some more
until
boiling, embroiling,
bubbling and troubling,
roiling and toiling,
shifting and shaping
the vital essence of our selves
is changed
into the elixir of holiness.

These are the blossoms of bones—
creativity born of desperation,
the roses opening from rotting marrow;
bloody drops become butterflies . . .
the great circle turning swiftly
as the wheel descends.

STEPPING INTO OURSELVES

Here is the arc of eternity,
the holy golden moment
this heartbeat, this breath, this delicious instant
stretching into the infinite now.

We are the hole in the stone,
the miraculous solitary point of focus,
the real magic of individual consciousness
penetrating the illusion.

Groups, Power and Priestessing*
By Shekhinah Mountainwater

I want to encourage you to look to future directions for your magic. Some of you may choose to work as solo witches, but some of you may feel a natural urge to expand into sharing your magic with others.

There are many ways you can reach out to share magic. You may wish to become a teacher and help others learn. You may wish to find a few friends to do rituals with and share support. You may be inspired to go at it in a big way and organize public events, publish a witch's newsletter, start a church or organize a political lobby. You may go into schools and bring magic to children, who are the seeds of our future world, or simply share with children what they know. All of these are valid ways to spread the energy. I do not wish to put any pressure on, however; just being a witch and living your life can be enough in itself, and sometimes difficult. Whatever path the Goddess takes you on must be the right one for you.

In case you should decide to get involved with a group, I am providing a few guidelines gleaned from my own experience as a priestess and feminist activist. Perhaps they will be of some use to you at a future time.

Guidelines for Leading Groups

Passing the Rattle
I have found it wonderfully whole-making to sit in a circle with a group of people of good will and pass a rattle or some sacred object that

---

* Originally published in a slightly different form in *Ariadne's Thread: A Workbook of Goddess Magic* (Freedom, CA: The Crossing Press, 1991).

designates each person's turn to speak. She who holds the rattle holds the power, in more ways than one. I'll never forget my early experiences with this process in sixties feminist consciousness-raising groups. We would select a topic, such as our experiences with marriage, children or other women. Each woman would talk for ten minutes or so about what she had been through. It was always staggering to me how transformed everyone in the room would be by the time we had gotten around the circle. We learned and saw things we had not seen before. We saw how much we had in common, and that our oppressions were shared oppressions. For me it was the budding of sisterhood, an abiding love for women and the beginning of my liberation.

Since then I have learned many things about communication and power and human beings through the process of passing the rattle. I have come to see that every voice must be heard before the whole story can be told, and that the truth resides not in one person but in the center—in the agreed-upon truth of all present. From this I learned the incredible power of agreement: it can move mountains.

Passing the rattle is a way for every member to take responsibility and participate fully in whatever may be happening. It is also a way for everyone to get support from someone who cares and is interested; after all, we all need to share our heartsongs, our ups and downs, our successes and our struggles. Passing the rattle takes us out of isolation into a safe and empowering intimacy. It gives us the advantage of many points of view. It is an excellent form for dealing with conflicts, making decisions, balancing communication, verbalizing visions, planning rituals and casting group spells.

Creating Safe Space

Doing magic together requires love and trust. Success depends upon all participants coming together in a spirit of sisterhood. People may disagree, but no one should be mean or antagonistic toward another. For a group to do well together, people should like and enjoy each other.

Sometimes it is best to keep groups small, so that there is room for close friendships to grow. There must be honesty, willingness to tell the truth about oneself and a promise not to repeat such revelations elsewhere. A woman feels safe in a group where she knows everyone there is glad to see her, interested in what she has to say, concerned if she is in trouble and happy when she is happy. A safe group is one you can turn to when the going gets tough to find healing, insight and the wonderful wisdom of woman. It is a place where you can expect honesty, but not put-downs, and where you know you will always be able to speak your mind freely.

Sharing Common Focus

Group sharing is the most rewarding when there is a shared focus. Random focus is nice for parties and other social occasions, but when a small group comes together to do magic, there needs to be time when everyone's attention is on the same things at the same time. The subject of the focus should be agreed upon to begin with, whether it be a shared vision, a poetic reading, a chant or teaching. Attention is a great power; we know from magic that whatever we pay attention to will eventually exist or manifest. When we synchronize this power in a group situation, we get a synergy of magic power. I think it is important for people to learn how to put their synchronized attentions together, without being coerced or talked down to, or having to play "audience." When people have a common focus, you can feel the energy of it; there is a glow, a tingle in the air. It feels good! We are taken out of ourselves, as our energies merge into a unified purpose.

Making a Commitment

Over the years of teaching women's groups, I have run the gamut from year-long commitments, to lifetime commitments, to no commitment at all, to nine months, to three months. I have found that those who make the greatest commitment to the Goddess usually reap the greatest rewards. However, people are varied and are pulled in many directions. Sometimes their spiritual process takes them elsewhere. I have found I must strike a compromise between their needs and mine. As a teacher, I have found that drop-in groups, where there was no commitment at all, drain me. I am there, week in and week out, keeping the energy going, while everyone else comes and goes. It is impossible to achieve continuity, share information or plan rituals. After doing drop-in groups myself in ithe past, I realized that some commitment on the part of students was necessary for the group energy to flow well. It takes at least three months, meeting once or twice a week, for a group to form a bond and feel like everyone knows each other. Many witches say that a year and a day is a good amount of time for studying the craft with an eye to initiation. I like that amount of time myself, and am overjoyed when people show their readiness for this. However, I don't think this is necessarily a rigid rule, and no one should be pressured or made to feel obligated.

Respecting Varying Viewpoints

One of the reasons I like the Neo-Pagan movement is because of its respect for the differing beliefs of its members. For a group to be successful, there must be mutual regard and basic human warmth. It is not necessary for everyone to agree on religious doctrine. I am pretty straightforward in my view that the Goddess is the center, but I have had sisters in circle with me who see the God in the center, or the God and the Goddess together, or even a life source that is neutral and nameless. Groups can be torn apart by bickering over what is the truth. Though I prefer to cast the seven directions or create a cone or sphere and declare it sacred space, some women prefer to cast four directions with four elements. Ritual can still be high and happy-making for everyone present, with each sister's magical views honored. The main thing is that we are together and sharing ourselves. We can enjoy one another's ideas and honor our own as well. We can even debate them in a spirit of enjoyment and learning. But when we forget that human love, sharing and an appreciation for the power of individual choice are central, we can lose the very purpose we began with.

Assuming Leadership

One of the best models I have found for successful group leadership is the mother/child model. Placing the Goddess at the center of all things not only relieves us of polarizing splits and authoritarian hierarchies, but gives us a new model of authority, that of Mother and Child, or the principle of nurturance. She or he who nurtures, who cares for the young, the old and the infirm, is the true authority. In authentic matriarchies, the mother was the center (not the top) of the tribe. Her authority was based on love and concern for those she nurtured, and her tribe held this gift in reverence. Social order was based on this mother-type authority.

This is a hairy topic and women especially (including me) have much to learn about giving and receiving leadership. I won't go into it extensively here, except for a few brief guidelines. The most successful groups are those where everyone feels empowered and a part of the decision-making process. A good leader is one who facilitates this, rather than simply imposing her own preconceptions on everyone. However, there are times when people need a strong person to take the energy and direct it for them, especially when they are new to the subject and to one another. When I direct groups, I usually make more decisions and initiate more of the format in the early stages, and try to phase out my leadership as the members learn to take these responsibilities themselves. The better people know one another, the more sensitive they are to one another, and the less leadership they require.

It is important to realize that leader and follower create another circle, and that both are equally powerful and depend upon one another to exist. I cannot lead you if you don't want me to, and nor do I wish to. Therefore, should you decide to become a group leader, I suggest you have very clear agreements with each member right from the start. Make sure there is mutual consent on all sides; that way no one feels they are being coerced. I have found it useful to begin each new group with individual interviews. This way, there is time for each person to state her needs and expectations, and to let others know what they wish to give. I have found it to be a pitfall to assume any of these things without discussing them first. Remember that mutual consent is essential, and leadership is a service, not coercion.[1]

Problems in Groups

I first began leading women's circles back in the early seventies. I was quite naïve about it at the start, of course, and had much to learn about group dynamics. I ran into pitfalls and patriarchal programming that I had no idea existed. I jumped in eagerly, innocently, with my heart open to women. I thought we were all perfect and that once we got together everything would be wonderful; we would "turn the world around," as Pat Parker says. I have experienced glory and healing as a leader, but I have also experienced hurt and disillusionment. I want to share these thoughts with you, not only so that you will be better prepared, but also to help you avoid some of the difficulties I have encountered. After all is said and done, I have no regrets: I am glad I made the plunge, felt the pain and learned the lessons because it has been a growth process for me and for many of the women I have worked with. Despite our problems, we have learned many things and moved a few inches closer to creating the world of our hearts' desires. I am committed to working in groups of women, more so now than ever before. The joy of seeing women flower and take wing, discover the Goddess in themselves, form bonds of understanding and love—these experiences are worth a great deal. And besides, with all the issues I have dealt with under my belt, I am now better equipped to lead groups successfully than ever before.

Naming Demons

Community is the ultimate force of healing, and magical community is the best of all. In a world that keeps us isolated, suppresses us, divides us and perpetuates scarcity of love, economic flows and community support, we urgently need to break down the barriers. But we can banish the problems that divide us. From a magical point of view, banishment is a helpful way to look for solutions. There are three steps to banishing: naming, dissolving and replacing. What follows are names for some of the problems/demons that can be destructive to groups:

- **Splits.** In circular theory, what seem like oppositions are ultimately connected, mutually creating, dependent upon one another to exist. Splits are usually caused by people taking sides and refusing to see the opposing point of view. It is a cutting of the circle and hence a breaking of the connection, and it is a frequent cause of divisions among people.
- **Scapegoating.** This is when one person, or a smaller group of people, become a focal point for venting the rage, frustra-

tion and hostility of a larger group, community or nation. The witch-burnings and Nazi holocaust are outstanding examples of large-scale scapegoating. Smaller-scale scapegoating occurs within groups, where one person, or a smaller group of persons, are accused, punished, ostracized or blamed for ills that many may be suffering. Individuals often scapegoat each other on a one-to-one basis, when they perceive one person as representing/containing the "enemy" or the oppressor.

- **The staircase.** The staircase is an insidious demon that attacks many groups. Everyone feels like she is on one step and trying to get to the highest, or the next highest. Those higher up are struggling to keep those lower down from climbing up, and those lower down feel inadequate and hate themselves. Everyone is always comparing themselves and each other, deciding who is more or less worthy of approval. Jealousies and competitions flourish and usually those at the top grow more powerful while those at the bottom feel more crushed. Like scapegoating, examples of the staircase effect can be found internationally, within groups and between individuals. The caste or class system is a staircase. "God over man over woman over child" is a staircase. "Man over nature" is a staircase. The United States over "underdeveloped countries" is a staircase. Staircases exist in most conventional forms of human interaction, from the school to the workplace to the church.
- **Pecking order.** This is an extension of the staircase, where several members join up on one step, others on another step and so on. They give one another clout, and support one another in conflict with people on the other steps. They also give an illusion of oneness within the order and help members to forget their connection to the whole. These in-groups generally rally around a leader whom they use to represent them—and whom they eventually sacrifice and topple from the pedestal.
- **The pedestal.** This is a modification of the staircase based on an either/or relationship between the boss/martyr and the slave/dependent. The pedestal is mutually created by members in both

positions.. It invariably explodes when an underling rebels and overthrows the person she has placed above her. This divides people; in the pain of it all, they flee from one another in rage, neither seeing how she, herself, has helped to create the game.
- **Discrimination.** This occurs when a person or group is rejected by another/others because of race, size, class, gender, religion, age, sexual preference, disability or just being "different."
- **Communication breaks.** Interruptions can be oppressive when less assertive people don't get to have their say. Some people are louder and more easily heard. But people can only make decisions on the basis of what has been communicated, and unspoken perceptions can go by the wayside. Remember things like, *As I have the strength to take the rattle, so do I have the understanding to pass the rattle on, and She who holds the rattle holds the power.* The power comes from the attention given to the one who is speaking. Aggressive people tend to jump in freely, which is good, but they sometimes forget to pay attention to those who are quieter. Quiet people often suppress their ideas and need to assume responsibility for speaking up.
- **Scarcity.** A feeling of scarcity occurs when some members feel there is not enough time, attention, support or interest for them to receive their share.
- **Personal insecurities.** There are uncountable numbers of these, but one of the most powerful in dividing groups is a personal fear of being considered strange, weird, different or unacceptable in some way. People who feel this way usually are afraid to contribute, and eventually disappear. Another personal insecurity is the illusion of powerlessness—the belief that the group is being created by others and that the individual has no power in decision making.

Banishing Demons

Having named these demons, the next step is to send them away. You can do this with ritual. Here are a few ideas on what forms could be used to replace the banished ones:

- **Splits.** Replace splits with circles and mediation. When caught in a conflicted two, find a third factor, look for the good or truth on either end, discard what is false and set up a flow. Remember that we are all connected and that the Divine is very helpful in preventing disagreements from becoming splits. If none of these things work, separating might be the best thing after all. We don't have to feel imprisoned with one another; there are always new patterns forming in the future, new connections to be made and lessons to be learned.
- **Scapegoating.** Replace scapegoating by remembering that the true enemies are the perpetrators of oppression. Instead of casting blame on one person or a small group, realize that this only plays into the hands of the oppressors, keeping us divided and blaming one another. Those who have been scapegoated, such as Jews, black people, witches, gay people, women, fat people, poor people and so on, can band together in mutual support instead of remaining divided. If you find yourself wanting to pick on one person, look inside yourself and see what old pain and anger you may be projecting. Realize that we all have faults, that no one has to be perfect and that we are not each other's enemies.
- **The staircase.** Replace the staircase with a circle of equality, in which every person is seen as beautiful, valuable, divine and essentially good. The circle of equality means that we each honor ourselves as well as one another, that no one is made more or less than another and that everyone has something precious and beautiful to give.
- **Pecking orders.** Pecking orders should not even exist in a group where people feel equal. However, there is sometimes a genuine need for people to pair off or meet in smaller clusters; this can be very nourishing and positive when based on good feelings rather than for the purpose of gossiping or consolidating divided power. Prevent divided energy by ensuring that smaller groups share their experiences with the larger group.
- **The pedestal.** Replace the pedestal with cooperation, and by dividing both responsibilities and rewards evenly.

- **Discrimination.** As with the staircase, replace discrimination using the circle of equality.
- **Communication breaks.** Replace communication breaks by being attentive and sensitive to one another, or by using the rattle process, which symbolizes this.
- **Personal insecurities.** It often takes prolonged work to heal personal insecurities, but you can begin by encouraging group members to give one another—and themselves—"strokes." Tell yourselves and each other how wonderful you are, affirm this and let yourself believe and enjoy it.
- **Scarcity.** Replace scarcity with abundance, which is created when all members give from whatever stores of energy they have, and allow all other members to receive.

Endnote

1 Starhawk has some fine material on group dynamics in her books *Dreaming the Dark: Magic, Sex, and Politics* (Boston: Beacon Press, 1997) and *Truth or Dare: Encounters with Power, Authority, and Mystery* (New York: HarperOne, 1989). She also has written on this subject in the newsletter *Reclaiming*, which comes out of the collective she helped to create (www.reclaiming.org).

As Within, So Without:
Some Psychological Aspects of Priestessing
By Kim Duckett

After more than twenty years as a high priestess in Dianic Goddess traditions, I have observed and noted our own and others' reactions to priestesses, both positive and negative—never indifferent. We have much to learn from these reactions, individually and collectively, regarding our personal biographical psychologies and, just as importantly, the transpersonal nature of some of these responses. Paying attention to, learning from and healing these dynamics can, as Vicki Noble suggested, "be used to further our work of reclaiming our lost heritage" as goddess people.[1]

It was Noble's article, "Authorizing Our Teachers: Teaching in a Feminist Spiritual Context," that named what I experienced during my early years as a teacher and priestess.[2] By the mid-nineties, I was a seasoned feminist activist and leader of women and, although I was sure I was to continue in these ways, I felt alone and confused by what I encountered in the circles and classes I was teaching and the spiritual community that grew up around me.

Although Noble's intent in writing the article was to highlight "some of the inherent problems and complexities involved in being a teacher of women," she was aware of the larger meaning of her endeavors and what she had encountered:

> The level of damage we have incurred in Western culture in the five thousand years that separate us from our ancient foremothers in the Goddess cultures of Anatolia and Old Europe is great, and, unfortunately, its influence has been felt in every

workshop or ritual journey to retrieve the past that I have conducted. It appears that a recapitulation of that loss, at times toxic, necessarily becomes part of our experience together, but I have found (that what) looks like pure pettiness (and sometimes escalates into attacks) can be used to further our work of reclaiming our lost heritage.[3]

Noble tells of her early experiences with women from the seventies to the nineties, including her activism in the women's health movement and her deep and abiding interest in yoga, women's spirituality and female shamanism. From the very beginning of her work with groups of women, Noble encountered dynamics she did not fully understand, including the "tendency towards psychological naming of things, the tendency to act out in psychological ways, and to want psychological attention."[4] Noble hired a psychologist to teach her "some of the basic psychological skills needed for group work" and realized "it was psychology with a vengeance that was slowly eroding my authority in my groups in the form of . . . unacknowledged resentment, competition, bids for power, jealousy."[5]

Others have noted the challenges inherent in being a priestess of women:

> Being a priestess does not lift one to the level described in fantasy novels. It is not a glamorous job. Most often it is the priestess who cleans up after everything is over and takes out the garbage in her ceremonial robes. It is a balancing act in which one tries to empower each woman while also making certain the day to day things get done . . . Those drawn to women's spirituality, like all women, have often been deeply affected by living in patriarchy and, sadly, being a priestess often makes one a target for others' issues.[6]

Another priestess agrees: "I first began leading women's circles back in the early 70s. I was quite naïve about it at the start, of course, and had much to learn about group dynamics . . . I have experienced glory and healing, and I have also experienced hurt and disillusionment."[7] Like Noble, others also honor the positive aspects inherent in their calling to priestess women: "After all is said and done . . . I am glad I made the plunge, felt the pain, learned the things I learned because the process was growthful (sic) for me and for many of the women I have worked with. Despite the problems, we learned many things and moved a few inches closer to creating the world of our hearts' desire." [8]

Both these sentiments—the undeniable call to do this work and the difficulties that arise from it—reflect my own experiences as a priestess in women's communities over the last two decades. Given my perspective as a woman who is trained in and teaches women's psychology, it is clear that there are dynamics to be recognized and dealt with regarding the complexity of what occurs when women gather together in a spiritual context. Our collective experience indicates that this complexity is an inherent part of what has been termed "the re-emergence of the Goddess," although perhaps we did not foresee what it would mean for those of us who would be called to actually priestess this re-emergence.[9]

Collision of Consciousnesses
One of the most common ways we "bump" with one another in women's circles is identified as a "collision of consciousnesses," which refers to conflicts that stem from radically differing perspectives, for example, regarding New Age tenets and the ideals of ancient goddess cultures that are being re-established today.[10] It is also applicable to conflicts that erupt between feminist and non-feminist perspectives. Another way it occurs is when conflicts arise over the "intent" of a group, one of the most common sources of contention within women's circles and communities. In all of these instances, it is often the priestess who ultimately bears the brunt of the conflicts. [11]

Some women's spirituality communities arise organically around or are created by one woman: a teacher/priestess. Others begin or are maintained as peer-led group endeavors. There has been a great deal of conflict regarding these different ways of growing and maintaining women's spiritual communities. Circles/communities with one priestess have the added potential for strong reactions toward her from those on the outside, as well as from those drawn to and surrounding her. It is important to respect and teach these different forms and structures as different "cultures" within the larger culture of goddess spiritualities, each with its own unique set of dynamics and potentials. Familiarizing women with examples and instances of these different kinds of cultures helps normalize a wide variety of organizational or communal structures.

Like many other leaders in women's circles/communities, Noble was concerned that if she actively answered the call she felt to teach/lead women, she would be accused of being "authoritarian" or "exerting 'power over' others"—that is, being patriarchal.[12] As has happened in other women's experiences, including my own, women she had hoped to empower ultimately used "their fledgling power to take (her) on as an opponent."[13] Concerns and conflicts regarding "feminist ideals of leaderlessness and equality"[14] have a long herstory.[15] Although these issues continue, the intervening years and experience on the part of many has resulted in a greater and more settled wisdom regarding the need for what Starhawk calls "responsive leadership."[16] I have found that proactively educating women about this herstory and the specifics of responsive leadership is helpful in lessening accusations and conflict about leadership and power.

Projections
Instances of personal psychological issues also arise in women's circles/communities. One of the most common is projection. Projection occurs when we place onto others those things we cannot see or own as parts of ourselves. Projection is a complex dynamic. Projections are often subconscious reactions. Discerning what is a projection and what is a genuine authentic reaction to someone is a learned skill:

> To have genuine regard for someone and the contribution she makes to the circle is not a projection. If I think or say, "(Sue) is a strong and steady presence today," and do not put (her) up, or myself down, but simply make the observation, I am having an authentic reaction . . . To have genuine difficulty with someone

and how s/he contributes to the group is not a projection . . . (Saying) "How Mary expresses herself is so different from how I express myself that it's difficult for me to wait patiently while she reaches the point of her story," (is) an authentic reaction . . . acknowledging the differences, not maligning her character or touting my own.[17]

Projections begin immediately at the convening of a class or circle. They intensify and become more problematic after the passing of the honeymoon stage of a circle or community. This is important for priestesses of circles to know and prepare for. "The reason to pay attention to projection in the circle is that resentment builds . . . If projections accumulate, the circle seems less and less holy or whole and can begin to shiver and shake with undercurrents that nobody understands."[18] Projection is a common reaction to the priestess, whether the reaction is idolization or highly critical. This is not surprising given that she is out there, front and center, often dynamic and charismatic, and leading/facilitating in a spiritual context. Projection has a draining influence and is hurtful to everyone. "In the energetic realm we can sense projection being laid on us, and have a natural tendency to resist it. We get tired of being honored or despised for fulfilling other people's fantasies."[19]

Shadow
The psychic material that we project onto others and subsequently act out, especially when conflict arises, is called "the shadow" in Jungian psychology. Shadow material includes all the unexplored or unresolved aspects of ourselves that we fear or are uncomfortable claiming. Rather than working on them as parts of ourselves, we project them onto others or onto groups of people. Maturation as a spiritual being includes recognizing and working on our own shadow material rather than projecting these attributes onto others.

Women's circles/communities are places where this work of becoming our authentic selves, with its accompanying accountability, takes place. Although not all circles are explicitly for healing or personal growth, it is imperative that participants in circles/communities be aware that their shadow material may be activated in circles, and therefore be alert to the very real potential for projecting this material onto one's circlemates, and especially one's priestess. Because we know first-hand the destructive impact that projection and the acting out of shadow material can have on women's circles/communities, one of our cultural expectations in the Mystery School and the WOTY circles I convene includes a commitment, whether internal or external, especially during times of conflict, to ascertain if one's shadow material is being activated and/or one is projecting onto others.[20] I offer a workshop to all Mystery School participants called, Womon Know Thyself: A Personal Practice and Communal Expectation, to familiarize participants with the dynamics and processes I speak of in this essay, and to gain their commitment to the personal practice and communal expectation of self-reflection and assessments that are foundational to the creed to "know thyself."

Projections and the activation of shadow material are inherent parts of the dynamic of circle/community. If they are recognized and understood as such, and not ignored or vilified, they can be used to further healing and growth on everyone's part.

Triggers

There is a fourth, and related, psychological process that is important in understanding not only circle/community dynamics, but especially women's reactions to priestesses. This is the experience of triggers. One can be triggered by encountering something (for example, a person, an event or a dynamic) that reminds one, often on an unconscious level, of a similar thing that was experienced in the past as a source of pain and trauma. The list of potential traumatic situations includes events that women commonly experience, such as sexual abuse and rape, domestic violence, being the victim of an alcoholic, drug-addicted or mentally ill parent or caregiver, experiencing discrimination based on gender/race/class/affectional preference, having life-threatening medical conditions and experiencing catastrophic events, whether natural (such as earthquakes and hurricanes) or man-made (such as war and poverty). Although trauma can be caused by many circumstances, research indicates that it is often the violation of a person's ideas about the world that puts the person in a state of extreme confusion and insecurity. This also occurs when people or institutions on which one depends for survival violate, betray or disillusion one in some way.[21] Simply living in patriarchy creates a constant state of trauma and PTSD[22] for many women.[23]

Although trauma can be ongoing and can happen at any time in one's life, for many of us the original trauma happened in our family of origin when we were young—that is, in our first experience of a "group" or "circle." Entering back into an intimate configuration like a circle/spiritual community, especially one with a strong female figure, may trigger original traumas. Reactivation of an original trauma can also arise in women's spirituality circles/communities due to many women's earliest spiritual experiences occurring in patriarchal religious institutions where they felt betrayed or disillusioned.

Being aware of the potential for triggering in women's spirituality settings is the first step in dealing with triggers. Proactive education is important. Articulating the potential for triggers should be a part of any prior communication about intent about a circle/community, workshop or event.

If a trigger affects an ongoing relationship that a woman wants to continue, it may be useful to share information about the trigger with the other person and find a mutually satisfying solution. For example, Barb had a circlemate who constantly jiggled her foot during circle. This nervous habit, which might for others be a simple annoyance, was a trigger for Barb due to traumatic events from her childhood. Barb tried sitting where she could not see the person in the circle, or shielding her view by turning her head, while simultaneously enlisting strategies to calm her PTSD, which manifested as feelings of irritability, distractedness and rage. Finally, however, in order to continue being in the circle with this woman, Barb decided to approach her to see if something could be worked out. Thankfully, the woman, who was at that time unaware of her nervous habit, was able to sit in such a way that she did not jiggle her foot.[24]

In another situation, a student approached me about a phrase I use to describe going into the deep/underworld time of the Wheel of the Year cycle. This phrase had abusive sexual connotations for her and she reacted negatively each time I used it. Because she knew herself so well and had paid attention to her charged feelings and growing tendency to project onto me, and because she valued both Mystery School and our relationship as teacher/student, she was able to tell me about her trigger and experience and we worked out a mutual solution. I was grateful to know and help in a way that allowed her to continue learning from me; because we were able to show care, this situation strengthened our bond with each other and contributed to our own individual healing processes.

This was one situation where I could respond in a helpful way, but there have been many other situations that could not be resolved so easily, or at all. It is important to remember that triggers are often associated with serious trauma and PTSD, and neither a priestess or a circle/community may be equipped to deal with these situations—and nor should they be expected to.

I want to stress that dealing with triggers is especially complex for the teacher/priestess. Because projection is often at work in situations involving triggers, a woman who becomes triggered in a circle/community often believes there is a "dynamic" going on between herself and the priestess (that is, the woman believes that the priestess is at fault or responsible in some way for what the woman is experiencing or feeling); in this situation, the woman may attempt to engage or involve the priestess in her personal psychological process or drama. Although the priestess may want to respond in a sympathetic way in the hope of helping or healing, she must be very careful about the way she engages with this situation. Triggers are usually the personal reactive process of an individual and, as such, do not involve another person or group or call for processing with others. Personal triggers are processes that are best dealt with on one's own or with a counselor.

Some women who come to our circles/communities/workshops are deeply disturbed, and their needs are beyond what we can deal with. A priestess may know or feel this immediately on an intuitive level, but it may also take time for her to discern whether the woman triggers her personally or has deep issues of her own, as well as the extent of any issues the woman may have. Determining whether a prospective student or ongoing participant is exhibiting issues we are not equipped to deal with is a learned skill and requires seasoned wisdom. Being able to recognize that there are some women we truly cannot work with in a circle/community and say, "I'm sorry, but this circle/community/experience does not seem to meet your needs," are essential skills for priestesses and priestesses-in-training.[25] Having a savvy co-facilitator—someone to discuss these situations with—is also extremely helpful.

Relational psychology and cultural theory (RCT),[26] a woman-centered psychology that I encourage my students to familiarize themselves with and practice in their priestessing, uses the term "disconnection" to talk about these same dynamics (projections, shadow, triggers) from a perspective based in women's experience and wisdom. We were born connected (literally) and thrive best in growth-enhancing connective relationships and situations. Instances of the kind of traumas listed above create an experience of "disconnection"—an unbearable but lived-with psychological distress. According to RCT, these disconnections are the cause of most mental and emotional illnesses, especially those common in women.

Like triggers, conflicts within women's circles/communities often replicate the original disconnects that we experienced in our early formative years or in other life experiences. There are times in the course of living one's calling as a priestess that one can be a part of a healing experience of "reconnection" for another. This takes time, patience and practice. One's natural relational healing tendencies can best be honed by studying and practicing the tenets of relational psychology. Clearly knowing if one has been called and has the desire and fortitude for this kind of healing work is imperative for a priestess. In my own situation, I had the gift of intuitive relationality and was able to engage in its healing application for the first thirteen or so years of my priestessing. However, my interest in and drive for this kind of healing dynamic waned as I reached mid-life and was called to focus my energies elsewhere and for the larger good; other priestesses report a similar experience.

I believe that all priestesses and priestesses-in-training should be familiar with basic psychology, though the kind of psychology is extremely important. Patriarchal psychology has not been kind to women and has been critiqued by feminists from its formal inception as a science in the 19th century. I encourage priestesses to familiarize themselves with the woman-centered psychologies I have mentioned, as well as others such as feminist therapy[27] and the work of the Jean Baker Miller Institute.[28]

One cannot expect all priestesses to be practicing psychologists. In fact, I've found that if I stress my experience regarding women's psychology in groups, it seems to call forth even more the kinds of dynamics described in this essay. I do ask that we not allow our students (or ourselves) to use the information discussed here against one another inappropriately—that is, to flippantly accuse each other of projecting shadow material, or to suggest someone is "triggered" when in fact they have a valid criticism.

What I have noticed in the literature and conversations with other priestesses is that part of what makes us priestesses is our dedication to working on our own personal issues.[29] For example, Noble notes her need for a "psychological understanding of my own unconscious projections" and the need to "retrain myself laboriously in the area of my own most basic compulsions and learned responses":

> I am more detached and less needy of personal contact myself, which allows me to be present for them in ways that are appropriate . . . I also ask women from the onset to take personal responsibility for the ways in which her personality may assert itself and together we craft an experience that allows us to bond yet stay individual enough to have autonomous experiences along the way . . . I am learning to take the rare failure with more humor and detachment. I am learning also to voice the truth as I see it in the moment, without holding on to negative feelings generated by personality clashes.[30]

Noble also changed the way she structured learning environments and formats to lessen the likelihood and impact of interpersonal psychology in groups, including shortening the teacher/student contact time; teaching in actual goddess culture settings in order to add the grounding and strength those places offer to the learning experience; and doing "a lot of ritual to keep spirits light and egos fed and calmed from the onset."[31] I have made similar changes over the years in my teaching/priestessing, including always having a "sacralized center"; this is the Spirit/Goddess to me and therefore the Spirit is always involved in any interactions I have with others.[32]

Most of what I've suggested in this essay in the way of how-to's applies specifically to circles/communities priestessed by one woman. Although much of this can be applied/adopted to peer-led groups, in collective circle/community endeavors each member is responsible for the circle/community. Having protocols proactively in place for when problems arise is necessary. When triggers or shadow material and their attending tensions and conflicts erupt in a peer-led circle/community, anyone can "shake the rattle"[33] to indicate that something has happened/is happening, so that an easy-to-follow protocol can immediately be put into place. Peer-led circles/communities also need scheduled assessment times to "keep your group healthy."[34]

Trashing

Whether due to unchecked projections, shadow or triggers, there have been instances of women's circles/communities taking undue collective action against their leaders/priestesses/teachers. This was true in some ways in Noble's case and is true in many other women's experiences, including my own. This group reactivity and the resulting action taken against other women, particularly women who step out to lead, is not new. In the early days of feminism, it was called *trashing*, "a feminist term for very public attacks on one woman."[35]

In 1976, Jo Freeman published, "Trashing: The Dark Side of Sisterhood,"[36] an essay that, like Noble's, should be read by all women who are involved in or priestess/lead/ teach women's circles and communities:

> Trashing is not disagreement; it is not conflict; it is not opposition. These are perfectly ordinary phenomena which, when engaged in mutually, honestly, and not excessively, are necessary to keep an organism or organization healthy and active.

> Trashing is a particularly vicious form of character assassination . . . it is not done to expose disagreements or resolve differences. It is done to disparage and destroy . . . There is, of course, a fine line between trashing and political struggle, between character assassination and legitimate objections to undesirable behavior. Discerning the difference takes effort.[37]

Trashing is a very painful and debilitating personal experience for those targeted. It is also an equally destructive, and often unconscious, collective experience that is used by patriarchy as a "powerful tool of social control."[38]

The term "trashing" is no longer commonly in use, though the practice continues today, including in women's/goddess spirituality circles/communities. Although the virulence surrounding trashing is explained by contemporary theories, Freeman offered the following rationale for this response to women leaders back in the mid-seventies:

> Rage is a logical result of oppression. It demands an outlet . . . While . . . the "system" (is) too big and vague, one's "sisters" are close at hand. Attacking other feminists is easier and the results can be more quickly seen than by attacking amorphous social institutions. People are hurt; they leave. . . Trying to change an entire society is a very slow, frustrating process . . . (in) trashing . . . one can feel the sense of power that comes from having "done something."[39]

Contemporary theories focus on the important research of Carol Gilligan that found that pre-teen and adolescent girls "lose their voice" (their truths) for the sake of maintaining relationships.[40] This idea was later expanded upon in Rachel Simmons' book, *Odd Girl Out: The Hidden Culture of Aggression in Girls*. Simmons describes girls' double bind of valuing relationships and, at the same time, being denied outlets for natural feelings of anger, jealousy and competition. Because girls are not taught to deal with conflict and yet encounter conflict and complex feelings in their interactions with other girls, a culture of indirect aggression develops, where girls destroy each other with silence and covert looks, turned backs and whispers.[41]

Girls grow up and become adult women and, unfortunately, often continue and intensify these behaviors with one another, in what Phyliss Chesler has called "woman's inhumanity to woman."[42] Chesler also identifies internalized sexism as a main culprit in women's ill treatment of one another: Like men, women unconsciously buy into negative images that can trigger abuse and mistreatment of other women ... women depend upon one another for emotional intimacy and bonding, and exclusionary and sexist behavior enforces female conformity and discourages independence and psychological growth.[43]

I believe some of our conflicts or experiences with one another, including the intense ones described in the preceding pages, are transpersonal in nature. Although there are many common instances of transpersonal experiences in goddess-women's lives, what is of import in the current discussion are those experiences that cannot be fully explained by the biographical life of an individual.[44] I believe that Western women have yet to fully address the psychological impact of the horrific loss of the goddess cultures that occurred some 6,000 years ago. This, and the innumerable other instances of dominator societies violently overtaking partnership societies, affects women collectively and as individuals today.[45] These unrecognized and unnamed transpersonal experiences can present in any number of ways, including serious and immobilizing psychological problems, such as anxiety, depression, post-traumatic stress disorder, phobias and so on.

A similar situation occurs regarding the experience known as "the burning times,"[46] when women were tortured and murdered *en masse*. Women often have transpersonal memory-experiences when they encounter information about the burning times, but they have no way of understanding or working through these within traditional psychological frameworks.

Transpersonal experiences also arise for some women regarding the ancient Amazons. Women find themselves deluged with memories of "the violent overthrow and loss of Goddess cultures," "the endless and lonely migrations in our attempts to stay ahead of the patriarchal hordes of marauding bands of torturers" . . . and "the constant warring, not for revenge or pleasure, but in a vain attempt to save our people and some vestiges of our peaceful Goddess cultures." [47]

I often imagine what we were made to do to one another in these instances and how that may affect our interactions with each other today. We know, for example, from copious trial records how we were made to betray each other during the European witch hunts by being forced under torture to "give the names of five other women in (our) village."[48] In doing so, we condemned those closest to us to the same fate of torture and death. Contemporary women often speak of their sense of "betrayal" on the part of other women in their spiritual circles/communities. I feel this is a clue that a response may, in fact, be a "memory" of an actual happening, whether it is an individual "past life memory," or some sort of lineage/collective memory.

Transpersonal "memories" come up in the psyche for healing in the here and now, just as they do with biographical trauma, memories and reactions. Acknowledging and working with the transpersonal realm is complex and filled with challenges.[49] As the transpersonal helper or guide, I give the same kind of support and suggestions in these situations as one might when working therapeutically with a personal, repressed biographical memory, but with the added perspective of transpersonal psychology and methods. Often the only way I have witnessed movement and healing in women's psyches and lives has been through this application of transpersonal psychology.

Many women's strong reactions to priestesses come from these and other traumatic or pivotal herstorical periods and events because we were the leaders/teachers/priestesses then, as we are now, whatever we were called, and whether we practiced formally or informally. I imagine that we encountered dynamics similar to the ones that have been discussed in this essay, though I believe that the dynamics may have been very different between us without the influence of patriarchy.

I also believe that, during times of great upheaval, and specifically at those junctures when dominator societies/patriarchy destroyed goddess/ partnership cultures, reactions to those recognized as leaders/teachers/

priestesses may have been especially tenuous. Patriarchy may have capitalized on those moments as a part of their psychological warfare against us. I am reminded of how the people of the Cherokee nation "lost faith in their shamans/healers after they could not heal the new diseases coming from Europe."[50] It is not hard to imagine that, in a similar way, the priestesses and leaders of ancient goddess cultures may have been blamed or held responsible, however irrationally, for the loss of their ways of life in the face of the incomprehensible horrors of the invaders. Perhaps this helps explain, in part, the sometimes odd and complex love/hate feelings some women seem to have toward priestesses today. It may also be another reason those who are called to priestess sometimes hesitate to step forward into that call.

Conclusion

Concurrent with all the hard experiences that can and do happen in women's circles/communities, there are also the many positive things that are an integral part of women's spirituality. These are the reasons we are drawn together and why we stay together, and why priestesses answer the call to teach and lead, even when things are challenging. How can one truly describe the life-changing psychological impact of encountering women's/goddess spirituality, or attending a women's circle for the first time and feeling that one is, finally, home? Or the soul-stirring impact of one's teachers and priestesses upon one's life, without, or even alongside, all the challenges that you may face together in the ways described in this essay?

It is, after all, these same priestesses who create and maintain the goddess-honoring, female-affirming circles/communities where these dynamics take place, who also activate and call forth the very best in us by encouraging and supporting us to find and live our authentic selves. It is all in hopes of moving "a few inches closer to creating the world of our hearts' desire"[51] and "further(ing) our work of reclaiming our lost heritage."[52]

Endnotes

1 Vicki Noble, "Authorizing Our Teachers: Teaching in a Feminist Spiritual Context," *Woman of Power*, 24 (Summer 1995): 71, accessed December 2, 2012, www.motherpeace.com/vicki_authorizing_our_teachers_1.html

2 Ibid.

3 Ibid., 71.

4 Ibid., 74.

5 Ibid.

6 "Women in Spiritual Leadership," Jade River, Gathering of Priestesses and Goddess Women, May 2010.

7 Shekhinah Mountainwater, *Ariadne's Thread: A Workbook of Goddess Magic* (Berkeley: Crossing Press, 1991), 359.

8 Ibid., 359–360.

9 Starhawk has provided those of us in feminist/Pagan/goddess groups an invaluable service in her adaptation and application of group dynamics and the added impact of sexism, racism, classism, heterosexism and hierarchy. See for example *The Spiral Dance: A Rebirth of the Ancient Religion of the Great Goddess* (New York: HarperCollins, 1999); *Dreaming the Dark: Magic, Sex, and Power* (Boston: Beacon Press, 1982); *Truth or Dare: Encounters with Power, Authority, and Mystery* (New York: HarperSanFrancisco, 1987); and *The Empowerment Manual: A Guide for Collaborative Groups* (Vancouver : New Society Publishers, 2011). Additional resources about group process from other women include: Robin Deen Carnes and Sally Craig, *Sacred Circles: A Guide to Creating Your Own Women's Spirituality Group* (New York: HarperCollins, 1998), 171–194; Christina Baldwin, *Calling The Circle: The First and Future Culture* (New York: Bantam Books, 1998), 143–165; Jean Shinoda Bolen, *The Millionth Circle: How to Change Ourselves and the World,* (Berkely: Conari Press, 1999), 62–66.

10 Vicki Noble, "Authorizing Our Teachers: Teaching in a Feminist Spiritual Context," *Woman of Power*, 24 (Summer 1995): 73, accessed December 2, 2012, ww.motherpeace.com/vicki_authorizing_our_teachers_1.html

11 To avoid the damage that can be done to ongoing or long-term circles and communities due to "collisions of consciousness," I offer an introductory course, Women's Spiritual Journeys, several times a year, wherein participants learn the basics of women's and goddess spirituality and familiarize

themselves, through experience, with circle and circle culture. This course is the prerequisite for all Mystery School, classes and rituals and is designed to proactively deal with the differing perspectives that participants may come in with by powerfully engaging/immersing participants in another culture—that is, a woman-centered goddess spirituality perspective. This course not only provides a way to gently and respectfully separate out those with radically differing views and needs, but also prepares women to enter the Mystery School culture with the same language and experience. Such a gateway course lessens the potential for serious and damaging collisions of consciousness later.

12 Vicki Noble, "Authorizing Our Teachers: Teaching in a Feminist Spiritual Context," *Woman of Power*, 24 (Summer 1995): 73, accessed December 2, 2012, www.motherpeace.com/vicki_authorizing_our_teachers_1.html

13 Ibid.

14 Ibid.

15 See Jo Freeman, "The Tyranny of Structurelessness," originally published in *The Second Wave*, vol. 2. no. 1, 1972, p. 20; revised version published in *Ms.*, July 1973, p. 76. Accessed PDF online, January 8, 2013, www.jofreeman.com/joreen/tyranny.htm

16 Starhawk, "Responsive Leadership," *Truth or Dare: Encounters with Power, Authority, and Mystery* (New York: HarperCollins, 1987), 268.

17 Christina Baldwin, *Calling The Circle: The First and Future Culture* (New York: Bantam Books, 1998), 152.

18 Ibid., 153.

19 Ibid.

20 WOTY is a conceptual model of the Wheel of the Year as a psychology for women. For an overview of WOTY, see my article, "The Wheel of the Year as a Spiritual Psychology for Women," in *The International Journal of Transpersonal Studies*, vol. 29, 2010, www.transpersonalstudies.org/Volume_29_2_2010.html

21 Anne DePrince and Jennifer Freyd, "The Harm of Trauma: Pathological Fear, Shattered Assumptions, or Betrayal?" in *Loss of the Assumptive World: A Theory of Traumatic Loss,* ed. J.Kauffman (New York: Brunner-Routledge, 2002), 71–82, accessed online, January 3, 2013, dynamic.uoregon.edu?~jjf/articles/defo2harm.pdf

22 Post-traumatic stress disorder. See the work of Jennifer Freyd, University of Oregon, Eugene Oregon, for new perspectives on trauma, and PTSD.
23 Lisa Garrett, "Supporting Battered Womyn to Somatically Re-member Themselves" (Master's thesis, Santa Barbara Graduate Institute, July 2004).
24 She later realized, however, because Barb brought it to her attention and in a way that did not move her into defensiveness, that wiggling in this way was a strategy of dealing with her own trauma and triggers about being in groups.
25 Conversation, via phone (January 8, 2013), with Jade River, Consistery Executive of the Re-formed Congregation of the Goddess, International, the oldest contemporary female-focused religious organization to formally train and legally ordain priestesses.
26 Relational psychology and cultural theory, developed by Jean Baker Miller and others, www.jbmti.org
27 See www.goodtherapy.org/feminist-therapy.html for information about feminist therapy.
28 See www.jbmti.org for information about the JBMTI, the Jean Baker Miller Institute.
29 Interview with Nancy VanArsdall, ordained priestess and psychotherapist, via phone December 8, 2013.
30 Vicki Noble, "Authorizing Our Teachers: Teaching in a Feminist Spiritual Context," *Woman of Power*, 24 (Summer 1995): 73, accessed December 2, 2012, www.motherpeace.com/vicki_authorizing_our_teachers_1.html
31 Ibid.
32 Christina Baldwin, *Calling The Circle: The First and Future Culture* (New York: Bantam Books, 1998), 150.
33 Ibid., 150.
34 Robin Deen and Sally Craig, *Sacred Circles: A Guide to Creating Your Own Women's Spirituality Group* (New York: HarperCollins, 1998), 171.
35 Jo Freeman (Joreen),"Trashing: The Dark Side of Sisterhood," Ms., April 1976, pp. 49–51, accessed December 4, 2012, www.jofreeman.com/joreen/trashing.htm (np).
36 Ibid.
37 Ibid.
38 Ibid.

39 Ibid.

40 Carol Gilligan, *In a Different Voice: Psychological Theory and Women's Development* (Cambridge: Harvard University Press, 1993).

41 Rachel Simmons, *Odd Girl Out: The Hidden Culture of Aggression in Girls* (New York: Mariner Books, 2003).

42 Phyliss Chesler, *Woman's Inhumanity to Woman* (Chicago: Chicago Review Press, 2009).

43 Woman's *Inhumanity to Woman*, description/review on author's website, accessed January 15, 2013: www.phylis-chesler.com/books/womans-inhumanity-to-women

44 Transpersonal experiences familiar to goddess women include: dreams, synchronicities, "knowings," "feelings," communing with nature, journeying, trance states brought on by focused intent, as when one does art, writing, weaving, knitting and so on. Transpersonal experiences can be induced by or result from drumming, chanting, rocking, dancing, music, the use of shamanic clicking sticks or bamboo staffs, ritual, divinations, mediations, spellwork and its impact—the list is endless.

45 Riane Eisler articulated the dominator/partnership models of societies and describes the takeover of partnership societies by dominator society invasions in *The Chalice and the Blade: Our History, Our Future* (New York: HarperOne, 1988). Marija Gimbutas researched and published the archeomythological evidence of the same in, for example, Language of the Goddess (NY: Thames and Hudson, 2001).

46 "The burning times" refers to a period of the witch hunts in early modern Europe.

47 Valeire Kim Duckett, non-published transcript of August 2010 session of WOTY-Guardian Psychology, a two-year research project on the dual identity of lesbian butch guardians using the WOTY model. See my article in the IJTS for a full description of this model.

48 *The Burning Times*, directed by Donna Read (Canada: National Film Board, 1990).

49 The most common challenges are the tendencies in some people to want to find a transpersonal reason for their issues rather than doing the hard work of healing in the here and now and the desire for a simple direct-causal relationship between past-life memories and associations and experiences with

people in the present. This may manifest as a simplistic "you did this to me in a past life and that's why I don't like or trust you in this life." It is also evident when one person tells another person what the latter "did" to the former in a "past life" based on the former's "memories." I have found it suspect, at best, to ascribe specific actions toward someone else based on one's own personal "past life memories." I believe it is often more a reflection of the "rememberer's" psyche, whether past or present, than of the other person who is being drawn into the past-life-memory dynamic.

50 Information from workshop with Barbara Duncan (2006), at the Cherokee History and Culture Institute, Cherokee, North Carolina.

51 Shekhinah Mountainwater, *Ariadne's Thread: A Workbook of Goddess Magic* (Berkeley: Crossing Press, 1991), 359.

52 Vicki Noble, "Authorizing Our Teachers: Teaching in a Feminist Spiritual Context," *Woman of Power*, 24 (Summer 1995): 71, accessed December 2, 2012.

Who Am I?
By Martina Steger

I am an amazingly
crazy, insane,
creative, analytical,
multi-talented
original masterpiece
designed by the Goddess herself.

A humanly divine vessel
with strengths and weaknesses
flawed but salvageable.

Under the artist's masterful hands
I am re-born, re-shaped, molded in her image
time and time again.

Gaining awareness
of my true beauty
with each touch of the artist's hands
or stroke of the artist's brush.

Emotions washing over me
like paint on a canvas
touching me,
changing me,
re-creating me.

Bringing me closer
to the divine human creation
that the Goddess intends
me to be.

Building a Working Relationship with Deity
By Mary Moonbow

Ask several modern Pagan priestesses how they define deity, and you're likely to get several different answers. While most Pagans agree on the sacred nature of the rhythms and cycles of the Earth, most witches will have a great explanation of why spellwork is a valid practice, and most followers of feminist spirituality will affirm empowerment of the feminine principle as essential to their spiritual viewpoint, all these folks may give very different answers when you ask them what the Goddess actually is. Most (though not all) priestesses who utilize the concept of deity in their worldview will identify as polytheistic, but views wildly diverge beyond that. With so many perspectives alive in our community, how do we decide upon or discover our own beliefs about deity? What personal practices can deepen our relationship with and understanding of the deities?

Happily, in thirteen years of priestessing, I have never heard a discussion of deity among Pagans become heated. I would go as far as to say that I've never heard an argument about the nature of deity; at most there has been polite sharing of diverse views. With gratitude for the blessing of tolerance and individuality in our Pagan community, let's examine a few common paradigms of belief:

- **Deity as abstract principle.** The Goddess/God/Universe/All-There-Is is an abstract, diffuse principle that animates our world. The idea that "all the gods are one god" (famously expressed in Marion Zimmer Bradley's classic novel, *The Mists of Avalon*) falls into this category as well.[1]

- **Deity as archetype.** The goddesses and gods are archetypes of the human experience, their mythic stories providing insight and guidance for how to navigate our lives.
- **Deity as product of belief.** What we believe defines the reality of the gods for us. If we believe in or focus on a deity, it becomes real in our lives, but does not necessarily exist for other people. Invoking deities in ritual or welcoming them more broadly into our lives will invite the energies and influence we associate with them to enter our experience. In essence, the gods are a coalesced form of human consciousness. (Neil Gaiman's conception of deity in his novel, *American Gods,* provides a fun bridge between this paradigm and the next.)[2]
- **Deities as real beings.** The gods are independent beings, with their own personalities, agendas, ideas, desires, needs, likes and dislikes. Many people with this view believe the gods exist on another plane of some sort, but interact directly and indirectly with our world (sometimes using their human priestesses as vehicles through channeling, aspecting or service work).

Many priestesses move from one deity paradigm to another over the course of their spiritual lives. I have personally progressed through all these paradigms in the order presented. Many priestesses seem to move in this same direction as I have, but it is also possible to skip around and move in different directions, and different paradigms can overlap or co-exist in a person's mind at times. I place no value judgment on which paradigm is better or truer; those are not the right questions to ask. Each practitioner must find the paradigm that fits them at the current time in their lives. As Diana Paxson suggests in her book, *Trance-Portation*, ask not whether something is true, but rather ask if it is useful.[3] The paradigm that is most useful and productive in your current spiritual work is the one is right for you.

The first paradigm is common in the New Age community and is fairly compatible with the monotheistic faiths that dominate religious belief in our Western culture; its adherents may or may not claim the label of Pagan or polytheist. The other three paradigms represent a continuum of increasingly polytheistic faith. Faith is not considered an intrinsic value by most Pagans: it is not demanded by our gods, but given freely or perhaps not given, as feels right to the individual practitioner. In our spiritual lives, we prioritize personal accountability and joyfulness in this present world, rather than requiring faith in a savior god who will rescue us at the end of our human lives. One can build a satisfying Pagan practice without faith, using only a scientific understanding of nature and an intellectual analysis of mythology. You can also choose, as Starhawk advises those first exploring Pagan religion, to simply "suspend disbelief" rather than develop faith in the effectiveness of magical spellwork and the reality of polytheistic deities. However, many people have a spiritual craving for something more numinous than these options provide. We want a mystery religion; we want to re-enchant our world. This requires discovering the relationship to faith and belief that helps us achieve our desired experience of the world.

In the modern world, deity is a challenging concept. Popular Western culture takes science as its god, and scoffs at that which cannot be measured and detected on the physical plane. Faith in the Judeo-Christian God is still marginally accepted, grandfathered into the cultural belief system after centuries of dominance in the religious and intellectual thought of the West. Discussions of faith in the context of Christianity are fairly commonplace in the American media and acceptable in many social circles. But turn to a stranger at a party and begin discussing your personal faith relationship with Artemis, Thor or Sarasvati, and reactions of confusion, dismissal or discomfort are common (if the person does not just assume you're joking). And yet, if we wish to re-enchant our world with spirits, elementals, fairies and gods, we must grapple with the concept of these unseen beings directly. Until we clearly determine our relationship to them, our practice will be plagued by an underlying ambivalence. Just as you can kiss someone even if you're not sure you're in love with them, you can ritually invoke a deity you're not sure you believe in, but both experiences are far more effective, satisfying and ecstatic once you've figured it out.

One way to explore your own relationship to deity is to work with a god or goddess directly and consistently in your spiritual practice.

Regardless of how you define these energies or beings at the outset, you can understand them much more deeply by building a working relationship. As with any relationship, this takes time, effort and consistency, and the rewards are in direct relationship to the amount of work you put in. You can work on this relationship alone, or with a circle of priestesses or covenmates. Other people's experiences can enrich and expand our study, and sometimes they can clash with our own observations and make us question the validity of our own experience. Many people find that a combination of solitary work and group work provides the richest results.

Here are some ideas for ways to build your relationship to a deity, loosely organized from easiest to most advanced:

- **Build an altar dedicated to a specific deity.** Use colors and symbols related to their myth. Locate the altar in a place where you will see it every day. Tend your altar daily or weekly, refreshing perishable elements and noticing any changes in it (a statue that falls over, a candle that won't stay lit, the fact that your cat loves to sleep under it). Sit at your altar on a regular basis and see what comes to you.
- **Do some academic research.** You can start with the internet, but get yourself to a library as well. Read material written by other modern Pagans, books and articles written for the academic community, children's books, fictional re-interpretations of myths, ancient and modern poetry, whatever you can get your hands on. To avoid cultural appropriation, be sure to read as many primary sources as you can and get the perspective of religious practitioners native to the deity's cult and culture whenever possible. The literature of archeology and art history can be very useful when the written record is scarce or non-existent. Always keep in mind the perspective of the writer, because some supposedly "primary" sources were written by Christian evangelists, sometimes centuries after the culture converted to Christianity; keep a critical eye on what seems intrinsic to the deity's cult and what may be an overlay added by the writer.

- **Write songs and prayers to the deity.** Sing and speak them at your altar on a regular basis, and at other relevant times throughout your day if it seems appropriate (upon rising in the morning, to bless a meal, to safeguard a journey, to inspire your work, to temper strong emotions).
- **Draw, paint or sculpt an icon of the deity.** Place these icons around your home or on your altar.
- **Meditate on your deity.** You can do this at your altar, at an appropriate place in nature, in front of a statue or shrine in a museum, or with a group of like-minded priestesses. You can chant a name or mantra associated with the deity, focus on a visual icon or sit in silence and see what comes to you.
- **Engage in conversational prayer with the deity.** Tell them your joys and concerns, ask for help solving problems—and don't forget to listen for an answer. Some people find it helpful to write the dialogue: divide the paper into two columns, write your questions in one column and write the answer that comes to you in the other.
- **Build a relationship with a deity.** If you are able to trace your family heritage, try building a relationship with a deity from a pantheon that was worshiped in the culture of your blood ancestors. While I believe we can all build relationship with deities from any culture (as long as we do so respectfully and avoid cultural appropriation), some people discover a particularly powerful connection with the gods of their ancestors.
- **Begin new projects or learn new skills with the intent of building a relationship with your chosen deity.** Learn to ski with Skadi, start an academic course of study with Athena or Sarasvati, start a new business venture with Lakshmi and Ganesh, study the runes with Odin, learn blacksmithing with Hephaestus or prepare for childbirth with Nuit. You can consciously dedicate your efforts in service to the deity you've chosen or wear a charm related to that deity while you work on the project or skill, and begin and end your work with a prayer of some sort if you wish.

- **Become a storyteller.** Tell the myths and stories of your deity at Pagan gatherings, to friends and family and especially to children.
- **Make a pilgrimage to a sacred spot associated with your deity.** If it is not possible for you to visit a particular sacred well, mountaintop, holy cave, temple or shrine that was associated with your deity in antiquity, find an equivalent of that place closer to home and make a pilgrimage there.
- **Invoke your deity in a group ritual.** I don't recommend that you do this until you've put in some significant time building a private relationship with the deity, at minimum doing both some academic research and some meditation on that deity. Create a costume to wear as that deity's priestess, memorize some poetry, perform a dance or song or some ritual theater. Be creative!
- **Go on a trance journey.** If you have the skills to do trance work (also known as shamanic journeying, pathworking, guided visualization, active imagination), go on a trance journey to meet your deity and speak with them. If you are new to this work, Diana Paxson's book, *Trance-Portation* provides a methodical, reliable and safe way to build your trance skills. It is good protocol to have a relevant question or request for the deity prepared ahead of time and to make an offering to them in gratitude afterwards (either in the spirit world or the mundane world, or both). Remember that you can negotiate with deities and set boundaries with them if they make demands that you are uncomfortable with. I have personally found this to be the most direct way to communicate with deity, and building a trance practice has radically changed my relationship with the gods, propelling me into literal belief in these beings.
- **If you have the skills and community support, try aspecting your deity.** Aspecting is an advanced priestessing skill in which you create space for the deity to step into your body, speak with your voice and move with your limbs, thus communicating very directly with other ritual participants. Before you attempt this work, build a strong set of trance and invocation skills and be

sure you have several priestesses present whose only job is to tend to your physical and energetic safety while you are aspecting. Be sure you have cast a strong circle to contain the work and prevent other, less benevolent energy beings from entering during this very vulnerable work. Ground yourself thoroughly after the work is done, and check-in with your support team for several days afterwards to help you integrate the experience. Occasionally, priestesses experience symptoms of physical illness for a day or so after aspecting, particularly if they were not appropriately prepared for the work or did not ground properly afterwards. Try to build some free time into your schedule for a few days after the aspecting to accommodate physical and spiritual integration.

Whatever paradigm of faith fits you at this time on your spiritual path, the practices I have listed above will help you explore your relationship to the gods and will enrich your practice immensely. Once you have built a strong relationship with one deity, don't be surprised if others show up in your life looking for some attention, too: the gods are drawn to people who are able to engage with them and help them do their work in the world. Enjoy your community of the Unseen Ones, but don't neglect to tend the relationships you have with your friends and family as well—they are just as important. Your deity relationships should enrich your human relationships rather than weaken them, just as having a wide circle of supportive friends strengthens your relationship with a life partner by giving you broad access to support in tough times. At the same time, you may find some of your human relationships changing as you are drawn to spend time with people who support and share your faith paradigm, thus enriching your deity work through the support of human community. Following Apollo's dictum to "know thyself" as a basis for wisdom, we can all enjoy this work of building rich relationships with our gods, and thus understanding our own personal faith more fully. Blessings and good luck to all who embark on this important work.

Endnotes

1 Marion Zimmer Bradley, The Mists of Avalon (New York: Knopf, 1983.)
2 Neil Gaiman, *American Gods* (New York: HarperTorch, 2002).
3 Diana L. Paxson, *Trance-portation: Learning to Navigate the Inner World* (Newburyport, MA: Weiser Books, 2008).

Sacred Vows
By Katie Anderson

Queen of the Night
All the worlds to hide from you
will not negate the shame in my heart.
So I knelt down before you
seeking to rekindle our covenant.

Taken away by your sons
to provide the truth in my devotion.
Walking in your wake
is to tread upon a path of uncertainty.
I chose to submit myself
to your two-sided embrace
And resume my rightful place
as a daughter to your mysteries,
A guardian to any secrets
you do not wish me to share.

And in that place
You whispered my name, once more.

What She Speaks When I Tend Her Flame
By Erin Lund Johnson

What She Speaks When I Tend Her Flame:

Grace.

That is what She whispered to me, after I laid out the offerings, lit the match,
said the prayers, and asked for guidance.
I transform, She said:
The raw meat into food,
The raw thoughts into poetry,
The raw materials into arts and crafts,
The raw ore into weapons, tools, and parts,
The water and plants into healing draughts.
In your heart, distress to peace.
In your mind, worry to reassurance.
In your body, death into life, and then life into growth.
In your life, suffering into power.
I transform, by the power of fire, and the power of Grace.
She said, You too can embody this Grace, in all the transformations in your life
you make:
From chaos to order,
From complacency to vigilance,
From suffering to healing,
From loneliness to togetherness.

From the Otherworlds to Thisworld,
From outside to in,
From self to others,
Like a gift.
Gift yourself, gift another, and then another.

Receive in grace,
Give in grace,
Become
Grace.

And then, we
Become
The Flame,
Her flame,
in this world,
for Her, for us, for all.

Re-Discovering Your Wild Priestess Power
By Gloria Taylor Brown

When I was a little girl in Florida, my Grampa Brown had a great garden. He grew vegetables and herbs and flowers, but the part of his garden I liked best was a small corner where everything grew wild. Separated by a small, foot-high fence, with a little gated opening, this corner of the garden was allowed to grow exactly as it pleased. There were overhanging branches from the tree next door, and even on the warmest summer day, this area was cool and shadowy. I would go into this corner to sit and watch. Sometimes butterflies would come and sit on my finger or small animals would scurry around in the underbrush. Every evening, my grandfather would place a small dish of food and a bowl of milk in the wild corner. He would tell me it was for the wild pixies and leprechauns.

I accepted this behavior as any child does, unquestioning, until I was six or seven years old; I thought everyone had a wild corner in their garden. About this time, I was sent for the summer to stay with my other grandparents. They had a large garden on a farm that produced all of their vegetables and enough left over to sell at the local market. But they had no wild corner. Everything was hoed and raked and the weeds were all pulled. I asked, "Where do the wild pixies live?" and was roughly told there were no such things!

Since I knew my Grampa Brown knew everything, I didn't believe this, and couldn't wait to get back home to tell my parents and grandparents that Grandma Anderson didn't know about pixies; she even said there were no leprechauns. My parents roared with laughter and told me those were just my Grandfather Brown's stories, like the stories I could read in books. But Grampa Brown said, "If you don't believe in pixies and give them a place to live, they won't come to visit. Or if they do, they will tear things up." Then he would snarl, and tickle me, acting like a wild thing, while I giggled and pretended to be scared. I knew he was right, for he always was!

This story inspired me many years ago when I was teaching metaphysical studies at the Centro de Arte Creativo, near San José, the capital of Costa Rica. I was a delegate to the International Women's Congress that was held that year at the nearby university. I wanted to create a special event to mark the successful completion of the Congress. We invited the attendees to come to the Centro to celebrate the community of women that had gathered together.

Seventy-five women from countries across the globe came to our small school grounds on a beautifully clear tropical night to celebrate the full moon. We shared our experiences, sitting around a large fire in the center of the courtyard. As we ended the ceremony, I led them on a meditation to where the wild ones lived. At the end of the meditation, I began to howl like a wolf at the rising moon and encouraged the others to join in. For fifteen minutes, the sound of women howling at the moon rose up to the heavens. All the neighboring dogs joined in. It was a beautiful, wild sound.

Later, many of the women came to me and told me that this experience had been the first time they had ever contacted that wildness that lives in all of us. Some shared that they were afraid we would be arrested. I found this so sad. Here were these bright, wonderful women from many countries who were terribly frightened to have a simple howl at the moon.

I thought about the story of my grandfather's garden again when I was preparing to teach a Wild Women! class at a women's conference in Seattle, Washington. I had envisioned this class as a way for women to transcend the tame and ordinary lives they lived as "good girls" and "nice ladies." I wanted them to get in touch with that wild, untamed and powerful corner of themselves, where Spirit lives. I wanted them to experience their Amazon power and embrace the wildness that I was sure was hidden in every one of them.

Then 9/11 occurred. Suddenly everything was much more frightful. People were terrified by what had come in out of the wild. How could I get women to explore their own wild nature when terrorists threatened to blow apart the world we knew and loved?

I regrouped. I rewrote. I took out the section on "confronting the beast within," removed "where the burrowing creatures live" as too scary, too much for them to experience in such a short class. In fact, I wimped out. I rigidly hoed and raked my class, until what weeds were left could easily be pulled up by my participants. Maybe I made the right choice, because the class went well and everyone seemed very satisfied with the results. Except me. I was unhappy with my performance and what we had achieved as a group. It just wasn't enough. The wild had nowhere to live in the cold, cavernous, hotel meeting room we had used. The wild is where nature can grow exactly as it pleases, just as in the corner of my grandfather's garden. I had pulled up some of my wild plants and tried to make my seminar safe and free of weeds. I realized this came from my own fears.

I vowed to let my teachings grow wild again. I determined to present these classes in natural settings near brooks and streams, where the creatures of the forest and wild birds live. There we could discover the wild flowers and animals, the weeds and the powers of nature as expressed by our Mother Earth. There we could safely discover and express our own wildness without being afraid. Since then I have presented this class in incredible wild and wonderful places around the world.

You see, the wild can be scary. We are trained from birth to suppress our wilder urges. In order to live in a society, there must be some rules, some agreement of civilized behavior. Yet when you push the wild out of your life completely, it has to find other places to live. If it can't be in you, it will exist outside of you and be much scarier than coming to terms with that inner wildness; no matter how hard you try to weed it out, it will still be there. My grandfather knew this, and gave it a place to live and something to eat, so that it never took over the whole garden.

In that wild, shadowy part of ourselves lives great power and great spirit. When we try to suppress and marginalize it, we end up losing a part of ourselves. We each need to have a wild corner, a place where pixies live, in the well-tended garden of our souls.

Explore your wildness. Go on hikes into nature, swim with dolphins, howl with wolves, walk in the woods. Create a place where you can explore the wild, in yourself and in your world. As you renew your connection with the wild, you will find that the wild power is growing within you.

We were never meant to live a tame, sedentary, boring life all the time. We were designed to seek the thrill of adrenaline, the rush that comes with excitement, the quickened pulse of doing something that scares us. This is what being physical is all about. Moving our bodies, exploring the physical world, creating a life filled with passion and purpose. This is where the power of the wild can come into our civilized world and be harnessed to help us get where we want to go. When we marginalize, ostracize and deny it, it comes through as disease, and unhappiness, violence against ourselves and others, for the wild will always find a place to live.

To the Wild Women

> Listen: Do you hear the sound of the drums, beating with the rhythm of your heart?
> Sniff: Do you smell the fires burning, the council fires that call you?
> Look: Do you see us dancing, walking, and moving to the sounds, in the fire light?
> We are waiting for you: Open your heart and feel the love of your tribe, your clan, and your lineage, welcoming you back from the long trip you have been on.
> "But where have I been?" you ask.
> Into the future, into the past, comes the answer. Remember.
> "Why must I remember?"
> Because if the lineage is lost, then the land is a wasteland, and the people perish.
> "What lineage?" you ask.
> The lineage of the Wild Ones, the ones who weave the inner world. An older woman, one of great power and spirit, comes to you, her arms held wide, "Welcome home, my daughter," she says, as you fall into her embrace.

You are home.

You are invited to take part in the council that will decide the course of the next year for yourself and for your world. Will you lend your strength, your courage, your knowledge, and your power that all may benefit?

As we convene the Gathering of Wild Women, we ask you to join us. You know who you are—the question is what will you become?

Come and explore the Wild.

Join the Clan of the Wild Women.

Your future is calling you.

Meditation to the High Priestess of the Wild Women

Close your eyes, relax your body and allow yourself to travel on the sound of your heart beat, beating like a drum, so regular, so comforting, beating, beating, beating like a drum.

Send down a grounding cord from the center of your body to keep you safe while you are traveling, traveling far beyond the bounds of space and time to the land of the Wild Women. Breathe deeply, breathing in the free air, the scent of cloves, allowing yourself to travel further and further with each breath, with each sound you hear as the drums grow louder.

You travel down a path, between trees reaching nearly to the sky, old growth, alive with power. You are going to visit the oldest of the old women, sometimes known as Hecate, sometimes called the Mother of Days, who is the Mother Creator Goddess of all beings and doings, including the sky and the earth, Mother Nyx who has dominion over all things from the mud and the dark, or Nut who is the Sky Goddess of Egypt.

She is the mother of us all and the one who sings us into being, the one who knows her people and has about her the smell of humus and the breath of the Goddess. She is the old one, the one who knows, and she is within each one of us. She lives in the deepest soul of women, the ancient and vital Wild Woman. She gathers rocks and bones, leaves and flowers, brings them home with her and croons a soft song, a song of becoming, a song of joy. She knows that bones represent the indestructible core of your being.

She gathers the bones, the bones of the wild creatures that have gone before, and she brings them back to her encampment, deep in the ancient woods. When she gets to her campfire, she arranges the bones and rocks, the leaves and flowers on her altar, stroking them, loving them, and singing to them. As she sings, the bones take shape, the shape becomes flesh, the flesh becomes new wild ones.

She preserves in the darkest of days that you may live again, that you may not be scattered to the winds, bringing together your soul and your flesh and singing the song that tells your story.

You hear her sing, "I am the oldest of the old, mother of the night, sister of the sun . . . I have been waiting for you, these long days to remember, to return, that I may teach you . . . that you may be trained in the way of the Wild. Will you accept the task I have for you? Will you join me as we raise up the power? The power of the wild—the power of women, pure and natural? . . . She sings her song of your becoming . . .

She continues to sing with a message for each individual woman, a precious gift for her daughters . . .

(Long Pause)

As she finishes her song, she reaches out her hands to you, and lifts you up into being, an individual, a part of the whole, a true Wild Woman, that she has sung into being. You may talk with her, or ask her questions, or you may just sit and sing together, beside the fire, the wild creatures of the forest drawing near to hear your song . . .

(Long Pause . . .)

As the singing draws to a close, the drums begin to fall silent, becoming only the beating of your heart once more. It is time to return, to come back from this time out of time, knowing it is not a parting, but only the beginning of a relationship that has always been and will always be. She is your mother, your creator and your friend. Her love surrounds you and supports you through all your days.

Thank her, and if you wish, give her a gift. She has a gift or word of advice for you to bring back with you.

Clutch it to your heart, as you leave the fireside, and return to this place and time, to be here now to celebrate your existence as a Wild Woman.

Rooftop Poem at Dendera
By Normandi Ellis

See how we walk into the temple together,
our rhythm moves these bodies as one—
a procession of lifetimes, spirits now manifest
in all of our known or unknown sacred names.
See how we move on the temple roof as one,
touching, wide-eyed, under the veil of night.
Your touch is the lighting of this temple fire;
My flesh is a veil you pierce with love.
Each atom in our bodies whirls & sizzles
like a galaxy of light. We are living stars.
My love, we have become night—a starry
blanket tucked beneath the chin of the world.
Move in me and through me as a god
moves in and throughout time and space.
See how we are one being—woman and man,
ever one, a universe making love with itself.

The Body is My Bible
By Vajra Ma

My experience as a priestess for over two decades is that the body is my bible, my holy book. I have experienced my body as the Tree of Knowledge and a treasure house of wisdom and bliss. It is my hope to encourage the 21st century priestess to discover this for herself at the deepest, most subtle levels and guide others to experience the same. I maintain that priestessing from the original sacred text, the wisdom of the female body, is our most potent antidote to the poison of patriarchy. It is time that, as women we take our seat of power—with no apology.

We are the natural spiritual authority of humanity by virtue of our female incarnation. Women author life, and what one authors (creates, births) one has authority toward. I say toward, not over, for natural authority is the antithesis of patriarchal authority. Patriarchal authority comes from a book, whereas the natural spiritual authority of woman arises from the power to give birth and unfolds from there into an inseparable matrix of responsibility and relationship to nurture, protect, teach and guide the life she has authored, and to do this not only physically, but emotionally and spiritually.[1] Authorship equals authority equals responsible relationship. This equation of authority extends not only to the physical, mental and emotional life of the child, but also the spiritual. Exalting book over body was the method used to wrest this natural spiritual authority away from women. The 21st century priestess may gain it back.

Reduced to its simplest terms, as well as its historical reality, male spiritual authority is based in written word: the "holy book." Female spiritual authority is based in reality: the Holy Body. When I speak of woman's body, I explicitly include the womb or wombspace (women who have had a hysterectomy retain the energetic imprint of the womb and its powers).[2] The modern-day priestess must lead the way in restoring respect for woman's body. Woman's body is the original Sacred Text or Holy Book.

In order to priestess unapologetically from our seat of power, we need to recognize very clearly how our innate seat of power has been obscured and, for all intents and purposes, stolen by a book. We need to free ourselves from the spell of the written word as authority.

Most people, when they hear the word "priest," have an association that includes a certain justification of the person's spiritual role by way of a scripture of sorts. This reference imbues the person, for centuries male only, with a superior authority, either because of having studied "the book" or because of having been ordained by a structure based in such a book. A book is a collection of words, a container of abstract concepts and definitions; "the book" is possessed by a few and it provides its authority to those few over a great many others. Most prominently, it discredits any claim to spiritual authority by people who are not referencing their authority in this book (as in mothers of children, matriarchs of clans). And it must do so, for if it allowed any kind of a spiritual free-for-all (just for being human), its book-based authority would cease to be exclusive. This extreme centralizing of spiritual power in a book and in its priests laid the groundwork for centralizing, and thus amassing, economic and political power.

The priest has a vested interest in an ever-increasing structure of control to maintain his power. And in the West, ever since Genesis 3:17, we have it all right there, in "the book," notwithstanding the fact that it is circular logic, justifying its own words by its own words. Jehovah provides a garden, places the Tree of Knowledge in it and then forbids Adam and Eve to eat its fruit. When Eve does eat the fruit, and shares it with Adam (as woman had for centuries before Genesis), Jehovah declares "Behold, the man has become like one of Us, to know good and evil," and kicks them out of the Garden of Eden.[3]

This is a territorial issue: all the knowledge, wisdom and life-generating powers woman possesses, just because she is a woman, become "forbidden fruit." Her powers become the territory of the male god, his male image and the male priest. This fundamental reversal—this assigning of women's power and wisdom over to men—is at the bottom of almost any perception of what a "priest" is.

This understanding becomes clearer when we realize that the tree(s) are the body and the serpent that urged Eve to eat the fruit is *kundalini*, which is often envisioned as a serpent goddess. When *kundalini* circulates fully through the body, it brings enlightenment. This explains why, from then on, englightenment must come from the the patriarch, not the woman; "the book," not the Body.

It is only by exalting a book over the body that patriarchy could establish a fundamental and ultimate reversal of reality: the myth of male "birth," the idea that a male god made a male, and then from this male made a female. What matters to our understanding of book versus body is that the myth of male "birth"—the penultimate usurpation of woman's natural spiritual authority—has been nailed in place for centuries through the "authority" of the "holy book" and under threat of physical or spiritual death. This includes not only the Bible, but many other myths and written misogynist codes and rules.[4] To priestess unapologetically from our seat of power, we need to realize how fundamentally the "holy book" usurped that seat of power: it assigned the power of the womb to the male. The 21st century priestess faces the task of reversing this centuries-long reversal, the task of taking us back to the original Tree of Knowledge: woman's body.

Reversing the reversal is a monumental task; yet it is amazing how quickly false notions and inhibiting mental and emotional patterns dissolve when we take the direct route of the body. I have found I can rely on bodyknowing to deliver unadorned reality. The body does not lie.

I define *bodyknowing* as a conscious awareness and participation with body energetics, an attunement to the body's language that gives a direct experience of spiritual awareness and wisdom. The body speaks through sensation, breath, sound, movement, shape and emotion. Through the body, we directly source innate knowing, which cannot be found in books. We awaken it neurologically, genetically, cellularly, molecularly; we awaken it within the body.

I do not include "visually" in the above list. Bodyknowing is a kinesthetic experience, not a visual one. Images arise, but we do not focus on them or let them lead. This is not to negate the true power of visualization to beneficially affect our subtle body; there is no hard division in the body. However, to enter the most subtle awareness, we focus on sensation.

It is important to understand that bodyknowing and using the body, whether in dance, song or ritual enactment, are not the same thing. As one who trained for decades as a dancer and classical vocalist, I know that such training is not bodyknowing. In fact, dance technique can pose an obstacle to bodyknowing: it can override sensitivity to the body's nuanced layers of knowing through feeling. This is also true of most yoga as it is taught in the West—that is, as a purely physical discipline. Bodyknowing, on the other hand, does not approach the body as a tool we use, but as a teacher to whom we are deeply and humbly receptive.

Bodyknowing covers a wide spectrum of degrees of subtlety and refinement. Anyone can drag a bow across a violin, but it takes skill to make music, and it takes highly refined skill to create music that touches the soul. So it is with priestessing through bodyknowing.

I began subtle body exploration in the mid-eighties with Continuum, a form of subtle, internal movement created by Emilie Conrad. I studied eighteen months with her close colleague Susan Harper. I had just stepped onto the goddess path and, in the Continuum explorations, I sometimes experienced sensations, movement and sounds that evoked what I felt were signature qualities of various goddesses: I somehow knew "this" was the energy of Yemaya, or "that" was a quality of Kali. Around the same time, I studied with a Middle Eastern dance teacher named Gena Reno; she was experimenting with how women in moving meditation could hold more energy in their bodies with more refined articulation, and how this put women in touch with "high frequencies" and "feminine knowledge."

During those early years, I facilitated ritual circles that included free-form movement; though not subtle-body oriented, it was potent, transformational bodyknowing in its own right. In these circles of about twenty women, we made our own music with drums, rattles and voices.

Each women, one at a time, came into the center of the circle; beginning from silence and stillness, each woman let anything come through that would from her bodyknowing. All the women in the circle were attuned to the body and breath of the woman in the center; they followed and amplified her experience with their music.

Gathering in circle generates a power vortex that enables us to access deeper levels of bodyknowing than we might by ourselves. The transformational power of circles greatly depends on the subtle body awareness and skill of the facilitating priestess. It is up to her to make the judgment calls, such as when a woman is breaking a natural silence to avoid depth of experience, or indulging in self-expression rather than listening to and feeling her body with humility, trust and courage. This kind of energetic "reading" is the responsibility of the priestess. How accurately she reads depends upon the level of her own subtle body cultivation.

It is at the subtle level that women understand the womb as a portal of wisdom. It is at the subtle level that we feel and hear what I call the "ancient future sisterhood"—the grandmothers, tribal women, dakinis, yoginis, priestesses, shamanesses, curanderas and others, who, from unseen dimensions, may gather around us in ritual. Many times I have felt-heard voices of women sounding around us. When I let what I hear vocalize through me, the sound electrifies and intensifies the dancer's experience and everyone is catapulted into expanded awareness.

The most direct access and integration of spiritual awareness is through subtle body awareness. I define spiritual awareness as the continually expanding consciousness that everything in and around us is alive, has spirit and is intrinsically sacred, and that we exist and unfold in a responsible relationship with it.

To fully describe the nature of the subtle body is difficult. On a basic level, it first requires an understanding that it is real—totally real. Though it's elusive compared to the dense, physical body, it is ultimately much more powerful. Subtle body awareness is refined awareness, not as in refined sugar where the potency is removed, but as in thousands of rose petals condensed into one drop of vitally potent essential oil.

We have all experienced the subtle body. At its most mundane, it is our "gut feeling." ("I had a funny feeling . . .") Often, the sensation is so fleeting that we ignore it, to our detriment. We also experience the subtle body when we feel an emotion, when tears well up, when anger simmers or flames inside; it is a warm surge of energy that flushes through us when we are comforted in an embrace. Every emotion is actually the subtle body in motion.

These common experiences give us a tiny glimpse into the vast inner landscape of the subtle body. When we focus on subtle sensations with reverence, receptivity and deep inquiry, without grasping for pleasure to stay or pain to go away, and without mentally rehearsing our "story" or conceptual thoughts, then we begin to enter the vast inner world of subtle bodyknowing. My experience is that the most potent subtle body experiences come to us when we rest our awareness in the womb.

The deepest spiritual embodiment women can engage in is rooted in the womb. The womb knows no racial, religious, cultural or political divide; there is no difference between the womb of a black, yellow, white, brown or red woman. The womb experience is the same. At the same time, this unity does not require any negation of diverse perspectives. In this, the womb, the original Sacred Text has the potential to unify us globally. This is of tremendous significance to the 21st century priestess. Let's take confidence, vision and authority from this reality.

All women experience the subtle body during menses, when our psychic sensitivity—our access to wisdom, guidance and spiritual awareness—is intensified.[5] I encourage priestesses to cultivate conscious communion with these womb/wombspace powers and teach other women how to do the same. I have done this for many years through a moving meditation called The Tantric Dance of Feminine Power, the womb-sourced yoga of feminine wisdom.[6] This devotional practice, which I originated and have taught for over two decades, has provided an immeasurable scope of wisdom and power, and it continues to do so; it can do so exactly because it is neither conceptualized nor circumscribed. It has been my most faithful and reliable teacher and it never deceives me. It has been more faithful to me than I have been to it.

The Tantric Dance of Feminine Power is sourced from the womb. It is both uncodified and uncodifiable because it comes from deep feeling, from feeling our deepest desires and emotions as manifest in the subtle sensations of pleasure in the body.[7] This is pleasure, not trivialized nor grasped onto and pumped up into an artificial "energy rush"; rather, it is pleasure surrendered to with reverence, received as a divine gift from the Mother, because pleasure is a portal into inner knowing, into spiritual awareness and awakening.

In The Tantric Dance of Feminine Power, we rest in the womb and allow the underlying tremoring vibration of Shakti to gather until we feel the impulse to move.[8] We feel our deepest feelings until they move our bodies into a spontaneous, living stream of shapes—precise shapes, that hold specific frequencies. "Frequency" is not a poetic expression but a concrete, tangible phenomenon. Everything in the universe has a frequency; every emotion, desire, thought and impulse has a frequency. Spiritual knowledge itself, and each spiritual awareness we have, holds a frequency. Frequencies are not a generalized feeling or state, but the direct experience of specific qualities and powers that shape the body in precise movements and postures. In The Tantric Dance of Feminine Power, we embody frequencies, literally, and this embodiment creates a biocircuitry in the body that transfuses the dancer with spiritual knowledge.

What we do in this practice is cultivate our capacity to absorb these frequencies and thus vibrate at their level. When we do that, we absorb the knowledge because this knowledge is not a concept or thought; it is a state of being. As we increase our capacity to absorb the frequencies, rather than escape through release, we transmute afflictive emotions, refine emotional intelligence and deepen spiritual awareness. Ultimately, what we cultivate in this moving yoga is coming back to our natural state of joy, the state of love. We enjoy direct experience of the wisdom of the Tantras, wherein the Divine Mother of the Universe says "I am your innermost self."

Here is an example of a subtle body experience in the dance: In the early nineties, before I knew anything about Tibetan Tantric Buddhism, during my witnessed Tantric dance in class, I held a body shape for several moments in which my breath ceased and I felt suspended in time and space. I felt I was moving swiftly yet perfectly still at the same time. It was simultaneously exhilarating and peaceful. I heard one of my students audibly gasp. Later in class, she told us she had been practicing Tibetan Buddhism and "the pose you were in is the exact pose of the flying dakini."

The subtle body awareness acts as a kind of Rosetta Stone from which I comprehend what I read in esoteric scriptures and teachings, things I would not otherwise be able to understand, because I recognize them as descriptions of what I have experienced directly in The Tantric Dance of Feminine Power. In the dance, we may experience an endless variety of epiphanies, *xiamanic* [9] workings, animal powers, karmic unfoldings, deity transmissions and spiritual empowerments. I have experienced the burning away of karma, soul retrieval and shamanic extraction. This happened not through deliberate intention, but through grace.

This grace was spelled out for me in 2003 while I was meditating at my altar to the Goddess Kali-Ma. She whispered in my heart, "This is the yoga of Shakti." She imprinted into my heart the realization that this practice, which had come through me, goes beyond its foundational components. It includes its living matrix of powers, phenomena and transmissions. Kali-Ma impressed upon me that it is this full matrix of manifested powers, phenomena and transmissions that defines The Tantric Dance of Feminine Power as The Yoga of Shakti. My responsibility, therefore, is to pass the practice on in its fullness, undiluted and uncodified.

Exalting a book over the body was a critical factor at the crossroads of the escalation of patriarchal dominance. As priestesses, we need to be aware of our own knee-jerk habits of bowing before books and pedigrees in general. Today, as priestesses, we come to a crossroads in restoring the natural spiritual authority of woman by taking our seat of power without apology, and embracing the Body as our Bible.

When we recognize how our religious myths determine our political, economic and societal structure, and that woman's body is the original Sacred Text, we understand that coming back to the body is not just a matter of priestessing at the fringes, but of changing the entire structure of how humanity lives. This is how we serve the healing of humanity: the power and wisdom of the female body and womb are universal and have the power to unify us globally, regardless of belief systems and societal constructs.

The body must be the fourth wave of feminism.

Endnotes

1 For a full discussion of what the natural spiritual authority of woman is and is not, and its historical reality, see the author's book, *From a Hidden Stream: The Natural Spiritual Authority of Woman* (2010). See also www.greatgoddess.org/library

2 In addition to the womb, the female body contains unique structures and evolutionary powers, including neurological, hormonal and chromosomal functions that distinguish it from the male body. These factors are beyond the scope of this article.

3 Genesis 3:22, King James Version.

4 Leonard Shlain, in his groundbreaking book, *The Alphabet Versus the Goddess* (NY: Penguin, 1998), documents the cross-cultural phenomenon that, when a holy book becomes dominant, women's lives and freedoms diminish.

5 The hormonal changes that afford this altered state continue on a sustained level when women enter menopause. Menopause is a gain in the powers of womanhood, not a loss; it is the "wise woman" phase of our lives.

6 While the term "tantric dance," as such, is a generic term, The Tantric Dance of Feminine Power® is a specific practice originated by the author, not to be confused with neo-tantra or with various "Tantric Dance of . . ." and "Womb-Sourced . . ." derivatives.

7 This is not necessarily sexual pleasure, but pleasure of any kind: enjoying the stretch of a muscle, a flush of emotion, the sensation of breath or the vast inner terrain of subtle sensation beyond words.

8 If a student does not feel subtle sensations yet, I have her begin moving; eventually, through practice, her sensitivity to subtle sensations increases.

9. *Xiamanic* signifies the innate shamanic knowing and power of Woman, unlimited by the restrictive associations of patriarchal lineages.

Dance With Me
By Martina Steger

Dance with me.
Set yourself free.

While the moonlight wantonly strokes
Anxiously awaiting bashful silken leaves,
With expectant wonder
I open myself to sense its will.

Forever abandoning myself
To its ebb and flow,
I absorb the energy of the drum
As it thunderously fills my aching soul.

Basking in its warm vibrating tone,
I sensually writhe;
casting taunting shadows as I go.

Over the fresh dew glistening earth,
I begin my spiral dance
With joyous tinkling bells upon my toes.

Set yourself free.

Quite simply,
dance with me.

Models of Leadership*
By Ruth Barrett

Many women have justifiable concerns about leadership, spiritual or otherwise. We have few models for leadership beyond the up/down, high/low, leader/follower examples of the dominator model of hierarchy in patriarchal culture. The patriarchal model for leadership is based in oppositional dualism: "leader" and "follower." Merely the use of the word "leader" implies that there are passive "followers"; due to patriarchal hierarchy, which is based on power over others, many women have knee-jerk resistance to anyone who establishes themselves, or is perceived by others, as a leader. Many women want nothing to do with "leadership" and close their minds to the possibility of it being based on egalitarian practices, mutual respect and appreciation for skills or knowledge gained and shared by all members of the community.

Sometimes hostility or disrespect is directed toward a woman who is experienced in a particular area or specialty and takes on a leadership role. Because many women are still learning to understand self-empowerment, some try to "take down" women whom they consider to have more power, in order to supposedly "level the playing field." Feminist writer Mary Daly, of blessed memory, describes this reaction as *horizontal violence*, where women and other oppressed people release their frustration by oppressing one another rather than focusing attention vertically (on the power structures of the dominant culture).[1]

A woman on the priestess path must be vigilant in examining the unconscious tendencies and unexamined habits she has learned from her

---

* Originally published in a slightly different form *Women's Rites, Women's Mysteries: Intuitive Ritual Creation* (Woodbury, MN: Llewellyn Worldwide, 2007).

culture. Another unexamined tendency, which is crucial to recognize, is that American culture is in all-out war against mastery. I use the word "mastery" as it is used in the martial arts. Mastering the physical, psychological and energetic skills required to achieve, for instance, a black belt in Aikido is a path that requires discipline, openness to learning and the patience and persistence to work through plateaus. The black belt is not a goal, it is a journey. The journey is the destination. A *sensei* (master) of a martial arts black belt is still a student. Mastery is a path, not a title or a credential. It is the process of recognizing and achieving potential. So it is with the priestess path. The more I know, the more I know there is to learn, and I must endeavor to have an open beginner's mind.

Many Americans, women and feminists included, haven't looked very closely at how colonized their minds are by patriarchy's powerful child: corporate culture. The corporate domination of our culture teaches that only the bottom line matters and demands instant results: fast temporary relief, just add water or take this pill. We live in an instant-gratification culture, where anyone can read a couple of self-help books and become an instant expert on any topic, including Wicca. Everything is available for purchase, preferably cheaply. We're supposed to get there fast and easy, and it's often easy to hide our resentment at the fact that there is no quick way to mastery.

Imagine if one of those same women who worried about level playing fields wanted to become a plumber and had the opportunity to apprentice with a master plumber. It would probably never occur to her to challenge her teacher if she made a recommendation about pipe sizes or diagnosis for a malfunctioning kitchen sink. She would never cry "Patriarchy!" or think to say "Who are you to tell me what I should be doing?" Becoming a priestess is similar to becoming a master plumber or carpenter, a concert pianist or a martial artist. It is a vocation of spiritual service based in acquired skills, experience, dedication, responsibility and continuing openness to more learning.

In her development of cultural transformation theory, Riane Eisler distinguishes between two kinds of hierarchies. One kind of hierarchy is based on threat or fear of pain. She calls this a *domination hierarchy*, inherent in a dominator model of social organization. The other type of hierarchy, an *actualization hierarchy*, is described as more flexible and far less authoritarian. This type of hierarchy is based on greater complexity of function and higher levels of function or performance.[2] In applying this theory to social systems, hierarchies of actualization equate the use of power with the power to create and to elicit from oneself and others their highest potential.[3]

It is Eisler's description of an actualization hierarchy that best describes the leadership role of the Dianic priestess and high priestess. As a high priestess, I am responsible for the perpetuation of my tradition even as I am empowered to evolve it. The traditional coven structure of most Wiccan traditions does not require nor aspire to a democracy. The high priestess is the teacher of the Mysteries who ideally supports and empowers her students/coveners to learn and grow until they know enough to form their own group. This is how the Craft was, and still is, perpetuated.

The branch of Dianic tradition revived by Z Budapest evolved out of a feminist movement determined to eradicate all patriarchal, power-over manifestations, including the notion of hierarchy. Unfortunately, the concept of an actualization hierarchy, based on acquiring greater levels of skill, experience and responsibility, has not been widely explored, understood or supported to a great degree. Instead, many feminists view all forms of hierarchy as inherently oppressive, and often insist that every woman's voice should be accepted as carrying the same weight as those with more experience. Consensus decision-making has been widely adopted in many Dianic and goddess spirituality circles as the only valid form of group process from which to resolve or decide anything. This is a wonderful ideal to aspire to, and one that can work especially well when a ritual group is comprised of women with similar or equivalent knowledge or skill. However, a circle comprised of peers is very different from a traditional coven model, where teachers are guiding their circle through a prescribed progression of learning and experiences.

The majority of women coming to the Goddess through the feminist movement have never had the benefits of apprenticing to elders in a coven structure, so the benefits of this learning model are outside the scope of their experience. It is understandable, especially as so many women have had to teach themselves in solitary or small group practices, but the reality is that mastering the subtle energies of magic, let alone the dynamics of a group and group ritual, ultimately requires critique and feedback.

Many women cannot imagine a hierarchical structure that might actually guide, support and empower them in their learning process. In a coven that is blessed with experienced teachers, all voices cannot carry the same weight because they cannot draw from the same level of experience to inform their choices or decisions. It bewilders me when women new to the Craft actually believe that their opinion about how a magical working should be carried out ought to be valued over the experience of their teacher. When less experienced women, who don't know what they don't know, argue with a more experienced woman or teacher, frustrations on both sides often ensue. Would you consent to brain surgery by an eager first-year medical student who has only read about how to do it? I certainly hope not, but you probably would feel safe coming to consensus about where to go out to dinner. Actualization hierarchy is about recognizing individuals who perform more complex functions, not about who is a better or more valued human being. The values of Dianic tradition acknowledge each woman's contribution of creativity and knowledge, while honoring and respecting our elders, teachers and priestesses. Shall we not also begin to honor their dedication to mastery?

How can we develop more egalitarian models for leadership? How do leaders emerge? For some, "leadership can be a function of charisma, seniority, knowledge, experience, consensus, or default (or more likely some mixture of these elements) . . . [For others,] the role of leader is fluid and can be borne by the right person for the given situation."[4] Women's groups, in general, often have very unrealistic expectations for their leaders. When a woman is, or is perceived to be, in a leadership role, and she makes a mistake or behaves outside of her community's expectations, the fallout is often severe. When our female leaders behave like humans, we are disappointed. We are too often quick to think the worst of our own leaders, assuming that the leadership in our groups and communities must be patriarchal. While it is vital to hold our leaders accountable for their actions, or for hurtful, unethical behavior (just as we must be responsible for our own behavior and actions toward others), we are quick to judge harshly, based on assumptions and too often without evidence that some oppressive act has actually been committed. Riane Eisler writes:

> Definitions of leadership in the context of the society that we are trying to leave behind, and definitions of leadership for the society we are trying to create, are very different. But we still have to function within society as it is, so we have to have standards that are realistic for our leaders and for ourselves.... Social movements reflect and even sometimes magnify the problems that they are trying to change, and this results in what psychologists call "displaced aggression." You don't dare attack the person who will really hurt you, so what do you do? You attack your own sisters, your own leaders, instead.[5]

It is important to understand that we are living in a crucial transition time in the world at large, where the patriarchal model for power, what Eisler calls the "dominator model," is being contrasted with a growing global movement toward a "partnership model." Women and men in many parts of the world are developing new models and theories for power that are based on equitable, relational ways of living.

Developing a greater understanding of how the dominator model manifests itself, both personally and globally, is a vital first step in developing new ways of being. These egalitarian ways of being must be practiced and lived on a daily basis by every person consciously involved in the process of this transformation of modern culture. Since spiritual, political, economic and social awareness is interconnected, this living experiment offers a great opportunity for participation. Through this experiment, and by sharing our processes and ideas, we will teach each other and ourselves what we need to learn about new models of power.

Endnotes

1 Mary Daly, *Outercourse* (San Francisco: HarperSanFrancisco, 1992), 233.
2 Riane Eisler, *Sacred Pleasure: Sex, Myth and the Politics of the Body—New Paths to Power and Love* (San Francisco: HarperSanFrancisco, 1996), 79.
3 Ibid., 404.
4 Robin Fisher, "The Priestess Path," *The Beltane Papers: A Journal of Women's Mysteries*, 2 (n.d.): 16.
5 Riane Eisler, *Woman of Power*, 24: 26.
6 Ibid.

The Wiccan Priestess as Initiator: The Psychology of the Initiatory Process

By Vivianne Crowley

The word "priestess" is evocative. It resonates of ancient temples, deep mysteries and a time when goddesses and gods were at the centre of people's lives. Being a Wiccan priestess today is more challenging. There is no fixed societal role. Our families, neighbours and work colleagues are unlikely to know what the word means and we must struggle to define it anew for the 21st century. We may offer ourselves as clergy to the many; as public ministers in a parallel role to that of a Christian cleric who fulfills a social role and provides spiritual comfort and leadership to all who need it. We may see ourselves as members of a mystery tradition appropriate only for a chosen few. Often, as priestesses, we find ourselves playing both of these roles, and others besides. We may act as teachers, counselors, healers, seers and ritualists, in much the same way as a minister of any faith; but we also act as initiators into the mysteries and into the priestesshood itself.

What draws us to become initiators? We may need to initiate others to create a coven, a group of people who can work Wicca together. For many people, one of the key attractions of Wicca is that it is a small group activity. Unlike large anonymous congregations, we interact with others in what can be one of the most intimate groups other than one's own family. For those whose families are scattered or where relationships have broken down, the Wiccan family may fulfill the psychological need that all humans have for bonding and interacting with others. We may belong to a strong committed group, but feel it is time to return what we have been given and to train and initiate others who would follow the path. Sometimes it is not a conscious decision at all. We find that others start to perceive us as people by whom they want to be taught and initiated. Some of us feel ready when people first approach us for teaching; others feel it is too soon, we don't know enough, the responsibility is too great. Some of us jump into it willingly; others have to be pushed. But for many it comes as a natural progression. Somehow we know that it is time.

Initiation is a new beginning, a new birth. In myths, and in their modern equivalents (fantasy novels, films and computer games), the challenges of initiation are expressed through the metaphor of a dangerous and adventurous journey to an unknown realm in search of a treasure. The treasure represents the hero's deeper self. The hero may begin the journey with companions but the final stage is his or hers alone. In our individual journeys of initiation, we too travel that final stage alone, but there are those who may accompany us part of the way. The initiating priestess is the companion, the way-shower and the guide. If we are initiating priestesses, this is the role we are called upon to play.

Choosing

In initiation, the initiate gives birth to a new potentiality from within herself. Her old self gives birth to the new initiated self, who is a Priestess of the Goddess. The initiator's role is to support and encourage, to give advice and to help the initiate make the right choices. The role of an initiating priestess is challenging. Training and initiating others on the Wiccan path is a "road less travelled"; for while Wicca is based on ancient ideas, the tradition in its present form is new and evolving. We are struggling to find a way to live out the mysteries in a skeptical and materialist age.

As pioneers of the Goddess Revival, our task as initiators can be daunting. It is often said that power brings responsibility; so, too, does responsibility bring power. As initiators, we have the power to decide whether to give or withhold initiation, and we have responsibility for the consequences of that decision. In taking such decisions, we are deciding whether or not someone is right for our particular tradition, as well as for the group she will join. Wiccan covens are small intimate groups that rely on love and trust between the members.

Covens are not perfect groups. As imperfect human beings, we must constantly work on and aspire to love and trust, but the basis must first be there. There must be mutual respect among the group members, and this is affected by personality dynamics. It is possible for someone to be right for the tradition, but incompatible with or even negatively disruptive to an existing group. Sibling rivalry can be a real problem in a group that functions as a quasi-family. Spacing between physical children is important. The same is true in a Wiccan coven. If people are too much in one another's space, there will be jealousies and rivalries.

We have to learn to beware of the charismatic initiate. Would-be initiates can be carried away by the charisma of the initiator, but the opposite is also true. When we are approached by the highly intelligent, beautiful and apparently highly dedicated, it is easy to be swept up by their enthusiasm and ardor. If we find ourselves bending the normal requirements and attempting to accommodate their individual needs in a way we would not normally consider, it is time to step back and seek the counsel of others—our peers or initiators—to sense-check what we are doing. Have we been psychologically seduced by the idea of having what appears to be a high-status initiate? If we lack academic qualifications, the imploring PhD professor may seem a highly desirable initiate. If we are not ourselves clairvoyant, a well-known psychic may seem a welcome addition to the tradition. But talent does not equal dedication, and those with persuasive powers who are used to getting their own way will not necessarily have the stamina to stay the course. As we grow more confident in our high priestesshood, we learn to recognize our personal weaknesses and to check with others when we are faced with those we find most attractive as initiates.

In some esoteric traditions, the earlier stages of initiation are open to any who ask. There can be a beguiling humility to this. As initiators, we can think, *It is not for me to decide whether the gods have chosen this woman; only she can decide. So if she asks for initiation, I will do it.* When initiation is practiced purely as a path of self-development, the rationale that only the seeker knows whether she or he should undertake initiation is strong. In Wicca and many other goddess traditions, however, initiation brings someone into a priestesshood. It confers powers that can affect the lives of others. Whether we view Wicca as an exoteric religion for all, or an esoteric practice for the few, when it comes to initiating priestesses or priests, we have a weighty responsibility.

If goddess religion is to flourish, it must have a firm foundation in those who are best fitted to carry it forward. We must endeavor to accept those capable of serving others, and refuse those who cannot carry that burden. Initiation is a catalytic process of change; if someone is not psychologically ready to assume the responsibilities of being a priestess, then, however much we would like to say yes, it would be wrong to agree to initiation. A difficulty with being an initiator is that it is much more pleasant to say yes than no. Within all of us is a desire to please and to gratify others. People are often overjoyed when they learn they have been accepted for initiation; on the other hand, they are sometimes devastated, and possibly angry, when we tell them we cannot initiate them. Saying no in a way that does not damage fragile egos is one of the first skills we have to learn as initiators.

Initiating

If you have experienced this, you will know that each time you perform an initiation rite the energy is different. Each initiate is different, and the time and place changes, as does our inner state and that of the others assisting in the ritual. Each initiation is a unique blend of human hopes and fears, and of subtle energies, such as the energy of the place and of seasonal and moon tides. As initiators, we want to make the experience as beautiful, moving and powerful as we can. For the first initiations we do, we may think if we get the format of the initiation right, the initiation will "work." We learn, after a time, that everything can go wrong. The incense will not light, the doorbell rings mid-way, the initiate is eaten alive by mosquitoes in the forest or we set up the rite only to find that an essential ritual tool is missing. Still, the initiate experiences the rite as profound and transforming. Conversely, everything can be word—and action—perfect, yet the energy does not flow. We sense an obstacle, a barrier. We learn that the essential ingredient, of course, is the initiate. If the initiate is sincere and open to the Divine, something transformational occurs that cannot be explained in words.

As initiators, we need to be able to set aside our egos and our ego needs. Our role is to create the symbolic "holding" structure of the ritual, which acts as a container and a safe space for interaction between the initiate and the Divine. In *Voices from the Circle*, I wrote:

> One hopes and fears, worries and relaxes, and one offers oneself to the Gods to act as a channel which will bring their power into the rite and make the initiation a thing of beauty and meaning for the initiate. The initiator is the channel, but it is the archetypal forces themselves which perform the initiation. The initiator is the mediator who links the initiate with the Gods. It is they and the initiate who determine what happens.[1]

In the journey of initiation, the initiate is the focus of the transformation, but as priestesses we act as catalysts in this process. We are change agents who encourage, facilitate and aid those who ask for our help so that they may transform themselves. In accepting someone for initiation, we must recognize the power of what we do, which is a power to allow something to occur. We can begin the process but we cannot predict its outcome. We can facilitate it, but we cannot truly control the initiatory energy once the process is started. We are powerful, yet the initiatory power moves as it wills; in the end, we are subject to it and, having initiated, we have a responsibility to assist the initiate in her journey.

The initiation rite is only a small component of the responsibility. The most challenging part of initiating someone is what happens after—the creation of an ongoing relationship that ideally evolves gradually from teacher to friend and spiritual co-worker.

Inflating, and Deflating

In Wicca, the power to initiate is usually conferred by a higher-degree initiation in which a priestess is given the title of High Priestess. The higher-degree initiations convey approval by more experienced elders: we are endorsed by those we respect as being worthy to teach and pass on the tradition. The first few times people ask us for initiation, we realize others see us as a repository of the Mysteries, a person of knowledge, a person of power. This can be scary but exciting, flattering and empowering too. Exalted titles, such as High Priestess, are tricky. There is a danger of the ego identifying with the title and imagined persona of a high priestess. People often speak of being "elevated" to a higher-degree initiation. As a newly elevated high priestess who has embodied the Goddess as seeker of the hidden wisdom, who has braved the underworld and overcome death, and who has had the symbols of power laid at her feet, one may feel compelled to become the Goddess outside the confines of the sacred container, the "safe space" of the ritual circle.

The dangers of ego inflation are obvious. Less obvious is the danger of ego deflation. We go through the exciting ceremony, which is possibly one that we have waited many years to experience. We are given the title; but deep down we sense our inadequacy and unfitness for the role. When all goes well, we cope well. When things go wrong, if our confidence in ourselves as initiators is not sufficiently well-rooted and grounded, our self-esteem will plummet to the depths.

Being an initiator is an up-and-down ride. Once we have taken the decision that we can see ourselves as initiators of others, it is easy to be swept up in enthusiasm. We have seen all the things our initiators did wrong; we will do better. We will be more discerning about who to initiate; we will give more as teachers; we will not develop the ego problems to which we have seen others succumb. And then we go through our first bad experience. Our most talented initiate walks out; our coven splits into acrimonious factions. That lovely stable couple who seemed ideal as potential coven leaders split up after one or both have launched into torrid affairs, sometimes with another member of the coven. People change in directions we could not predict and we feel tempted to give the whole thing up, thinking we may not have what it takes to be an initiator, after all. We may even spend a while in solitary practice. Then, somehow, our confidence rebuilds. Wiser, and somewhat emotionally battered, we take on new initiates; we have less excitement than before, but also less of a burden of expectation.

Relating

In intimate relationships like that of initiate and initiator, we transfer to the new relationship emotions that we have experienced in the past. In the early stages of the initiatory journey, the initiate is a novice in a new territory in which the initiator is the expert guide. The relationship has elements of teacher and pupil, and of parent and child. Initiates often transfer to their initiator feelings, issues and problems that they have had with authority figures in the past.

In the initiate-initiator relationship, it is easy also for counter-transference to occur, and for us, as initiators, to project onto our initiates feelings that belong elsewhere. We are all familiar now with the sexual relationships that sprang up between the early (usually male) psychotherapists and their female clients. The same dynamic can be present between initiate and initiator. The heady combination of spiritual hierarchy with a strong initiatory relationship can lead to emotional and sexual feelings that would not otherwise arise, and which have nothing to do with people's everyday lives. Counter-transference can lead us to fall in love with our initiates, and this is a major pitfall of the early stages of being an initiator. Partnerships have broken up and relationships have been shattered when initiate and initiator succumb to the heady transference and counter-transference that the initiatory bond can create.

Initiatory relationships are fraught with difficulty, partly because they are unusual in contemporary society and we have few role models. It is not often in everyday life that we are called upon to create such a close bond with someone. A professional musician or sports star may have an intimate relationship with their teacher or coach; but the added glamour of the spiritual dimension means that, in Wicca, a magical relationship is grafted onto what is already a potentially deep involvement. Few initiates will have the psychological insight to realize that the relationship they are having with their initiator is laden with transference. The initiator, too, may lack this insight.

Some traditions of Wicca are practiced as Women's Mysteries. Others are mystery traditions open to women and men. For a priestess who initiates men, it can be hard to avoid taking on a male initiate's *anima* projection, at least for a time. The priestess can be, for many, the ultimate *anima* figure—the mysterious and elusive "eternal feminine."

Every man carries within him the eternal image of the woman—not the image of this or that woman, but a definite feminine image. This image is fundamentally unconscious, a hereditary factor of primordial origin engraved in the living organic system of the man; an imprint or "archetype" of all the ancestral experiences of the female; a deposit, as it were, of all the impressions ever made by woman; in short, an inherited system of psychic adaptation.[2]

Men, in particular, may wish to enter Wicca, consciously or unconsciously, seeking the Goddess, who is at once mother and lover, prophetess and queen—and, of course, totally engaged with the seeker.

"Good Enough" Mothering

"Mother" is an archetype and we are pre-wired, as it were, with a set of expectations around "mother" that are expressed symbolically in images such as the Great Goddess, the Church and Mother Nature. In a religion such as Wicca, which is so mother-focused, mother issues are activated and mother archetypes projected onto those who best fit them—namely the priestesses, and especially a teaching or initiating priestess. New initiates may be narcissistic and need affirmation of their specialness and difference. Indeed, the feeling of being special and different can be one of the attractions of a spiritual path like Wicca, which gives its members labels like "witch" and "priestess." The labels can become ways of explaining our feelings of difference and our difficulties in relating to the everyday world. The narcissistic ego of the initiate may seek therefore to be nurtured by the seemingly all-benevolent High Priestess/Spiritual Mother with her unconditional love. As recipients of the projection, there is a strong temptation to slip into the role of ". . . the Great Mother, the All-Merciful, who understands everything, forgives everything, who always acts for the best, living only for others, and never seeking her own interests, the discoverer of the great love . . ."[3]

Once our new initiates project onto us an idealizing transference[4] and experience us as transcendentally positive and nurturing, it is all too easy for us to fall into trying to fulfill their expectations. It is, however, an effort doomed to failure: we cannot be, and should not strive to be, the perfect high priestess of their dreams. If we fall into the trap and collude with the flattering delusion, all may be fine for a while. Inevitably, however, the initiate will begin to test the unconditionality of the Great Mother's love and is likely to be disillusioned by the result, and then angry about the disillusionment. Young children adore their parents and think they are perfect. Older children are embarrassed by their parents and think they are stupid, ridiculous, old fashioned and out of touch. As reality seeps into the relationship, our initiates begin to see our faults and, suddenly, the perfect mother is the terrible mother: authoritarian, uncaring, selfish and focused on self rather than the initiate. The "bitchcraft" found in Wiccan communities is much more understandable if we see those communities as hothouses that take people quickly from spiritual childhood into spiritual adolescence. The aim, of course, is to work through all this and to come out as spiritually mature adults.

I was helped greatly in my early years as a high priestess by an elder in a parallel tradition who, when I was daunted by the demands put upon me, asked me simply, "If you don't do it, who will?" The answer was, of course, that there wasn't anyone else. Whatever I was, inadequate as it was, I was as good as it got. Donald Winnicott's concept of the "good-enough mother" is important for the priestess.[5] We need to be "good enough" to mediate the archetype of the mother without being pressured into pretending to be something we are not, which is damaging both to us and to our initiates.

> The good-enough mother . . . starts off with an almost complete adaptation to her infant's needs, and as time proceeds she adapts less and less completely, gradually, according to the infant's growing ability to deal with her failure.[6]

One aspect of being a good-enough mother is truthfulness. People welcome easy answers, especially in times of uncertainty. Fundamentalist branches of all the major religions are flourishing as people search for security and stability in the face of the social and economic stresses of a rapidly changing world, while true spirituality and spiritual truth wither.

The truthfulness we must practice as initiators is not just about ourselves and our deficiencies, but about the deficiencies of our spiritual path. Unlike fundamentalist religions, we are truthful in that we do not offer ultimate certainties about rewards in heaven or an exalted status in an afterlife open only to those who share our beliefs. We can be more open than other clergy regarding the limitation of human knowledge about the universe and humankind's place in it. We can demonstrate, through our own lives, our willingness to live with that uncertainty and the ambiguity it brings. We are not prepared to compromise by pretending that we know all the answers, that we can open the gates of heaven or that following our practice will bring material rewards; in fact, the opposite may be the case. To follow a demanding spiritual path such as ours may take away some of the desire and competitiveness that drives people to see material success as the highest good. In being honest with ourselves about the inadequacies and limitations of our current vision of spiritual reality, we can better help our initiates as their own doubts and crises of belief emerge—as inevitably they will—and lead them to reconnect with the mystical and spiritual impulses that first drew them to the path.

Renewing

Carl Jung saw in his psychological work a parallel with the art of alchemy. Alchemy, he argued, had evolved over the centuries from a quest to transform base matter into gold into a quest that resulted in the transformation of the alchemist her- or himself. Wiccan initiation is a rite of passage to a new status of priestess, but it also begins a process of personal transformation toward individuation and wholeness to help fit us for the role we are learning to undertake.

The process of individuation is largely a process of "letting go." By allowing the boundaries of the ego to become permeable to the "waters" of the unconscious—our dreams and fantasies, our hopes and fears—we take up the anchor that keeps us chained to the here and now, and we cast ourselves adrift on the current of the collective psyche. At the mercy of archetypal forces, in a dynamic interplay between ego and archetype, the new centre of consciousness is born.[7]

The role of the initiator is to help, support and encourage the initiate in that endeavor. The role is similar to that of parent and child, though over a much shorter time period, but the desired result is the same—that the initiate will ultimately transcend the need for the initiator. As initiators, our role is to make ourselves redundant, while hopefully forging a new relationship with the initiate, one in which we are equal. This is not unlike launching an adolescent into the world. We contain but do not constrain and, in creating a safe space for the psyche to grow, we help give the fledging the strength to fly.

In becoming initiators, we are ourselves transformed by the initiatory process. Each new initiate, and the interactions we have with her, make new demands upon us that force us to grow. Jung saw this in alchemical terms: "For two personalities to meet is like mixing two different chemical substances: if there is any combination at all, both are transformed."[8] As initiators, we throw ourselves into the crucible. If we want the initiate to change, we are part of the elemental matter that will be consumed in the process. Jung comments in the context of psychotherapy that it is painful to live up to what we want others to experience.[9] This is equally true of initiation: part of us is consumed in the process, and the dangers of burn-out are ever present.

As initiators, we must help our initiates turn away from external authorities in order to find the true voice of the self within. This is an important part of spiritual maturity. To do so, we must be prepared to move forward in our own development. As initiators we will need to renew our sources of inspiration and continue to grow. If we become stuck in our spiritual development, we can become a blockage for our initiates, trying unconsciously to prevent them from overtaking us. It is as though we stand upon our pedestal, as does the Devil in the Tarot, binding our initiates to us so they cannot grow. The card of the Devil can be seen as a shadow side of the Tarot card of the High Priestess. Instead of creating a free exchange of energies and ideas with those we teach, we create emotional dependencies either overtly or, more damagingly, covertly. The role of teacher becomes an end in itself, and one that we need in order to affirm our self-worth, rather than being a route to the spiritual growth of ourselves and others. When our initiates reach the right point, the role of the initiator is to sit back, close the book, point to the veil behind the throne of the high priestess and encourage them to walk through.

Grandmothering
A final stage of being an initiator is "grandparenting": recognizing when it is time for us to lay down the role of initiator and to let others step forward to carry that burden. In the initiatory traditions, we act as vehicles, mediums or channels for the initiatory process. The process takes place through the interaction of the initiate and the Divine. We are simply the facilitators, but such a role requires energy and cannot be carried out forever. Jung commented: ". . . each of us can carry the torch of knowledge but a part of the way, until another takes it from him."[10] We reach a point when we sense it is time to stand back. In academic life, we take sabbaticals from teaching every few years in order to do new research, to make sure we are in touch with the latest thinking and simply to rest from the demands of students. Often, if we step back from initiating for a while, we feel ready again some years later; those last initiates, when we are older, wiser and our own ego needs are much less strong, can be the most rewarding.

As older priestesses, we can play another more important role, which is that of mentoring those who are running covens and initiating. The model of Wicca taught by Gerald Gardner and his immediate heirs was appropriate for a society in which Wicca had to be kept secret. Covens were to be separate, autonomous and have little communication with one another. This must have created great strain on those who led those groups. It is easy to imagine, when we are going through difficulties with an initiate, that no one else ever had such a difficult and stressful problem; but, of course, this is not true. Building strong relationships with a community of supportive elders is an important part of the structure Wicca needs to create if it is to flourish in future generations. These relationships need not be hierarchical. A "top-down" power structure does not meet the aspirations of people today, who are used to flatter organizations, people who are more used to making decisions for themselves and who are more suspicious of authority figures. We do, however, need to interact with communities of peers who have gone through the same processes as we are going through as initiators.

If we spend too long isolated on the throne of the High Priestess, it can be difficult to step down from it and sit in a circle of equals. Fortunately, many Wiccan communities have now evolved circles of elders who meet as covens of peers who are either running or have run covens. In these circles, free of the responsibilities of being teachers, we can nourish our own spiritual and magical development in order that we may have more to give. These second- and third-degree gatherings are times for replenishment and renewal. As teachers, we need to constantly learn and grow, if we are not to stagnate and allow our teaching to become sterile and out of touch with the needs of new generations.

In Wicca, we work with a seasonal cycle of conception, birth, maturation, mating, death and rebirth; so, too, in our spiritual lives as priestesses we need to allow time and space for this cycle of activity, rest and renewal. Retreats, sabbaticals and time spent with other elders are important parts of our journey of initiation and must be accommodated if we are to be spiritual wellsprings, facilitators of the Mysteries and living embodiments of the goddess traditions we are so privileged to represent.

Endnotes

1 Vivianne Crowley, "The Initiation," in *Voices from the Circle: The Heritage of Western Paganism*, ed. P. Jones and C. Matthews (Wellingbrough: Aquarian, 1990), 65–82.

2 C. G. Jung, "Problems of modern psychotherapy" in *The Collected Works of C. G. Jung*, vol. 16, *The Practice of Psychotherapy* (London: Routledge & Kegan Paul, 1929/1966 ed.) 53–75, para. 338.

3 C. G. Jung, "The Relations Between the Ego and the Unconscious; Part 2: Individuation," in *The Collected Works of C. G. Jung*, vol. 7, *Two Essays on Analytical Psychology* (London: Routledge & Kegan Paul, 1916/1928/1935; 1966 ed.), 173–241 para. 379.

4 H. Kohut, *The Analysis of the Self* (New York: International Universities, 1971).

5 D. W. Winnicott, "Transitional Objects and Transitional Phenomena" in *International Journal of Psychoanalysis* 34 (1953): 89–97.

6 Ibid.

7 Vivianne Crowley, "The Mystery of Waters" in *Deep Blue: Critical Reflections on Water*, ed. S. Shaw and A. Francis (London: Equinox, 2008), 177–194.

8 C. G. Jung, "Problems of Modern Psychotherapy" in *The Collected Works of C. G. Jung*, vol. 16, *The Practice of Psychotherapy* (London: Routledge & Kegan Paul, 1929/1966 ed.) 53–75, para. 163.

9 Ibid., para. 170.

10 Ibid., para 157.

On Ordination[*]

By Andrea Goodman

Here you are
Stepping into yourself,
Once again—
A series of step after step,
Leading secretly to this one—
This step into this self—
This you—the opening lotus
Into your many petals—
Your other priestess lives
Returning to celebrate,
Your many-armed hands
Touching, holding, shaping
Your families, your creations,
Your gardens, nests, worlds,
Your layers of dream petals,
Vibrational petals vibrating.

Your precious head
Receives now
Your crown of starlight
Illuminating your inner circuitry

---

[*] Written on November 15, 2008, Lifebridge Sanctuary, High Falls, NY. For Jane, Lisa, Sadee & Jacqueline.

STEPPING INTO OURSELVES

Lighting sight, thought and memory,
Lighting the way.

The friend and the seeker
Come to your door.
The pain of the world
Comes to your table.
As your lap widens to hold them
You find yourself held
On the Great Lap of the Mother,
Enfolded by Her wings,
Warmed by Her heart.
Her words come through your lips,
Her wisdom, Her love,
Her nurturing, Her gifts
All pour to you and through you,
River of Life, the Milky Way,
Unlimited Source and
You are the vessel.

STEPPING INTO OURSELVES

Stepping Into Ourselves

We draw the title of the book from Andrea Goodman's poem, "On Ordination":

> Here you are
> Stepping into yourself,
> Once again—
> A series of step after step,
> Leading secretly to this one—
> This step into this self—
> This you—the opening lotus
> Into your many petals—
> Your other priestess lives.

Through poem and story, our concluding section describes the joys, agonies, ecstasies, hopes, dreams and sheer humanity of being a priestess.

The Book of Earth
By Jill Hammer

R. Meir used to say:

> Adam—the dust out of which he was made was gathered from
> the whole earth.
> —Babylonian Talmud, Sanhedrin 38b

No part of you is alien to me,
no red dust of the desert,
no rotting mulch,
no sunless ocean floor,
no cave soil rimed in frost.
Touching you, I am not lost.
I feel my way along the walls of what is,
no need for sight.

Of you,
I am rooted in you.

Where I lie down,
there you will hold me.

Where I fall,
there will I come
to you.

STEPPING INTO OURSELVES

Always, you take what is hers.
Sometimes you know it.

Womb and grave,
she requires no other name.

I have only to pull out
the roots of the grass
to see how she quickens
and kills.

I only ask that she use my bones
to grow something beautiful.

I summon the spirit of earth
flowing like water,
curving and rising like a mansion,
curling like an embryo of stone.

Volcano: fire within earth.
Wellspring: water within earth.
Geode: air within earth.
Seed: earth within earth.

I summon the ground of life
to life.

> The one hundred thirty years
> when Adam and Eve stayed aloof
> from one another,
> Eve warmed the male demons and bore offspring
> and the female demons were inflamed by Adam
> and bore offspring.

STEPPING INTO OURSELVES

One view:
House spirits are benevolent
because they grow up with humankind.
Another view:
They are harmful,
for they understand our evil inclinations.

One view:
The spirits of the field are benevolent,
for they do not grow up with humankind.
Another view:
They are harmful,
for they do not understand our evil inclinations.
—Genesis Rabbah 20:11

Spirits of homes
and spirits of meadows,
spirits of study-houses
and spirits of rabbit-holes,
spirits of seats of government
and spirits of the wilderness,

come into this circle
of stones and fire,
of beautiful things
you love.

Come into this circle
of circulating blood
of daily chores
of the hunt
and the long winter sleep.

Come and teach us
of the invisible life

that hides in the mirror,
our own secret life.

Come, or pass by without harm
to the unknowable palaces you inhabit.

If you want an animal spirit,
go out to the forest
or to the lake.

If you want a house spirit,
clean your windows
and let the moon shine in on your furniture.

If you want both,
leave your door open
for a month.

Things will go in and out
and soon it will become your habit
to be inside and outside.

And if you want neither,
say your prayers in a closed room
out of a closed book.

A recipe for divination:
use something you can leave to chance:
cards, runes, petals.

Cast one
if you wish to know what gift
your day will bring.

STEPPING INTO OURSELVES

Cast two to know
who walks on either side of you.

Cast three
if you wish to weave
past and future
into the present.

Cast seven
if you want to see
Divine faces.

Cast eleven
if you want knowledge
of your roots and branches.

Cast thirteen
if you are the high priestess
and you want to know
the fate of the world.

A warning:
cast none
if you have already decided
what you must do.

From the earth, a rising-up blessing.
From the water, a seeping-in blessing.
From the wind, a diving-down blessing.
From the fire, a breaking-through blessing.

Circle, open:
release this soul
into the larger circle.

The Mother of Us All
By Tamis Hoover Rentería

She had not wanted to come. The house would be peaceful without her mother's constant, swarming buzz of students and followers, and an evening at home alone would be such a luxury. But here she was at the door of the hall, drawn irresistibly by the lure of a Brigit ritual. She stepped through the arch of evergreen branches and caught a pungent whiff of burning sage and a shiver of energy surged up through her chakras. Maybe the ritual would help her make a decision. Brigit was, after all, the season for change.

She liked Winter Hall for rituals. Its low ceilings and arched wooden beams gave the room a cozy, witchy feeling. It was still early; women wandered singly or hovered in clusters, talking, stretching, dancing languidly. A lone conga beat pumped out its welcome from a back corner. She wondered who was drumming and who else would be coming to join them. Her mother had insisted that she drum tonight. "You can't miss Brigit, Gaia. The drumming stinks without you." When she had hesitated, thinking how pleasant and quiet the house would be, Serenity's lips formed a pout and her large, half-moon eyes drooped pitifully. "You've got to come, Gaia. You're the best. Mommy needs you."

She despised herself for falling prey to her mother's manipulations. A therapist once told her it was a problem of boundaries. There simply weren't any between them. At the moment of birth, Serenity had metaphorically hoisted Gaia to her maternal hip, wrapped the umbilical cord several times around her wrist, and charged ahead with what she felt was their inseparable feminine/feminist destiny.

The woman ahead of Gaia was standing on tiptoe. The greeters passed their smoking sage wands up and around her, chanting softly, wisps of smoke swirling around the vintage sixties paisley skirt and tangling in the woman's spiky, bleached hair. Gaia didn't recognize her, but she knew the greeters as her mother's latest witchcraft students. Dancer was newly arrived from Massachusetts, an herbalist with large upper teeth and a quirky smile. The other—wispy, blonde Demetria—had been wandering around the West Coast Pagan scene for years, but had recently begun to hang out at the house. She came to the Monday night Introduction to the Goddess class. Gaia had suffered an excruciating crush on her all through high school.

She closed her eyes and tried to focus as the girls began to cleanse her, feeling the soft pulses of air against her skin as they gently stroked the heavy smoke toward her with long, stiff turkey feathers. Gaia tried to relax but the image of her mother's anxious face kept intruding. She would be nervous and difficult tonight because she was presenting a new Asherah dance and song with her students and wasn't secure about it. That morning in the kitchen she had ranted on about one of the girls singing off key. The real problem, however, was not the student's voice, but Serenity's, which was adequate but reedy and in no way capable of competing with the robust vocal instruments of her two rival priestesses in the county—Morgaine Merriwether of the Celtic vibrato and Rachel Lillith of the soaring soprano.

Many, perhaps most, of their mornings were like this, Serenity raving about some alleged slight or imperfection in one of her priestesses, drummers or lovers and Gaia trying to catch a moment of peaceful awakening. That morning, her mother's nervousness had spilled into the farthest reaches of the tiny, rented house. It flowed past Gaia into the bathroom with its heaped baskets of shells, crystals and herbal beauty products, and seeped under the closed door of her tiny bedroom off the porch with its mattress on the floor and vintage sixties art nouveau posters of fairies and princesses thumb-tacked to the wall. When Serenity was in one of her moods—and when wasn't she in one?—it was impossible to hide. You almost had to laugh, if it wasn't too painful, at the irony of it. Her mother, Serenity Waters, née Sharon Renee Feldman, formerly of Manhattan, father Walter in the sweater manufacturing business and mother Esther on the Beth Israel synagogue board, was in the business of teaching women to empower themselves, and she often did an amazing job of it. Or so many of her students claimed. However, it only worked with women who departed right after the weekend seminar or the weekly class. If you had to live with her, or be her friend for any period of time, you soon learned that there was no room for anyone else's power or energy in a relationship with the local reigning queen of feminist witchcraft.

But it was undeniably true that her mother had a gift for creating and leading powerful rituals that brought badly needed magic into women's lives, including her own. Gaia thanked the greeters and moved deeper into the room, anticipating the elation and release she would feel as the evening progressed. No one could build energy in a crowd of pagans better than Serenity Waters. An evening of dancing, singing and drumming with Serenity was almost as good as sex.

But Gaia wanted something more than dancing, trance and the simple release of tension tonight. She needed conviction and courage. She needed to feel the Goddess inside her, to be filled with her own power and the certainty that it was time to untie the intricate maternal knot and go her own way.

She walked around the perimeter of the room, her latté-colored hair falling like a curtain across her slender back. Her sapphire rayon gown, sprinkled with silver stars, snaked behind her. The long train could be looped to her skirt for drumming or dancing, just like the dresses of southern belles she'd seen in movies. Like her mother, she designed and sewed her own ritual gowns. She was proud of her creativity; besides sewing, she dabbled in clay and paints and photography, but it was hard to compete with Serenity. Just look at the directions tables tonight. Serenity had outdone herself, decorating with a designer's flair for color and detail. She must have hit up most of her friends for their better altar paraphernalia. Sarongs of appropriate colors had been draped at angles across the tables, fringe dangling artfully over the edges, and the large, pillar candles—blue for east, red for south, green for west, and brown for north—were surrounded by beautiful handmade goddesses and ritual objects. On the south table, a brown and yellow ceramic snake twined around a Medusa statue Gaia hadn't seen before. She could tell by the style of the sculpture that Raven had created it. Serenity must have made amends with Raven. They had been feuding recently.

She felt drawn to the blue and green magic of the west. Tonight she needed water's power to move things. The wonder of water was that it could work two ways. The gentle tenacity of repeated motion over time as with dripping water on a stone was handy for long-term projects and goals, but she needed more drastic energy tonight, the raw force of a single moment of irresistible urgency, like a tidal wave. *That's what I need tonight, the power of tsunami. Only that would be potent enough to confront my mother.* She approached the altar wreathed in blue and green sarongs and heaped with seashells and several rare, aqua-colored, glass Japanese fishing-net floats that belonged to Redhawk, who had collected them on the Oregon coast when she was a young girl. Interspersed among the shells and floats were statues of Aphrodite, Quan Yin and Oshun.

She reached over and picked up the athalme lying at Oshun's feet. It belonged to Jane Littlecreek, who collected these ritual knives. She ran its double blades across her palm, gathering its strength to herself. *I need to ground before I go to the drummers. Meditate.* She closed her eyes and inhaled deeply, but was immediately interrupted by the sensation of someone approaching. She peered up through her lashes, not raising her head.

Susan Johnson, a.k.a. Rainbow, another of her mother's acolytes, stood next to the table, her face pinched with confusion. She was obviously on a mission from Serenity. Gaia felt sorry for this middle-aged, sad-eyed woman whose ritual garb—a mishmash of garage sale lace and curtain fabric in pastel colors—made her look like an overweight, slightly retarded fairy. She must have been abused. Abuse victims were often attracted to the fey world with its promise of dancing and enchantment. Rainbow had been her mother's slavish follower for years; that kind of masochism was a sure sign of being accustomed to the role of kicked dog at the bottom of the hierarchy. Gaia watched as the poor woman struggled to come to some decision. She could guess what was bothering her. She was torn between Serenity's command to fetch her daughter and her own polite reluctance to disturb anyone trying to meditate. Finally she blurted out miserably, "Gaia? Your mother's waiting for you. She needs to give you guys the drumming instructions." Her eyes pleaded forgiveness for the interruption.

"Okay, okay. I'm coming. Don't singe your wings about it, Rainbow, okay? Chill."

"Hunh? Oh! Singe my wings? Hunh? Gaia, you really better hurry." Rainbow's face crumpled as she delivered her last words and fluttered off heavily, trailing frothy loops of lace behind her.

The poor thing was such a literalist. It was impossible to resist teasing her, although Gaia suspected that her own mean pleasure in doing so was born of uneasiness with Rainbow's devotion to Serenity. It was a pathetic attachment too similar to her own.

"I'll come when I'm ready," she muttered guiltily under her breath. *I need to meditate. Mom can just wait. We wait for her all the time.* Serenity was chronically, legendarily late for everything, and half the time entirely forgot to keep her commitments. She forgot dental appointments, her daughter's school events (she never made it to Gaia's high school graduation), and even her own classes sometimes. At least once a session, a gaggle of laughing women would arrive at the doorstep ready for their next lesson in herbal magic, altar arrangement or spell-casting and find no Serenity. Gaia would usually invite them in for tea or chai, and a few of them would stay, hoping that the teacher would eventually arrive. Sometimes she did.

Gaia planted herself in front of the Quan Yin and breathed deeply, focusing on the peaceful face of the Goddess, but feeling the disturbing forces of her mother's energy on the other side of the room, pulsing outward in concentric circles and lapping like waves against her resolve. "Help me, Lady. I need to shift energy tonight. Fill me with your strength and courage." She looked back over her shoulder. No messengers were on their way across the room, but her mother was making large, angry gestures near the drummers. Gaia refused to speculate about what might be the problem. She breathed deeply, closed her eyes and began a tree-grounding. She had practiced this meditation from the time she was three; it was the classic witch's visualization for entry into active meditation. She planted her feet firmly on the floor and concentrated on her heels and arches. After a few seconds, she felt a jolt. A massive, hairy taproot shot out of her left foot, and another from her right. They thrust down through the linoleum, urgent and hungry, pushing down, breaking through the sub flooring and down through the foundation to the cold, wet clay and sharp gravel below, down, down, curling around stones, stretching tendrils into crevices of yielding soil, encountering earthworms and pill bugs, breaking through at last to the water table, where they plunged into the cool, receiving dark of the Mother's womb.

She lingered there for a moment. Peace. For a moment, peace. She began to draw the cool water energy up through the roots and into her feet, her calves, her thighs, the delicious cool curling around and through her *yoni* and up through her trunk and limbs. New buds broke through the top of her skull and pushed up through her tangle of hair, reaching out with their fresh, tender branches, trembling with new, achingly green leaves, reaching urgently, hopefully toward the endless possibility of sky.

She was on the brink of an orgasmic rush when a gust of cold air broke her concentration. She knew before she opened her eyes or heard a word that it was her mother, and that she was angry.

"Gaia! What are you doing?!" Serenity's voice shattered what remained of the tree; fragments of leaf and bark fluttered limply to the floor. Gaia raised her eyes slowly and looked deliberately at the Quan Yin on the table before shifting her energy toward Serenity and acknowledging the question. Her mother was always partially hysterical before a ritual. It would have to be endured.

"I'm grounding, Mother. Like a good drummer should before a ritual."

Serenity was wearing a new gown, an eggplant-colored velvet that hugged her slightly bulging, middle-aged curves and draped dramatically with long, Renaissance sleeves. Last week she'd been yelling that there was no money for groceries, so where or how had she conjured up enough cash or credit for four yards of $15.00-a-yard crushed cotton velvet to make that dress?

"We haven't got time for grounding." Serenity's hands perched dangerously on her hips, her lips pressed tightly together. "Everything's a mess. Redhawk and Rita don't have a clue what I want from them."

Gaia felt the last dregs of her grounding energy rush out of her chakras, sucked as though through a straw into her mother's angry aura. Serenity's pre-ritual energy was too intense to resist; it was futile to try. But Gaia could refuse to look at her directly. That might hold her off a little.

"I need to go over the rhythms with you. And I want you to use the dumbek for the Asherah dance, just you, no other drums, got that?" Serenity's impatience was palpable. "Are you coming?" Her eyes focused to pinpoints and darted to either side of her daughter. "Where are your drums?" It was more an accusation than a question, which was typical of her interrogations. The subtext was: How dare Gaia come unprepared? How dare she in any way, or even partially by her forgetfulness or irresponsibility, threaten any of her mother's carefully laid plans? Gaia watched the matriarchal eyebrows arch dangerously. "Gaia, I asked you. Where are they?"

A deep breath from the third chakra. "I'm borrowing Rita's tonight. Mine are at a friend's."

"Where?" Serenity's eyes bored down on her. She had given the expensive set of congas to Gaia at her menses celebration and preferred their tawny sound to any others. She was not going to be happy about their absence at the ritual.

"A friend's house, I said."

"Who?" Serenity was relentless when she wanted information.

Gaia felt the last drop of tree energy shiver down her back and dribble to the floor. She didn't even have the strength to withhold his name. "Kyle. They're at my friend Kyle's house."

And then it was the usual dance, her mother getting larger and more invasive, and Gaia shrinking to infant size, barely able to speak. They were making a scene and Serenity was pleased as usual to be the center of attention, no matter what the occasion. But Gaia had always hated these public family dramas. She felt a piece of her break off and float up like a bubble to hover just above them. From here she could safely watch herself explain that he was just a guy from her photography class, and then try to put her mother's question off about where she'd been the night before —was it Karen's or "that guy's" house?—and then she was trying to visualize Quan Yin, but the goddess had deserted her in the face of a greater force.

Serenity abruptly ended the tableau by throwing her hands up in disgust and whirling away, "Good Goddess, I can't believe you, Gaia. After all I've told you about men! You'd better get over here with the drummers now! I need you."

Rita, Redhawk and Jane Littlecreek were standing behind their drums, but only Rita was pumping out the single congolese beat on her red conga set. Gaia slipped in beside her and tried to avoid direct eye contact, although she did catch a glimpse of a new gemstone in Rita's left nostril that looked outrageously sexy. Serenity was now standing with her hands on her hips, gesturing for the drumming to stop.

"Tonight I want Gaia to take the lead. Keep it steady. Don't speed it up until I say to. Gaia, you keep an eye out for my signals, unless you're too busy tonight, hunh?"

Gaia ignored the jab, lowered her head and swung it around heavily in the opposite direction. All the drummers were familiar with her mother's moods. It was part of the territory. Every once in a while, someone would get fed up and quit coming to Serenity's rituals, but not often. Drummers were willing to put up with a lot because they knew her events were the most ecstatic Pagan scene around. Her pet phrase was Z Budapest's injunction—"The Goddess hates a boring ritual"—and she was known to flounce away dramatically from community events led by other priestesses simply because she felt they were dull.

Gaia listened passively as her mother finished her instructions to the drummers and then whisked off into the crowd, heading for the back door and her pre-ritual toke in the back of her VW van. The habit was irritating. She wouldn't be back for at least ten minutes. If she took longer than that—as she often did—the crowd might get restless and bored.

Gaia suddenly felt reckless. She nudged Rita and started up a fast congolese rhythm they'd learned in congo drum camp last summer. It had several parts and would be irresistible to the other drummers. She knew it would tick her mother off when she found everyone all wound up with a hot drum rhythm when she returned, but she suddenly didn't care. Besides, they could tone it down before she got back.

Redhawk let out a yelp and women began circling around the central altar where fire burned inside a large cauldron. Everyone began dancing and leaping to the rhythm. Gaia quickly slipped into drum trance. She was remembering the night before at Kyle's house. He had built a fire in his little stucco-covered fireplace and cracked open a bottle of some wonderful organic red wine. There was even brie and crackers laid out neatly on a blue ceramic plate that he'd made himself in a pottery class. "Don't you think it's time you moved in with me?" he'd asked, kissing the back of her neck under her ear, making her dizzy with pleasure. Of course, it was time. She wanted to. She was ready. But the problem was breaking it to her mother.

Serenity didn't know anything about Kyle, even though they had been seeing each other for six months now. She remembered the first night they'd slept together. Kyle had put out candles and incense and she'd said, "Don't try to seduce me with that stuff; that's too much like my mother," and he'd said, "I thought you liked all that." "I do," she'd said, "but it's not really you. I want you to be you—you know—different."

What she'd really meant was, *I want you, a man, totally distinct from the feminine world I grew up in: hard edges, scratchy face, smelly tennis shoes, sports channel, basketball, husky voice, hard-on, Male and completely Other.*

And being with him had been wonderful that night, at least at the beginning. All warm and wet and soft, just like sex with a girl, only he smelled different, but just as tender. Then there came the urgent hard pelvis and her fear suddenly overcame her. Kyle had been sweet about it, clearly frustrated but not pushy, which had made her even more confused. "They'll take advantage of you; men don't respect no," her mother had always said. But Kyle had kissed and held her afterward and they'd slept all night in the bed together, curled up safe like kittens. In the morning, he'd even cooked her breakfast.

Her mother was extra sensitive about the whole hetero thing, because she had been abused by an uncle in her early teens, and although she hadn't rejected men completely, she was never comfortable around them. Gaia had noticed, over the years, that she was either edgy and rude with them, or strangely pliant and passive. It was always disconcerting to be around Serenity when she related to men. And she was worse about Gaia's relationships to them. Girlfriends were never a problem. They could sleep together, make out in front of her, it didn't matter. But if Gaia even mentioned a guy, her mom went ballistically intrusive, wanting to know everything about him: was he a feminist, did he respect his feminine side, was he involved in a patriarchal religion? Etcetera, etcetera, etcetera. She'd kept Kyle secret for months, just like she'd kept that box of treasures out in the garage behind the old lawnmower when she was a kid—a peacock feather, a perfect round white rock, and a picture of her father in his long, hand-woven robe. Her mother would never think of looking for anything there; she didn't believe in mowing lawns.

But now that Kyle wanted her to move in with him, she would have to bring him out into the dangerous matriarchal light.

The energy in the room was rising. A flurry of purple at the edge of the crowd alerted her to Serenity's arrival. She had forgotten to slow the rhythm down before her return. Serenity's face was taut with anger as she whirled in and gestured for the drummers to stop. She cast a swift I'll-talk-to-you-later look at Gaia.

She arrives like a new planet, pulling everyone into her orbit and assuming that we'll all begin to revolve around her just because she's there. And we do. Even me. Gaia watched Serenity step into the center of the circle with her arms raised, wielding a handmade broom in her left hand and moving the crowd smoothly into the opening summons of the four directions. She beckoned and four priestesses emerged from the crowd to position themselves near each table.

It was always interesting to see who had been chosen for these positions of honor—who was in and who was out, who was being seduced into the orbit, who was being placated for a former offense. There were no surprises tonight. Jane Littlecreek, her mother's former lover and one of Gaia's favorite people, opened in the east, her raspy ex-smoker's voice ringing out over them as she called in air: breath, wind and song, Artemis, Oya and Aradia.

The opening continued with more familiar faces, each priestess walking from her own direction to the next after she called her invocation, handing the broom over to the outstretched arms of her sister witch. Excitement crackled in the air, and Gaia realized with guilty pride that it was partly because of her own drum rhythm introduced at the propitious moment while Serenity was out of the room. You needed to stir the cauldron when the fire was hot. Her mother wasn't infallible; sometimes she missed the cues from the crowd, too involved in her own rhythm to notice what was happening around her. Energy could easily dissolve and dip before things got started. Gaia wondered idly if perhaps she'd make a better priestess than her mother, being more in tune with people. But she didn't want to be a priestess, always in the center of the circle stirring things up. She liked the more discreet roll of drum mistress, working with rhythms in the background.

She was glad she'd come now. Women loved Brigit. Tonight the crowd whooped, whistled, whinnied and shouted during the invocations, and the air bristled with energy and excitement. It boded well for the year. Brigid was the ritual for beginnings, the first joyful peepings of spring and the promise of relief from bleak winter. Gaia was ready for release from her mother's dark hold. But she needed strength: the fire energy of Pele and Kali, lending her the power to will, and the water energy of Yemaya and Oshun, giving her the power to dare. She chanted a prayer as she watched her mother take up the broom and hold it over her head now that the circle was cast, singing out in her thin, pushed voice. "Earth my Body, Water my Blood, Air my Breath and Fire my Spirit." The women began singing loudly with her in unison.

She's good, thought Gaia. Even when she's slightly off, like tonight, she's the best. No one could move energy like Serenity did, or bring out the wild side in all those bourgeois housewives, spangle-eyed college girls and abused women drifting on the edge of sanity who came flocking to her classes in search of feminist Witchcraft. The problem was, she couldn't work with anyone without eventually abusing them. "The abused becomes the abuser." That's what Serenity herself had taught Gaia since childhood. It's not that she didn't realize how she'd screamed and taunted and ignored her daughter all those years. But consciousness was not the same as reparation or healing or change. Serenity was addicted to the anger, the release and relief of venting on someone smaller and helpless. Her own parents, numbed by generations of alcoholism, narcissism and patriarchy, had never let her have a feeling of her own and never believed her stories about Uncle Joel's predatory visits. And Serenity had done a little bit of everything in search of peace. Drugs, of course, that went without saying; almost all the priestesses used drugs for mood and mind enhancement. She'd also worked with rolfers, yoga gurus, color therapists, former-lives hypnotists and nutrition experts; she'd even done a few angry sessions with a trained psychoanalyst. "I don't do well with therapists," she'd said after the fourth appointment, explaining to Gaia why she wasn't planning to return.

It was time for the Asherah dance. On a signal from her mother, Gaia lifted the small wooden dumbek to her side and began the rhythm, slowly and seductively building the beat. Someone lowered the lights and the women began to stroll deosil around the center, where Demetria stood singing a slow, sensuous song about Asherah, the ancient Hebrew Goddess. It was one of her mother's better song-writing efforts, all about leafy groves and laughing women worshiping the Goddess in the Judean hills. Serenity and two other acolytes began to move sinuously to the song in a prepared dance, weaving themselves around Demetria as her warbling voice rose above the drums.

Gaia watched as the circling women shifted into trance. Some had removed their tops and the light of the fire in the central cauldron bathed their breasts in a soft, coral glow as they joined the dance. She loved being part of such a woman-centered community; until recently with Kyle, she'd never known anything else. There had never been any men around her house, except the landlord and an occasional repairman. Her Mother's experiments with the male sex had ended with Gaia's father, a Pagan priest in the Druid tradition who had long ago disappeared out of their lives. "He was a sexist pig," explained Serenity. "He thought the only role for a priestess was to wash his dirty laundry and weave flower wreaths for the rituals. When I read Mary Daly, I washed my hands of all patriarchal religion and men, whether Pagan or mainstream."

STEPPING INTO OURSELVES

The dance had reached its height, Gaia now beating out a fast rhythm and the women swirling around each other, their skirts flying like dandelion fluff in a spring wind. At the peak of the energy, Serenity raised her hands above her head and let them fall gracefully to her sides, the signal for everything to stop. Gaia obediently halted her drumming and several of the circling women dropped to the floor, laying their foreheads and palms on the linoleum to ground the excess energy.

Maybe I should try to contact my father, thought Gaia as the next phase of the ritual began. The circle tightened around the central fire and women began stepping toward the cauldron to make their pledges to Brigit. *No, why borrow trouble? I don't need him. He's never tried to contact me, so he probably is a pig, like mom says. But my mother doesn't know everything about men, just because she's probably right about my father. Kyle isn't like any man she's ever described to me, or any man I've ever met, for that matter. Why shouldn't I move in with him? I love him; he loves me. I'm eighteen. It's simple, isn't it? But Mom is going to have a fit.*

The other drummers had come out from behind their drums and joined the circle. Gaia stepped to the side, away from her friends, not willing to join in. She watched as each woman stepped forward and dipped her hands in the warm water and held them up to feel the heat of the flames.

"I promise to be truer to myself this year."

"I pledge to Brigit that I will take my activism for the earth more seriously."

"I promise to open myself up to love."

They looked so solemn and beautiful. She made her own silent pledge without going forward: *I promise to be open to something new, Brigit. I'm ready for changes.*

Someone came up behind her and began gently massaging her back. She knew who it was before she turned. Jane Littlecreek was a masseuse and acupuncture therapist with a gentle touch that was unmistakable. She and Serenity had been lovers almost ten years ago when Gaia was little. It had been lovely while it lasted. Jane was a Hestia Witch of hearth and home who loved to cook and keep her domestic surroundings cozy and organized. For the three years she had lived with them, Gaia had learned the pleasures of dinner fixed every night, clean sheets on her bed and fresh vegetables from a backyard garden. She had kept up the relationship with Jane even after she and her mom broke up, sometimes spending weekends with her in her little one-room house in the redwoods.

"Thanks, Jane." She shrugged and forced a smile, trying not to look ungrateful, but feeling an urgent need to be alone. Jane patted her sympathetically and wandered off. Unlike Serenity, she could respect other people's moods and boundaries.

Women were still making their pledges. Gaia felt a sudden urge to go outside, to feel the night air and be released from her mother's presence. She sidled around the back of the circle, cutting her way out of the energy field with a slice of her hand, and heading for the back door.

The February evening enveloped her in a brisk embrace. It was a cloudless night, the stars unusually brilliant in the inky blue-black sky. She immediately located Orion, and thought how ironic it was that she could always find the hunter, the warrior, more easily than Cassiopeia the queen, or even Draco, the primeval Goddess Dragon. She pulled a cigarette out of the pouch hanging from her waist and lit up. It was a stupid habit, but it suited her need for oral satisfaction—her mother said she'd been a greedy breast feeder—and it delighted her to rouse Serenity's self-righteous outrage. Her mother was such a hypocrite, inhaling pot almost every day, taking 'shrooms and sometimes peyote and calling it a spiritual experience and not an addiction to mind-altering substances. "Marijuana," she loved to say, "is a natural substance sacred to the Goddess. Tobacco is a capitalist plot to addict people."

Gaia exhaled and flicked her ashes. She pulled her shawl around her shoulders, tangling her moonstone ring in its intricate fringe. Her grandmother had knit the shawl years ago when they still went for visits to New York. Soon afterward, Serenity participated in some hypnotherapy sessions and discovered that her uncle had sexually abused her. When she confronted her parents, they denied the possibility and ridiculed her. Her response was unequivocal: she cut off all communication with them. Gaia hadn't seen her grandparents or any other relatives in ten years.

Occasionally she fantasized about the relationship she might have had with her grandmother, Esther, if things had worked out differently, but she was essentially relieved that her mother had been so ruthless in breaking the ties. Who knows what might have happened to her in the occasional care of people who refused to admit the possibility of patriarchal evil in the form of sexual abuse? For all her faults as a mother, Serenity was as fierce as a wildcat in protecting her offspring.

But why can't I stop thinking about her? It's like a wheel that always comes back to the same spot—my mother. I'm so sick of it. Wasn't that the whole problem here? She couldn't get away from her mother. Even when she acted independently, it was usually in rebellion to something her mother harped about, like the smoking, and now, Kyle.

Or was Kyle really just a rebellion? She remembered the way he'd awakened her with a kiss that first morning, his breath as sweet as warm milk and honey. And how she'd wanted him so urgently until her mother's voice in her head had interrupted the flow of their lovemaking. "Rape isn't just some stranger in a parking lot, you know. Date rape is the most underreported crime in the United States. Women are just so ignorant and afraid they don't tell. And it happens all the time."

Of course, her mother was right. Women and girls all over the world were still at the mercy of men and patriarchy, but it wasn't rape when a man wanted you and you wanted him. There was such a thing as mutually consensual heterosexuality. And it could be very good, as she knew from experience now.

She heard the door open behind her and dropped the cigarette, waving her hand to dissipate the smoke. Demetria of the wispy blonde locks stood poised awkwardly at the threshold, a twist of hair twined around her finger near her rosebud mouth. She looked like a little girl standing there tentatively on tiptoe in her white, laced-up ballet shoes. She must have trained as a ballerina: her portion of the Asherah dance that evening had been unusually graceful. "Gaia. Your mother is looking for you. They're going to start the spiral dance and she needs you to lead the drummers."

It was a reasonable request, but the juvenile quality of that high, elfin voice made Gaia suddenly angry and unreasonable. "Tell my mother I'm not coming in right now. She'll have to ask Rita."

A look of incredulity passed briefly over Demetria's face, and she scuttled back through the door. Gaia laughed and stretched her arms over her head luxuriously like a cat. She stepped out into the parking lot. Next door in the city park, a priestess from Bodega Bay had inlaid a brick labyrinth in honor of the mothers of Plaza de Mayo and all the other mothers of the *desaparecidos* throughout the world. Gaia walked toward it under the street lamps, feeling sheepishly brave about walking alone at night. Goddess knew how many derelict rapists might lie in wait in the bushes. She laughed at the image, shaking off her clinging fear like an annoying cobweb.

The labyrinth was sheltered in a corner of the park by a circle of English lavender shrubs. They were gray and bare of bloom now, but she imagined them in the rich purple of early summer, full of bees and sharp, sweet scent. The labyrinth pattern had been created by sinking bricks into the soil and interplanting them with fragrant chamomile and thyme. It was a Cretan labyrinth pattern, asymmetrical and looking something like a human brain. Following its path, the walker was led back and forth as though integrating the left- and right-brain aspects of herself until she found harmony and wholeness in the center. Very Pagan. She preferred it to the medieval ones that the Catholic Church had adopted; they were beautiful but rigid and symmetrical in their rhythms and requirements.

She entered at the slightly tapered opening and began to walk it slowly, letting herself sink into trance, imagining herself as a Cretan priestess in a white linen gown seeking enlightenment from some long forgotten goddess. Back and forth the pattern took her, in and out, and then back in. The scent of thyme and chamomile wafted up from where her light suede shoes crushed the aromatic leaves beneath them. She dropped her train and it trailed behind her, snagging gently on stray leaves and twigs. She sank deeper and deeper into trance, her mother's image receding and her own inner column of light growing in intensity as she centered herself.

When she came to the heart of the labyrinth, she dropped down to sit on the flat white stone, letting her consciousness dive deeper, seeking images of the Goddess. She needed the fire of Pele and the nurturing of

Quan Yin. It would take all the power of multiple goddesses to help her break away from her mother. But the image of Serenity with her white-streaked hair and black eyes kept merging into Gaia's conjured pictures of feminine deity. How could she ever be rid of her? She spoke to the image directly, faintly recalling this method from a therapy session: *You know, I love you, Mom, and I understand about your uncle fucking you, and your mother's coldness and betrayal, and I'm really sorry, Mom, but I'm tired of carrying it for you.*

The words reverberated in her head like they had been spoken by someone else, someone wiser and older inside of her who had been waiting for her summons to speak this truth. It was simple. Her mother needed her now; she didn't need her mother. It was time for both of them to grow up.

She started to cry. It began softly but built in intensity until huge sobs heaved up from her chest, rolling like relentless waves, hurtling their protest and grief into the night. When the sobs turned to wailing, she was half experiencing it and half hearing it as though she were eavesdropping. The wails at first sounded like an abandoned, angry baby and then grew in volume until the sound was more like the cry of a mountain lion that she'd once heard on a camping trip, eerie and wild and lonely, calling desperately, but powerfully, out into the darkness for an answering voice.

And then, just as suddenly, the crying was done. She hung her head down between her legs and let the mucous and tears drip freely, hot and wet, from her face to the chamomile below, and a feeling of quiet liminality encompassed her. It was a peaceful, voiceless state of comfort she had never reached through meditation. She lifted her head, still afloat in that solemn space of emptiness and peace, and felt something touch the top of her hair, light and gentle, like the faintest brush of a soft hand. A moth? A bat? Before she could look up to see what it was, she felt a sensation that was almost physical, but not quite, of being enfolded in a great pair of arms, or was it wings?

It was only for a moment; she heard and saw nothing, but the sensation was real and unmistakably maternal. She had never felt anything like it. Touched by an angel? By an archetype? By the Goddess? By a figment of her own imagination? It didn't ultimately matter. She was stunned with a feeling of well-being and love.

This is what it must have felt like inside the womb, rocked in a cradle of comfort and protection. It was slightly embarrassing to be so infantile and vulnerable, but it felt wonderful. She wasn't alone in the world. There was someone, or something, out there, or inside herself, that was uniquely concerned for her and full of love.

She drifted in and out of trance. Eventually the awed feeling faded and she returned to the moment and the uncomfortable awareness of cold, hard rock beneath her. She had no idea how long she'd been gone from the hall. The ritual would soon be breaking up or was already over, and her mother would be looking for her. She would be furious and possibly frantic. The familiar feeling of anxiety about her mother began to wash through her, making her stomach tighten and her breath sharp. It was happening again. She took a deep breath, willing the air to fill the farthest reaches of her body as she'd learned to do in yoga. Her breath eased and the wave of fear ebbed slowly away until it vanished. She replanted her feet on the ground and steadied herself, reaching over to pluck a piece of chamomile from where her tears had fallen. She pressed it between her fingers and held it to her nose, inhaling deeply. The sweet pungency reminded her of childhood tea parties and Jane's after-school ministrations. Her panic subsided. Life was sweet. The Goddess was good. She could almost feel the wings around her again.

Kyle lived just around the corner. His little green house with the wisteria vine, three cats, the guitar and the big, warm bed were waiting for her. She would call her mother and leave a message on the machine. There wasn't any need for a big scene any more. She knew what she needed to do. Kyle was probably sitting in his candlelit living room with grungy socks and unshaven face, playing and singing to her this very moment. His energy called to her across the dark streets.

"Mom will just have to handle it," she said out loud to herself and anyone else who might be listening. She gathered her shawl tightly around her and headed across the park. He was waiting. She was ready. Her heart was a basket of chamomile, thyme and lavender, a brimming, fragrant offering of love to the Mystery, the Goddess and the Mother of us all.

Credits and Acknowledgements

Acknowledgments

An anthology is an image composed of the perspectives of many artists. Those who together crafted *Stepping Into Ourselves: An Anthology of Writings on Priestesses* are an exceptional and rare array of priestesses who offer vastly differing perspectives that come together to create a harmonious work of art. We extend our heartfelt gratitude for their vision, creativity, grace and individual experiences. We are forever thankful for their patience throughout the lengthy and tedious editing process, which helped to create this distinctive and quality work.

We would like to acknowledge all of those who have helped bring this book to fruition. First, thanks go to Soujanya Rao (www.soujanya.net), whose artistic sensibilities matched with technical skill bring beautiful and readable formatting to this publication. Heartfelt thanks to Lynne Melcombe (www.lynnemelcombe.com) for attentive copy editing and proofreading and patience with the ever-changing production schedule. Many thanks go to Betty LaDuke (www.bettyladuke.com) for the cover art, and to Katlyn Breene (www.mermadearts.com) for the inside artwork.

Birthing a book requires a team of doulas. Our thanks go out to Joanie Sather for help with promotional copy and Sid Reger for advice and counsel. Of course, our deepest heartfelt thanks go to our long-suffering husbands, Jim Kant and Ben Kuehn. Their continued support and belief in this project, from the moment they were ordering more drinks at the bar in the Doubletree Hotel until now, continues to sustain us.

About the Editors

Anne Key and Candace Kant are both practicing priestesses, academics, writers and teachers.

Dr Key is a graduate of the Women's Spirituality Program of California Institute of Integral Studies, where her investigations centered on Mesoamerica. She was the priestess at the Temple of Goddess Spirituality Dedicated to Sekhmet from 2004–2007. She is an adjunct faculty member in Women's Studies and Religion at the College of Southern Nevada and in the Women's Spirituality department of California Institute of Integral Studies. She continues to lead ritual and to priestess in her new home of Albuquerque, New Mexico, where she lives with her husband, his four cats and her snake.

Dr Kant served as one of the priestesses at the Temple of Goddess Spirituality Dedicated to Sekhmet, participating in creating and leading rituals. Her teaching background at the College of Southern Nevada includes classes such as the History of Witchcraft, Goddess Traditions, Introduction to Modern Western Paganism and Modern Pagan Thought, all of which she developed. She conducts rituals with a small group in her home and occasionally in more public venues with larger groups. Upon her retirement, she was awarded the title of Emerita and continues to teach a few classes a year. She is now the Dean of Students of Cherry

Hill Seminary, the first Pagan seminary in the United States. She lives in Las Vegas with her husband and an elderly spoiled cat.

As the founders and managing editors of Goddess Ink, the greatest joy Drs Key and Kant experience is bringing more books on the female divine and women's spirituality into existence. Find out more at www.goddess-ink.com.

About the Contributors

Abbi Spinner McBride is a high priestess of the Family of Fire. She is a musician and artist based in Las Vegas, Nevada, where she helps focus the Vegas Vortex, a community of artists, wisdom-keepers and seekers of truth and beauty. Abigail is a highly skilled facilitator of fire-circle technology and the co-author of *Universal Fire Circle Alchemy*. Her latest album, *The Family of Fire,* is a collection of her original music, inspired by the fire circles. She spends her time performing magic, belly dancing and teaching drumming, chanting and movement workshops. She also enjoys gardening, cooking and practicing the art of levitation with her loving husband, magician Jeff McBride. Contact Abbi through www.cdbaby.com/Artist/AbbiSpinnerMcBride or www.vegasvortex.com

ALisa Starkweather is a visionary with formidable commitment to women's leadership from 28 years of facilitating women's empowerment. She is the founder of the Red Tent Temple Movement, Daughters of the Earth Gatherings, the Women's Belly and Womb Conferences and the acclaimed Women's Mystery school, Priestess Path, founded in 1998. A long-time certified facilitator of Shadow Work, ALisa is the co-founder of Women in Power: Initiating Ourselves to the Predator and Prey Within, an international women's initiation with radical premises that help women free themselves using the archetypal portals that hold deep transformation. She is co-producer of the new documentary film featuring her work, *Things We Don't Talk About: Healing Stories from the Red Tent,* and is a published author in the award-winning anthology, *Women, Spirituality, and Transformative Leadership: Where Grace Meets Power.*

She also teaches an online course called Answering the Call: Birthing Your Fierce Feminine Life. ALisa has three CD recordings of her chants and spoken word and she is sure to move your hearts from love into action. One of the most important aspects of her work is to bring the priestess back to women's consciousness to remind women of the power of being with the mystery. Contact ALisa through www.alisastarkweather.com

Andrea Gale Goodman lives in Boothbay, Maine, where she is the director of Ruby-Throated Spirit: Sanctuary, Studio and Labyrinth. There she offers voice instruction, astrology and Tarot readings, Reiki/sound-healing sessions, retreats, ceremonies and cosmic harmony classes. Ordained in 1998, Andrea is a High Priestess and co-founder with Director and Reverend Mother IONE of the Ministry of Maåt, Inc. She considers all her work to be her ministry. She has co-facilitated Women's Mysteries retreats with Rev. IONE since 1990 as an astrologer and vocal initiator, including journeys to Egypt. Her career as a pioneer in vocal mysteries began as a performer with Meredith Monk Vocal Ensemble (1974–1991), including world-wide theater, concert touring and recording, singing mostly without words in a language of sound. She currently performs "Nightingale" with Figures of Speech Theatre (premiered in 1994), for which Andrea composed the music. She has recorded a CD with percussionist Gerry Hemingway called *Divine Doorways*, comprising improvised expressions of Tarot cards. Andrea is the author of numerous poems and *Lightning Holds My Hand: A Woman's Journal of Guidance*, published in 2008, taken from her journals of dialogue with her guidance during the difficult passage of divorce. She has one daughter, Rose Beverly, born in 1992.

Anne Key, PhD, is Adjunct Faculty in Women's Studies and Religious Studies at the College of Southern Nevada. She is a graduate of the Women's Spirituality Program of California Institute of Integral Studies, where her investigations centered on Mesoamerica. Co-founder of the independent press Goddess Ink, Anne was Priestess of the Temple of Goddess.

Spirituality Dedicated to Sekhmet, located in Nevada, from 2004–2007. She is the author of the award-winning *Desert Priestess: A Memoir* (a finalist for the 2012 New Mexico Book Awards) and co-editor of *The Heart of the Sun: An Anthology in Exaltation of Sekhmet*. Anne resides in Albuquerque with her husband, his four cats and her snake, Asherah. Find out more about Goddess Ink at www.goddess-ink.com or contact Anne through www.annekey.net

Asia Shepsut is the pen-name of Asia Haleem, an art historian, archaeologist and freelance writer based in the London, England area. After extensive travels in most countries of the Middle East some years before the increased present-day turbulence, her interest in priestesses arose as a byproduct of her current research on the canon of ancient Near Eastern Art (visit her website at www.layish.co.uk) and resulted in two books produced for HarperCollins. *Journey of the Priestess* (1993) brought together the huge amount of fascinating written and pictorial evidence about individual priestesses and their lives in the ancient world, while *Year of the Goddess* (1990) was an edited and picture-researched version of Lawrence Durdin Robertson's *Calendar of Festivals of the Goddess*; both are now out of print, but obtainable second-hand on Amazon. She continues to monitor the activities of spiritual women and their influence worldwide, seeing authenticity in all traditions, ancient and modern, monotheistic and polytheistic. Rather than run for public office, she tries to operate invisibly in life situations as agent for the *dea ex machina* to help others trapped in materialist labyrinths find their way to higher worlds.

Breyn Marr Hibbs: *Once there was a girl who sang to the bones of who she was meant to be. Growing up, she played in the realms of magic, mystery, spells and incantations because her intuition told her they would someday be necessary in creating new realities. Continually cutting loose from the chains that tried to bind her, she danced, healed and loved herself into a way of being that answers not only the deepest desires of her heart, but also meets a great need in the world. Her soul commitment is to the restoration the Divine Feminine. When she looks in the mirror, she sees into the eyes of the women who have come before her, as well* *as those who will come after. Blessed be.* Breyn Marr Hibbs *is a priestess whose soul is lifetimes older than her 26 years. You will not see my credentials here, because I do not want to give in to the ways society tells me I am only worth what I do and produce, thus ignoring the Truth of who I am—my true value and true brilliance. I have a significant capacity and desire to contribute to the world.*

Calypso was not stranded on a desert island, although she did have some unfortunate experiences with men in early adulthood. Despite that, she has led an ordinary but blessed life. Retired now from her mundane profession, she focuses her energies on family and priestessing.

Carmen Roman: *I am a priestess. I use words, my hands, some tea or a meal to heal those who come for help. I am a Ph.D. Candidate in clinical psychology with a specialization in creative arts therapy at the Institute of Transpersonal Psychology in Palo Alto, CA and a licensed psychotherapist in Mexico with an MS in gestalt therapy from INTEGRO in Mexico, and a MA in transpersonal psychology from the US. I have consulted with public and private agencies as well as maintaining a private practice for individuals, families and groups over a period of twenty years. I've also been a group facilitator for therapy workshops in human development, creativity and parenting skills. Spirit calls me often to serve those in recovery from trauma due to domestic violence or sexual abuse experiences as well as the struggles of being an undocumented immigrant. Fostering the emotional and spiritual growth of Jesuit seminarians and counselors in training has been my opportunity for service during my career. My self-care practices include dancing, painting, yoga, hiking, and Aikido. Swimming and drinking tea with friends are my passions as well. Read me at www.morningswithcarmen.com or carmelitaroman@gmail.com, and see me in lecciones de vida at youtube.com/user/cafecitovirtual or tell me at carmelitaroman@gmail.com*

Chandra Alexandre is a Tantric Bhairavi, an initiator in the tradition of Kali. Founding director of SHARANYA, a *devi mandir* (goddess temple) dedicated to social justice through engaged spirituality, she resides in

San Francisco with her family and *kaula* (spiritual family) offering *puja* (teachings and spiritual guidance). For more information or to contact Chandra, visit www.SHARANYA.org or www.KaliVidya.org

Delphyne Platner is a Doctor of Women's Spirituality and a psychotherapist, who believes we all possess an innate ability to heal ourselves. She aspires to help clients awaken to their inherent wisdom, empowering them with tools to facilitate their own healing. Delphyne works with girls and women, sowing the seeds of conscious resistance against the barrage of negative messages that impact girls throughout adolescence. Her work strives to galvanize girls and women toward personal freedom and empowerment, to realizing that they have choices about how they perceive themselves and interact with the world. This realization is a significant and integral step in beginning to dismantle the foundation of the elaborate and insidious structure that is internalized oppression. Years of clinical experience have repeatedly demonstrated that possessing an understanding of Women's Mysteries and spirituality can fortify a girl's or woman's self-esteem to the extent that she can avoid or begin to subvert some of the damaging psychological effects of female socialization. Delphyne is wholeheartedly dedicated to re-embracing the sacred feminine and elevating women's experience within popular culture. Contact Delphyne through www.drplatner.com

Deirdre Pulgram Arthen has been a priestess for over thirty years. She is an elder of the Glenshire Order of Witches and executive director of EarthSpirit, an international non-profit organization sustaining and building community around the spiritual traditions of old Europe. Deirdre is a ritualist, speaker and teacher who has led workshops and ceremonies involving hundreds of people on four continents including the Parliament of the World's Religions in Chicago, Capetown, Barcelona and Melbourne. A singer and instrumentalist, Deirdre writes chants and songs for ritual use, many of which she has recorded with EarthSpirit's performance group, MotherTongue. Deirdre has an MA in counseling psychology from Lesley University, and a BA in theater and history from Tufts. She is author of *Walking with Mother Earth*, a children's book, and numerous published articles. She served on the national and regional boards of Covenant of the Goddess and has been recognized for her work in several national directories. Deirdre lives in Massachusetts with her husband Andras Corban Arthen in a small, rural, intentional community, and is the proud mother of two remarkable young adults, Donovan and Isobel. You can find out more about Deirdre at www.earthspirit.com, www.earthspiritvoices.wordpress.com, www.cdbaby.com/cd/mother-tonguemusic and www.cdbaby.com/cd/mothertonguemusic2. Contact Deirdre at deirdre@earthspirit.com

D'vorah J. Grenn, PhD, is Director and Assistant Professor, Women's Spirituality MA and Certificate Programs at Sofia University in Palo Alto, California (www.sofia.edu/academics/low-residency/wsma.php). She was founding *kohenet*/priestess of Mishkan Shekhinah (2007), a movable sanctuary honoring the Sacred Feminine in all spiritual tradition, and also founded The Lilith Institute in 1997. Dr Grenn's dissertation, *For She Is A Tree of Life: Shared Roots Connecting Women to Deity,* was an inquiry into Jewish women's religious/cultural identities, beliefs and ritual practices among the South African Lemba and United States women. Her other writings include *Lilith's Fire: Reclaiming our Sacred Lifeforce* (Universal Publishers, 2000) and *Talking To Goddess* (2009), an anthology of sacred writings from 72 women in 25 spiritual traditions, which includes blessings, prayer-poems, chants, oriki, meditations and invocations. Her research includes ongoing explorations of thea/theology as methodology, the role of the ancient and contemporary priestess, women's contemporary ritual practices and *midrash* as a liberating literary genre.

Erin Lund Johnson is Mother Priestess of Nigheanan Brìghde (Brìde's Daughters in Gaelic), Brigidine Order of Priestesses and Flamekeepers, which fosters service and sisterhood through tending the Sacred Flame and Healing Waters of Brìde, and through offering both a shared spiritual tradition called Slìghe Brìghde, and an ongoing study circle called Griannán Brìghde. The Order also sponsors the Directory of

Brigidine Flametending Orders online, and the public Facebook groups, Friends of Nigheanan Brìghde and Flametenders International. To view the Directory and learn how to submit an entry, please visit www.flamtendersdirectory.wordpress.com. To learn more about Nigheanan Brìghde and how to apply for the Order, please visit www.nigheananbrighde.wordpress.com. When not in her role of priestess, Erin is wife, mother, homeschooler, writer, poet, gardener and urban homesteader in beautiful Cascadia on the Mighty Columbia River. She practices the Creideamh Sí, the traditional Irish religion of the Aos Sí, with a small circle of families in her area, and she writes and blogs about the Creideamh Sí at www.gaelicfolkway.webs.com. Her writing has recently appeared in Goddess Ink's anthology *Brigit: Sun of Womanhood,* and will be appearing in an upcoming anthology by Moon Books featuring essays discussing various Pagan traditions, due to print in 2014.

Rabbi Geela Rayzel Raphael is a visionary artist and award-winning songwriter/liturgist with five recordings to her credit. She is an "unorthodox" rabbi teaching about "the Jewish Mysteries"—angels, dreams, Kabbalah and more. Her most recent creation is a deck of Shechinah Oracle cards. Rabbi Rayzel counsels interfaith couples and their parents in the Philadelphia area. She has also been the spiritual leader of two congregations and worked for many years organizing campus programs for Jewish students. She was ordained at the Reconstructionist Rabbinical College and studied Religion at Indiana and Brandeis Universities. Rabbi Rayzel studied in Israel at Pardes, and at the Hebrew University of Jerusalem. Contact Rabbi Rayzel through www.shechinah.com

Gloria Taylor Brown has always been a Wild Woman, and a Priestess of the Goddess. Her travels have taken her to many wild places, from Alaska to Egypt. She is the author of *Invoking the Scribes of Ancient Egypt,* co-authored with Normandi Ellis, released in 2011. She is a contributor to numerous books, including *Heart of the Sun: An Anthology in Exaltation of Sekhmet,* published by Goddess Ink (2011).

Gloria teaches classes, seminars and workshops. Contact Gloria through www.gloriataylorbrown.com. To download the meditation, go to www.gloriataylorbrown.com/wildmeditation.com

Hava Montauriano *Born in Israel in 1969, now handfasted to my beloved, I am a new mother to my first-born, Tom. I hold a Bachelor of Literature Poetics and Education from Tel Aviv University, and am a senior librarian and a Tuina practitioner. Since year 2000, I have been an active Pagan, mostly as a priestess in coven "Tehom" (Abyss), based in the center of Israel. As such, I have served as a priestess in private, semi-private and open rituals. In recent years, I have also been a teacher of the Pagan path, teaching a class called In the Bosom of Earth and Moon: a Journey to the Re-Emerging Pagan Religion. This year, I am learning the face of the Goddess first-hand, as a mother, with the many lessons, joys and adventures this situation enfolds. I am Eve, Priestess of the Goddess, and I bring forth children with hardship and joy as a gift of life, with the wisdom of the body as a sacred tool of the Goddess. Blessed Be.*

HD Artemis is a priestess, poet and producer. Heather considers herself a relational artist and primarily explores the intersection of experiences between subject and object, the mystical and the mundane, and people, places and things. She uses various forms in order to provide an outlet for her creative expression, including creating images in stained glass, folding origami, writing and producing events that bring people together for meaningful reasons. She was ordained as a priestess in both the Dianic and Green traditions in 1991. She holds a BS in psychology, an MS in community health administration and an MBA. She lives in exotic Brooklyn.

IONE is the director of the Ministry of Maât, Inc a spiritual organization specializing in women and community with goals of world harmony and balance. She is also Artistic Director of Deep Listening Institute, Ltd. As a dedicated educator and counselor specializing in dreams and the creative process, she conducts seminars and retreats throughout the world. IONE is a noted author, playwright and poet whose works include the critically acclaimed memoir, *Pride of Family: Four Generations of American Women of Color Listening in Dreams* and *This is a Dream!* Her recent book of texts and poems is entitled *Nile Night: Remembered Texts from the Deep*. She is the author of *Spell Breaking: Remembered Ways of Being, An Anthology of Women's Mysteries*. She is the playwright and director of *Njinga the Queen King* and the dance opera *Io and Her and the Trouble with Him,* and director and writer of *Dreams of the Jungfrau,* a twenty-minute experimental narrative film. IONE is also an improvising spoken-word performer and sound artist who performs with Pauline Oliveros and other artists internationally.

Jade River is co-founder of the Re-formed Congregation of The Goddess, International, the first legally incorporated tax-exempt religion serving the women's spiritual community. She is the creator of the Women's Thealogical Institute, the first organization to nationally offer in-depth training for women seeking training in goddess religion and, for some of its graduates, ordination as priestesses. She is the author of several books including: *Tying The Knot: A Gender-Neutral Guide to Handfastings or Weddings for Pagans and Goddess Worshippers; Delphi: A Goddess Oracle; To Know: A Guide to Women's Magic and Spirituality;* and a number of other publications dealing with the goddess and women's spirituality: www.rcgi.org

Jalaja Bonheim, PhD, was raised in Austria and Germany and is now a speaker, teacher and workshop leader. Trained as a temple dancer in India, her circle gatherings have helped thousands of women reconnect with the priestess within. Jalaja is the founder and director of the Institute for Circlework (www.circleswork.org), and one of the world's foremost experts in the use of circle gatherings as a tool for empowering women. In Israel and Palestine, she works with Jewish and Arab women, inspiring them to serve as agents of peace in their communities. She is the author of five books, including *Goddess: A Celebration in Art and Literature* and *Aphrodite's Daughters: Women's Sexual Stories and the Journey of the Soul. Aphrodite's Daughters* explores the central role of sexuality in women's spiritual journey and has changed the lives of women everywhere. Her new book, *Evolving Towards Peace: Awakening a New Consciousness for a New World*, explains why we are failing to live in peace, what we can do to support the evolution of a peaceful global community and why honoring the feminine is a critical key to human survival at this time. Contact Jalaja through www.jalajabonheim.com

Janine Canan has written many books of poetry, including *Ardor: Poems of Life, Changing Woman*, which was a Small Press Review pick; *Of Your Seed*, for which she received an NEA grant; the award-winning anthologies *She Rises like the Sun: Invocations of the Goddess by Contemporary American Women Poets* and *Messages from Amma*; major translations of German-Jewish poet Else Lasker-Schueler and French poet Francis Jammes; two illustrated storybooks, *Journeys with Justine and Walk Now in Beauty: The Legend of Changing Woman*; and Canan's collected essays, *Goddesses Goddesses*. Janine lives in the Valley of the Moon, where she practices holistic psychiatry. She is a graduate of New York University School of Medicine and graduated Stanford University *cum laude*, and she is a follower of Divine Mother Amritanandamayi. Janine has given countless readings and occasionally appears at California Institute of Integral Studies Women's Spirituality Program. Contact Janine through JanineCanan.com

Jennifer Jones loves the sociality and culture of the city and the nature and horses of the country. Libra that she is, she requires both to feel balanced. Jennifer is passionate about bringing greening and gardening to the city and also about demonstrating how to communicate with horses, as many people do not recognize their efforts to communicate with us humans. She likes creating community with other people, preferably in person but also over the internet for those who live far away. She will talk to just about anyone who is friendly. Her email is PhilaWriterJennifer@comcast.net and her blog is www.jenniferjoneswriter.wordpress.com

Jezibel Anat is a Wiccan High Priestess, poet, actress, belly dancer, teacher, songwriter and drummer who moved to Augusta, Georgia from Manhattan at the end of 2007. She is currently a Worship Associate at the Unitarian Universalist Church of Augusta, where she also facilitates monthly Pagan circles and the drum group, Bardic Fire. She directs Eastern Star Dance Theatre and has performed goddess belly dance at local Pagan events. She acts in local theatre and movie productions, and is on the board of the Greater Augusta Arts Council. In Manhattan, she and her husband, Joseph Zuchowski, taught Pagan Way Grove and led Kyklos ton Asterion Coven. Her poetry and articles have appeared in *Nomad's Choir, Our Pagan Times, The Beltane Papers, Circle Magazine, Bennu* and *Gilded Serpent*, and she is a feature writer for *Carpe Nocturne*. Two of her pieces were published in the new UU meditation anthology *Falling into the Sky,* and her "Invocation to Sekhmet" was published in Goddess Ink's *Heart of the Sun: An Anthology in Exaltation of Sekhmet*. Contact Jezibel on Facebook as Jezibell Anat.

Rabbi Jill Hammer, PhD, is the Director of Spiritual Education at the Academy for Jewish Religion (www.ajrsem.org) and co-founder of the Kohenet Institute, a program in Jewish women's spiritual leadership (www.kohenet.org). Rabbi Hammer is the author of three books: *Sisters at Sinai: New Tales of Biblical Women* (Jewish Publication Society, 2001), *The Jewish Book of Days: A Companion for All Seasons* (Jewish Publication Society, 2006) and *The Omer Calendar of Biblical Women* (Kohenet Institute, 2012). Her academic work has appeared in *Religion and Literature, Nashim: A Journal of Jewish Women's Studies and Gender Issues, The Journal of Applied Social Psychology and G'vanim: The Journal of the Academy for Jewish Religion*. She has presented at the 2010 conference of the Association for the Study of Women and Mythology. Rabbi Hammer's literary writing has been published in a variety of journals and newspapers such as *Zeek Magazine, Lilith Magazine, The Journal of Feminist Studies in Religion, Natural Bridge, The Torah: A Women's Commentary* and *The Forward*. She has been published online at ritualwell.org, myjewishlearning.org, telshemesh.org and other websites.

Johanna H. Stuckey, PhD (Yale), is a Professor Emerita in Humanities, Women's Studies and Religious Studies at York University. Until recently, she taught courses on ancient goddess worship, feminist theology and female spirituality at York University and at the School of Continuing Studies at the University of Toronto, and wrote quarterly articles on ancient goddesses, which are archived at www.matrifocus.com. Her book, *Women's Spirituality: Contemporary Feminist Approaches to Judaism, Christianity, Islam and Goddess Worship*, was published in 2010. At present, she is readying for press a jointly written dictionary of deities of the ancient Near East. If age allows (she turned 80 in 2013), she plans to return soon to working on and finishing a book on Ancient Eastern Mediterranean goddesses and "dying gods." Contact Johanna at jstuckey@yorku.ca

Josephine MacMillan has worked as a priestess, clairvoyant and trance-medium in Berkeley, California since 1991. She's also the executive director of Belladonna Sanctuary and FairyCamp, an ecomagical arts and sciences program for children.

Kathryn Ravenwood (Raven) is the author of *How to Create Sacred Water: A Guide to Rituals and Practices*, published by Inner Traditions/Bear & Co. Kathryn is a Priestess for the Water and for the Trees, a ceremonialist, shamanic guide and teacher. She has studied in the Egyptian Mystery School tradition with Nicki Scully, Normandi Ellis and Gloria Taylor Brown, and is an initiated member of the Lineage of Thoth. She reads Tarot, bringing through the guidance of the Great Council of Tarot for personal alchemical transformation. She has studied the Mysteries for over forty years. She grew up in Casper, Wyoming, lived many years in Seattle, Washington and now resides in Albuquerque, New Mexico.

Kathy Jones is a Priestess of Avalon and Priestess of the Goddess. She is founder and webster of the Glastonbury Goddess Conference, and founder and creative director of the Glastonbury Goddess Temple. She has lived on the Isle of Avalon in Glastonbury for over 35 years and loves this sacred land of the Goddess. She is a ceremonialist, teacher, author, initiator, wounded healer, Temple Melissa, sacred dramatist and international pilgrim traveler and speaker. She is the author of several acclaimed goddess books, including *Priestess of Avalon, Priestess of the Goddess,*

The Ancient British Goddess, In the Nature of Avalon and *Spinning the Wheel of Ana*. Kathy offers, with Priestess Erin MacCauliff, a three-year training to become a Priestess or Priest of Avalon, and other goddess and soul-healing trainings. Contact Kathy through www.kathyjones.co.uk, www.goddessconference.com or www.goddesstemple.co.uk

Katie Anderson is a poet and scholar living in Saint Louis, Missouri, US. She earned her BA in psychology and an MA in history from the University of Missouri, Saint Louis. Her work has appeared in *The Global Goddess Oracle, The 19th Annual Saint Louis Pagan Picnic Program Guide, Anointed: A Devotional Anthology to the Deities of the Near and Middle East* and *Mandragora: An Anthology of Esoteric Poetry*. Katie is deeply passionate about the study of ancient and prehistoric mythologies, and about the development of personalized mythologies in the modern world.

Katlyn Breene has been creating sacred art and incense for forty years. Her arts are a manifestation of her spiritual path and can be experienced in homes, on altars and in temples around the world. She is the creator of Mermade Magickal Arts and has handcrafted natural incense and oils since 1984. She is the author and illustrator of books and articles on spiritual arts, incense, magic and folklore. Her work includes cover art and illustrations for many music CDs, books and magazines here and abroad. She was the co-founder of the Road to Eleusis, an initiatory and transformational retreat based on the Mysteries of Ancient Greece at Eleusis. Now in Nevada, Katlyn is the founder and priestess of Desert Moon Circle, a spiritual community based on the Sacred Wheel of the Year with over 100 active members. DMC has met every month for the past twenty years and supports the growing Fire Circle tradition. She and her husband Michael, known as "Zingaia," create techno-trance dance music dedicated to sacred lovers and to the living goddess in every woman. Contact Katlyn through www.mermadearts.com

Reverend Le'ema Kathleen Graham is a Priestess Hierophant in the Fellowship of Isis and the Temple of Isis, and is founder of the Temple of Isis Serpentarius. As a visionary dancing priestess, Ms. Graham has choreographed nearly 100 dances dedicated to the Great Mother in all her faces. She has been a snake priestess for 25 years, and teaches and initiates students as both dancing priestesses and snake priestesses. She was given the honor to be Priestess of the Muse Terpsichore in the Nine Muses Symposium by Lady Olivia Robertson, co-founder of the Fellowship of Isis. Le'ema is the author of *Dancing the Inner Serpent: Memoirs of a Suburban Snake Priestess*, which made the bestseller list on Amazon in 2012 for shamanism. Her instructional DVD, S*nake Yoga: Sacred Feminine Wisdom*, is a cutting-edge healing yoga practice for awakening the *kundalini*. As a master teacher with over thirty year's expertise in the field of somatics, Le'ema has helped people of all ages embody their inner serpent. She lectures and teaches internationally, and lives in the San Francisco Bay area.

Kim Duckett has a PhD in Women's Studies and Transpersonal Psychologies from The Union Institute, 1997. She is the Spiritual Director/Priestess of WHISPER: Land of the Sky Chapter of RCG-I, and founder of A Year and a Day Sacred Mystery School for Women, a three-year feminist spirituality curriculum, established in 1993. Kim taught Women's Studies in university for thirty years, including courses on women and psychology. She has been a shamanic ritualist, and a presenter at annual Priestess Gatherings, National Women's Music Festival, Hullaballoo and the Association for the Study of Women and Mythology conferences. Currently completing a book on the Wheel of the Year (WOTY) as a psychology for women, her personal and professional focus is now solely on the psychology of her people: goddess women.

Leilani Birely is a Hawaiian Kahuna and Dianic High Priestess who brings ancient Hawaiian healing and goddess wisdom to the community. She is the founder and ritual director of Daughters of the Goddess Women's Temple in the San Francisco Bay Area. She has conducted workshops and ceremonies in Hawaii and Canada, at the Michigan Women's Music Festival, the Hopland Women's Music Festival, the Goddess Temple of Orange County, the Sekhmet Temple in Nevada, Spiral Door

Priestess Training Faculty at the Temple of Diana, the New College of San Francisco, the Institute of Transpersonal Psychology and the California Institute of Integral Studies. She is on the faculty of the women's spirituality MA program at Sophia University, and co-authored with Luisah Teish *On Holy Ground: Commitment and Devotion to Sacred Lands*. She is also a *hula haumna (*student) of Kumu Patrick Makuakane in Na Lei Hulu I Ka Weiku Halau. Contact Leilani through www.daughtersofthegoddess.com or Leilani@DaughtersoftheGoddess.com

Linda Johnsen is an author on yoga and other aspects of Hinduism. She earned a Master's degree in Eastern Studies and did post-graduate work in comparative religions at the Graduate Theological Union in Berkeley. In addition, she spent decades studying Eastern traditions with Shakta and Shaivite yogis in India and North America. Her books include *Daughters of the Goddess: The Women Saints of India, The Living Goddess* and *The Complete Idiot's Guide to Hinduism*.

Lorraine Schein is a New York poet and writer. Her poetry has appeared in *Sagewoman, Witches & Pagans, Vallum, Hotel Amerika, Women's Studies Quarterly, the We'Moon Calendar* and *New Letters*. Her fiction and humor are included in the anthologies *Alice Redux*, an anthology about Alice in Wonderland, and *The Unbearables*. *The Futurist's Mistress*, her poetry book, is available from Mayapple Press. She is currently working on a graphic novel.

Martina Steger is a devotee of Sekhmet, a reiki master/teacher, artist and medium who continues to learn more about herself each day, thanks to the Goddess. Martina currently resides in Wisconsin, with her three cats, Cali Mae, Molly and Pumpkin.

Mary Moonbow has circled with Pagan groups across the United States, including Vermont Witch Camp, WomenCircles, CAYA Coven and Collectively. She spent eleven years developing the Gathering Tradition with fellow priestesses in Western Massachusetts and beyond. These days, she is putting down roots in central Vermont as a founder of

Dragon's Nest Cooperative Homestead, where she facilitates local moon circles and is creating a Women's Mystery school and retreat center. She also runs Mountainsong Expeditions, a spiritually rooted wilderness trip company that offers the popular Huntress Intensive class on the sacred hunt (www.mountainsongexpeditions.com). Her personal practice centers around trance work, collaboration with deity, rune magic, mantra meditation, working with energetic boundaries, time in the wilderness, building empowered community and embodying the Warrior and Huntress archetypes.

Reverend Nan Brooks is a graduate of Indiana University and the Women's Thealogical Institute. She is a priestess, healer, writer, editor, theatre artist, activist, stitcher, mother and grandmother. Nan has led public rituals for festivals, families, rallies and conferences. Whether there are a few present or thousands, her intention is to empower women and thereby heal the world. Nan co-founded WomanShine Feminist Theatre in the seventies, for which she wrote and performed original pieces. In "Scars," women participate in ritual theatre by telling the stories and honoring the wisdom stored in their physical scars. Nan's acclaimed one-woman portrayal of Eleanor Roosevelt toured nationally for over twenty years. Ordained by the Re-formed Congregation of the Goddess, International, Nan is an advisor and teacher for the Women's Thealogical Institute and at the Indiana Women's Prison. She also teaches workshops on a variety of subjects related to Dianic Wicca, creativity and healing. Nan lives with her beloved Margarette in Indianapolis, where she provides pastoral ministry to the larger community and cares for her mother and chosen family.

Reverend Nano Boye Nagle, MLA, Ziji Salaam, Interfaith Minister and Drum Guardian, grew up in London amidst a predominately Irish-Catholic community. She escaped to Seattle in 1989 and now makes her home in Austin, Texas. Writer, actor, musician, scholar and poet, she is honoured to be included in this anthology. Former columnist and poetry editor for Matrifocus (www.matrifocus.com) and current poetry editor for *Seasonal Salon*, (www.rcgi.org/news/seasonal-salon), Boye's poetry appears in anthologies and journals and on her blog (www.poetryfishing.blogspot.com). Her essay "Beautiful Boy'" in *Looking Queer: Body Image and Identity in Lesbian, Bisexual, Gay, and Transgender Communities* (Routledge, 1998) is widely read in gender studies programs. She is completing her first novel and planning the second. Boye's thriving private practice, "EFT2BME," offers spiritual direction, mediation, EFT (tapping) and coaching for women with ADD and other creative eccentricities. She facilitates workshops for women around the country, offering expansive conversations about full, fluid gender expression, spiritual practice and the possibilities of queer spirituality. She has been teaching ritual drumming at the Re-formed Congregation of the Goddess, International gatherings (www.rcgi.org) for five years and is evangelical about the role of drummers and drumming in ritual. She offers group or private sessions in person or via teleconference. Contact Boye through www.eft2bme.com or at eft2bme@gmail.com

Pamela Eakins, PhD, DD, is a sociologist, visionary cosmologist, mystic, poet, lover and priestess. She has lectured widely and taught at Stanford University, the University of Colorado, the California Institute of Integral Studies and Pacific Center. She teaches emerging priestesses in her classes called Women of Power. She is also Mistress of the Pacific Mystery School, which teaches Tarot and Kabbalah onsite and online. Her books include *Mothers in Transition; The American Way of Birth; Passages for a Spiritual Birth; Tarot of the Spirit; Priestess; Heart, Breath and Graceful Movement; Wild Voracious Love; The Lightning Papers; 10 Powers of Evolution;* and *Cosmic Interiors*. *Tarot of the Spirit* is currently being used to help American veterans with PTSD. *Heart, Breath and Graceful Movement* and *Wild Voracious Love* are being used to teach poetry in homeless shelters. Contact Pamela through pamelaeakins.com for online and onsite classes, events and study guides.

Patricia Monaghan passed away at her home, Brigit Rest, in Wisconsin on November 11, 2012. Patricia was a scholar, poet, teacher, spiritual path-breaker and leader, and friend and mentor to many people and communities. She created visions of a new and better world in her art and scholarship; moreover, she created networks and organizations to make that vision come true. Her writings were used by many in their practice, rituals and personal life. Her books on goddesses of the world provided a resource and inspiration for connecting with those whose history has been taken away and suppressed. Her work continues in her books and in the organizations she helped found in more recent years, including the Association of the Study of Women and Mythology, and the Black Earth Institute. In addition to her many publications during her life, two more have come out since her death: *Sanctuary* is a collection of poetry about the Driftless area of Wisconsin, and about Ireland, both of which were close to her life and her heart and *Brigit: Sun of Womanhood* is an anthology of writings about the goddess/saint Brigit/Brigit/Brighid/Brihde, which she co-edited with her husband, Michael McDermott, and which was published by and is available through Goddess Ink. Though Patricia has gone from us, her influence and presence continue.

Rachel Koenig, L. ac, CH, is a practitioner of Oriental Medicine specializing in holistic women's health, fertility and pediatrics. She apprenticed with Jeffrey Yuen, a Taoist Priest in the Jade Purity Tradition, as well as De Ying Huang. Her homeopathic mentors include Alize Timmerman and the late Dr Edward Whitmont. Founder of Aurora Healing Arts in Park Slope, Brooklyn, Rachel has treated families in the community for eighteen years. She is co-author of the first published collection of *Interviews With Contemporary Women Playwrights* (1987); her novel, *The Ravens' Bridge*, set in Prague during three eras, is forthcoming. She is the ninth priestess ordained in the Ministry of Maat, and in February, 2012 she was ordained High Priestess in the Great Pyramid, Giza, Egypt.

Ruth Barrett is an ordained Dianic High Priestess and elder who has taught magical and ritual arts at festivals and conferences across the United States, Canada and Great Britain since 1980. She is author of the critically acclaimed *Women's Rites, Women's Mysteries: Intuitive Ritual Creation* (Llewellyn, 2007). She was honored as recipient of the 1997 LACE award for outstanding contributions in the area of spirituality by the Gay and Lesbian Center in Los Angeles. Ruth is the co-creator of

The Spiral Door Women's Mystery School of Magick and Ritual Arts, and co-founded Temple of Diana, Inc., a national Dianic temple with groves in California, Michigan and Wisconsin. Ruth is an internationally known fretted-dulcimer recording artist, singer and songwriter, and an award-winning recording artist of original goddess songs. Since 1980, her numerous recordings have been among the pioneering musical works in the Pagan and Goddess Spirituality Movements. She is best known for her original folk music, inspired by folklore, goddess mythology and magic, celebration of nature, and her arrangements of traditional folk music. At the 2011 National Women's Music Festival, Women in the Arts presented Ruth with the Jane Schliessman Award for outstanding contributions to women's music. Contact Ruth through www.dancingtreemusic.com

Shauna Aura Knight is an artist, writer, leader, teacher, event organizer, environmental activist and ecstatic spiritual seeker. She travels nationally, offering intensive education in the transformative arts of ritual, community leadership and spiritual growth. She is the author of the ritual facilitation book *Spiritual Scents* and the paranormal romance *Werewolves in the Kitchen*, as well as a columnist on ritual techniques for *Circle Magazine*. Shauna's writing will also appear in several forthcoming publications on spiritual seeking, urban fantasy and paranormal romance. Her artwork is used for Pagan magazines and book covers, and decorates many Pagan shrines and altars. Artwork is a deep part of Shauna's spiritual practice and explores myth, transformation, story and archetype. Shauna finds herself on a Grail Quest, seeking the mystical cup that brings transformation and healing to make our world a better place. She is passionate about creating rituals, experiences, spaces and artwork to awaken mythic imagination and inspire creativity. She is inspired by Joseph Campbell's mythology, Carl Jung's archetypes, psychology, sacred geometry, the design of temples, archaeoastronomy, communication and community-building techniques as well as shamanic techniques of ecstatic ritual and transformation. She welcomes questions and conversation about ritual techniques. Contact Shauna through http://shaunaaura.wordpress.com or at shaunaaura@gmail.com

Susan Levitt is an astrologer, tarot reader, and feng shui consultant in San Francisco, CA. She is the author of five books that are published in many languages including international best-sellers *Taoist Astrology* and *The Complete Tarot Kit*. Visit her web site www.susanlevitt.com for free astrology information and updates.

Sylvia Brallier is co-director of Army of Good Girls, a women's entrepreneurial and philanthropic organization focused on e-learning courses in entrepreneurship and personal development. AGG supports sustainable development focused on women in developing nations. Sylvia is also on the development team for Global Resolutions, a social-change media company whose mission is to create cause-driven media content to inspire a sustainable global culture. GR focuses on special events, entertainment, social platforms and cause marketing. As well, Sylvia is a personal-growth educator who is deeply interested in the relationship between the body, mind, emotions and spirit, and especially in unique and fun ways to help people shift their perspectives in order to empower and transform lives. She has a school for practitioners of integrative medicine, called The ShamaSoma Method, a healing modality, incorporating energy medicine with somatic hypnotherapy, which Sylvia developed. Syliva is the author of *Dancing in the Eye of Transformation*, a guide to wholeness and inner peace through the integration and balancing of aspects of one's being, and co-author with Master Wang, a Chinese Shaolin and Daoist Master from Yunnan China, of *Ancient Wisdom for Total Vitality*. Contact Sylvia through www.armyofgoodgirls.com, www.globalresolutions.org or http://ShamaSoma.com

Tamis Rentería is an author and anthropologist who writes novels and short stories about people struggling with different religious, spiritual and cultural traditions. In the story in this anthology, "The Mother of Us All," she draws on her life-altering experiences with northern California goddess communities. Tamis is part of a small but growing movement of women and men exploring and promoting feminist spirituality within Judaism, including a revived interest in the Goddess Asherah. Her new novel, *The Prophet's Woman*, is a story about women, prophets and goddess worship in ancient Israel. Tamis currently lives with her husband and youngest son in Tucson, Arizona, where she types on a Mac, cooks ethnic food and gardens among the *sahuaros*. Look for Tamis's novel on Amazon in the fall of 2013, and contact her through tamisrenteria.com

Vajra Ma has not studied in India, Nepal or Tibet. The Dalai Lama has never heard of her and probably never will, although she has heard of him and thinks quite highly of him. She did have a sudden awakening at age three-and-a-half when she awoke to a bright light, but it was just her mother switching on the light in her room. She comes from an ordinary town and went to ordinary schools but, though she was an "A" student, she was repressed, depressed and much too obedient. You won't find a PhD behind her name because, foolishly, after completing her BA and grad work in Theatre Arts, she dashed off to Los Angeles for an acting career. Perhaps you have seen her in an occasional TV movie. You might as well know she has not taken any weekend workshops with the Federation of Landed Spaceships or the Galactic Shamanic-Tantric-Metaphysical Mystery School Reincarnation of the Light-Bearers of the Submerged Continent of Atlantis, but she has explored the female body and its capacities as a treasure house of wisdom, knowledge and creative power. Her knowledge is direct, original, detailed and unapologetic. If you want the real deal, Vajra is it, although the jury is still out on whether she is enlightened. Contact Vajra through www.GreatGoddess.org

Vivianne Crowley, PhD, is a psychologist by profession. She was formerly Lecturer in Psychology of Religion at King's College, University of London. She is now a member of the Faculty of Pastoral Counseling at Cherry Hill Seminary. She has been teaching Wicca, Kabbalah and spiritual journeying for forty years and has Wiccan initiates and daughter covens in many countries. She is the author of many books on Wicca, Pagan spirituality and psychology, including *Wicca: The Old Religion in the New Millennium, Jung: Journey of Transformation* and *A Woman's Kabbalah*.

APPENDICES

Suggested Readings

Adelman, Penina. *Miriam's Well.* Fresh Meadows, NY: Biblio Press, 1986/1996.

Amazzone, Laura. *Goddess Durga and Sacred Female Power.* Lanham MD: Hamilton Books, 2010.

Baldwin, Christina. *Calling The Circle: The First and Future Culture.* New York: Bantam Books, 1998.

Bancroft, Anne. *Women in Search of the Sacred: The Spiritual Lives of Ten Remarkable Women.* London: Penguin, 1997.

Barnard, Mary, trans. *Sappho.* Berkeley: University of California Press, 1958/1999.

Barrett, Ruth. *Women's Rites, Women's Mysteries.* Woodbury, MN: Llewellyn Publications, 2007.

Berrin, Susan, ed. *Celebrating the New Moon: A Rosh Hodesh Anthology.* Northvale, NJ: Jason Aronson, 1977/1998.

Birnbaum, Lucia Chiavola, ed. *She Is Everywhere: An Anthology of Writing in Womanist/Feminist Spirituality,* vol. I. New York: iUniverse, Inc., 2005.

Bolen, Jean Shinoda. *Goddesses in Everywoman: A New Psychology of Women.* New York: Harper & Row, 1984.

Bolen, Jean Shinoda. *Goddesses in Older Women: Archetypes in Women over Fifty.* New York: HarperCollins, 2002.

Bolen, Jean Shinoda. *The Millionth Circle: How to Change Ourselves and The World.* Berkeley, CA: Conari Press, 1999.

Bonheim, Jalaja. *Aphrodite's Daughters: Women's Sexual Stories and the Journey of the Soul.* New York, NY: Simon & Schuster, 1997.

Bonheim, Jalaja. *Goddess: A Celebration in Art and Literature.* New York: Stuart, Tabori & Chang, 1997.

Brooten, Bernadette J. *Women Leaders in the Ancient Synagogue.* Chico, CA: Scholars Press, 1982.

Brown, Karen McCarthy. *Mama Lola: A Vodou Priestess in Brooklyn.* Berkeley: University of California Press, 1992/2011.

Budapest, Zsuzsanna E. *Grandmother Moon: Lunar Magic in our Lives.* CreateSpace Independent Publishing Platform, 1999/2011.

Budapest, Zsuzsanna E. *Grandmother of Time: A Woman's Book of Celebrations, Spells, and Sacred Objects for Every Month of the Year.* New York: HarperCollins Publishers, 1989.

Budapest, Zsuzsanna E. *Summoning the Fates: A Guide to Destiny and Sacred Transformation.* New York: Three Rivers Press, 2013.

Budapest, Zsuzsanna E. *The Feminist Book of Light and Shadows.* Feminist Wicca, 1976.

Budapest, Zsuzsanna E. *The Holy Book of Women's Mysteries.* San Francisco, CA: Weiser Books, 1980/2007.

Canan, Janine, ed. *She Rises Like the Sun: Invocations of the Goddess by Contemporary American Women Poets.* Freedom, CA: The Crossing Press, 1989.

Cardin, Nina Beth. *Tears of Sorrow, Seeds of Hope: A Jewish Spiritual Companion for Infertility and Pregnancy Loss.* Woodstock, VT: Jewish Lights, 1999.

Cardin, Nina Beth, ed. *Out of the Depths I Call to You: A Book of Prayers for the Married Jewish Woman.* Northvale, NJ: Jason Aronson, 1992.

Carnes, Robin Deen and Sally Craig. *Sacred Circles: A Guide to Creating Your Own Women's Spirituality Group.* New York: HarperOne, 1998.

Christ, Carol P. *Rebirth of the Goddess: Finding Meaning in Feminist Spirituality.* New York: Routledge, 1997.

Christ, Carol P. *She Who Changes: Re-Imagining the Divine in the World.* New York: Palgrave MacMillan, 2003.

Christ, Carol P, and Judith Plaskow. *Womanspirit Rising: A Feminist Reader in Religion.* San Francisco: Harper, 1992.

Connelly, Joan Breton. *Portrait of a Priestess: Women and Ritual in Ancient Greece.* Princeton, NJ: Princeton University Press, 2007.

Cooey, Paula M., William R. Eakin and Jay B. McDaniel. *After Patriarchy: Feminist Transformations of the World Religions.* Maryknoll, NY: Orbis Books, 1998.

Crowley, Vivianne. "The Initiation." In *Voices from The Circle: The Heritage of Western Paganism*, edited by P. Jones and C. Matthews, 65–82. Wellingborough: Aquarian Press, 1990.

Crowley, Vivianne. *Wicca: A Comprehensive Guide to the Old Religion in the Modern World.* London: Element/HarperCollins, 2003.

Crowley, Vivianne. "Women and Power in Modern Paganism." *In Women as Teachers and Disciples in Traditional and New Religions*, edited by Elizabeth Puttick and Peter B. Clark, 125–140. Lewiston, NY: Edwin Mellen Press, 1993.

d'Este, Sorita, ed. *Priestesses, Pythonesses and Sibyls: A Collection of Essays on Trance, Possession and Mantic States from Women Who Speak For and With the Gods.* London: Avalonia, 2008/2012.

Della-Madre, Leslene. *Midwifing Death: Returning to the Arms of the Ancient Mother.* Austin, TX: Plain View Press, 2003.

Dexter, Miriam Robbins. *Whence the Goddesses: A Source Book.* New York: Teachers College Press, 1990.

Diamant, Anita. *Saying Kaddish: How to Comfort the Dying, Bury the Dear, and Mourn as a Jew.* New York: Schocken Books, 1999.

Downing, Christine. *The Goddess: Mythological Images of the Feminine.* New York: Continuum, 2000.

Eakins, Pamela. *Priestess: Woman as Sacred Celebrant.* New York: Samuel Weiser, Inc., 1996.

Eisler, Rianne. *Sacred Pleasure.* New York: HarperCollins, 1995.

Eisler, Rianne. *The Chalice and the Blade.* San Francisco: HarperSanFrancisco, 1987/1995.

Ellis, Normandi. *Feasts of Light: Celebrations for the Seasons of Life Based on the Egyptian Goddess Mysteries.* Wheaton, IL: Quest Books, 1999.

Faulkner, Mary. *Women's Spirituality: Power and Grace.* Charlottesville, VA: Hampton Roads Publishing Company, Inc., 2011.

Ferguson, Marianne. *Women and Religion.* Upper Saddle River, NJ: Prentice Hall, Inc., 1995.

Firestone, Tirzah. *The Receiving: Reclaiming Jewish Women's Wisdom.* San Francisco: HarperOne, 2004.

Fischer-Rizzi, Susanne. *The Complete Incense Book.* New York: Sterling Publishing, 1998.

Fleming, Daniel E. *The Installation of Baal's High Priestess at Emar: A Window on Ancient Syrian Religion.* Atlanta: Harvard Semitic Studies, 1992.

Fortune, Dion. *The Sea Priestess.* San Francisco: Weiser Books, 1976/2003.

Frymer-Kensky, Tikva. *In the Wake of the Goddesses: Women, Culture and the Biblical Transformation of Pagan Myth.* New York: Fawcett Columbine, 1992.

George, Demetra. *Asteroid Goddesses: The Mythology, Psychology, and Astrology of the Re-Emerging Feminine.* Lake Worth, FL: Ibis Press, 2003.

Goodrich, Norma Lorre. *Priestess.* New York: HarperCollins Publishers, 1989.

Goldstein, Rabbi Elyse. *Revision: Seeing Torah Through a Feminist Lense.* Woodstock, VT: Jewish Lights Publishing, 1998.

Gottlieb, Lynn. *She Who Dwells Within: A Feminist Vision of a Renewed Judaism.* New York: HarperCollins, 1995.

Graham, Le'ema Kathleen. *Dancing the Inner Serpent: Memoirs of a Suburban Snake Priestess.* Goddesswork: 2009/2013.

Grenn, D'vorah J. *Talking to Goddess: Powerful Voices from Many Traditions.* Napa, CA: The Lilith Institute, 2009.

Grenn, D'Vorah J. *Lillith's Fire: Reclaiming Our Sacred Lifeforce.* San Mateo, CA: The Lilith Institute, 2000.

Griffin, Wendy, ed. *Daughters of the Goddess: Studies of Healing, Identity, and Empowerment.* New York: AltaMira Press, 2000.

Hammer, Jill, and Holly Shere. *The Hebrew Priestess.* Teaneck, NJ: Ben Yehuda Press, 2013.

Harding, M. Esther. *Women's Mysteries Ancient and Modern: A Psychological Interpretation of the Feminine Principle as Portrayed in Myth, Story and Dreams.* Boston: Shambala Publications, Inc., 1971.

Harrow, Judy. *Devoted To You: Honoring Deity in Wiccan Practice.* New York: Citadel Press, 2003.

Harrow, Judy. *Spiritual Mentoring: A Pagan Guide.* Toronto, Can: ECW

Press, 2002.

Harrow, Judy. *Wicca Covens: How to Start and Organize Your Own*. New York: Citadel Press, 1999.

Henshaw, Richard A. *Female and Male, the Cultic Personnel: The Bible and the Rest of the Ancient Near East*. Allison Park, PA: Pickwick, 1994.

IONE, ed. *Spell Breaking; Remembered Ways of Being: An Anthology of Women's Mysteries*. Kingston, NY: Deep Listening Publications, 2013.

Ingerman, Sandra. *Medicine for the Earth: How to Transform Personal and Environmental Toxins*. New York: Three Rivers Press, 2000.

Johnson, Buffie. *Lady of the Beasts: The Goddess and Her Sacred Animals*. Rochester, VT: Inner Traditions, 1994.

Jones, Kathy. *Priestess of Avalon, Priestess of the Goddess: A Renewed Spiritual Path for the 21st Century*. Glastonbury, Eng: Ariadne Publications, 2006.

K. Amber, and Azrael Arynn K. *Covencraft: Witchcraft for Three or More*. Saint Paul, MN: Llewellyn Publications, 1999.

K. Amber, and Azrael Arynn K. *Ritual Craft: Creating Rites for Transformation and Celebration*. Woodbury, MN: Llewellyn Publications, 2006.

Kaltsas, Nikolaos, and H.A. Shapiro. *Worshipping Women: Ritual and Reality in Classical Athens*. Onassis Foundation, December 31, 2008.

Kant, Candace C, and Anne Key. *Heart of the Sun: An Anthology in Exaltation of Sekhmet*. Las Vegas, NV: Goddess Ink, Ltd., 2011.

Key, Anne. *Desert Priestess: A Memoir*. Las Vegas, NV: Goddess Ink, Ltd., 2011.

Kraemer, Ross Shepard. *Her Share Of The Blessings: Women's Religions among the Pagans, Jews, and Christians in the Greco-Roman World*. NY: Oxford University Press, 1992.

LaGalliene, Eva. *The Mystic in the Theatre: Eleonora Duse*. New York: Farrar, Straus and Giroux, 1966.

Laura, Judith. *Goddess Matters: The Mystical, Practical and Controversial*. Kensington, MD: Open Sea Press, 2011.

Laura, Judith. *Goddess Spirituality for the 21st Century: From Kabbalah to Quantum Physics*. Kensington, MD: Open Sea Press, 1997/2008.

Laura, Judith. *She Lives: The Return of Our Great Mother*. Kensington, MD: Open Sea Press, 1989/1999/2010.

Lapinkivi, Pirjo. *The Sumerian Sacred Marriage in the Light of Comparative Evidence.* (State Archives of Assyria Studies XV). Helsinki: Neo-Assyrian Text Corpus Program, 2004.

Levine, Elizabeth Resnick, ed. *A Ceremonies Sampler, New Rites, Celebrations, and Observances of Jewish Women.* Women's Institute for Continuing Jewish Education, 1991.

Livingstone, Glenys. *PaGaian Cosmology: Re-Inventing Earth-Based Goddess Religion.* New York: iUniverse, Inc., 2005.

Marcus, Joyce. *Women's Ritual in Formative Oaxaca: Figurine-Making, Divination, Death and the Ancestor.* Ann Arbor: University of Michigan Press, 1998.

Matthews, Caitlin. *Ladies of the Lake.* London: Thorsons, 1992.

Matthews, Caitlin, ed. *Voices of the Goddess: A Chorus of Sibyls.* Northhamptonshire, UK: The Aquarian Press, 1990.

Mountainwater, Shekinah. *Ariadne's Thread: A Workbook of Goddess Magic.* Berkeley: Crossing Press, 1991.

McLaren, Karla. *Emotional Genius: Discovering the Deepest Language of the Soul.* Columbia, CA: Laughing Tree Press, 2002.

Meador, Betty De Shong. *Inanna, Lady of Largest Heart: Poems of the Sumerian High Priestess Enheduanna.* Austin, TX: University of Texas Press, 2000.

Monaghan, Patricia, and Michael McDermott. *Brigit: Sun of Womanhood.* Las Vegas, NV: Goddess Ink, Ltd., 2013.

Monaghan, Patricia and Eleanor G. Viereck. *Meditation: The Complete Guide.* Novato, CA: New World Library, 2011.

Monaghan, Patricia. *O Mother Sun! A New View of the Cosmic Feminine.* Freedom, CA: The Crossing Press, 1994.

Monaghan, Patricia. *The Goddess Path: Myths, Invocations, and Rituals.* Woodbury, MN: Llewellyn Publications, 2011.

Monaghan, Patricia. *The Goddess Companion: Daily Meditations on the Feminine Spirit.* Woodbury, MN: Llewellyn Publications, 2000.

Monaghan, Patricia. *The New Book of Goddesses & Heroines.* St. Paul, MN: Llewellyn Publications, 2000.

Monaghan, Patricia. *Seasons of the Witch: Poetry and Songs of the Goddess.*

Cottage Grove, WI: Creatrix Books, 2004.

Neal, Carl F. *Incense: Crafting and Use of Magickal Scents.* Woodbury, MN: Llewellyn Publications, 2003.

Neal, Carl F. *Incense Magick: Create Inspiriting Aromatic Experiences for Your Craft.* Woodbury, MN: Llewellyn Publications, 2012.

Nicholson, Shirley. *The Goddess Re-Awakening: The Feminine Principle Today.* Wheaton, Ill.: Quest Books, 1989.

Noble, Vicki. *Motherpeace: A Way to the Goddess through Myth, Art and Tarot.* New York: HarperCollins, 1983/1994.

Novick, Rabbi Leah. *On The Wings of Shechinah: The Divine Feminine.* Wheaton, Ill.: Quest Books, 2008.

Orenstein, Rabbi Debra. *Lifecycles: Jewish Women on Life Passages and Personal Milestones,* Vol I. Woodstock, VT: Jewish Lights Publishing, 1998.

Ozaniec, Naomi. *Daughter of the Goddess: The Sacred Priestess.* London: The Aquarian Press, 1993.

Pagano, Cathy. *Wisdom's Daughters: How Women Can Change the World.* Bloomington, IN: Balboa Press, 2013.

Paper, Jordan. *Through the Earth Darkly: Female Spirituality in Comparative Perspective.* New York: Continuum, 1997.

Patai, Raphael. *The Hebrew Goddess.* Detroit: Wayne State University Press, 1978.

Paxson, Diana. *Trance-Portation: Learning to Navigate the Inner World.* San Francisco, CA: Weiser Books, 2008.

Paxson, Diana. *The Way of the Oracle: Recovering the Practices of the Past to Find Answers for Today.* San Francisco: Weiser Books, 2012.

Perera, Sylvia Brinton. *Descent to the Goddess: A Way of Initiation for Women.* Toronto: Inner City Books, 1981.

Peskowitz, Miriam. *Spinning Fantasies: Rabbis, Gender, and History.* Berkeley: University of California Press, 1997.

Plaskow, Judith, and Carol P. Christ. *Weaving the Visions: New Patterns in Feminist Spirituality.* New York: HarperCollins Publishers, 1989.

Raphael, Melissa. *Introducing Thealogy: Discourse on the Goddess.* Cleveland, Ohio: The Pilgrim Press, 2000.

Raphael, Melissa. *Thealogy and Embodiment: The Post-Patriarchal*

Reconstruction of Female Sacrality. Sheffield, UK: Sheffield Academic Press, Ltd., 1996.

Redfield, James M. *The Locrian Maidens: Love and Death in Greek Italy.* Princeton, NJ: Princeton University Press, 2003.

Redmond, Layne. *When the Drummers Were Women: A Spiritual History of Women.* New York: Three Rivers Press, 1997.

Roberts, Wendy Hunter. *Celebrating Her: Feminist Ritualizing Comes of Age.* Cleveland, OH: The Pilgrim Press, 1998.

Rose, Michael. *The Way of Wild Sage.* Encinitas, CA: The Sage Council, n.d.

Rose, Sharon. *The Path of the Priestess.* Rochester, VT: Inner Traditions, 2002.

Saracino, Mary and Mary Beth Moser, eds. *She Is Everywhere: An Anthology of Writings in Womanist/Feminist Spirituality,* Vol. 3. Bloomington IN: iUniverse, Inc., 2012.

Schlain, Leonard. *The Alphabet Versus the Goddess.* New York: Penguin, 1998.

Sered, Susan Starr. *Priestess, Mother, Sacred Sister: Religions Dominated by Women.* New York: Oxford University Press, 1994.

Sered, Susan Starr. *Women as Ritual Experts: The Religious Lives of Elderly Jewish Women in Jerusalem.* New York: Oxford University Press, 1992.

Shepsut, Asia. *Journey of the Priestess: Priestess Traditions of the Ancient World.* London: The Aquarian Press, 1993.

Spretnak, Charlene, ed. *The Politics of Women's Spirituality: Essays on the Rise of Spiritual Power within the Feminist Movement.* New York: Doubleday, 1982.

Starhawk. *The Spiral Dance: A Rebirth of the Ancient Religion of the Great Goddess.* San Francisco: HarperSanFrancisco, 1999.

Starhawk. *Dreaming the Dark: Magic, Sex, and Politics.* Boston: Beacon Press, 1997.

Starhawk. *Truth or Dare: Encounters with Power, Authority, and Mystery.* New York: HarperCollins Publishers, 1987.

Starhawk. *The Empowerment Manual: A Guide for Collaborative Groups.* Gabriola Island, Canada: New Society Publishers, 2011.

Starhawk and M. Macha Nightmare. *The Pagan Book of Living and Dying.* San Francisco: HarperSanFrancisco, 1997.

Stein, Diane. *Casting the Circle: A Women's Book of Ritual.* Freedom, CA: The Crossing Press, 1990.

Stein, Diane, ed. *The Goddess Celebrates: An Anthology of Women's Rituals.* Freedom, CA: The Crossing Press, 1991.

Stein, Diane. *Guide to Goddess Craft.* Freedom, CA: the Crossing Press, 2001.

Stewart, Iris J. *Sacred Woman, Sacred Dance.* Rochester, VT: Inner Traditions, 2000.

Stone, Merlin. *Ancient Mirrors of Womanhood: A Treasury of Goddess and Heroine Lore from Around the World.* Boston: Beacon Press, 1990.

Stone, Merlin. *The Paradise Papers: The Suppression of Women's Rites.* London: Virago with Quartet Books, 1976.

Stone, Merlin. *When God Was A Woman.* New York: Harcourt Brace & Company, 1976.

Stuckey, Johanna H. *Women's Spirituality: Contemporary Feminist Approaches to Judaism, Christianity, Islam and Goddess Worship.* Toronto, Canada: Inanna Publications and Education, Inc., 2010.

Sweely, Tracy L., ed. *Manifesting Power: Gender and the Interpretation of Power in Archaeology.* New York: Routledge, 1999.

Tate, Karen. *Walking an Ancient Path: Rebirthing Goddess on Planet Earth.* UK: O Books, 2008.

Tedlock, Barbara. *The Woman in the Shaman's Body: Reclaiming the Feminine in Religion and Medicine.* New York: Bantam Books, 2005.

Teubal, Savina. *Sarah the Priestess: The First Matriarch of Genesis.* Athens, OH: Swallow Press, 1984.

Torjesen, Karen Jo. *When Women Were Priests.* San Francisco: HarperCollins, 1995.

Ulanov, Ann Belford. *Receiving Women: Studies in the Psychology and Theology of the Feminine.* Philadelphia: Westminster John Knox Press, 1981.

Van der Meer, Annine. *The Language of MA, the Primal Mother: The Evolution of the Female Image in 40,000 Years of Global Venus Art.* The Netherlands: Pan Sophia Academy, 2013.

Walker, Barbara G. *Restoring the Goddess: Equal Rites for Modern Women.* New York: Prometheus Books, 2000.

Walker, Barbara G. *Women's Ritual: A Sourcebook.* San Francisco: Harper & Row, 1990.

Wehr, D.S. *Jung and Feminism: Liberating Archetypes.* London: Routledge & Kegan Paul, 1988.

Willowhawk, Alfred. *I Am Healer, Storyteller, and Warrior Priest: Learning from Arianrhod.* Jupiter Gardens Press, 2013.

Williams, Annette Lyn, Karen Nelson Villanueva and Lucia Chiavola Birnbaum, eds. *She Is Everywhere: An Anthology of Writing in Womanist/Feminist Spirituality,* Vol 2. New York: iUniverse, 2008.

Wolkstein, Diane and Samuel Noah Kramer. *Queen of Heaven and Earth: Her Stories and Hymns from Sumer.* New York: Harper & Row, 1983.

A Guide to Incense Botanicals
By Katlyn Breene

Botanicals include all types of organic plant material, but not all produce the same scent when burned as when fresh. There are four main types of botanicals used in incense: resins (including balsams and gums), herbs and plants, precious woods and spices.

Resins, balsams and gums are basically tree sap (*Elixir vitae*), the blood of trees, or a sticky plant balsam extracted from a plant or shrub. The drops of sap are known as "tears" and they are the base of a blend. Resins are great healers and have chemical components that have antiseptic and antimicrobial properties, repel insects, bind wounds and soothe the soul; just think what they do for the trees.

Herbs and plants include aromatic plant material. Only certain ones translate well into scent when burned, but you may include any herb in blends for energetic and symbolic reasons. Also consider using essential oils, instead of fragile herbs or flower petals, to give a more potent opening scent. They are the "top notes" of a blend.

Precious woods are the "body and binder" of a blend. Woods are best used in powder form or sawdust, but small chips are traditionally used as well. Try dipping a sliver of fragrant wood in your favorite essential oil and then burning it as incense.

Spices are highly aromatic seeds and barks. They can sweeten and warm a blend. Try buying your spices from a big online supplier instead of the grocery store. They will be fresher and more potent, and there will be a wider selection.

These four botanical types are traditionally burned in combination and come from every place on the planet; you will even find them in your own backyard. They can be more costly than gold, but many with the most wonderful scents are very reasonable and are now easily obtainable.

There are good *formularies*, or recipe books, now available, and there are many sources for incense sticks and blends, but it is good to know what the pure ingredients smell like and try blending them yourself. Finding all natural incense is very difficult; just because it says "natural" on the label doesn't make it so. You can describe an incense blend as natural if it has no artificial binders or ignition chemicals in it, but most on the market have synthetic fragrance oils added to them. These can smell lovely, but for sacred work you might want to consider mixing your own. Here is a place to start your explorations.

Recommended Resins and Balsams

Benzoin Styrax (*Styrax benzoides*) Known also as gum benjamin, benzoin is very aromatic with an amber-vanilla odor. Sourced from Asia, it is used widely in perfumes as a fixative; it is remarkably sweet and enlivening, often used as a mental stimulant to promote creativity. *Ben* means "branch" in Hebrew and "fragrant" in Arabic, while *zoa* means exudation, or "to ooze." Benzoin is often combined with frankincense to make Byzantine incense used for religious ceremonies. Add benzoin to sweeten any blend like adding "aromatic honey." True benzoin also gets confused with many sweet aromatic gum resins called *jawi*, from the Middle East and India.

Breuzinho (*Breu Claro*) Tree resin from Brazil, this resin is sacred and traditionally used in shamanic work. It is collected from the forest floor to use in ceremony and has an earthy, smooth, rainforest scent. This is the incense used for the Ayauasca ceremonies of Brazil, a wonderful earth offering that is harvested without wounding the tree.

Copal (*Bursera*) Copal literally means "tree sap," and there are many types of copal from all over the Americas. My favorite is *copal blanco* from Mexico. It is white, sticky and aromatically potent. *Copal negro* is also lovely, sweeter and darker. Other types such "gold," are generally not as fragrant, but are very pleasant. The clean fresh scent of copal has a long history of sacred use in Mesoamerican cultures. Gazing through its smoke is said to reveal energetic patterns and carry messages to the spirit world. It is known as "food for the gods" and is burned for Day of Dead ceremonies to guide the spirits home. Copals are a very good choice to burn for almost any type of work from divination to purification.

Dragon's Blood Resin (*Daemonorops draco*) This is a deep red resin used for banishment and protection. The Sumatran dragon's blood used for incense is from a climbing rattan palm of Eastern Asia. It is most commonly found in a hard fist-size ball stamped with a gold impression. Its alchemical properties will make a blend more potent.

Elemi (*Canarium luzonicum*) The name *elemi* comes from the Arabic phrase "above and below." There are many types of *elemi*, but the one most often used in incense is from the Philippines. It has a beautiful fruity, pine-wood scent with herbal notes. It inspires creativity and fertility and is lunar in nature. It is white and sticky when fresh, but dries and ages to become brittle and dark. It is perfect for full moons and visionary work.

Fir Balsam (*Abies balsamea*) This resin is secreted by the balsam firs of northeastern North America. The raw conifer balsams are best found by folks who live in the forest. They are hard to find on the market, but they are so lovely. You can sometimes find "fir balsam absolute," which is a thick, fragrant syrup with an unforgettably forest-like, sweet, fruity scent. It is like the essence of the green world, nurturing and calming—a balm for the spirit.

Frankincense (*Bosellia sacra* or *carteri*) Frankincense (especially *sacra* of Oman) is one of the finest aromas incense has to offer. It is expensive but worth every penny. If you have not tried *hougary*, the best frankincense of Oman, you have a treat in store. The most prized is white or greenish in color and translucent like a gemstone. Also known as *olibanum*, frankincense is harvested by hand from the resin tears exuded from trees in Africa and the Middle East. This resin is the gold of the ancient world; it eases stress and relieves anxiety. The cost can vary greatly. Look for large, white-to-pale-yellow tears to start; it should have a nice scent when rubbed between your fingers. There are many types and grades, from green to black. This is a universal solar medicine.

Labdanum (*Cistus creticus*) Labdanum was an important ingredient in ancient Egyptian incense and perfumery. This amazing earthy resin comes from the rockrose or cistus bush. It is sexy and dark, with scents of leather, oakmoss, wood and flowers in honey. In the past, it was collected by goats that had been let loose in the fields. After feasting on the bushes, they returned with resin sticks in their beards and coat. The sticks were later combed out of their coats and cleaned by boiling. Long rakes of leather strips are also used to harvest labdanum in Crete. The false beards worn by Egyptian pharaohs were actually goat's hair held together by labdanum. If you cannot find the resin in its raw form, try the oil—it is remarkable. Labdanum is an earth scent: seductive, animalistic and underworld.

Mastic (*Pistacia lentiscus*) In ancient Egypt, mastic was called "the fragrance that pleases the gods." Most mastic, or *mastiha in Greek,* is from Chios, a Greek island, and is a rare and pure incense experience. Its properties are mercurial and healing, and its fragrance soft and subtle. Burning it as incense is a very soothing but uplifting balm to the soul. Since ancient times, mastic has been used as a natural medicine. A leaf fossil from a mastic tree has been found that dates back six million years. The incense makers of ancient Egypt used mastic resin in their *kyphi* mixtures. *Mastiha* is a stimulant with a mysterious virtue and power to feed the pleasures of Venus and to arouse in a remarkable way. One of the original ingredients in holy oil, mastic was the first chewing gum used to sweeten the mouth.

Myrrh (*Commiphora myrrha*) This is one of the oldest and most renowned of the incense resins. Myrrh is amongst the first scents used in both prayer and perfumery as far back as 4,000 years ago. Most myrrh is sourced from Somalia or Yemen. It has been used in incense mixtures since antiquity to heal, to honor the Goddess and to strengthen and transform the spirit. Used in its pure form as incense, it is rather smoky and bitter, but it is an important element nonetheless. Try adding the essential oil if you want the true, rich, myrrh scent to come through in smoke. It has energetic ties to funerary rites and, for me, dark moon rituals. It has an air of solemnity, yet it is also referred to as a balm of passion in the Song of Solomon 1:13: "A bundle of Myrrh is my beloved to me." The word "myrrh" comes from the Hebrew *murr* or *maror*, which means "bitter." Burn it gently.

Piñon Pine (*Pinus edulis*) *Piñon* pine is a smooth, warm, and easily obtained resin from the Southwest. It can be very sticky when fresh, but dries with time and ages well. It is lovely burned on its own. This is a very different scent from other pine saps (some can be slightly sour). *Piñon* is used in the Native American tradition for protection and blessing. One of my favorite scents comes from burning resi- rich *piñon* pine logs in the fireplace during the desert winter. It surrounds our home with the protective scent of incense, and smudges the neighborhood.

Peru Balsam (*Myroxylon balsanum*)This balsam is from a tall tree in Central America. It has a warm dark, reddish-brown syrup, with a cinnamon-vanilla scent. It was considered by the early Church to be sacred and used as a sacramental oil in ordination. A great healer, it is used to make things sweet and comforting.

Salupati or **Sal** (*Shorea robusta*) India and the Himalayas are known as "the deliverer of intoxicating resin." This resin is *salu pat*, a resin from the tropical sal tree. The sal tree is an object of worship among Buddhists and Hindus in India and adjoining countries. It is considered sacred because of its characteristics: it is nearly indestructible, attains a great stature and produces copious amounts of resin by the scarring the bark. It is used by shamans as a traveling agent for its psychoactive properties. When placed on coals, the resin gives forth billows of white smoke. Many shamans enter deep trances through this incense, and all in its presence are uplifted. It is said that the Buddha was born under a sal tree.

Storax (*Liquidambar orientalis*) This is obtained from a small tree, which is now mostly found in Turkey. The balsam and the bark are both used in incense. The smoke is sweet and cinnamon-like and warms any blend. It is sometimes mistakenly known as the Balm of Gilead due to its remarkable healing properties. Mesoamerican cultures held other types of storax sacred, using them in smoking blends and incense, as well as to carve votive images. The Turkish storax bark makes wonderful incense, thought to have been used in *kyphi*.

Tolu Balsam (*Myroxylon balsamum*) This is from a tree of Venezuela, Colombia and Peru. Incisions with a V-shape are made in the trunk and the balsam exudes slowly and is collected in gourds. It is a brown brittle resin which looks and smells like brown sugar and vanilla. It has been used for salves and ointments as well as incense. Like benzoin, it has great fixative powers and sweetens any blend. Rich and caramel-like, it reminds one of the sweetness of life.

Recommended Herbs and Plants

Artemisia(s) Named after the Greek goddess Artemis, artemisias include mugwort, wormwood and sagebrush, or desert sage, which have wonderful green herbal scents. Desert sage (not to be confused with white sage) is a traditional herb used in Native American incense for smudging and sweat lodges. Wormwood and mugwort are used in trance, lunar and dreaming blends. Though very bitter herbs, they add a note of moon magic and sorcery. Wormwood is the herb used in absinthe and "flying ointments." It is best to grow your own; all artemisias are easy to cultivate.

Bay Laurel (*Laurus nobilis*) Thought to be a gift from Gaia grown by the Greek Oracle of Delphi, it is said that bay leaves were burned and ingested by priestesses to bring on trance. Bay was also burned in Greece as a fumigant for protection and good fortune. Bay is traditionally a symbol of triumph, wisdom and victory, with a warm, sweet scent—very pleasant and meaningful in incense. Use the branches as incense for rites of divination, and for asperging (to purify ritually by sprinkling with salt water).

Lavender (*Lavandula*) Lovely lavender is the herb of peace, healing and learning: the mother of aromatherapy. The stems are traditionally used for strewing and asperging. The fresher the lavender, the more aromatic it is, so try to harvest it yourself. When burned, it may not carry a lot of its true scent into smoke, but it will give your blend freshness and an uplifting feel. Because it's a natural antidepressant and stress reliever, it's a good idea to add a few drops of essential oil to the buds for incense or a dream pillow. I remember Anne Key throwing bundles of home-grown lavender on the temple fire, and the fabulous scent that surrounded us.

Mexican Tarragon or **Marigold** (*Tegetes lucida*) This is a euphoric incense herb widely used by the Mesoamerican cultures. It has a lovely anise-like scent and is used in incense, teas and smoking blends. Used to promote visions and for guided meditation, it also has a mild psychotropic effect; the Aztecs used it as a sedative and to grant "closed-eye visuals." The Huichol Indians from the Sierras Madre worked with this plant as ritual incense. Used since pre-Hispanic times, the scent will take you back in time.

Orris Root (*Iris florentina*) This is a classical incense ingredient to add sweet scent and act as fixative to let blends hold their scent longer over time. It is the quintessential plant of the moon and of lovers' magic. For a root, the scent is very floral, much like violets. Use it in a powdered form. Orris root is my first pick for full moon incense blends.

Patchouli (*Pogostemon cablin*) The herb of the patchouli plant is a classic incense scent and is a potent aphrodisiac. Use patchouli to add depth and a very earthy sweet note to sensuous blends. Consider adding some essential oil to the herb to empower the scent. The name comes from India, *patch ilia*, which means green leaf. Patchouli is wonderful as a sachet to scent bedding, shawls and intimate apparel, and it gets better with age.

Rosemary (*Rosmarinus officinalis*) This great, all-purpose incense has been used for purification, cleansing and sanctification since ancient times. It is especially nice as purifying incense when mixed with juniper berries. The scent of rosemary increases concentration and memory when studying. Combine it with lavender, roses and mugwort for a dream pillow. It is a helpful herb, and easy to grow. The fresh stalks make wonderful wands to use for blessing and asperging (sprinkling with holy water).

Sweet Grass (*Hierochloe odorata*) Sweet grass is a traditional blessing and smudging herb that is sacred to the divine feminine and has a lovely vanilla scent. Sweet grass is good for earth offerings. Also known as seneca grass or holy grass, sweet grass is braided and burned for blessing ceremonies. The braids smolder slowly and need to be re-lit often. It can also be cut into small bits and added to blends or burned on charcoal.

Vetiver (*Chrysopogon zizanioides*) Vetiver is a hardy grass with very long roots that gather the scents of the earth. It is woody and deep, and mixes beautifully with patchouli for the potent scent of green earth. It is easiest to find in an oil form, known as the "oil of tranquility." The roots are used in incense and are also woven into aromatic mats. Vetiver was used historically to scent water for ritual. It is very grounding and calming. Use in incense to help process grief and loss.

White sage (*Artemisia apiana*) Sage is often used to bless our homes, our communities and our personal energy. White sage is a panacea of healing and clearing. It can be used not only for smudging but as a tea, in mist and in our medicine bags. Whenever healing is needed, sage is our ally. The smell of fresh white sage is intensely therapeutic, and maintains it potency when dried. It will lose some scent over time, but compared to other herbs it is very long-lasting. Store sage bundles (as well as all types of incense) in an airtight container. "At Equinox we dance, and at Solstice, we light wands of Sage that make showers of sparks as we strike our wrists together."[1]

Recommended Trees and Woods

Cedar (*Thuja plicata* or Spruce/Cedar species) This is the perfect base for all types of blends with its wonderful deep-green forest scent. A few drops of any type of cedar oil mixed with the powdered wood and green bough tips makes a universal earth-blessing incense. There many kinds of cedar; it is a broad family of varying trees known for their strengthening aromatic foliage and wood. The best for incense are red cedar, Port Orford cedar, eastern cedar, *arbor vitae*, *siskiyou* cedar and incense cedar. You can find powdered *arbor vitae* and red cedar from many suppliers, which makes them easy to use in blends. Cedar boughs are often used in smudge blends and bundles.

Cypress (*Cupressaceae* family) Called *thyia* in ancient Greece, the resin was thought to be burned at Delphi by the oracle priestesses, and perhaps was the origin of the *thyrsus* wand carried by the female followers of Dionysus, the Greek god of ecstasy. It has a long and important history, and is an incense of queens and priestesses. The cypress tree is also a symbol of Artemis and the moon.

Juniper (*Juniperus*) Aromatically potent, with medicinal and spiritual properties, juniper needles have long been used by Native Americans for smudging. The berries were used widely in the ancient world for holy incense, most notably in Egyptian *kyphi*. Himalayan juniper wood is used as a base in many Nepalese, Tibetan and Ayurvedic healing incenses.

Palo Santo (*Burserea graveolens*) Literally translated as "holy wood," *palo santo* is very healing and cleansing with a clear, sweet, clean scent. Sticks of the wood are lit and burned for purification; the powdered wood makes a great base for healing incense blends. *Palo santo* is excellent for shifting the energy in a room for those who need a healing atmosphere. Burn the incense in a space or room as a preparation. I recommend buying this wood from Ecuador's Pacific coast, where it is ecologically and sustainably harvested. This product is produced without harming the living *palo santo* tree, as only wood found to have died naturally in the forest is processed. Every country in every part of the world has its botanical treasures, the greatest of which are so important to the society that they become pillars of the culture. *Palo santo* is one such medicine. Its healing powers are so numerous that it has served as a panacea in areas of South America for centuries. Its use in sacred ritual is so important that it is an essential tool for shamans and priestesses. Its aroma is so uplifting that it stands among the greatest of the world's fragrant woods. Bestowing great blessings, it gives good fortune to all who use it. Over time, plant teachers such as *palo santo* reach divine-like status in hearts and minds.

Pine (*Pinus*) The sawdust from pine wood makes a pretty good incense base when combined with essential oils and resins. In its rosin form, it is often known as "colophony" (*Colophonium* or *Colophonia resina*), a translucent, amber-like material with a balsamic, woody scent, and a powerful incense of the elements of fire and air. Lodgepole pine (*Pinus contorta*) is one of the widest ranging pines in the Americas and the resin/sap is known as Mayan copal; it has a lovely, sweet fragrance.

Sandalwood and **Agarwood** (also known as Aloeswood) The most precious of incense woods, sandalwoods and agarwoods are very expensive and endangered.[2] I encourage incense lovers to explore and research the world of fine woods but proceed with caution; there are many pricey and false suppliers out there. That said, there is nothing as incredible, spiritually and sensually, as these fine woods when they are genuine. Their scent connects us with the ancients and invokes thoughts of the sacred temples of all ages. If you decide to experiment with these woods I recommend that you burn them gently on a heater; you do not want to waste a single whiff. Volumes could be written on the beauty, use and history of these rare jewels; I will leave it to you to discover their mysteries.

Recommended Spices

Cardamom (*Amomum subulatum, Amomum costatum*) Cardamom is the scent of the exotic, the far away and the sensual. These seed pods run from green to black and all are aromatic delights. To use as incense, grind them in a spice or coffee grinder. They enhance the erotic and invigorate sexuality. They are aphrodisiac in nature and an offering to the goddesses of love. Serve cardamom tea with milk and honey to one you love.

Cinnamon (*Cinnamomum verum*) This is true cinnamon, one of world's most beloved spices, and has been a very important ingredient in sacred incense and holy oil throughout time. Many types of amazing cinnamon are available now; my favorite is from Saigon. The fragrant bark is warm and brings the abundance of the sun. The phoenix made its nest of cinnamon and precious resins, there to be reborn. Burn cinnamon for creativity and inspiration. Cinnamon is used universally in fine incense to open the heart as well as the head. In Sappho's poetry, cinnamon grew in Arabia, beside incense, myrrh and labdanum, and was guarded by winged serpents.

Clove (*Eugenia caryophyllata*) Clove is an important incense ingredient. Not only is the scent warming and protective, it also helps incense to burn better. It is said to bring prosperity and comfort the heart, making us think of hearth and home and things baking in the oven. It is used in many Japanese incense blends. Clove adds body and depth to any incense.

Star Anise (*Illicium verum*) These elegant star-shaped seed pods carry the scent of the moon, dreaming and clairvoyance. Aromatically potent, their magical attributes are as beautiful as their scent. They are used in many Japanese incense blends. To use as incense, grind them in a spice or coffee grinder. Carry one in your pocket or medicine bag for luck and goddess blessings.

Kyphi Burned in the evening in the ancient world, Kyphi was said to restore sexuality and delight the body and mind. In temples, of the ancient world it was an offering to the gods. The creation of this incense was a long process, considered the work of the priesthood. This famous compound incense was made of sixteen ingredients.

> Most of the ingredients that are taken into this compound, in as much as they have aromatic properties, give forth a sweet emanation and a beneficent exhalation, by which the air is changed, and the body moved gently and softly by the current, acquires a temperament conducive to sleep. The distress and strain of our daily cares, as if they were knots, these exhalations relax and loosen without the aid of wine.[3]

Creating kyphi is a long process and was considered the work of the priesthood. Now there are many good sources of information on its creation and the varying ingredients used. A lifelong search for *kyphi* has been a big part of my work. Every year, I dedicate many months to making my own version of *kyphi*, using the ancient formulas that have been made available to us. I highly recommend getting involved the process of incense-making. The making of *kyphi* is a journey. Finding and preparing the ingredients, putting your love and devotion into its blending, waiting for it to cure (sometimes six months), forming the small pellets and finally burning it as an offering—it is a labor of love and a divine offering for the Goddess.

Recommended Sources for Powdered Wood, Resins and Botanicals Used in Incense

Essence of the Ages: www.essenceoftheages.com. Beth carries all types of incense from around the world, an important reliable source
Scents of Earth: www.scents-of-earth.com. Here you can find a wide selection of incense materials and hard to find resins Mermade Magickal Arts: www.mermadearts.com. "We provide the very best in natural incense."

Endnotes

1 Michael Rose, *The Way of the Wild Sage* (Encintitas, CA: The Sage Council, n.d.).

2 Please note that these woods are endangered. However, you can find sustainable sources; just be aware so future generations will be able to enjoy them. Cultivated agarwood can be found from Vietnam; you can get sustainably grown and harvested sandalwood from Australia.

3 From Plutarch, *Moralia,* "Isis and Osiris."

Stepping Into Ourselves:
An Anthology of Writings on Priestesses
A Goddess Ink Reading Group Guide

About this Guide

We hope this Reading Group Guide fosters discussion and encourages exploration into the various themes presented in *Stepping Into Ourselves: An Anthology of Writings on Priestesses*. Additional information may be found on our website: www.goddess-ink.com

STEPPING INTO OURSELVES

Questions for Discussion

- Consider the roles of the ancient priestesses and modern applications outlined in "Job Descriptions for the Priestess" and "Mourning-Woman/Priestess." Where do you find your calling? Looking at the chart Asia Shepsut lays out with each role inspired by a chakra, which role appeals to you? Explain why.

- "I, Enheduanna" (Jezibel Anat), "Inanna's Chants"(Janine Canan), "Sacred Prostitutes" (Johanna Stuckey) and "Job Descriptions for the Priestess" (Asia Shepsut) all discuss Enheduanna, often considered the first historical priestess and author, and she is the earliest priestess of record. How does she inspire you? How do her life and work inform your ideas about priestesses?

- After reading "The Kohanot: Keepers of the Flame" (D'vorah Grenn), "Mourning-Woman/Priestess" (Jill Hammer), "Shechinah" (Geela Rayzel Raphael) and "Temple Weaving: Jewish Weaver-Priestesses and the Creation of the Cosmos" (Jill Hammer) discuss the roles women played in ancient Judaism. How do they compare to the roles played by women in Judaism today?

- After reading "The Stuff of Life: Clay, Figurines and Priestesses in Mesoamerica" by Anne Key, consider how women's duties in ancient times were interpreted by male scholars who did not have a framework for seeing women in positions of religious and spiritual authority, leadership and power. How do you see women now in roles of spiritual/religious authority outside structures that don't recognize them?

- After reading "Yoginis of Ancient India" and "The Path of Priestess and Priest: Initiation into an Ancient Tradition" by Jalaja Bonheim, "Priestess of Kali" by Chandra Alexander and

"Ammachi: In the Lap of the Mother" by Linda Johnsen, how do you think modern women can find a legacy of priestessing in living traditions, such as Hinduism?

- How do priestesses such as ALisa Starkweather ("Walking the Priestess Path") and Deidre Arthen ("I Am the Earth: The Priestess in Service to Community") negotiate being outside of structured religion?

- A number of women wrote about their relationships with trees; consider "Wisdom of Elders" (Patricia Monaghan), "On Becoming a Tree Priestess" (Kathryn Ravenwood), "The History of My First and Second Urban Street Trees" (Jennifer Jones) and "Forest Rules" (Patricia Monaghan). Do you have a special story or experience with a tree, or in nature? How has that informed your identity as a priestess?

- Consider the questions Ruth Barrett raises in her essay "The Dianic Priestess." She writes: "The role of the priestess is being revived in contemporary times. It is most often through attending rituals that women become attracted to the role that the priestess represents. With growing interest in ritual making and more women gaining experience in facilitating ritual, we must ask ourselves many questions." Where are the role models for contemporary women who are on the ritual priestess path? When you imagine yourself as a ritualist, a priestess or a ritual priestess, what are your expectations for yourself and others? What are your expectations based on? Do you have any models for spiritual leadership other than religious leadership models from patriarchal religions?

- How are rituals used to address issues, such as Hava Montauriano has done with the "Reclaiming Adam and Eve" ritual? How does this ritual re-work the old into something new?

Can you give another example of a ritual that you have created or would like to create that would address a contemporary issue?

- Consider the essays "Hearing the Call" (Ruth Barrett), "Priestessing with Integrity" (Sylvia Brallier) and "Priestesses I Have Known" (Calypso). What are the roles of priestesses, how do they affect the people they work with and what are some of the responsibilities?

- Looking again at the essays mentioned in the previous question, what seems to work in priestessing and what doesn't work?

- Describe the effects of the feminist movement on spiritual practice, especially as described by Ruth Barrett ("The Dianic Priestess," "Answering the Call of Service: Dianic Tradition and Women's Mysteries"), Jade River ("Three Times a Priestess"), Nano Boye Nagle ("It is Easier to be a Priest than a Priestess") and Shekhinah Mountainwater ("Groups, Power and Priestessing").

- Read about the history of Inanna in the first two essays, and then read about the modern experience of the descent of Inanna in "Discovering the Priestess Within: The Origins of a Thriving Women's Mystery" by IONE. Comment on how IONE's article affected you personally in the light of the historical depiction of the descent of Inanna.

- Read "As Within So Without: Psychological Aspects of Priestessing" (Kim Duckett), "The Mother of Us All" (Tamis Rentería), "Groups, Power and Priestessing" (Shekinah Mountainwater), "The Wiccan Priestess as Initiator: The Psychology of the Initiatory Process" (Vivianne Crowley) and "Models of Leadership" (Ruth Barrett). Discuss group dynamics and the role of the priestess. What ideas do these authors have in common? How do they differ? Which ideas and suggestions were the most helpful to you?

- Read "I Am the Earth: The Priestess in Service To Community" (Deirdre Arthen) and "On Becoming a Tree Priestess" (Kathryn Ravenwood). In what ways do priestesses act as doorways or portals?

- Read "My Family's Lineage of Priestesses" (Carmen Roman), "Aloha Priestess Path" (Leilany Birely) and "The Mother of Us All" (Tamis Rentería). What role does family lineage and culture play in priestessing?

- Read "Holy Bite" and "Minoan Snake Priestess" (both by Le'ema Kathleen Graham). How do animal and spirit guides assist in the art of priestessing? Do you have animal or spirit guides that you depend upon for advice, comfort and counsel? In what way do they assist you?

- Of all of the ritual techniques addressed in this book—the use of incense and altars, rhythm and chanting, the effect of theater, working with energy—which have you found to be the most effective? Explain why. Which have you found to be the most difficult? Explain why.

- Read "Priestess Me" (H.D. Artemis), "Generating Stillness: Creating Sacred Space" (Kathy Jones), "Priestessing Yourself" (Ruth Barrett) and "Who Am I" (Martina Steger). Why is it important to take care of yourself? How does that impact your effectiveness as a priestess?

- Do you recognize yourself in any of the pieces in the anthology? If so, which one or ones?

- Which of the poems spoke most to your heart?

www.ingramcontent.com/pod-product-compliance
Lightning Source LLC
Chambersburg PA
CBHW020630230426
43665CB00008B/104